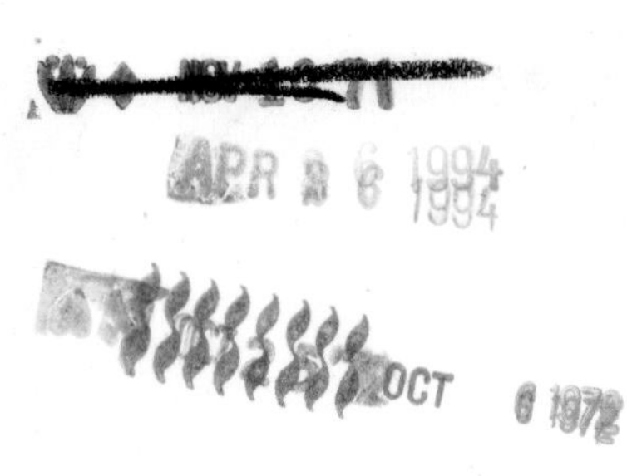

# Libraries

Michael Brawne

# Libraries

## Architecture and Equipment

Praeger Publishers
New York · Washington · London

PRAEGER PUBLISHERS, INC.
111 Fourth Avenue, New York, N. Y. 10003, U.S.A.
5 Cromwell Place, London S.W. 7, England

Published in the United States of America in 1970
by Praeger Publishers, Inc.


Library of Congress Catalog Card Number: 73-89609

Printed in Germany
Translated into German by Antje Pehnt

CONTENTS | INHALT

## Preface

Communication has been recognized as one of the key elements of present-day society, and its high development as one of the distinguishing marks of contemporary culture. This book, like its predecessor, *The New Museum*, deals with the physical enclosure of one of the media of communication and does so by analysing the conditions which it is thought should be fulfilled if this enclosure is to be successful in furthering the communication. It also illustrates a number of recently built examples even though only some meet the criteria suggested in the analysis. The nature of the media being stored is at present undergoing change as are the demands of society for information. The implications of both these changes are discussed at the end of the book. There appears, however, as yet to be no built example which could be used by way of illustration of these trends. They can only be described in words.

A book such as this cannot be written unaided. I am, therefore, very grateful to all the architects and librarians who supplied plans, photographs and descriptions of their buildings, only a proportion of which could be shown; to the very many librarians who spent a great deal of time showing me their buildings and discussing library design; to Verlag Gerd Hatje and particularly Gerd Hatje and Ruth Wurster who, with tact and patience, accumulated photographs and plans; to Colin St. John Wilson, one of the architects of the British Museum Library, and Nicholas Childs, formerly of the Department of Printed Books, British Museum, now University Librarian, Brunel University, with whom I discussed library problems on a study tour of some libraries in the Soviet Union; to A. N. L. Munby who, when Librarian, King's College, Cambridge, drew my attention to some medieval examples; to Edward Carter, one time Librarian to UNESCO, who made it possible for me to meet a number of specialists, including S. R. Ranganathan of the DRTC, Bangalore, who happily confirmed so many of my views in discussion; to my wife who painstakingly read the manuscript and proofs.

## Vorwort

Kommunikation ist eines der wichtigsten Elemente der heutigen Gesellschaft, und der hohe Entwicklungsstand der Kommunikationstechniken charakterisiert unsere zeitgenössische Kultur. Wie der Band *Neue Museen*, der dieser Publikation vorausging, behandelt auch das vorliegende Buch das architektonische Gehäuse eines Kommunikationsmediums, indem es untersucht, welche Voraussetzungen erfüllt sein müssen, damit die Bauform sich fördernd auf die Kommunikation auswirkt. Der Abbildungsteil, der sich anschließt, vereinigt Bauten aus jüngster Zeit, auch wenn nur wenige den Kriterien der Analyse entsprechen. Zur Zeit verändern sich sowohl die Beschaffenheit des gespeicherten Materials wie auch die Ansprüche, die die Gesellschaft an die Information stellt. Die Konsequenzen, die beide Entwicklungen nach sich ziehen, werden am Ende des Buches diskutiert. Offensichtlich ist bisher jedoch noch kein Bauwerk entstanden, das als Beispiel für diese Tendenzen dienen könnte, so daß ich mich auf eine verbale Darstellung beschränken mußte.

Ein Buch wie dieses kann nicht ohne fremde Hilfe geschrieben werden. Ich danke deshalb allen Architekten und Bibliothekaren, die Pläne, Photographien und Beschreibungen ihrer Bauten zur Verfügung gestellt haben (nur ein Teil des Materials konnte gezeigt werden); den zahlreichen Bibliothekaren, die viel Zeit darauf verwandten, mir ihre Gebäude zu zeigen und mit mir über Bibliotheksplanung zu diskutieren; dem Verlag Gerd Hatje und besonders Gerd Hatje und Ruth Wurster, die mit Takt und Geduld Foto- und Planmaterial beschafft haben; Colin St. John Wilson, einem der Architekten der Bibliothek des British Museum, und Nicholas Childs, früher an der Abteilung für Bücher im British Museum, heute Bibliothekar an der Brunel University, mit denen ich auf einer Studienreise Bibliotheken der Sowjetunion besuchte und Probleme des Bibliothekswesens diskutierte; A. N. L. Munby, der als Bibliothekar am King's College in Cambridge meine Aufmerksamkeit auf mittelalterliche Beispiele lenkte; Edward Carter, ehemals Bibliothekar bei der UNESCO, der mich mit mehreren Fachleuten in Verbindung brachte, darunter S. R. Ranganathan vom DRTC, Bangalore, der glücklicherweise viele meiner Ansichten bestätigte; und meiner Frau, die Manuskript und Korrekturen sorgfältig gelesen hat.

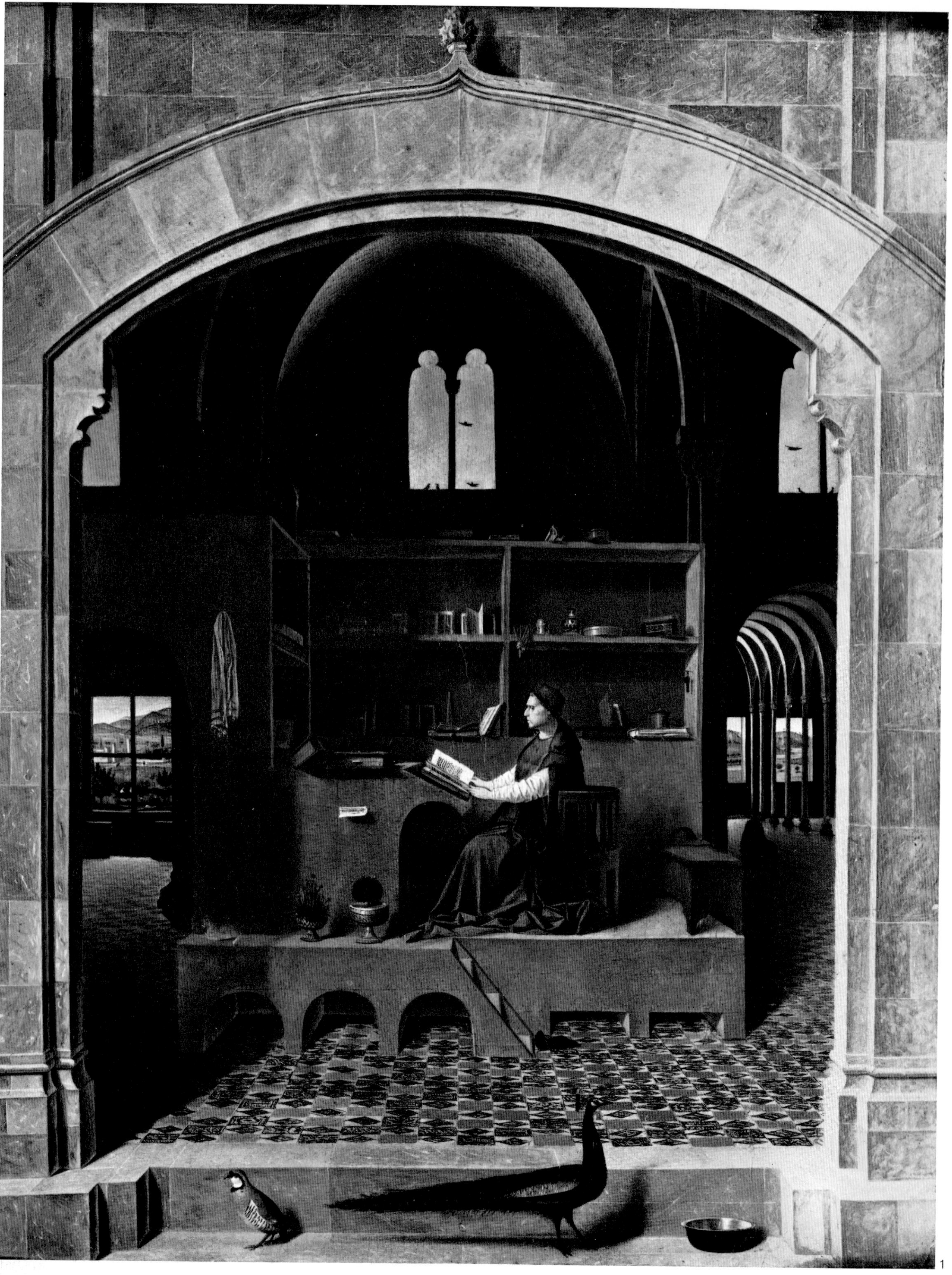

1

There is a small painting by Antonello da Messina (Fig. 1) which shows St. Jerome in his study; the Saint is sitting in an armchair in front of a sloping desk surrounded on two sides by book shelves. The desk and shelves are part of a wooden construction raised three steps off the floor which stands within a great vaulted Gothic hall. Through the upper windows the sky and flying birds are visible, through the lower windows an Italian landscape of hills, buildings and a river. Framed in an arch on the right there is a lion, curled up to the left of the Saint there is a cat asleep on the podium.

The picture, now in the National Gallery in London, is not only a painterly study of receding planes seen in perspective and of the quality of light falling on these – from the stone arch to the most distant mountain top – but also an accurate and brilliant portrayal of the characteristics most needed if there is to be a successful communication between the accumulated store of knowledge and the reader. The problems and solutions are present in that single picture.

St. Jerome has something like thirty volumes within reach and obviously room for a good many more. Although any monastic library of Antonello's time, the second half of the 15th century, would have housed a very much greater collection than this, it seems likely that these thirty books satisfied the Saint's needs for a considerable period of study and that they could have dealt with a sizeable part of the then available knowledge. Storage, accessibility and expansion had thus simple and direct solutions; they in fact hardly existed as problems.

The wooden platform and its furniture are also both a kind of work station and an aedicule; an individual and particular space delineated and in some measure separated from the greater space beyond. The distractions of the outside world – the fishermen in their boats, the birds wheeling against the sky – are shielded but not wholly excluded. Concentration on the essential task is possible and in fact encouraged by the organization of the surroundings. Furniture, enclosure, space, light, outlook, are all manipulated to aid the communication between the book and its reader.

The Saint, like the sleeping cat, has not only made a place for himself but has at the same time detached himself from what must frequently have been a cold floor and a windy hall. He has retreated into a protecting niche and appropriately surrounded himself with wooden surfaces which would absorb little body heat.

The desk and the book are lit from the left; the surrounding surfaces, a little darker than the manuscript page, are also illuminated but there is no bright object within the field of vision as St. Jerome reads or as he looks up. The lion's padded foot falls are unlikely to be disturbing, only the peacock's cry could startle. Body comfort, which includes appropriate conditions for eye and ear, is vital if the message of the book is to be easily understood; its absence is a serious distraction, an interference in the system of communication.

Antonello painted St. Jerome in his Study only a few years after Gutenberg in 1455 printed his first Bible using movable type. An important library in the century preceding Antonello's time might have had something like 1500 volumes – the Papal library at Avignon, for instance, had 1,677 codices in 1377, the Sorbonne 1,722 codices in 1338 – a number perhaps not more than twice that which a reasonably well-read family might own and keep in their house today. A lesser library would have had a very much smaller number; the catalogue of the library of Lincoln Cathedral of about 1450 lists 107 works. Comparable libraries would now count their volumes in hundreds of thousands, frequently in millions. The local public library

Antonello da Messina hat ein kleines Tafelbild gemalt (Abb. 1), das Hieronymus in seinem Studierzimmer zeigt; der Heilige sitzt auf einem Stuhl vor einem abgeschrägten Pult, das an zwei Seiten von Bücherregalen umgeben ist. Pult und Regale sind Teile einer Holzkonstruktion, die – drei Stufen über dem gekachelten Fußboden – inmitten einer hohen, gewölbten gotischen Halle errichtet ist. Durch die oberen Fenster sieht man Himmel und vorbeifliegende Vögel, durch die unteren Fenster eine italienische Landschaft mit Hügeln, Häusern und einem Fluß. Unter den Arkaden zur Rechten nähert sich ein Löwe, zur Linken des Heiligen auf dem Podest schläft zusammengerollt eine Katze.

Das Bild, das heute in der Londoner National Gallery hängt, ist nicht nur eine malerische Studie perspektivisch verkürzter Flächen und der Qualitäten des Lichts – vom Steinbogen bis zum fernsten Berggipfel –, sondern liefert auch eine exakte und brillante Darstellung der Voraussetzungen, die für eine Kommunikation zwischen dem Leser und dem angehäuften Vorrat an Wissen am wichtigsten sind. In diesem einen Bild offenbaren sich die Probleme und ihre Lösungen.

Der heilige Hieronymus hat schätzungsweise dreißig Bände in seiner Reichweite und könnte offensichtlich noch weit mehr unterbringen. Obwohl zu Antonellos Zeit – der zweiten Hälfte des 15. Jahrhunderts – jede Klosterbibliothek eine weitaus größere Sammlung besaß, ist anzunehmen, daß diese dreißig Bücher dem Heiligen für eine längere Zeit des Studiums genügten und daß sie einen beträchtlichen Teil des damals verfügbaren Wissens enthielten. Unterbringung, Zugänglichkeit und Vermehrung fanden also einfache, direkte Lösungen; als Probleme existierten sie praktisch nicht.

Die hölzerne Plattform und ihre Einrichtung bilden eine Art Arbeitsraum oder Nische, einen individuellen, abgeschirmten Bereich, der aus dem größeren Raum ausgegrenzt und in gewissem Maße von ihm abgetrennt ist. Zwar ist die Außenwelt – Fischer in ihren Booten, Vögel, die vor dem Himmel ihre Kreise ziehen – nicht ganz ausgeschlossen, doch kann sie nicht ablenkend wirken, denn die Umgebung ist ganz darauf eingerichtet, die Konzentration auf die wichtigste Aufgabe zu ermöglichen und zu fördern. Raum, Möblierung, Licht, Abschirmung und Ausblick dienen der Kommunikation zwischen Buch und Leser.

Der Heilige hat sich, wie die schlafende Katze, nicht nur einen Ruheplatz geschaffen, sondern wahrscheinlich auch Zuflucht vor dem zweifellos kalten Fußboden und der zugigen Halle gesucht. Er hat sich in einen geschützten Winkel zurückgezogen und sich zweckmäßigerweise mit Holzflächen umgeben, die wenig Körperwärme absorbieren.

Pult und Buch sind von links beleuchtet; auch auf die umgebenden Flächen, die ein wenig dunkler sind als die Manuskriptseite, fällt Licht, doch wenn Hieronymus liest oder aufblickt, findet sich kein heller Gegenstand in seinem Blickfeld. Daß das Geräusch der leisen Löwenpfoten ihn stört, ist kaum anzunehmen, nur der Schrei des Pfaues könnte ihn aufschrecken. Physische Bequemlichkeit, die angemessene Bedingungen für Auge und Ohr einschließt, ist entscheidend, wenn die Botschaft des Buches den Leser erreichen soll; fehlt sie, so wird der Leser abgelenkt und das System der Kommunikation gestört.

Antonello malte seinen Hieronymus im Studierzimmer nur wenige Jahre, nachdem Gutenberg 1455 seine erste Bibel mit beweglichen Lettern gedruckt hatte. In dem Jahrhundert vor Antonellos Zeit enthielt eine bedeutende Bibliothek ungefähr 1500 Bände – die Päpstliche Bibliothek in Avignon umfaßte zum Beispiel im Jahre 1377 1677 Codices, die Sorbonne im Jahre 1338 1722 Codices –, also

1. Antonello da Messina (c. 1430–79): St. Jerome in his study. (Reproduced by courtesy of the Trustees, The National Gallery, London). Saint Jerome (c. 340–420) – Ciceronian scholar, Christian scholar, for four years hermit in the desert of Chalcis, priest, papal secretary, pioneer in biblical archaeology, translator of the official "Vulgate" Bible of the Roman Catholic Church – was a frequent subject for painters of the Middle Ages and much of the Renaissance. He is usually shown in the desert or in an imaginary situation of the latter part of his life in Bethlehem where he presided over a monastery devoting his time to study and writing. These paintings often give a very clear indication of the kind of space then in current use by scholars.

1. Antonello da Messina (etwa 1430–79): Der heilige Hieronymus in seinem Studierzimmer (abgebildet mit Genehmigung der National Gallery, London). Der heilige Hieronymus (etwa 340–420) – hervorragender Kenner der klassischen und christlichen Literatur, vier Jahre Eremit in der Wüste von Chalkis, Priester, päpstlicher Sekretär, Pionier der christlichen Archäologie, Übersetzer der »Vulgata« – war ein beliebtes Motiv für die Maler des Mittelalters wie der Renaissance. Er wird im allgemeinen in der Wüste oder als Abt eines Klosters in Bethlehem gezeigt, wo er sich am Ende seines Lebens mit seinen Studien beschäftigte. Diese Darstellungen vermitteln häufig eine klare Vorstellung von den Räumen, in denen die damaligen Gelehrten arbeiteten.

of the suburban community of Hillerød outside Copenhagen has 90,000 books, 35,000 of which are in the Children's Department; the John Crerar Library of the Illinois Institute of Technology in Chicago has a book capacity of 820,000 volumes; in the centre of Moscow, within walking distance of the Kremlin, the Foreign Language Library has 3½ million volumes, the Library of the Social Sciences 7 million and the Lenin Library 23 million.
It is this quantitative change, and the continuity of that change, which has disrupted the idyllic situation evident in the picture of St. Jerome in his Study and which has brought with it qualitative differences which library design must now attempt to solve. These attempts are being made in the organization of space and the organisation of the documented store of knowledge. The first is the main topic of this book, the second will be discussed in so far as it has obvious architectural implications. Most experiments in this latter field, like project Intrex now under way at the Massachusetts Institute of Technology, are in fact attempts through the use of computers to give a user at a console the degree of immediate accessibility at his private place of work which St. Jerome found in his Study.

### The Historical Sequence

Until Gutenberg invented movable type, and literacy and the printed book had their effect, becoming one of the distinguishing attributes of Western Society, the concept of the library as a special building type was rare. This was especially true in the centuries preceding Gutenberg's invention despite the existence of many monastic collections (Fig. 3). The great change came after 1500 when printing became not only much more general but works began to be specially written for the wide circulation made possible by the new printing presses; until then they had mainly been concerned with converting existing manuscripts into printed books.
In the eighteen centuries between the creation of the library which was known to have been part of the Royal Palace of Ptolemy II in Alexandria in the early part of the third century B.C. and the start of Michelangelo's Biblioteca Laurenziana in Florence in 1524 (Fig. 8), two traditions can be distinguished. Both of these have had considerable influence on library planning.
The first is typified by the Roman colonial library at Ephesus in Asia Minor (Fig. 2) where a single large room was lined with shelving for the rolls of papyrus, perhaps 20 to 30 feet long, which were kept in cylindrical boxes about a foot deep and three inches in diameter. There had of course been earlier Roman and Greek libraries but it is difficult to discover what their internal arrangements were. The best known of these was probably the library at Pergamon, also in Asia Minor, where the Greek successors of Alexander the Great established a library as part of the acropolis complex at the beginning of the second century B.C. Plutarch claims that it contained 200,000 rolls. The library was linked to the temple through the north stoa which enclosed the Sanctuary of Athena on two sides and from this colonnade there was a long view down the valley to the Aegean.
The notion of the large room in which books and possibly sculpture fitted into the recesses of the wall, exemplified by the library at Ephesus, placed considerable emphasis on the book and a symbolically important room in which to house it; book and space became an architecture.
The second tradition, which was largely a monastic development, gave very much greater emphasis to the reader. It was due no doubt to the considerably smaller number

kaum mehr als doppelt so viele Bücher, wie eine einigermaßen kultivierte Familie heute besitzt und im Hause aufbewahrt. Eine kleinere Bibliothek verfügte natürlich über sehr viel weniger Bücher; so führt der Katalog der Lincoln Cathedral um 1450 nur 107 Werke auf. Heute zählen die Bände vergleichbarer Bibliotheken nach Hunderttausenden, häufig nach Millionen. Die Volksbücherei der Vorortgemeinde Hillerød bei Kopenhagen besitzt 90000 Bücher, davon 35000 in der Abteilung für Kinder- und Jugendbücher; die John Crerar Library des Illinois Institute of Technology in Chicago verfügt über 820000 Bände; die Bibliothek für Fremdsprachen im Zentrum Moskaus, nicht weit vom Kreml entfernt, hat 3½ Millionen, die Bibliothek für Gesellschaftswissenschaften 7 Millionen und die Lenin-Bibliothek 23 Millionen Bände.
Diese stete quantitative Zunahme hat der Idylle, wie sie noch in dem Bild von Hieronymus in seiner Studierstube dargestellt ist, ein Ende gesetzt und qualitative Probleme mit sich gebracht, die heute die Bibliotheksplanung zu lösen versuchen muß. Sie befaßt sich sowohl mit der Organisation des Raumes – dem Hauptthema dieses Buches – als auch mit der Organisation des gespeicherten Wissensstoffes, die hier nur behandelt wird, soweit sie sich auf die Architektur auswirkt. Die meisten Experimente auf diesem Gebiet – etwa das Intrex-Projekt, das zur Zeit am Massachusetts Institute of Technology erprobt wird – zielen dahin, dem Leser mit Hilfe von Computern die Bücher an seinem Arbeitsplatz ebenso direkt zugänglich zu machen, wie sie es für den heiligen Hieronymus in seinem Studierzimmer waren.

### Historischer Abriß

Bis Gutenberg die bewegliche Letter erfand, bis das gedruckte Buch und der steigende Bildungsstandard ihre Wirkung taten und zu einem Charakteristikum der abendländischen Gesellschaft wurden, war die Bibliothek als spezifischer Gebäudetyp nur selten anzutreffen. Das gilt besonders für das Mittelalter, obwohl in jenen Jahrhunderten viele Klöster Sammlungen von Handschriften besaßen (Abb. 3). Der große Wandel setzte nach 1500 ein, als nicht nur der Druck immer größere Verbreitung fand, sondern auch Bücher eigens für die hohen Auflagen geschrieben wurden, die das neue Druckverfahren ermöglichte; bis dahin hatten die Druckpressen hauptsächlich dazu gedient, vorhandene Handschriften in gedruckte Bücher zu verwandeln.
In den achtzehn Jahrhunderten zwischen der Entstehung der Bibliothek, die zu dem königlichen Palast des Ptolemäus II. in Alexandria gehörte (Anfang des 3. Jahrhunderts vor Christus), und dem Baubeginn von Michelangelos Biblioteca Laurenziana (Abb. 8) in Florenz im Jahre 1524 lassen sich zwei Traditionen verfolgen. Beide haben einen starken Einfluß auf die Bibliotheksplanung ausgeübt.
Für die erste Tradition ist die Bibliothek der römischen Kolonie von Ephesus in Kleinasien kennzeichnend (Abb. 2): ein einziger großer Raum mit Nischen für die Papyrusrollen in den Wänden. Die etwa 6 bis 9 Meter langen Rollen wurden in zylindrischen Behältern aufbewahrt, die ungefähr 30 cm tief waren und einen Durchmesser von 7,5 cm hatten. Es hatte natürlich auch schon früher römische und griechische Bibliotheken gegeben, doch läßt sich heute schwer feststellen, wie die Innenräume gegliedert waren. Am bekanntesten ist wohl die Bibliothek von Pergamon, ebenfalls in Kleinasien, wo die griechischen Nachfolger Alexanders des Großen zu Beginn des 2. Jahrhunderts vor Christus eine Bibliothek innerhalb des Akropolis-Komplexes errichteten. Plutarch behauptet, daß sie 200000 Rollen umfaßte. Die Bibliothek war mit dem Tempel durch

2. Library at Ephesus, Asia Minor, c. A. D. 115. A large room lined with shelves for scrolls and with sculpture in niches; readers used the open central space.

2. Bibliothek in Ephesus, Kleinasien, etwa 115 n. Chr. Eine Halle mit Regalen für Schriftrollen, die ebenso wie die Skulpturen in Wandnischen untergebracht waren; den Lesern stand der offene Raum in der Mitte zur Verfügung.

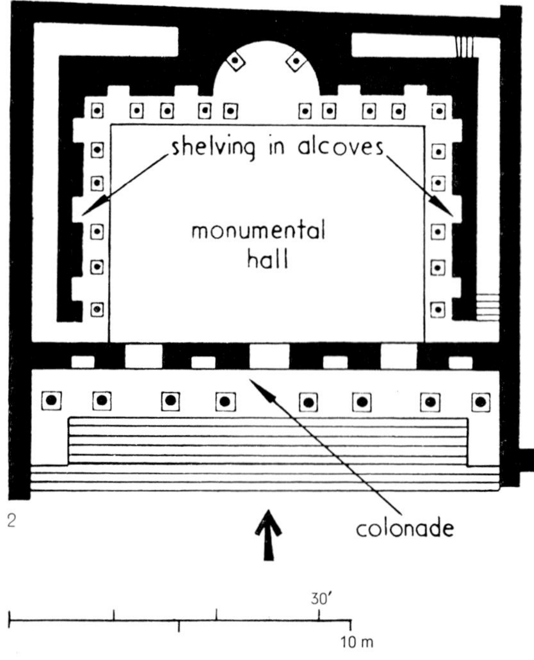

3. Tomb of Galla Placidia, Ravenna. The fifth century mosaic shows the kind of book cupboard which was then current and which continued in use into the Middle Ages for the safe keeping of codices. Libraries were for a long time furniture rather than buildings.

3. Grabmal der Galla Placidia, Ravenna, 5. Jahrhundert. Auf dem Mosaik ist ein Bücherschrank zu sehen, wie er damals gebräuchlich war. Solche Schränke dienten bis zum Mittelalter zur sicheren Unterbringung von Handschriften. Bibliotheken waren lange Zeit entsprechend möblierte Räume, ehe sie zu selbständigen Gebäuden wurden.

3

of volumes which had to be kept, and to the perhaps rather prolonged periods of study in a harsh environment which the monks pursued in the monasteries of Northern Europe. This emphasis is typified by the carrel. This was at first no more than a small sheltering niche such as is to be found in the group of twenty in the south range of the cloister of Gloucester Cathedral (Fig. 5) built between 1370 and 1412 when it was still an abbey. Each recess was 6′9″ high, 4′0″ wide and 1′7″ deep and allowed a reader to sit sideways to a window. It was not unlike the aedicular space which a Gothic cathedral would have for the statues of the saints; an individual enclosure delimited from the general space. Within this system, the definition of the space of each reader, together with its relation to light, and the subsequent aggregation of such spaces became an architecture.

When during the Middle Ages buildings, or parts of buildings, began to be designed specifically as libraries, these were as a rule thought of as an accumulation of such carrel-like spaces. This was particularly true of the college libraries which were built at Oxford and Cambridge from the early part of the 14th century onwards (Fig. 4). The enclosure was created there by the disposition of furniture – book case, bench and a reading shelf – placed at right angles to the solid parts of the wall between the regularly spaced windows.

Such a system worked well as long as the number of readers and books was small. Each user could have almost immediate access to the whole collection; access was only difficult in so far as the book was still such a rarity that elaborate precautions were taken to preserve it. It was in the early part of the period kept in book-cupboards or sometimes locked in a chest which might require two keys to open it such as at Peterhouse in Cambridge where the statutes of 1344 ruled that the Master was to have one key, the Senior Dean the other. Later in the period it was usually chained (Figs. 6, 9).

It was after 1500 that a change occurred caused both by

die nördliche Stoa verbunden, die das Heiligtum der Athena auf zwei Seiten umschloß. Von dieser Kolonnade aus bot sich ein Ausblick hinunter ins Tal bis zum Ägäischen Meer.

Das in Ephesus angewandte Konzept des großen Raumes, in dem Bücher und manchmal auch Skulpturen in Wandnischen untergebracht sind, mißt dem Buch und dem symbolhaft ausgezeichneten Raum, der es aufnimmt, besondere Bedeutung zu; Buch und Raum werden zu einer Architektur.

Die zweite Tradition, die sich hauptsächlich in den Klöstern entwickelte, legte sehr viel mehr Wert auf den Leser. Das lag zweifellos daran, daß eine weitaus geringere Zahl von Büchern aufbewahrt werden mußte und daß die Mönche in den Klöstern Nordeuropas vergleichsweise langwierige Studien in ihrer asketischen Umgebung trieben. Typisch für diese Tendenz sind die *carrels*. Sie waren zunächst nicht mehr als kleine schützende Nischen, wie sie sich im südlichen Teil des Kreuzganges der Kathedrale von Gloucester finden (Abb. 5), der zwischen 1370 und 1412 errichtet wurde, als Gloucester noch eine Abtei war. Jede dieser zwanzig Nischen war 2,05 m hoch, 1,20 m breit und 0,50 m tief und erlaubte es dem Leser, seitlich neben einem Fenster zu sitzen. Im Prinzip ähnelten sie den Baldachinen, in denen in gotischen Kathedralen die Statuen der Heiligen aufgestellt wurden – ein individueller Bereich, der vom umgebenden Raum abgesondert ist. Bei diesem System entstand Architektur aus der Definition des dem einzelnen Leser vorbehaltenen Raumes, aus der Orientierung zum Licht hin und schließlich aus der Addition solcher Bereiche.

Wenn im Mittelalter Gebäude oder Gebäudeteile von Anfang an als Bibliotheken geplant wurden, bestand die Entwurfsidee gewöhnlich in der Aneinanderreihung solcher nischenähnlicher Bereiche. Das gilt besonders für die College-Bibliotheken, die seit dem frühen 14. Jahrhundert in Oxford und Cambridge errichtet wurden (Abb. 4). Die Raumtrennung wurde den Einrichtungsgegenstän-

the great increase in the number of books and the return to Roman architectural prototypes. Books were again made to line walls and as their numbers grew, the presses in which they were kept were made taller and the rooms correspondingly higher until even ladders became awkward and galleries and balconies were introduced. The principle of the great book-lined room remained constant however. It was established in Philip II's library at the Escorial in 1567 (Fig. 10) where the 18,000 volumes were placed in presses against the walls. This was a significant departure from the earlier Renaissance libraries like the Malatestiana or even the Laurenziana (Figs. 7, 8) which had kept the medieval plan within a Renaissance enclosure.
The Biblioteca Ambrosiana in Milan of 1603–09 founded by Cardinal Federigo Borromeo was an early example of the great room, 74 ft. (26 m) long and 29 ft. (13,6 m) wide with a barrel vaulted ceiling, in which it became necessary to design an intermediate level in order to simplify access. The lower set of presses was 13 ft. (4 m) high, then there was a gallery which could be reached from a staircase in each corner, and this was lined by further bookcases 8′6″ (2,6 m) high. The concept of the library as a unified single great room whose walls held books and occasional sculpture, as they had done at Ephesus, continued into the 18th Century and had its most exuberant expression in the monastic libraries of Southern Germany and Austria. The libraries of St. Florian, Melk, Ottobeuren, Wiblingen and many of the other baroque monasteries of the Upper Danube (Figs. 11–13) were rooms in which light, sculpture, painting, book-storage and the manipulation of space were considered together and where this total space was thought to be symbolically important within the building group.

It was in many ways an idyllic situation, a situation which was, however, to be short lived. Two changes had a disrupting effect. The first was due to a considerable increase in the number of books being printed; the second to an equally important increase in the number of readers wanting to use the collections. Göttingen University for instance had 12,000 volumes in 1737 but in 1786, less than

den – Büchergestell, Bank und Lesepult – übertragen, die rechtwinklig zur Wand zwischen die regelmäßig angeordneten Fenster gestellt wurden.
Ein solches System funktionierte reibungslos, solange die Zahl der Leser und der Bücher klein blieb. Jedem Benutzer war die ganze Sammlung nahezu direkt zugänglich; erschwert war der Zugang nur insofern, als das Buch in jener Zeit noch so kostbar war, daß alle möglichen Vorsichtsmaßnahmen ergriffen wurden, um es zu erhalten. Es wurde zunächst in Bücherschränken aufbewahrt oder auch in Truhen eingeschlossen, die manchmal nur mit zwei Schlüsseln zu öffnen waren – wie zum Beispiel im Peterhouse in Cambridge, wo die Satzungen von 1344 vorsahen, daß der Rektor den einen und der Dekan den anderen Schlüssel besaß. Später wurden die Bücher gewöhnlich angekettet (Abb. 6, 9).
Erst nach 1500 trat ein Wandel ein, den die ständig zunehmende Menge der Bücher wie auch der Rückgriff auf römische Bauformen verursachten. Die Bücher wurden wieder an den Wänden entlang aufgestellt, und als ihre Zahl ständig wuchs, wurden die Schränke, in denen man sie aufbewahrte, immer größer und die Räume immer höher, bis sogar Leitern nicht mehr ausreichten und Galerien oder Balkone eingezogen wurden. Das Prinzip des Saales, der an den Wänden von Büchern umgeben war, blieb jedoch bestehen. Es war zum erstenmal in der Bibliothek Philipps II. im Escorial (1567) angewandt worden (Abb. 10), wo 18000 Bände in Schränken an den Wänden entlang aufgestellt waren. Die Bibliothek des Escorial unterschied sich darin von den früheren Bibliotheken der Renaissance wie der Malatestiana oder auch der Laurenziana (Abb. 7, 8), die innerhalb ihrer Renaissance-Architektur den mittelalterlichen Grundriß beibehalten hatten.
Ein frühes Beispiel der Saalbibliothek ist die Biblioteca Ambrosiana in Mailand (1603–1609), die von Kardinal Federigo Borromeo gegründet wurde. Sie war 26 m lang und 13,60 m breit und mit einer Tonne gedeckt, in die ein Zwischengeschoß eingezogen werden mußte, damit die Bücher leichter zugänglich waren. Die unteren Bücherschränke waren 4 m hoch, und darüber lag eine Galerie, die über eine Treppe in jeder Ecke zu erreichen war und ihrerseits 2,60 m hohe Büchergestelle trug. Das Konzept

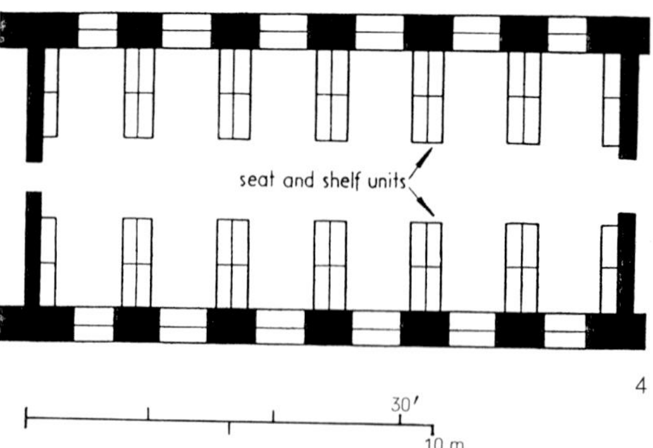

4

5

4. Library of Queens' College, Cambridge, 1448. Shelving is placed at right angles to the wall and used to create carrel-like enclosures within the larger space.
5. South walk of the cloister, Gloucester Cathedral, late fourteenth or early fifteenth century. Twenty carrels were built down one side, each allowed a monk to sit within a secluded lit space.

4. Bibliothek des Queens' College, Cambridge, 1448. Die Regale sind im rechten Winkel zur Wand angeordnet und schaffen so abgesonderte Studienplätze innerhalb des Gesamtraums.
5. Kathedrale in Gloucester, Südseite des Kreuzgangs, spätes 14. bis frühes 15. Jahrhundert. Zwanzig *carrels* ermöglichten den Mönchen ungestörtes Studium in geschlossenen, durch Fenster belichteten Räumen.

6. Library of St. Walburga, Zutphen, Netherlands, 1561–64. The chained medieval library in which the similarity between reading desks and church pews is still extremely evident.
7. Biblioteca Malatestiana, Cesena, c. 1452. The interior shows a medieval arrangement of books and seating within an early Renaissance building; unlike the college libraries of Oxford and Cambridge these are still very much adapted churches.
8. Biblioteca Laurenziana, Florence, 1524; by Michelangelo. Michelangelo still preserves within his Mannerist interior the established plan of the Middle Ages; the ratio of books to readers has not yet reached the stage where there is a need to increase shelf space.
9. University Library, Leyden, 1610. (Reproduced by permission of the Syndics of the Fitzwilliam Museum, Cambridge.) The chained books are now on shelves above the the reading desks; on the right there is a book cupboard, on the left some of the new information sources which were introduced into libraries.

6. Bibliothek St. Walburga, Zutphen, Holland, 1561–64. In der mittelalterlichen Bibliothek waren die Bücher häufig angekettet; die Verwandtschaft zwischen Lesepult und Kirchenbank ist hier noch deutlich erkennbar.
7. Biblioteca Malatestiana, Cesena, etwa 1452. Die Innenansicht zeigt die mittelalterliche Anordnung von Büchern und Pulten in einem frühen Renaissance-Bau; im Gegensatz zu den College-Bibliotheken in Oxford und Cambridge handelt es sich hier noch um umgewandelte Kirchenräume.
8. Biblioteca Laurenziana, Florenz, 1524. Erbaut von Michelangelo. Michelangelo hält sich in diesem manieristischen Innenraum noch an die mittelalterliche Anordnung. Das Verhältnis von Büchern zu Lesern hatte sich noch nicht so sehr verändert, daß eine Erweiterung der Regalflächen notwendig geworden wäre.
9. Universitätsbibliothek, Leyden, 1610 (abgebildet mit Genehmigung des Fitzwilliam Museum, Cambridge). Die angeketteten Bücher stehen nun auf Regalen über den Lesepulten. Rechts ein Bücherschrank, auf der linken Seite einige der neuen Informationsquellen, die damals in die Bibliotheken eingeführt wurden.

6

7

8

9

10

11

fifty years later, the number had grown to 110,000. The Bodleian at Oxford possessed about 150,000 volumes by 1817, the British Museum about 250,000 by the 1830's. Concurrent with this quantitative increase there occurred a separation of the library as an institution invariably attached to the Court, the Church or the University. Although the Ambrosiana had times at which it was open to the public and Cardinal Mazarin's library of 1643 in Paris was open one day a week, it was a long time before the library was considered to serve a public function and was designed as such. The move was perhaps typified, as Nikolaus Pevsner has commented when "in 1774–78 Frederick the Great built a library for Berlin, at right angles to Unter den Linden and on a plan and an elevation adapted from a design of Fischer von Erlach's for the Hofburg. It was from the start intended as a public library and it carries the inscription *Nutrimentum Spiritus,* a telling testimony to the new, universally educational function of libraries in general."

These new problems of the library were explored by the French visionary architects of the late 18th century and particularly by Boullée between 1785 and 1788 in three projects for the Bibliothèque Nationale in Paris (Figs. 15–17). Both size and the new symbolic importance of the library as a shrine of knowledge had an immediate appeal and rationalized the monumental strivings of Boullée, Ledoux and Lefebvre who, for instance, was premiated in the Academy's Grand Prix of 1787 when, significantly, the subject set was a Bibliothèque Publique.

It is an Italian, however, Leopoldo della Santa who in 1816 is generally assumed to have made new solutions possible by devising an alternative principle, namely that of separating stack space, reading room and offices. The plan (Fig.20) shows three clearly differentiated zones: a central reading room adjacent to a catalogue area; a group of offices which can be reached from the catalogue room, the stacks and particularly the rare book collection; and finally two long wings of stacks on either side of the central group of rooms. This three zone separation was to become the accepted organisation of library space for very many of the large libraries which were to be built during the next hundred years.

Della Santa's type plan "was reproduced by Christian Molbech in a Danish book *Om Offentlige Bibliotheker* in 1829, and this was translated into German in 1833" (Pevsner) so that by the 1830's the idea was known in some parts

des großen Einheitsraumes, an dessen Wänden Bücher und gelegentlich auch – wie schon in Ephesus – Bildwerke untergebracht waren, blieb bis ins 18. Jahrhundert hinein bestehen und wurde am großzügigsten in den süddeutschen und österreichischen Klosterbibliotheken verwirklicht. Die Bibliotheken von St. Florian, Melk, Ottobeuren, Wiblingen und vielen anderen Barockklöstern des oberen Donaugebiets (Abb. 11–13) waren Säle, in denen Licht, Skulpturen, Bilder, Bücher und Raumorganisation als Einheit betrachtet wurden. Innerhalb der Gebäudekomplexe spielten sie eine symbolisch bedeutsame Rolle.

Dieser Zustand war in mancher Hinsicht idyllisch, doch sollte bald ein Wandel eintreten, der durch zwei Faktoren bedingt war: Zum einen nahm die Zahl der gedruckten Bücher ständig zu, zum anderen wuchs auch die Zahl der Leser, die sich in den Bibliotheken zu informieren suchten. Die Göttinger Universität besaß zum Beispiel im Jahre 1737 erst 12000 Bände, doch 1786, weniger als fünfzig Jahre später, war der Bestand auf 110000 gestiegen. Die Bodleian Library in Oxford verfügte 1817 über etwa 150000 Werke, das British Museum um 1830 über 250000 Bände. Gleichzeitig begann sich die Bibliothek, die bis dahin stets dem Hof, der Kirche oder einer Universität angegliedert war, zu einer selbständigen Institution zu entwickeln. Obwohl die Ambrosiana zu bestimmten Zeiten dem Publikum offenstand und Kardinal Mazarins Bibliothek in Paris (1643) an einem Tag in der Woche geöffnet war, dauerte es lange, bis die Bibliothek als öffentliche Einrichtung angesehen und entsprechend geplant wurde. Ein Markstein dieser Entwicklung war – wie auch Nikolaus Pevsner aufzeigte – der Berliner Bibliotheksbau, »den Friedrich der Große in den Jahren 1774 bis 1778 errichten ließ. Er lag rechtwinklig zur Straße Unter den Linden, Grundriß und Aufriß gingen auf einen Entwurf Fischer von Erlachs für die Wiener Hofburg zurück. Die Berliner Bibliothek war von Anfang an als öffentliche Institution gedacht und trug die Inschrift *Nutrimentum Spiritus*, ein beredtes Zeugnis für die neue allgemeinbildende Aufgabe der Bibliotheken.«

Mit den neuartigen Problemen der Bibliothek setzten sich zunächst die visionären französischen Architekten des späten 18. Jahrhunderts auseinander, vor allem Boullée, der zwischen 1785 und 1788 drei Projekte für die Bibliothèque Nationale in Paris entwarf (Abb. 15–17). Die Größe

12. Library, Freising, Oberbayern, 1732–38. ▷
13. Library, Wiblingen, near Ulm, Wurttemberg, 1744; by Christian Wiedemann. The baroque monastic libraries of Southern Germany and Austria raised the classical tradition of a book-lined space decorated with sculpture and painting to new levels of virtuosity; the emphasis was however on books and their display rather than on readers.
14. Trinity College Library, Cambridge, 1677–99; by Sir Christopher Wren. Wren combines the medieval plan based on putting books at right angles to the light with the Renaissance need for shelving along a wall reaching as high as possible; he does this by raising the windows above the top line of the presses.

12. Klosterbibliothek Freising, Oberbayern, 1732–38. ▷
13. Klosterbibliothek Wiblingen bei Ulm, 1744. Erbaut von Christian Wiedemann. Die barocken Klosterbibliotheken in Süddeutschland und Österreich führten die klassische Tradition des von Bücherwänden begrenzten Raumes, der mit Skulpturen und Gemälden dekoriert wurde, zu neuen Höhepunkten. Das zur Schau gestellte Buch spielte in diesen Bibliotheken freilich eine wichtigere Rolle als der Leser selbst.
14. Bibliothek des Trinity College, Cambridge, 1677–99. Erbaut von Sir Christopher Wren. Wren kombinierte den mittelalterlichen Grundriß – Regale im rechten Winkel zur Lichtquelle – mit der Konzeption der Renaissance, die Bücher in möglichst hohen Wandregalen unterzubringen: Die Fenster sind oberhalb der Regale angeordnet.

◁ 10. The Library, Escorial, 1567. This royal monastic library built by Philip II is likely to have been the first aisleless space which had tall shelves lining the walls to cope with the increase in the size of book collections; there were about 18,000 volumes in the Escorial library.
11. St. Florian, near Linz, Austria, 1744–50; by Jakob Prandtauer and Gotthard Hayberger. Bookshelving and wall become the same thing; a gallery is built to make high level access possible.

◁ 10. Bibliothek des Escorial, 1567. Diese königliche Klosterbibliothek, unter Philipp II. erbaut, ist wahrscheinlich die erste Bibliothek ohne Mittelgang und mit hohen Wandregalen, in denen die ständig wachsende Zahl der Bücher – der Escorial verfügte bereits über 18000 Bände – untergebracht werden sollte.
11. St. Florian bei Linz, 1744–50. Erbaut von Jakob Prandtauer und Gotthard Hayberger. Bücherregale und Wände werden zu einer Einheit; die Bücher in den oberen Regalen sind über eine Galerie zu erreichen.

12

13

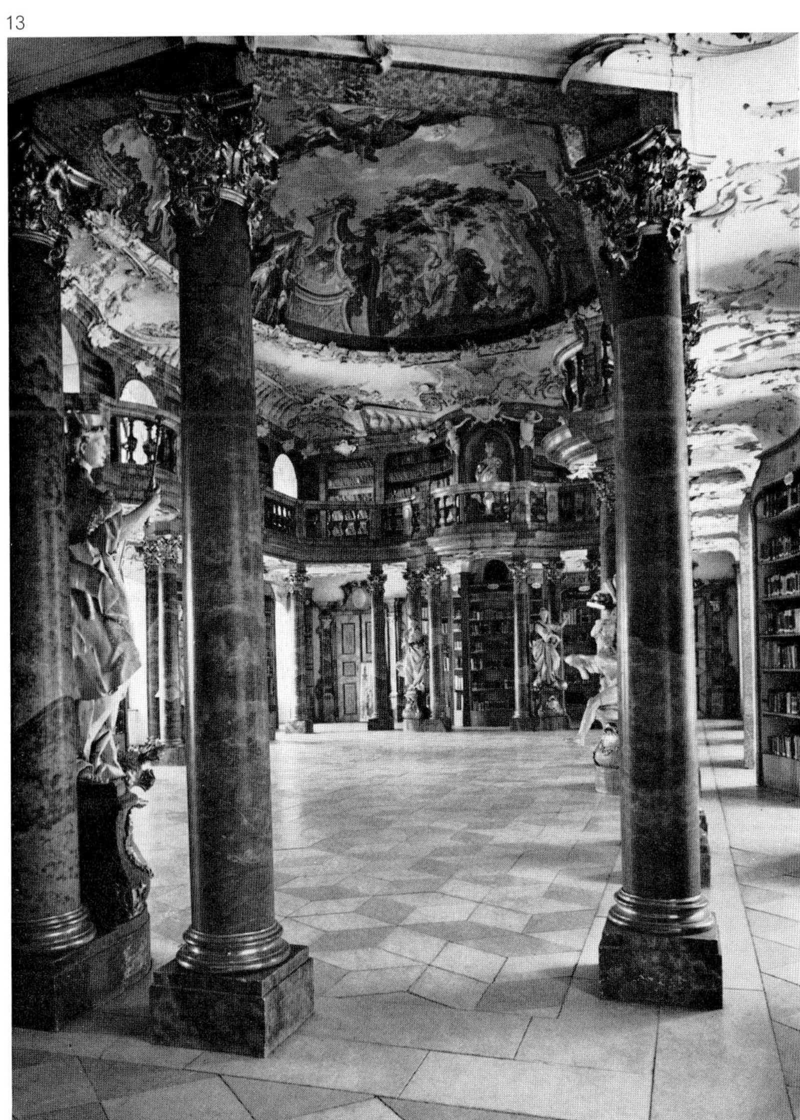

14

of Europe. The tripartite division which was suggested need not of course occur only horizontally but can equally well do so vertically. It was such a separation on section which was the organisation of Labrouste's design for the Bibliothèque Sainte Geneviève in Paris of 1843–51 (Fig. 19). Here a large top-lit reading room seating 600 readers is placed on the upper floors, a range of tall stacks on the lower floor. This also conformed closely to the needs of these two areas, of readers for light – this was before the invention of gas or electric artificial lighting – and of stacks for adequate support of the heavy load imposed by the book storage.

Horizontal separation was used in the two important library designs of the 1850's, that of the British Museum in London (Fig. 21) an d of the Bibliothèque Nationale in Paris (Figs. 22, 23). At the British Museum Sydney Smirke, working on the suggestion of Panizzi who was then Librarian, created a great central circular reading room seating 364 readers surrounded by stacks all made of iron with floors only 8 feet apart. Labrouste's design for the Bibliothèque Nationale divided a large and

wie auch die neue symbolische Bedeutung der Bibliothek als Schrein des Wissens machten sie zu einem interessanten Planungsobjekt und entsprachen den monumentalen Vorstellungen von Boullée, Ledoux und Lefebvre, der bezeichnenderweise den Grand Prix im Jahre 1787 erhielt, als die Akademie eine Bibliothèque Publique ausgeschrieben hatte.

Es war jedoch der Italiener Leopoldo della Santa, der 1816 den Weg zu neuen Lösungen wies. Della Santa schlug ein Prinzip der Dreigliederung vor und trennte Magazine, Publikumsräume und Verwaltung voneinander. Sein Idealplan (Abb. 20) zeigt drei klar abgegrenzte Zonen: einen zentralen Lesesaal, an den sich der Katalog anschließt; eine Reihe von Büroräumen, die sowohl vom Katalograum wie vom Magazin wie vor allem von der Sammlung seltener Bücher aus erreichbar sind; und schließlich zwei lange Magazinflügel zu beiden Seiten des Zentralbereichs. Diese Dreigliederung wurde in den meisten großen Bibliotheken angewandt, die im Laufe der nächsten hundert Jahre entstanden. Della Santas Idealplan »wurde 1829 von Christian Molbech in dem dänischen Buch *Om Offent-*

15

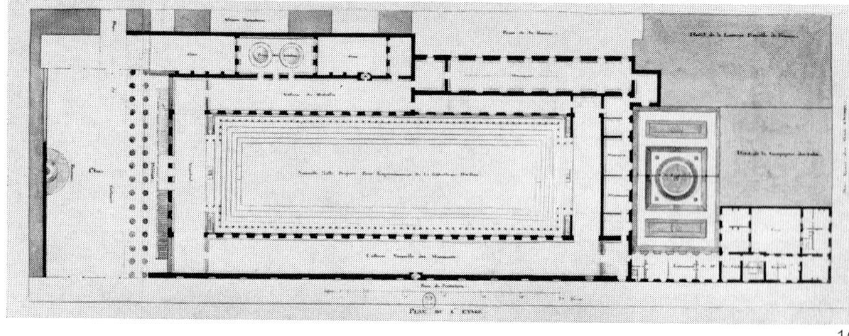

16

17

15–17. Design for the Bibliothèque Nationale, Paris, 1785; by Etienne-Louis Boullée. To house the accumulated store of knowledge became one of the design tasks which greatly appealed to the French architects of the late eighteenth century; the desire for size and monumentality could in some way be rationalized for book collections were now vast and their symbolic standing high. The section shows that books are being stored both in the tiered reading room and the tall first floor rooms on either side.

15–17. Entwurf für die Bibliothèque Nationale, Paris, 1785. Erbaut von Etienne-Louis Boullée. Die Unterbringung des angesammelten Wissensstoffes war eine Bauaufgabe, mit der die französischen Architekten des späten 18. Jahrhunderts sich häufig auseinandersetzten. Ihre Vorliebe für Größe und Monumentalität war auch rational zu erklären, denn die Büchersammlungen wurden nun immer umfangreicher und hatten große symbolische Bedeutung. Der Schnitt zeigt, daß die Bücher sowohl in dem stufenförmig ansteigenden Lesesaal wie auch in den hohen Räumen zu beiden Seiten des Obergeschosses aufbewahrt werden.

18

18. Carl Ludvig Engel's great neo-classical Library facing the cathedral in Helsinki was finished in 1840. It is one of the significant monuments of the nineteenth century testifying to the civic and national importance accorded to the idea of learning. It was enlarged and renovated by Aarne Ervi in 1954.

18. Die große neoklassizistische Bibliothek von Carl Ludvig Engel, gegenüber der Kathedrale in Helsinki, wurde 1840 vollendet. Sie gehört zu den bedeutendsten Baudenkmälern des 19. Jahrhunderts und ist ein Zeugnis dafür, welche wichtige Rolle Stadt und Staat der Idee der Gelehrsamkeit beimaßen. Aarne Ervi hat das Gebäude 1954 erweitert und renoviert.

remarkable reading room seating about 360 readers, from a multi-storey top-lit stack with only a great glass window. The columns and floors of the book storage space were iron, the stacks themselves were wooden. The roof immediately above the stacks was of glass and the floors were iron grating so that a multi-level luminous space was created.

Despite the considerable originality of the stack space in Labrouste's design, the main visual emphasis in this new type of library occurred in the reading area. This was as true for the domed space of the British Museum Reading Room as for Labrouste's two libraries where he used cast iron to produce apparently insubstantially supported domed roofs over large enclosures. This emphasis on the reading room reversed of course the development of the great book-lined room which had been pursued by the architects of the Baroque. The reader, as in the medieval period, was again paramount. He also surrounded himself with a small selection of books within a very much larger space, only now the degree of enclosure became very much less. His detachment had to some extent to be felt by seeing himself as a very small unit within a very large volume. Height, which had been principally a device

*lige Bibliotheker* reproduziert, das 1833 in deutscher Sprache erschien« (Pevsner), so daß dieses Gliederungsprinzip nach 1830 in einigen Teilen Europas bekannt war. Es konnte natürlich nicht nur in der Horizontalen, sondern ebenso gut in der Vertikalen angewendet werden. Eine solche vertikale Trennung der Funktionen lag zum Beispiel Labroustes Entwurf für die Bibliothèque Sainte Geneviève in Paris (1843–51) zugrunde (Abb. 19). Hier nimmt ein großer, durch Oberlicht erhellter Lesesaal für 600 Benutzer das obere Geschoß ein, während die hohen Regale des Magazins im Erdgeschoß untergebracht sind. Diese Disposition entsprach den Funktionen beider Bereiche, denn die Leser brauchten Licht – Gaslicht oder elektrische Beleuchtung waren noch nicht erfunden –, und die schwere Bücherlast in den Magazinen erforderte auf diese Weise keine aufwendigen statischen Maßnahmen.

Horizontale Differenzierung kennzeichnet die beiden wichtigen Bibliotheksentwürfe um 1850, die Bibliothek des British Museum in London (Abb. 21) und die Bibliothèque Nationale in Paris (Abb. 22, 23). Im British Museum schuf Sydney Smirke auf einen Vorschlag des damaligen Bibliotheksdirektors Panizzi hin einen zentralen kreisförmigen Lesesaal für 364 Benutzer. Den Lesesaal umgeben

19

19. Bibliothèque Ste. Geneviève, Paris, 1843–51; by Henri Labrouste. The first floor reading room placed over a ground floor stack area; della Santa's separation is achieved here vertically.
20. Plan for a Library by Leopoldo della Santa, 1816. First published in his *Della costruzione e del regolamento di una Pubblica Universale Biblioteca,* della Santa's plan shows a clear tripartite division: readers in the centre, catalogue area and offices also in the centre, stacks on either side.
21. Reading Room, British Museum, London, 1854–56; by Sydney Smirke. The caption to the plan and view shown in *The Illustrated London News* for 9th May 1857 draws attention to the technical innovations of the structure and the method of ventilation and gives great praise to the conception of a single structure – built inside an existing courtyard of the Museum – due to Panizzi, the Librarian. The idea of a central circular reading room surrounded by bookstorage space was to be influential for a long time.

19. Bibliothèque Ste. Geneviève, Paris, 1843–51. Erbaut von Henri Labrouste. Der Lesesaal im ersten Stock liegt über einem Büchermagazin im Erdgeschoß; della Santas Gliederungsprinzip ist hier in der Vertikalen angewandt worden.
20. Plan für eine Bibliothek, 1816. Leopoldo della Santa. Della Santas Idealplan, der zuerst in seinem Werk *Della costruzione e del regolamento di una Pubblica Universale Biblioteca* veröffentlicht wurde, zeigt eine klare Dreigliederung: Lesesaal, Katalog und Verwaltungsräume im Zentrum, Magazine zu beiden Seiten der Mittelzone.
21. Lesesaal in der Bibliothek des British Museum, London, 1854–56. Erbaut von Sydney Smirke. Der Text zu Grundriß und Ansicht in *The Illustrated London News* vom 9. Mai 1857 hebt die technischen Neuerungen der Konstruktion und der Klimatisierung hervor und lobt besonders die Tatsache, daß alle Funktionen in einem einzigen Bauwerk untergebracht wurden, das auf Anregung Panizzis in einen vorhandenen Hof des Museums eingebaut wurde. Die Idee eines zentralen, kreisförmigen Lesesaals, der von Bücherregalen umgeben ist, beeinflußte spätere Planungen.

to assist monumentality, became also a psychological aid towards isolation and thus concentration.
The books which the reader was able to have around him were brought to him by a member of the library staff; in this sense the tripartite division of the 19th century library plan created new problems while it solved existing ones. The degree of accessibility between the user and the information source, security precautions apart, was less than it had been in a college library of the 15th century or a baroque monastic library of the 18th century. The problem was again largely one of numbers.
This numerical increase was part of the technological change which took place in the 19th century and, as far as printing is concerned, happened largely between 1800 and 1820. During these two decades the metal press, the foot-operated cylinder press and the mechanical steam-press all came into use. These made large printings possible and these in turn tended to increase the number of titles published. In the 18th century the average printing in England was thought to have been between 500 and 1000 copies; by 1814 Byron's *The Corsair* sold 10,000 copies on the day of publication.
Attempts were therefore made to subdivide the number of books and readers, and also to separate out different library functions. This occurred perhaps for the first time at the Saltykov-Shchedrin Public Library in St. Petersburg – now one of the very large libraries of not only Leningrad but the Soviet Union – when it was extended in the early 1830's; "to satisfy the varied needs of many different categories of readers, there were not only general reading rooms but also specialized reading rooms for research, for journals, newspapers etc. These in turn were divided up according to the fields of knowledge" (from *Putevoditel po gos. Publichnoi Biblioteke,* Leningrad 1956, quoted by Thompson).
One of the principal functional subdivisions which was made was between lending and reading within the building. The character of the two activities was radically different and mutually conflicting. Such a separation was made at Marburg in 1840. This general trend continued throughout the second half of the 19th century not only within large libraries, but led also to the establishment of

an der Peripherie eiserne Büchergestelle mit Laufstegen in Abständen von nur 2,45 m. Labroustes Entwurf für die Bibliothèque Nationale trennte den eindrucksvollen großen Lesesaal, der ebenfalls etwa 360 Besucher aufnimmt, von dem mehrgeschossigen, durch Oberlicht beleuchteten Magazin durch ein einziges großes Glasfenster. Stützen und Böden des Magazinbereichs waren aus Eisen, die Gestelle selbst aus Holz. Das Dach unmittelbar über den Bücherregalen war verglast, und da die Böden aus eisernen Rosten bestanden, ergab sich ein mehrgeschossiger lichterfüllter Raum.
Wenn auch die Magazinzone in Labroustes Entwurf von bemerkenswerter Originalität war, lag der Hauptakzent bei diesem neuen Bibliothekstyp gewöhnlich auf dem Lesebereich. Das gilt ebenso für den kuppelgedeckten Lesesaal des British Museum wie für die beiden Bibliotheken Labroustes, bei denen er Gußeisen verwandte, um die weiträumigen Säle mit scheinbar schwebenden Kuppeldächern überspannen zu können. Diese Akzentuierung des Lesebereichs führte natürlich von der büchergesäumten Saalbibliothek der Barockarchitekten fort. Wie im Mittelalter spielte der Leser wieder die Hauptrolle. Auch er umgab sich innerhalb eines sehr viel größeren Raumes mit einer kleinen Auswahl von Büchern, nur war nun der Grad der Abgeschlossenheit sehr viel geringer. Isolation kam jetzt dadurch zustande, daß der Leser sich selbst als sehr kleine Einheit in einem sehr großen Ganzen empfinden mußte. So wurde die Höhe der Räume, die ursprünglich um der Monumentalität willen eingeführt worden war, zu einem psychologischen Hilfsmittel, das Isolation und damit Konzentration förderte.
Die Bücher, mit denen sich der Leser einst an seinem Platz umgab, brachte ihm jetzt ein Bibliotheksangestellter; insofern schuf die Dreigliederung des Bibliotheksgrundrisses im 19. Jahrhundert neue Probleme, während sie andere gelöst hatte. Für den Benutzer war die Informationsquelle weniger leicht zugänglich – von Sicherheitsvorkehrungen einmal abgesehen –, als sie es in einer College-Bibliothek des 15. Jahrhunderts oder einer barocken Klosterbibliothek des 18. Jahrhunderts gewesen war. Wieder ergaben sich die Schwierigkeiten hauptsächlich aus der wachsenden Zahl der Bücher und der Benutzer.

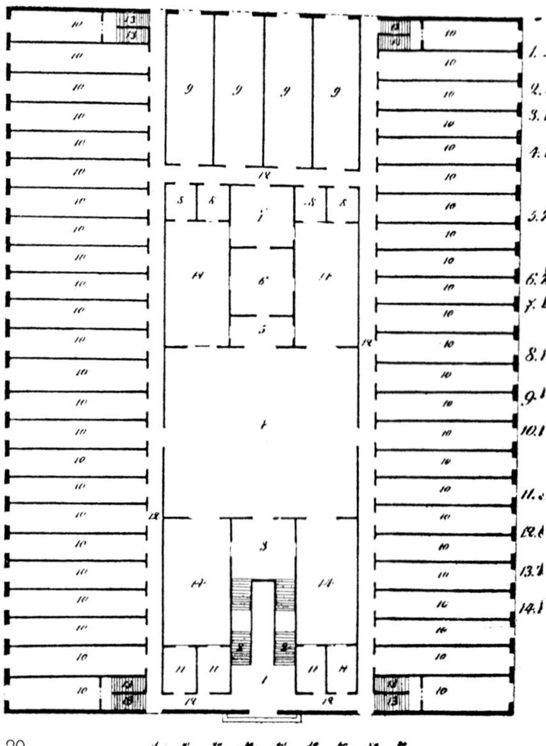

20

THE NEW READING-ROOM, BRITISH MUSEUM.

rounding libraries, 750,000. The building is constructed principally of iron, with brick arches between the main ribs, supported by 20 iron piers, having a sectional area of 10 superficial feet to each, including the brick casing, or 200 feet in all. This saving of space by the use of iron is remarkable, the piers of support on which our dome rests only thus occupying 200 feet; whereas the piers of the Pantheon of Rome fill 7477 feet of area, and those of the Tomb of Mahomet 5593. Upwards of 2000 tons of iron have been used in the construction. The weight of the materials used in the dome is about 4200 tons—viz., upwards of 200 tons on each pier. The roof is formed into two separate spherical and concentric air-chambers, extending over the whole surface: one between the external covering and brick vaulting, the object being the equalisation of temperature during extremes of heat and cold out of doors; the other chamber, between the brick vaulting and the internal visible surface, being intended to carry off the vitiated air from the reading-room. This ventilation is effected through apertures in the soffites of the windows, and partly by others at the top of the dome; the bad air passing through outlets provided around the lantern. In order to obviate the effects of condensation, all the skylights, lanterns, and windows throughout the building are double. The quantity of glass used amounts to about 60,000 superficial feet.

The main entrance into the new Reading-room is direct from the Great Hall, and there are secondary entrances viâ the King's Library and the Great Northern Library rooms.

To Mr. Panizzi is due the merit of the first conception of a single and sufficient structure. His indefatigable industry and his untiring interest in the Museum have been devoted to the daily inspection of the works, and he has originated constant and valuable suggestions in the course of their progress.

The architect, Mr. Smirke, has his merit in the preparation of the original and first designs. The contractors, Messrs. Baker and Fielder, share no common deserts in their professional labours. Indeed, the skill, perseverance, and ingenious resources of their managing partner, Mr. Fielder, have been beyond all praise. All worked together, we understand, without vanity or jealousy, to complete a public reading-room worthy the Museum and their country.

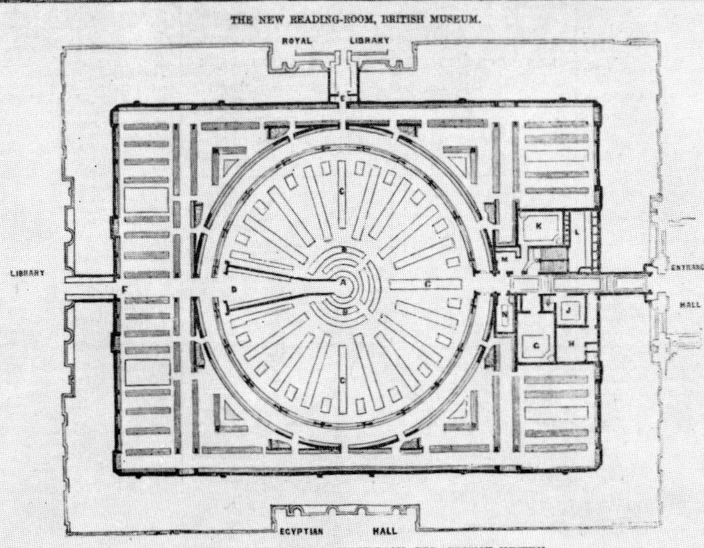


GROUND-PLAN OF THE NEW READING-ROOM, ETC., BRITISH MUSEUM.

REFERENCES TO THE GROUND-PLA

A Superintendent.
B Catalogues.
C Readers' Tables.
D Access for Attendants.
E Entrance from Royal Library.
F Entrance from North Library.
G For Registration of Copyrights
H Ladies' Cloak room.
J Attendants' R[illegible]m.
K Gentlemen's Cloak-room
L For Gentlemen.
M Umbrella-room.
N Assistants' Room

22

23

22, 23. Bibliothèque Nationale, Paris, 1868; by Henri Labrouste. The reading room, top lit through partially glazed saucer domes, is only separated from the stack area by a large glazed opening seen behind the issue desk.

22, 23. Bibliothèque Nationale, Paris, 1868. Erbaut von Henri Labrouste. Der Lesesaal mit seinen teilweise verglasten kuppelförmigen Oberlichtern ist vom Magazin nur durch ein großes Glasfenster hinter der Bücherausgabe getrennt.

different kinds of separate libraries, both institutional and public. This diffusion was greatly influenced by the 19th century emphasis on the value of knowledge and particularly on its value as a means of improving the mind and morals of the growing urban population. In England for example the Act of Parliament brought in by William Ewart which authorized the establishment of public libraries dealt with towns over 10,000 only. The Act which was in any case permissive and not compulsory was extended to Scotland and Ireland in 1853 but it was not until the Public Libraries Amendment Act of 1918 that the county became the administrative unit and a library service could be provided in rural areas.

During the 19th century libraries were also frequently seen as philanthropic institutions which, like museums, were part of an attempt to make possible the "improvement", through education, of the less privileged. They therefore appeared in the Utopian proposals put forward at the beginning of the century and occupied a central place in these. Robert Owen (1771–1858) putting forward his thesis based on the proposals established at New Lanark describes the centre of an ideal village in his *Report to the Committee for the Relief of the Manufacturing Poor,* March 1817, as "the central building contains a public kitchen, mess-rooms and all the accommodation necessary to economical and comfortable cooking and eating. To the right of this is a building, of which the ground floor will form the infant school, and the others a lecture-room and a place of worship. The building on the left contains a school for the older children, and a committee room on the ground floor; above a library and a room for adults." A very similar description appears in Charles Fourier's (1772–1837) *Traité de l'association domestique-agricole* in which a single communal building, the Phalanstery, becomes in effect a town. Within it again "the central part ought to be appropriated to public uses, and contain the dining halls, halls for finance, libraries, study etc." (both quotations from Leonardo Benevolo *The Origins of Modern Town Planning,* London 1967). At the end of the century some of these suggestions were, in greatly modified form, actually put into effect. H. H. Richardson for example built the Oakes Ames Memorial Library in North Easton, Massachusetts (Fig. 24), between 1877–79 as part of a new central group of buildings within a manufacturing town as a memorial to Oakes Ames. The building was commissioned according to H.-R. Hitchcock *(The Architecture of H.H. Richardson and His Times,* Hamden, Connecticut, 1961) "by the heirs of two of the most famous and, indeed, notorious magnates of the period." Library buildings became one of the public gestures which might somehow balance the moral accounts of an industrial society.

At the turn of the century the public libraries of the English speaking countries gained greatly through the financial aid given by Andrew Carnegie (1835–1919), the Scottish-born American manufacturer, and his charitable trusts. Carnegie undertook to build and equip public libraries if the local authority gave the site and maintained the service; by 1918 he had erected 2,505 such buildings throughout the world. He also helped to influence the character of these libraries, particularly through a pamphlet published in 1911 by the Carnegie Corporation, *Notes on the Erection of Library Buildings* which suggested rather more informal library spaces than were then current and which considered the library building as a potential community centre with an auditorium and rooms for other educational activities.

By the beginning of the 20th century there existed therefore a hierarchy of libraries within most countries. This had a single national library at one end of the scale, a large

Diese quantitative Zunahme war auf die technischen Umwälzungen zurückzuführen, die sich auf dem Gebiet des Buchdrucks hauptsächlich zwischen 1800 und 1820 vollzogen. In diesen beiden Jahrzehnten kamen die Metallpresse, die fußbetriebene Zylinderpresse und die mechanische Dampfpresse in Gebrauch, die den Druck hoher Auflagen ermöglichten. Damit wuchs auch die Zahl der Titel, die veröffentlicht wurden. Im 18. Jahrhundert dürfte in England die durchschnittliche Auflagenhöhe zwischen 500 und 1 000 Exemplaren gelegen haben; aber schon 1814 wurden von Byrons Verserzählung *The Corsair* am Tage des Erscheinens 10000 Exemplare verkauft.

Es wurden Versuche unternommen, Bücher wie Leser in Gruppen aufzugliedern und außerdem verschiedene Funktionen der Bibliothek auszusondern. Dies geschah wahrscheinlich zum erstenmal in der Saltykov-Shchedrin-Bibliothek in St. Petersburg – heute eine der größten Bibliotheken nicht nur Leningrads, sondern auch der Sowjetunion –, als sie um 1830 erweitert wurde. »Um die unterschiedlichen Bedürfnisse der vielen verschiedenen Leserkategorien zu befriedigen, wurden nicht nur allgemeine Lesesäle eingerichtet, sondern auch besondere Leseräume für wissenschaftliche Arbeit, für Zeitschriften, Zeitungen usw. Diese Räume waren wiederum nach Wissensgebieten unterteilt.« (Aus *Putevoditel po gos. Publichnoi Biblioteke,* Leningrad 1956, zitiert nach Thompson.)

Eine der wichtigsten Funktionstrennungen war die zwischen Ausleihe und Lektüre an Ort und Stelle, zwei grundsätzlich verschiedene Tätigkeiten, die im Konflikt miteinander standen. Eine solche Trennung wurde beispielsweise 1840 in Marburg vorgenommen. In der zweiten Hälfte des 19. Jahrhunderts setzte sich diese Entwicklung fort; sie führte nicht nur zur Aufgliederung innerhalb großer Bibliotheken, sondern auch zur Errichtung verschiedener Spezialbibliotheken, die entweder bestimmten Institutionen angeschlossen waren oder dem Publikum offenstanden. Von Einfluß war dabei die Tatsache, daß das 19. Jahrhundert dem Wissen besonderen Wert beimaß, vor allem, da es geeignet schien, das geistige und moralische Niveau der ständig zunehmenden Stadtbevölkerung zu heben. In England bezog sich beispielsweise das Gesetz über die Errichtung von Volksbüchereien, das William Ewart dem Parlament vorlegte, nur auf Städte mit mehr als 10000 Einwohnern. Das Gesetz, das freilich fakultativ und nicht obligatorisch war, trat 1853 auch in Schottland und Irland in Kraft; doch erst mit der Gesetzesnovelle für Volksbüchereien vom Jahre 1918 wurden die Grafschaften als Verwaltungseinheiten anerkannt, so daß auch in ländlichen Gebieten Bibliotheken eingerichtet werden konnten.

Im 19. Jahrhundert wurde die Bibliothek häufig auch als philanthropische Institution betrachtet; ähnlich dem Museum sollte sie die weniger Privilegierten durch Erziehung »fördern«. So spielten Bibliotheken eine wichtige Rolle in den utopischen Projekten, die zu Beginn des Jahrhunderts publiziert wurden. Robert Owen (1771–1858), dessen Thesen auf den in New Lanark formulierten Reformvorschlägen beruhten, beschreibt in seinem *Report to the Committee for the Relief of the Manufacturing Poor* vom März 1817 das Zentrum eines idealen Dorfes folgendermaßen: »Das zentrale Gebäude enthält eine öffentliche Küche, Speisesäle und alle Einrichtungen, die für wirtschaftliches und bequemes Kochen und Essen erforderlich sind. Rechts davon liegt ein Gebäude, das im Erdgeschoß die Schule für die kleineren Kinder und in den anderen Geschossen einen Vortragssaal und eine Andachtsstätte aufnimmt. Das Gebäude links enthält im Erdgeschoß eine Schule für die älteren Kinder und einen Versammlungsraum; darüber sind eine Bibliothek und ein Raum für Erwachsene

number of highly local public libraries at the other. Intermediate to these were the regional or county libraries and the central town libraries. In many countries all these facilities as well as specialized institutions dealing with science or art, for instance, were linked by an inter-library loan service. What emerged from this was an inter-locking library service by which the demands of readers could be met not only from local sources but normally from the library resources of the whole country. Occasionally international loans were also possible. This complex service was in England and many other European countries largely housed in buildings of the 19th century, most of which were from the 1880's and 1890's. This association between a large proportion of the library service and late Victorian institutional buildings was to be an unfortunate legacy for many years to come. The idea of reading a book in the sort of environment envisaged for St. Jerome in the 15th century seemed far removed. The problem which most recent library design has thus set itself is how to provide an environment of that quality for large numbers and how to make the activity of using a library part of an everyday existence while at the same time coping with the very considerable technical problems produced by the rapid increase in the quantity of information.

24. Oakes Ames Memorial Library, North Easton, Massachussetts, 1877–79; by H. H. Richardson. Library building in the nineteenth century became in many instances a charitable activity for the improvement of the working poor; the Oakes Ames Memorial Library commemorated a somewhat infamous North American magnate of the middle of the century.

24. Oakes Ames Memorial Library, North Easton, Massachussetts, 1877–79. Architeckt: H. H. Richardson. Bibliotheksbauten des 19. Jahrhunderts waren häufig Stiftungen zum Wohle der ärmeren Bevölkerungsschichten; die Oakes Ames Memorial Library wurde von den Erben des berühmt-berüchtigten nordamerikanischen Magnaten in Auftrag gegeben.

24

untergebracht.« Eine sehr ähnliche Beschreibung findet sich in Charles Fouriers (1772–1837) *Traité de l'association domestique-agricole*, der aus einem einzigen kommunalen Gebäude, dem Phalanstère, eine ganze Stadt entwickelt. Auch hier »sollte der zentrale Bereich allgemeinen Zwekken dienen und die Speisesäle, die Räumlichkeiten für Bankgeschäfte oder Studien, Bibliotheken usw. enthalten«. (Beide Zitate nach Leonardo Benevolo, *The Origins of Modern Town Planning*, London 1967.) Am Ende des Jahrhunderts waren einige dieser Vorschläge tatsächlich verwirklicht, wenn auch in stark abgewandelter Form. So baute zum Beispiel H. H. Richardson die Oakes Ames Memorial Library (Abb. 24) in North Easton, Massachusetts (1877–79), die dem Andenken an Oakes Ames gewidmet war und Teil einer neuen zentralen Gebäudegruppe in einer Industriestadt bildete. Nach H.-R. Hitchcock (*The Architecture of H. H. Richardson and His Times*, Hamden, Conn., 1961) wurde das Gebäude »von den Erben der beiden berühmtesten und zugleich berüchtigtsten Magnaten jener Zeit« in Auftrag gegeben. Ein Bibliotheksgebäude zu errichten, war also häufig eine Geste der Öffentlichkeit gegenüber, mit der sich in einer Industriegesellschaft die moralische Bilanz ausgleichen ließ.

Um die Jahrhundertwende wurde das öffentliche Bibliothekswesen der englischsprechenden Länder durch Andrew Carnegie (1835-1919), dem amerikanischen Fabrikanten schottischer Herkunft, und seine karitativen Stiftungen großzügig unterstützt. Carnegie verpflichtete sich, Volksbüchereien zu bauen und auszustatten, wenn die örtliche Verwaltung das Grundstück zur Verfügung stellte und die Instandhaltung übernahm; bis 1918 errichtete er 2505 Bibliotheken in der ganzen Welt. Er beeinflußte auch den Charakter dieser Bibliotheken, vor allem durch die Schrift *Notes on the Erection of Library Buildings* (Anmerkungen zur Errichtung von Bibliotheksbauten), die 1911 von der Carnegie Corporation herausgegeben wurde. Diese Schrift setzte sich für eine weniger einseitige Auffassung der Bibliotheken ein; das Bibliotheksgebäude sollte zu einem Gemeindezentrum mit einem Vortragssaal und Räumen für andere pädagogische Zwecke werden.

Zu Beginn des 20. Jahrhunderts existierte in den meisten Ländern eine Hierarchie der Bibliotheken, von der großen Nationalbibliothek bis zu den zahlreichen lokal orientierten Volksbüchereien; dazwischen rangierten die regionalen Bibliotheken und die zentralen Stadtbibliotheken. In vielen Ländern waren alle diese Bibliotheken wie auch spezialisierte Institutionen, die sich beispielsweise mit Naturwissenschaften oder Kunst befaßten, durch Fernleihverkehr miteinander verbunden. Daraus ergab sich ein engmaschiger Leihdienst, so daß die Leser die Bücher nicht nur aus der Bibliothek ihres Ortes, sondern gewöhnlich auch aus den Bibliotheksbeständen des ganzen Landes beziehen konnten. In besonderen Fällen war sogar internationaler Leihverkehr möglich. Diese komplizierte Organisation war in England wie in vielen anderen europäischen Ländern häufig in Gebäuden des 19. Jahrhunderts untergebracht, von denen die meisten aus den achtziger und neunziger Jahren stammten – ein unseliges Erbe, das noch auf Jahrzehnte die Arbeit der Bibliotheken erschwerte. Es schien unmöglich, Bücher unter Umweltbedingungen zu lesen, wie das 15. Jahrhundert sie sich für den heiligen Hieronymus vorgestellt hatte. So setzte sich die moderne Bibliotheksplanung das Ziel, großen Besucherzahlen ähnlich angenehme Arbeitsmöglichkeiten zu verschaffen und den Bibliohekbesuch zu einem Bestandteil des täglichen Lebens zu machen. Zugleich muß sie sich mit den außerordentlich schwierigen technischen Problemen befassen, die sich aus der schnellen Zunahme des Informationsmaterials ergeben.

A good deal of the present day contribution originated in Scandinavia both as regards library services and library buildings. Both have held an important position there for a considerable period and there was a precedent for innovation. Sweden was, for instance, one of the first European nations to institute legal deposit for its Royal Library in Stockholm in 1661; Norway was, in 1841, the first country to give State aid to public libraries; Denmark was probably the first country to open a library school, in Copenhagen, in 1918. But perhaps most important of all has been the Scandinavian contribution towards making libraries both important and everyday places in the community and giving this notion an acceptable architectural expression.

When in 1927 Alvar Aalto won the first prize for the design of the municipal library at Viipuri (Figs. 25–30), then part of Finland, he was working in the Scandinavian tradition as well as in the more newly established one of the modern movement in architecture. The library, and particularly its book room and lecture hall were to become famous after the completion of the building in 1935 for the way in which these two key spaces of a public library had been handled.

The user, if he was not going to the auditorium or the children's library, was led by a series of half flights to the highest level in the library where the control desk was placed overlooking both the book stack and reading room (Fig. 25). This arrangement made supervision easy but also created a number of distinct though connected spaces separated by changes in floor level within a single volume all top-lit through round conical skylights about two metres in diameter. The placement of the book shelving on two levels created, moreover, as in the Baroque library, additional accessible wall surface and made the books an integral part of the space enclosure. This division also produced two natural areas for that casual reading which occurs when choosing a book, one on the edge of the upper gallery, the other within the pit-like area formed at the centre. Alvar Aalto was to explore this organization in his subsequent library designs, such as that for the seminar and reading room in the Finnish National

Eine wichtige Rolle für die Entwicklung des Bibliotheksbaus spielten die skandinavischen Länder, die großen Wert auf Organisation und Konstruktion von Bibliotheken legen und häufig als erste Neuerungen eingeführt haben. So war zum Beispiel Schweden eine der ersten europäischen Nationen, die im Jahre 1661 die Abgabe von Pflichtexemplaren für die Königliche Bibliothek in Stockholm gesetzlich festlegte; Norwegen war 1841 das erste Land, das öffentlichen Bibliotheken staatliche Subventionen gewährte; in Dänemark wurde 1918 die wahrscheinlich erste Bibliothekarschule eröffnet. Vor allem aber haben die skandinavischen Länder die Bibliothek zu einem alltäglichen und zugleich bedeutsamen Ort des Gemeindelebens gemacht und dieser Konzeption auch zu einem akzeptablen architektonischen Ausdruck verholfen.

Als Alvar Aalto 1927 den ersten Preis für den Entwurf der Stadtbücherei in Viipuri (Abb. 25–30) gewann, das damals zu Finnland gehörte, folgte er der skandinavischen Tradition ebenso wie der modernen Bewegung in der Architektur. Die Bibliothek und vor allem ihr Hauptraum und ihr Vortragssaal wurden nach der Vollendung des Bauwerks im Jahre 1935 weltberühmt, weil Aalto für diese beiden Schlüsselbereiche einer öffentlichen Bibliothek neuartige Lösungen gefunden hatte.

Wenn der Benutzer sich nicht zum Vortragssaal oder zur Jugendbücherei wandte, wurde er über eine dreiläufige Treppe zum höchsten Niveau der Bibliothek geführt, wo vom Aufsichtspult aus Büchermagazin und Lesesaal zu überblicken waren (Abb. 25). Diese Anordnung erleichterte die Kontrolle und schuf zugleich innerhalb eines einzigen Volumens abgegrenzte Bereiche auf verschiedenen Ebenen, die dennoch miteinander in Verbindung standen. Für die Belichtung sorgten konische Oberlichter von etwa 2 m Durchmesser. Die Anordnung der Regaleinheiten in zwei Ebenen ermöglichte es wie in der Barockbibliothek, die Wandflächen weitgehend auszunutzen, und ließ die Bücher zu einem Bestandteil der Raumhülle werden. Dem Leser, der ein Buch auswählte und darin blättern wollte, standen durch die Unterteilung in zwei Niveaus zwei verschiedene Bereiche zur Verfügung, der eine an der Brüstung der oberen Galerie, der andere in dem grubenähnlichen Raum im Zentrum des Lesesaales. In Alvar Aaltos späteren Bibliotheksentwürfen ist diese Idee der Raumorganisation konsequent fortentwickelt, zum Beispiel im Seminar und der Bibliothek der Staatlichen Volkspensionsanstalt in Helsinki (Abb. 31) und in der Bibliothek der Pädagogischen Hochschule in Jyväskylä, wo der Raum zu den Seiten hin in abgestufte Terrassen mit Bücherregalen und Leseplätzen übergeht, die an Boullées Entwurf für die Bibliothèque Nationale erinnern. In den neueren Projekten nahmen diese abgestuften Raumteile eine komplexere fächerartige Form und einen in sich

25–30. Municipal library in Viipuri, Finland, 1935. Architect: Alvar Aalto. This was Alvar Aalto's first library design won in competition in 1927. Local political problems prevented its completion before 1935.
25. The staircase leading to the control desk at the upper level.
26. First floor plan.
27. Ground floor plan.

25–30. Stadtbücherei, Viipuri, Finnland, 1935. Architekt: Alvar Aalto. Alvar Aalto gewann mit seinem ersten Bibliotheksentwurf 1927 den ersten Preis in einem Wettbewerb. Lokalpolitische Schwierigkeiten verzögerten die Fertigstellung bis zum Jahre 1935.
25. Die Treppe führt zum Aufsichtspult im Obergeschoß.
26. Grundriß Obergeschoß.
27. Grundriß Erdgeschoß.

25

26

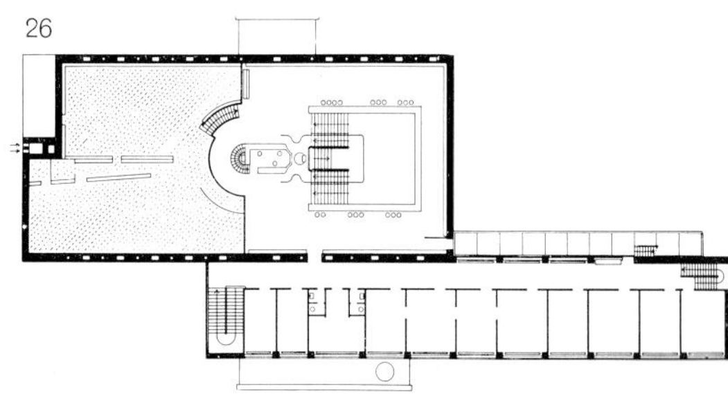

27

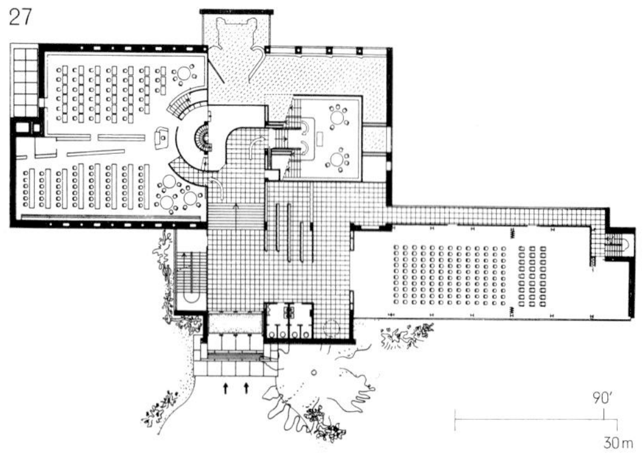

31

31. Library in the National Pensions Institute, Helsinki, 1956. Architect: Alvar Aalto. Some of the elements of Viipuri, particularly the top lighting and the sunk enclosure, were adapted here for use within an office building.

31. Bibliothek der Staatlichen Volkspensionsanstalt, Helsinki, 1956. Architekt: Alvar Aalto. Einige Charakteristika von Viipuri wie die Oberlichter und der umschlossene Lesebereich kehren hier in der Fachbibliothek eines Verwaltungsgebäudes wieder.

28. Aerial view of library in the town park.
29. Entrance.
30. Detail of the ceiling in the lecture room, the speaker's end.

28. Luftansicht der Bibliothek im Stadtpark.
29. Eingang.
30. Deckendetail des Vortragssaals auf der Seite des Rednerpultes.

28

29

30

Pensions Institute in Helsinki (Fig. 31) and the library of the University of Jyväskylä where the sides of the room become stepped terraces with books and reading places reminiscent of Boullée's design for the Bibliothèque Nationale. In later projects this stepped space was to assume a more complex fan-shaped form, was to become more centred on itself and secluded, and thus perhaps a more appropriate library space. It can be seen in the Wolfsburg Cultural Centre in Germany (Figs. 32, 33), in the library at Seinäjoki (Figs. 34–37) and in that of the civic centre at Rovaniemi in northern Finland (Figs. 38–49). In each of these rooms there is an apparently paradoxical situation of openness and seclusion – there is the ability to orientate oneself within the visible total enclosure yet feel anchored to a particular part of it; there is the possibility of supervision by the staff yet no sense of being left exposed in some great space. It is exactly this phenomenon of "both – and", as Robert Venturi, borrowing a phrase from Cleanth Brooks, has described such ordered contradiction, which gives these rooms their meaning and functional appropriateness.

Something similar happened in the other room at Viipuri which was to become famous, the lecture hall. This was a long narrow room immediately to the right of the entrance lobby. It had large windows overlooking the park which was heavily wooded. Curtains could be drawn over the windows, a screen pulled across the width to reduce its size, some of the seats were upholstered armchairs, the floor was wood; the room felt in many ways like an enlarged living room. Yet what made it a public place in both a symbolic and a usage sense was a wave-shaped ceiling of 30,000 knotless strips of pine which started above the entrance doors at one end and culminated in a surf-like crest behind the speaker at the other end (Fig. 30). The function of the wave formation was, however, not only to direct the eye to the lectern and to reflect the speaker's voice to the far end of the room, but equally to distribute the voice of a speaker anywhere in the audience up and down the room. A visual and acoustic form was thus directed towards the purpose of both lecture and discussion.

What Aalto was able to suggest at Viipuri and in his later work, and what has now been taken up in many other library buildings, is that it is possible to create a public building which though unmistakably such in character and function is yet domestic, everyday, at the same time. It is a complexity which, though important in many kinds of spaces, seems particularly apposite in the case of libraries.

selbst zentrierten, abgeschlossenen Charakter an. Insofern entsprachen sie noch besser der Bestimmung eines Bibliotheksraumes. Beispiele finden sich im Wolfsburger Kulturzentrum (Abb. 32, 33), in der Bibliothek von Seinäjoki (Abb. 34–37) und in der des Gemeindezentrums von Rovaniemi in Nordfinnland (Abb. 38–49). Jeder dieser Bibliotheksräume vereint auf scheinbar paradoxe Weise Offenheit und Abgeschlossenheit – der Benutzer kann sich innerhalb des überschaubaren Gesamtraumes orientieren und sich doch in einem abgesonderten Bereich isolieren. Dem Personal ist eine Aufsicht möglich, ohne daß das Gefühl des Exponiertseins in einem riesigen Raum aufkäme. Das Phänomen des »Sowohl-Als-auch«, wie Robert Venturi in Anlehnung an einen Satz Cleanth Brooks' eine solche organisierte Widersprüchlichkeit beschrieben hat, verleiht diesen Räumen ihre Bedeutung und ihre funktionale Angemessenheit.

Etwas Ähnliches geschah in dem anderen Raum in Viipuri, der berühmt werden sollte, in dem Vortragssaal, einem langen schmalen Raum rechts vom Haupteingang. Er hatte große Fenster, die auf den Park hinausgingen; vor die Fenster konnten Vorhänge gezogen werden, der Raum war durch eine Trennwand zu verkleinern, einige Sitze waren gepolsterte Sessel, der Fußboden bestand aus Holz: So wirkte der Raum in mancher Hinsicht wie ein vergrößertes Wohnzimmer. Was ihn aber in symbolischem wie in funktionellem Sinn zu einem Ort der Öffentlichkeit machte, war eine wellenförmige Decke aus 30000 astlochfreien Kiefernholzstäben, die auf der einen Seite über den Eingangstüren ansetzte und in einem Wogenkamm hinter dem Rednerpult kulminierte (Abb. 30). Die Wellenform sollte nicht nur das Auge auf das Pult lenken und die Stimme des Redners bis ans andere Ende des Raumes tragen, sondern auch die Stimme eines Diskussionsteilnehmers aus dem Publikum an allen Stellen des Raumes vernehmbar machen. Aalto benutzte also eine visuelle und akustische Form, um sowohl den Zwecken des Vortrags als auch denen der Diskussion gerecht zu werden.

Aaltos Bibliothek in Viipuri und seine späteren Bauten beweisen ebenso wie viele andere moderne Bibliotheksgebäude, daß es möglich ist, ein öffentliches Bauwerk zu schaffen, das zwar seinen Charakter und seine Funktion keineswegs verleugnet, zugleich aber privat wirkt und selbstverständlicher Bestandteil des täglichen Lebens wird. Eine solche Komplexität entspricht zahlreichen Bauaufgaben, ist jedoch der Bibliothek besonders angemessen.

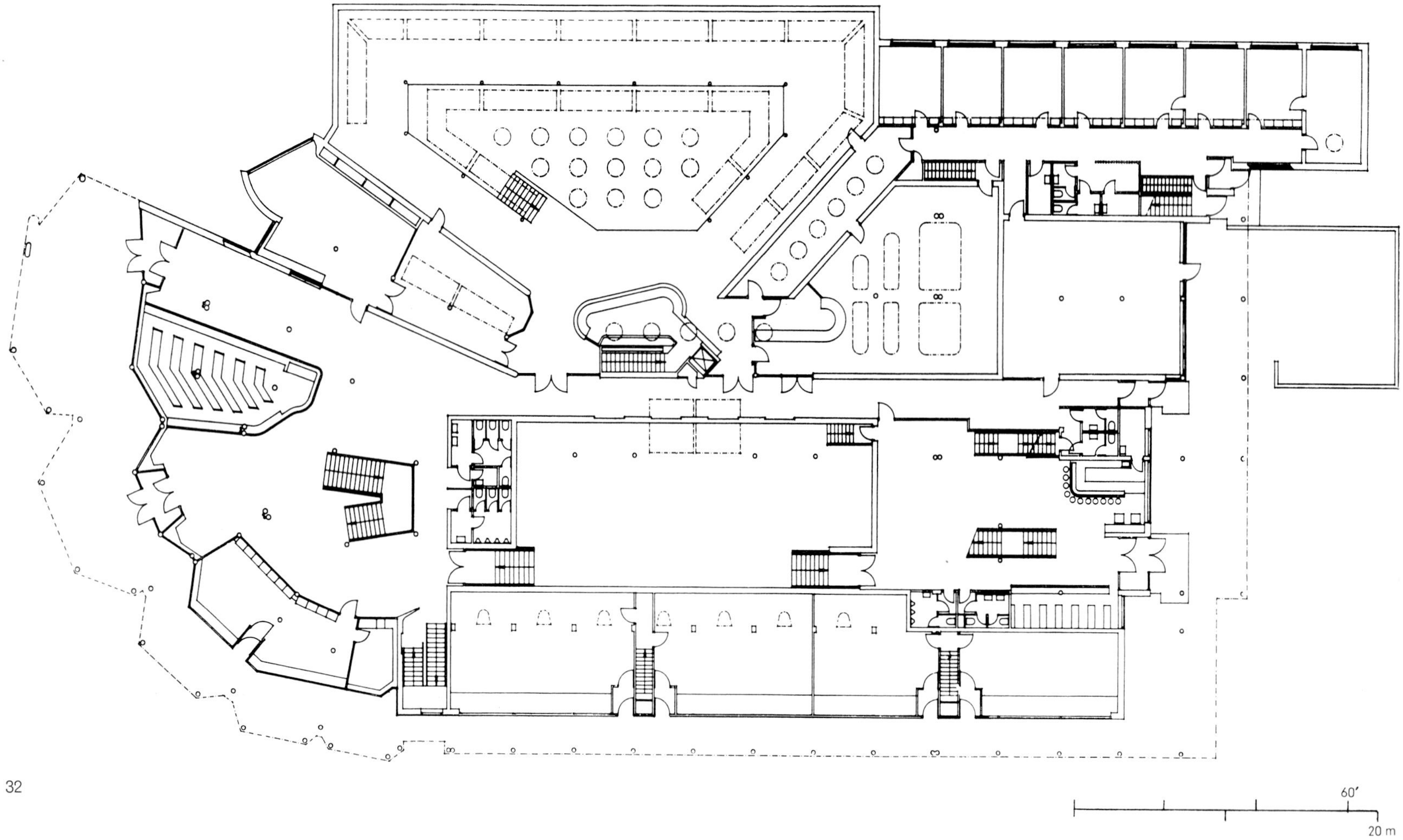

60'
20 m

32

33

32, 33. Library in the Cultural Centre, Wolfsburg, Germany, 1962. Architect: Alvar Aalto. The cultural centre of the Volkswagen town of Wolfsburg forms one side of the Town Hall Square and contains lecture halls, studios, workshops, clubrooms, and a youth centre as well as a library for adults, teenagers and children.
32. Ground floor plan.
33. The adults' lending library.

32, 33. Bibliothek des Kulturzentrums, Wolfsburg, 1962. Architekt: Alvar Aalto. Das Kulturzentrum der Volkswagenstadt schließt den Rathausplatz an einer Seite ab. Es umfaßt Vortragssäle, Werkstätten, Clubräume und ein Jugendzentrum sowie Büchereien für Erwachsene, Jugendliche und Kinder.
32. Grundriß Erdgeschoß.
33. Leihbücherei für Erwachsene.

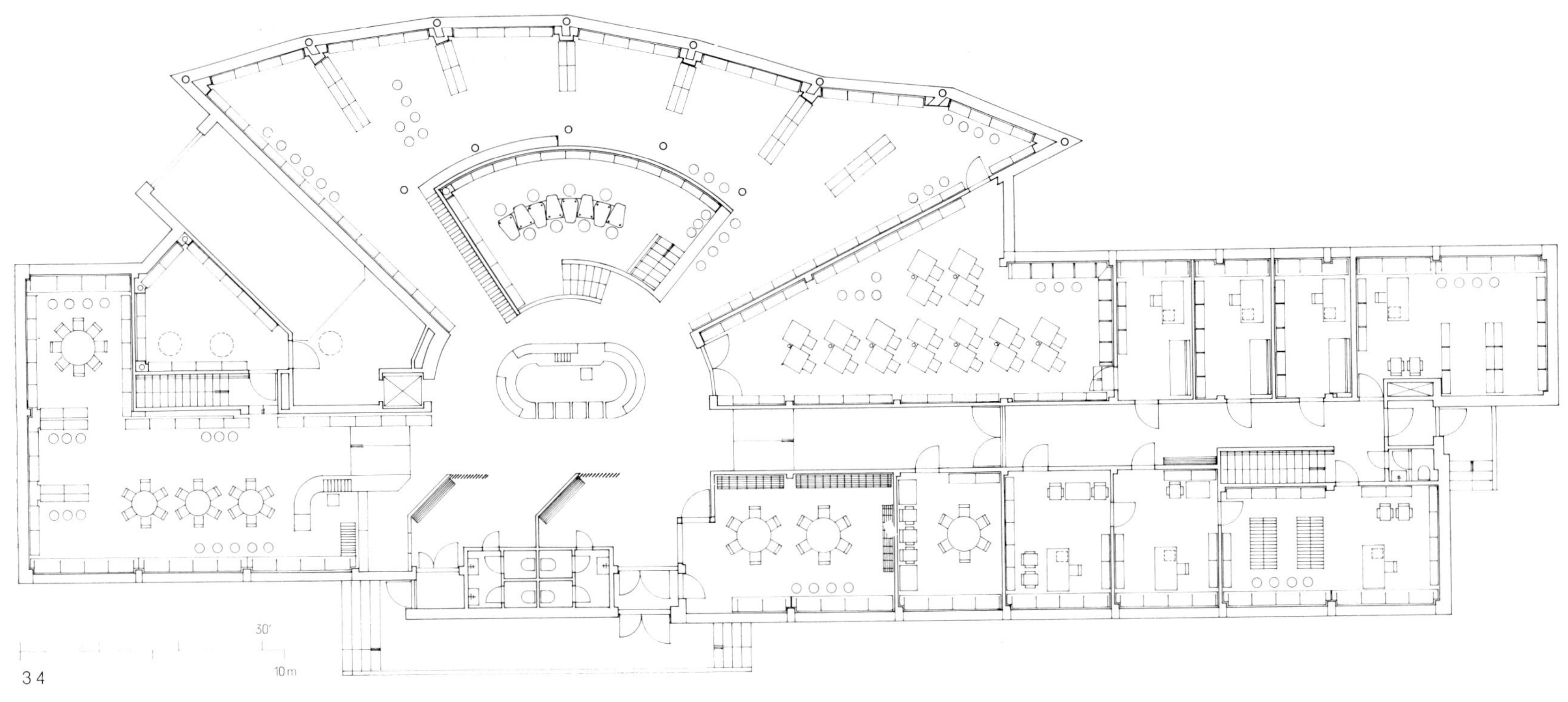

34

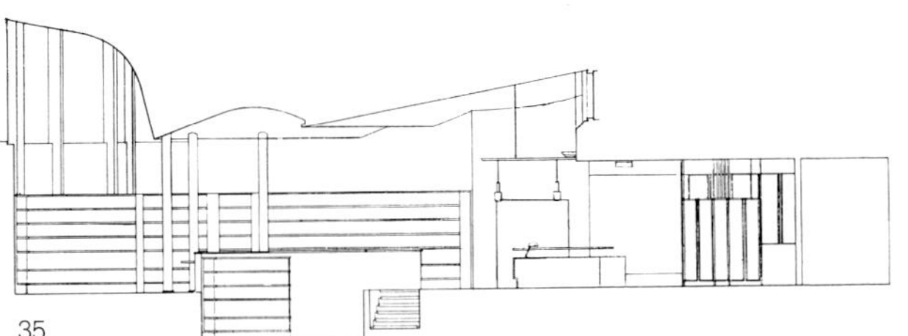
35

34–37. Library, Seinäjoki, Finland, 1965. Architect: Alvar Aalto.
34. Ground floor plan.
35. Section through the lending library and issue desk.
36. Exterior.
37. The main room.

34–37. Bibliothek, Seinäjoki, 1965. Architekt: Alvar Aalto.
34. Grundriß Erdgeschoß.
35. Schnitt durch Leihbücherei und Ausleihe.
36. Außenansicht.
37. Der große Lesesaal.

36

37

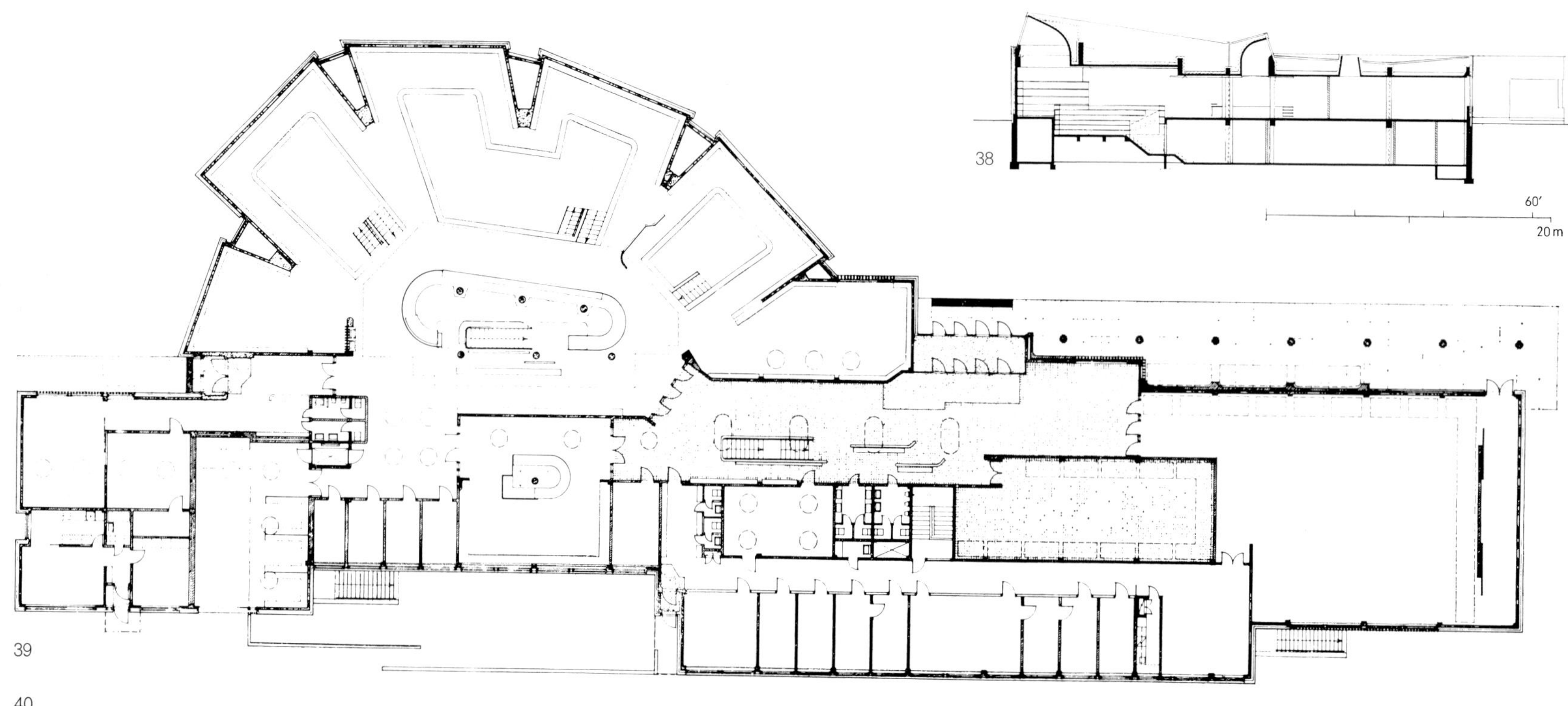


40

41

38–49. Library for the Civic Centre, Rovaniemi, Finland, 1965. Architect: Alvar Aalto. The Rovaniemi Library brings together the ideas which Alvar Aalto has pursued in library design since 1927; the completed building establishes a new level of design and at the same time, a new departure point.
38. Section through the lending library.
39. Ground floor plan.
40. Entrance side.
41. Main entrance.

38–49. Bibliothek des Gemeindezentrums, Rovaniemi, 1965. Architekt: Alvar Aalto. In der Bibliothek von Rovaniemi sind alle Konzeptionen verwirklicht, die Alvar Aalto seit 1927 entwickelt hatte; zugleich weist dieses Gebäude dem Bibliotheksbau neue Wege.
38. Schnitt durch die Leihbücherei.
39. Grundriß Erdgeschoß.
40. Eingangsseite.
41. Haupteingang.

42. One of the enclosed lower areas.
43. Control counter.
44. The two levels of the library; stools and the shelf which forms the balustrade allow for casual reading.

42. Einer der tiefer liegenden Leseräume.
43. Kontrolltisch.
44. Die beiden Geschosse des großen Lesesaals; Hocker und das Regal, das die Balustrade bildet, laden zum »Schmökern« ein.

42

43

44

45

46

47

◁ 45. The two levels seen from below.
46. The children's room which forms one of the off-shoots from the main room.
47. The stepped shelving suggests both openness and enclosure.

◁ 45. Die beiden Niveaus von unten gesehen.
46. Die Kinderbücherei ist in einer der Apsiden des Hauptleseraums untergebracht.
47. Die übereinandergestaffelten Bücherregale vermitteln ein Gefühl der räumlichen Kontinuität und sorgen zugleich für Abgeschlossenheit.

48

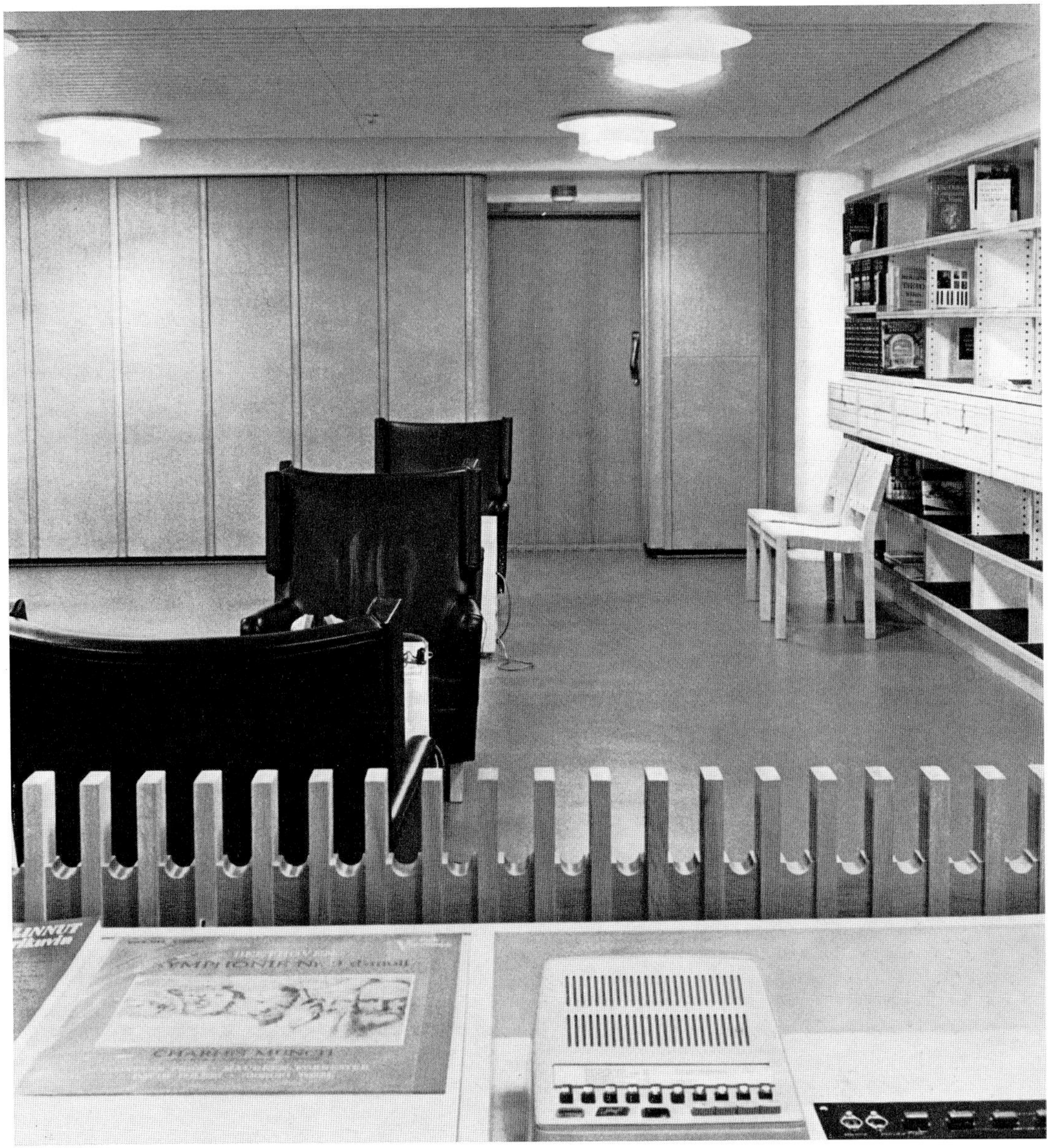

49

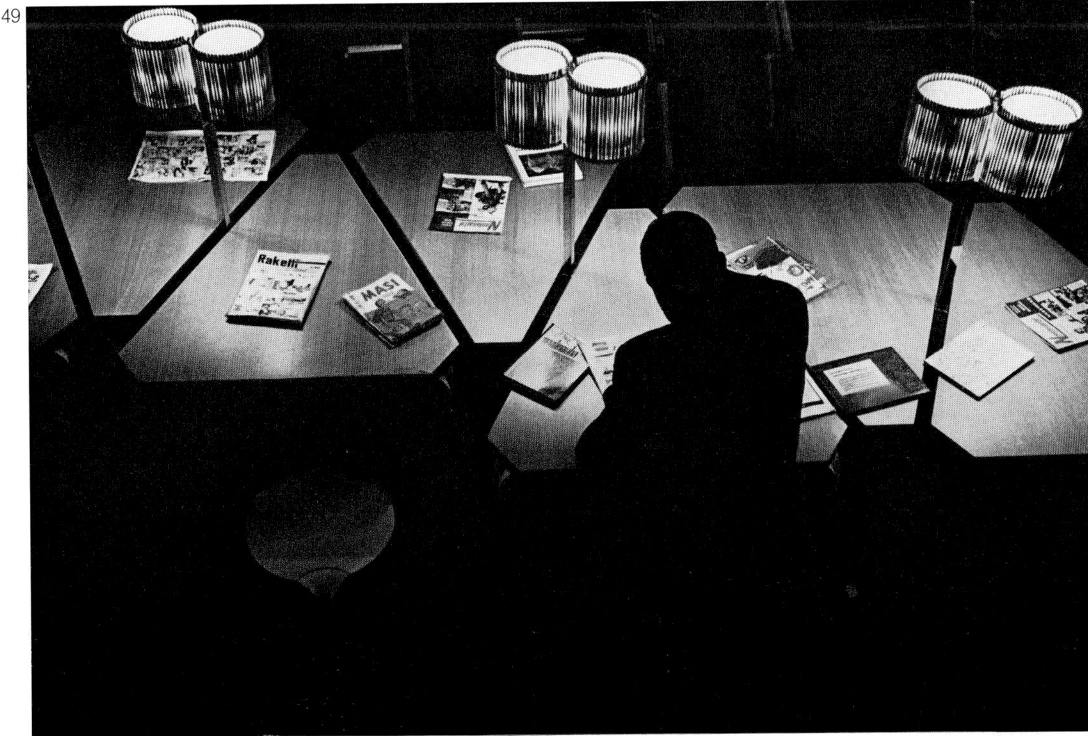


48. The music room with facilities for listening to recorded music.
49. Lighting and furniture were also designed by Alvar Aalto.

48. Blick in den Musikraum mit den Abhöranlagen für Schallplatten.
49. Lampen und Möbel wurden ebenfalls von Alvar Aalto entworfen.

## Analysis of Functions

The library has in the past had to fulfil a definable function and despite technical innovations it continues to do so today. This is in the main concerned with making stored information available to an individual. Up to now the bulk of this information has been in the form of words, printed on paper and issued in the shape of books, pamphlets, magazines or newspapers. Although there have been changes in the method of recording and storing information (among which the invention of movable type and electronic data processing may be the most significant so far) four distinct operations can be distinguished in the primary function of a library which are largely independent of the means used to produce the information store. These four operations, which also constitute a cycle of use, could be described as follows:

1. the location of the information,
2. the retrieval of the information from storage,
3. the communication of the information to the user,
4. the return of the information to storage.

This particular cycle is independent of the size of the library though certain parts of it may increase in complexity with an increase in the size of the information store. The cycle occurs of course even in the home; we remember a book, look for it on the shelves, take it down, read it and finally return it to its place. The location/retrieval/communication/return sequence of operations is, it is important to recognize, equally critical to the understanding of library design where the information is contained in books and where it is stored in some other form. In terms of the design of a building each sequence in the cycle, each characteristic operation, is likely to need its characteristic space based on the particularity of that function. The organizational and architectural aspects of these particular spaces will be discussed in a subsequent section which deals in detail with each of the four operations in turn.

The design of these spaces and of their relation to each other will, however, also depend on the relative importance which is to be assigned to each of them within any one building. This difference in emphasis is very dependent on the general function of the library and could in fact be said to be the distinguishing mark of each type of building within the library service. It is this shift in emphasis within the cycle of use which has the greatest repercussions on the architectural organization. This is perhaps best demonstrated by looking at three typical categories of library building as regards the functions they have to perform, and then to illustrate some of the solutions which have been produced recently. The label which each category carries is however only a kind of shorthand based on the library type most likely to form the bulk of that group, and the understanding of any one group also depends not only on the analysis of that type but equally on recognizing its differences.

## Analyse der Funktionen

Trotz aller technischen Neuerungen hat die Bibliothek nach wie vor eine klar definierte Funktion. Ihre Hauptaufgabe liegt darin, dem Individuum gespeicherte Information verfügbar zu machen. Bis heute besteht diese Information zumeist aus gedrucktem Material, das in Form von Büchern, Schriften, Zeitungen oder Zeitschriften publiziert wird. Wenn auch in der Art der Veröffentlichung und der Aufbewahrung Veränderungen eingetreten sind (die Erfindung der beweglichen Letter und die elektronische Datenverarbeitung sind wohl die einschneidendsten Ereignisse auf diesem Gebiet), lassen sich doch in der Grundfunktion einer Bibliothek vier Vorgänge unterscheiden, die von den Methoden der Informationsspeicherung weitgehend unabhängig sind.

Diese vier Vorgänge, die zugleich einen Zyklus der Benutzung bilden, sind wie folgt zu definieren:

1. Lokalisierung der Information,
2. Beschaffung der Information aus dem Magazin,
3. Kommunikation der Information an den Benutzer,
4. Rückgabe der Information ans Magazin.

Dieser Zyklus ist nicht von der Größe der Bibliothek abhängig, obwohl einzelne Phasen sich komplizieren können, wenn die Quantität der gespeicherten Information zunimmt. Der gleiche Zyklus vollzieht sich übrigens auch zu Hause: Wir erinnern uns an ein Buch, suchen es im Regal, nehmen es heraus, lesen es und stellen es schließlich an seinen Platz zurück. Die Abfolge der Phasen Lokalisierung / Beschaffung / Kommunikation / Rückgabe spielt bei der Planung einer Bibliothek eine entscheidende Rolle, gleichgültig, ob die Information in Büchern enthalten oder auf andere Weise gespeichert ist. Jede Phase des Zyklus, jeder charakteristische Vorgang erfordert im allgemeinen einen charakteristischen Raum, der den Eigenarten dieser Funktion entspricht. Von den organisatorischen und architektonischen Problemen dieser Räume wird in einem folgenden Abschnitt dieses Buches, der sich eingehend mit allen vier Phasen befaßt, die Rede sein.

Die Planung dieser Bereiche und ihre Verbindung untereinander hängt freilich auch davon ab, welche Bedeutung ihnen innerhalb eines bestimmten Gebäudes beigemessen wird. Je nach der allgemeinen Funktion der Bibliothek ist der eine oder der andere Bereich besonders wichtig, so daß sich die Gebäudetypen innerhalb des Bibliothekswesens danach unterscheiden lassen, auf welcher Phase des Benutzungszyklus das Hauptgewicht liegt. Diese Akzentverschiebung hat starken Einfluß auf die architektonische Organisation der Bauten. Als Beispiel dafür mögen drei in ihren Funktionen typische Kategorien von Bibliotheksbauten dienen, die durch einige Lösungen aus neuester Zeit illustriert sind. Die Bezeichnung, die jede dieser Kategorien trägt, ist freilich nur eine Art Stenogramm und entspricht dem Bibliothekstyp, der innerhalb der jeweiligen Gruppe am häufigsten vertreten ist. Im übrigen kommt es darauf an, nicht nur die einzelnen Gruppen zu analysieren, sondern auch die Unterschiede zu anderen Typen festzustellen.

In the small public library dealing very largely with fiction and forms of literature read in much the same way, information location will be relatively random. A book will be found by browsing, by the reader having some favourite authors, by its newness. It will in most cases be located by the reader without recourse to a catalogue. Retrieval is again performed by the reader and this normally happens immediately after location; the two occur almost simultaneously. Some initial communication of a sampling kind may be done as soon as retrieval has taken place but the bulk of the communication is likely to occur outside the library building; the book is taken home to read. The return of the book to storage is done by the library staff from a control position where it has been checked out and in. A large proportion of the operations are thus performed by the user—and the most prolonged takes place mainly elsewhere—and conditions have therefore to be created where these actions by the user are simple and where they can be guided fairly unobtrusively.

The problems of such a library serving a small community are in many ways akin to those of a supermarket; like the self-service store its problems are movement, supervision, storage, enticement. The degree to which the first of these three represent difficulties to be solved in terms of design is greatly dependent on the intensity of use which may occur at any one time and the distribution of that use throughout the books being stored. The size of the spaces will be governed by this. As in the supermarket the width of the aisles will depend on the numbers going through and the numbers stopping to pick up an article, as well as the desire on the one hand to get the users near the shelves to attract their attention, and on the other hand to avoid overcrowding which is at the same time likely to make supervision difficult. There must thus be a resolution of potential conflicts. This applies also to the kinds of users who will be coming to the library and who may have not only different interests in the sense of wanting different books, but may also have different abilities to locate information.

The simplest possible division in use is between adults and children as in a very small library at Koforidua in Ghana with an area of 1350 sq. ft., not much bigger than a medium-sized house. Adults are on one side, children on the other, staff, control, entrance and exit are in the middle. An alternative simple division is between those who have come to borrow material and those who intend to read it in the library. The Hansaviertel library in Berlin makes this separation on either side of the entrance hall: the book area is straight ahead, the magazine reading room on the right. A further stage of differentiation is reached at the very much larger Hampstead Central Library, London, where there is a distinction between age groups and between books, periodicals and music as well as between books going out on loan and books to be read in the library. These separations into zones—adults, youths; loan, reference;books, magazines—can of course also occur within a simple large enclosure by means of almost suggested subdivisions as in the Public Library at Hørsholm, in the suburban area just north of Copenhagen. This preserves the ability to supervize from a near central position and deliberately blurs what may otherwise be overly rigid demarcations. The space acquires the double meaning of a large public room with domestic enclaves. The design assumes that these aspects are more important than seclusion since this will in any case be achieved at home when the book is read; it recognizes in other words the distinction between a public library of this kind and other libraries where the communication of the information occurs within the building. The four operations of the normal cycle of library use thus receive different

In der kleinen öffentlichen Bücherei oder Volksbücherei, die sich hauptsächlich mit Romanen und verwandten Literaturformen befaßt, ist die Lokalisierung der Information häufig vom Zufall abhängig. Der Leser entdeckt ein Buch, indem er in den Regalen stöbert, er hat einen Lieblingsautor, oder das Buch ist gerade neu erschienen. In den meisten Fällen wählt er das Buch aus, ohne einen Katalog zu Hilfe zu nehmen. Auch für die Beschaffung der Informationsquelle, die normalerweise unmittelbar nach der Lokalisierung vollzogen wird, sorgt der Leser; beide Vorgänge finden nahezu gleichzeitig statt. Danach kann, noch in der Bibliothek, beim ersten flüchtigen Durchblättern des Buches eine kurze Kommunikation eintreten, doch im allgemeinen vollzieht sich die Kommunikation außerhalb des Bibliotheksgebäudes; der Leser nimmt das Buch mit nach Hause, um es dort zu lesen. Für die Rückgabe des Buches an das Magazin sind die Bibliotheksangestellten verantwortlich, die Ausgabe und Rückgabe an einer Kontrollstelle überwachen.

Die meisten erforderlichen Vorgänge führt also der Leser selbst aus, während die zeitraubende Tätigkeit, das Lesen, zum größten Teil an anderer Stelle stattfindet. Deshalb müssen Bedingungen geschaffen werden, die dem Benutzer die Ausübung seiner Tätigkeiten erleichtern und eine unauffällige Führung ermöglichen.

Die Probleme einer solchen Bibliothek, die eine kleine Gemeinde versorgt, sind in mancher Hinsicht denen eines Supermarktes ähnlich; wie beim Selbstbedienungsgeschäft spielen Zirkulation, Überwachung, Lagerung und Anregung eine Rolle. In welchem Maße die Planung für die ersten drei Faktoren Lösungen finden muß, hängt weitgehend von der allgemeinen Benutzungsfrequenz und von ihrer Verteilung auf die vorhandenen Bücher ab. Die Größe wird durch diese Daten bestimmt. Wie beim Supermarkt richtet sich die Breite der Gänge danach, wie viele Benutzer hindurchgehen und wie viele stehenbleiben, um ein Buch in die Hand zu nehmen. Einerseits sollen die Benutzer nahe an die Regale herangeführt werden, damit ihre Aufmerksamkeit erregt wird, andererseits soll kein Gedränge entstehen, das die Aufsicht erschweren würde. Es müssen also gegensätzliche Faktoren miteinander in Einklang gebracht werden. Das gilt auch für die verschiedenen Gruppen der Bibliotheksbenutzer, die nicht nur unterschiedliche Interessen haben, sondern deren Fähigkeit, den Standort der gewünschten Information auszumachen, auch sehr unterschiedlich ausgebildet ist.

Die einfachste Unterteilung nach Benutzergruppen ist die in einen Bereich für Erwachsene und einen für Kinder. Eine solche Unterteilung findet sich zum Beispiel in einer sehr kleinen Bücherei in Koforidua, Ghana, die eine Fläche von etwa 125 qm umfaßt und damit nicht viel größer ist als ein mittelgroßes Einfamilienhaus. Den Erwachsenen ist die eine Seite zugewiesen, den Kindern die andere, und Verwaltungsräume, Kontrollstelle, Eingang und Ausgang befinden sich in der Mitte. Ähnlich leicht läßt sich eine Trennung zwischen den Benutzern vollziehen, die Material ausleihen, und jenen, die es in der Bibliothek lesen wollen. Wer beispielsweise die Eingangshalle der Bibliothek des Hansaviertels in Berlin betritt, findet geradeaus die Buchausleihe und rechts vom Eingang den Zeitschriftensaal. Eine noch weitergehende Differenzierung ist bei der wesentlich größeren Zentralbücherei Hampstead, London, erreicht, wo nicht nur zwischen den einzelnen Altersgruppen unterschieden wird, sondern auch zwischen Büchern, Zeitschriften, Noten und schließlich zwischen Büchern, die für die Ausleihe und solchen, die für die Lektüre in der Bibliothek gedacht sind. Diese Unterteilung in Einzelbereiche – Erwachsene, Jugendliche; Ausleihe, Leseraum; Bücher, Zeitschriften – läßt sich

1. Regional Library, Koforidua, Ghana, 1957. Architects: Kenneth Scott Associates. A typical basic plan: central control and offices, adults on one side, children on the other. The small steel framed building is 1350 sq. ft. (126 sq. m.).

1. Bezirksbücherei, Koforidua, Ghana, 1957. Architekten: Kenneth Scott Associates. Ein typischer Bibliotheksgrundriß: Kontrolle und Büros in der Mitte, Erwachsene auf der einen, Jugendliche auf der anderen Seite. Der kleine Stahlskelett-Bau hat eine Grundfläche von 126 qm.

Ground floor plan / Grundriß Erdgeschoß.
1 Foyer
2 Control desk / Kontrolle
3 Adults / Erwachsene
4 Children / Jugendliche
5 Staff / Personal
6 Store / Lagerraum
7 W.C.

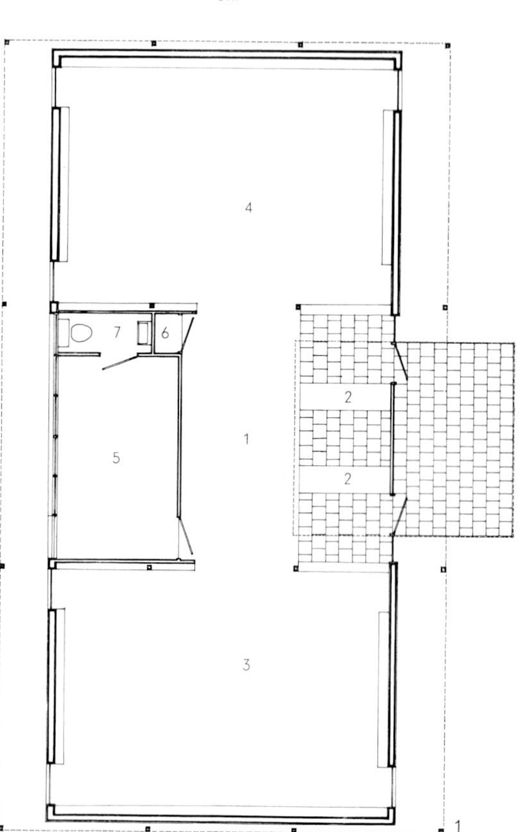

2, 3. Hampstead Central Library, London, 1964. Architects: Sir Basil Spence, Bonnington & Collins. The library and its adjacent swimming baths are the first part of a Civic Centre being built next to an underground station and immediately adjacent to a very busy shopping street. The organization of the building differentiates between adults and children, between users borrowing and those reading within the library and between different kinds of library material.

2, 3. Zentralbücherei, Hampstead, London, 1964. Architekten: Sir Basil Spence, Bonnington & Collins. Die Bücherei und die benachbarten Schwimmbäder entstanden im ersten Bauabschnitt eines Stadtzentrums, das in der Nähe einer Untergrundbahnstation und einer Hauptgeschäftsstraße errichtet wird. Die räumliche Organisation des Gebäudes unterscheidet zwischen Abteilungen für Erwachsene und Kinder sowie zwischen Bereichen für die Ausleihe und für die ungestörte Lektüre von Büchern.

First floor plan and section A–A / Grundriß erstes Obergeschoß und Schnitt A–A.

1 Lending library / Leihbücherei
2 Bibliography / Bibliographie
3 Workroom / Arbeitsraum
4 Periodicals / Zeitschriften
5 Reference library / Nachschlagewerke
6 Exhibition / Ausstellung
7 Exhibition foyer / Foyer des Ausstellungsbereichs
8 Opening in the floor over / Doppelgeschossige Raumzone
9 Children's library / Kinderbücherei
10 Entrance hall / Eingangshalle
11 Book stack / Magazin
12 Upper lending library / Leihbücherei im zweiten Obergeschoß
13 Research / Studienräume
14 Louvres / Sonnenschutz

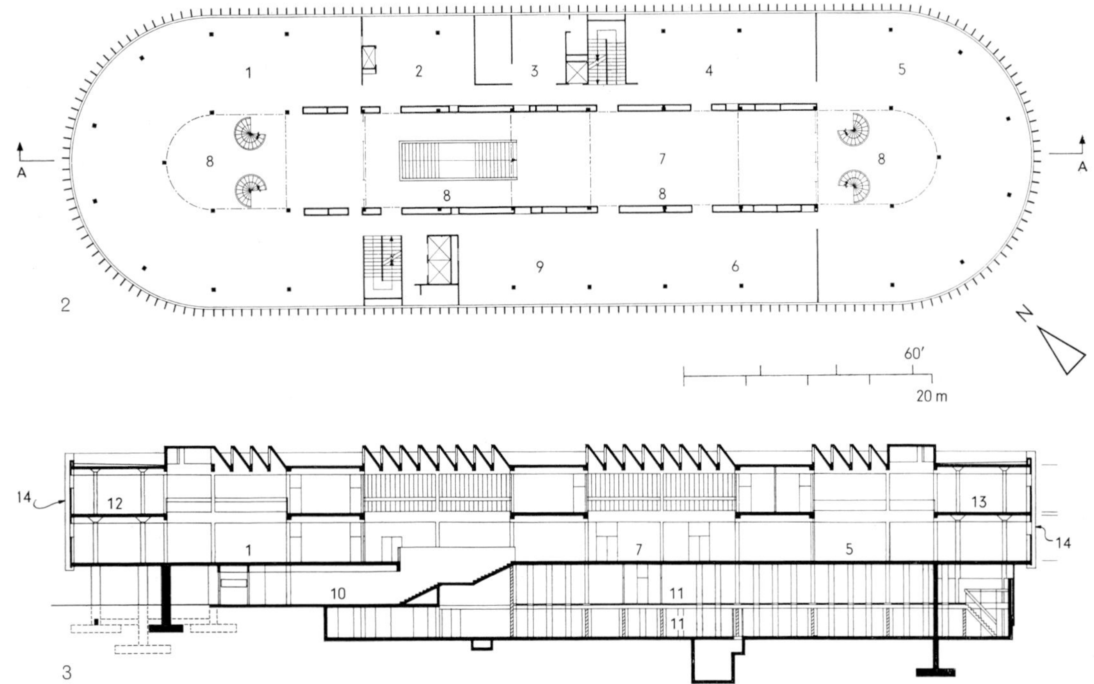


degrees of emphasis and these differences influence the planning of the building. It is this, rather than that the library falls within a size range, which is important.

A public library is also part of the service which a community expects to receive. It must therefore be possible to make use of it in a simple way. Like the supermarket again, the library depends a good deal for its success on easy accessibility. Siting is therefore of the first importance as soon as it is assumed that the user comes to the book rather than the book to the user as in the mobile library service of many rural areas.

The public library deserves a location which puts it immediately adjacent to the normal routes of movement, which puts it, for instance, in the midst of pedestrian flow and makes it as easily reached as a Woolworth. Its placing ought to be such as not only to cater for the confirmed user but to attract and hold the reluctant reader. Such a situation is moreover not incompatible with the acknowledged need for quiet and the equally important possibility of future expansion. Both of these conditions may be satisfied by working in depth and on the section. Thus the Children's Library at Pimlico in London (see page 172) uses two bays in a row of shops which form the ground floor of a seven storey building on an important local street. The small library opens onto an enclosed garden to the south which corresponds to the rear service area of the shops which are on either side. A chair store, staff room and lavatories and the entrance face the street and shield the inner room. The same principle of achieving a gradation from public activity to the virtually private pursuit of reading a book can be achieved by vertical separation as in the library for the Danish minority of South Schleswig in Flensburg (see page 172) where the building makes contact with the street at ground floor level, but books and reading areas are at a higher level yet opening onto a garden at the back of the sloping site. Detachment and participation are both possible through a proper manipulation of the spaces.

Such integration with other activities and particularly everyday ones like shopping or going to school, is important for many libraries and especially very small facilities

natürlich auch mit Hilfe nur angedeuteter Trennelemente innerhalb eines einzigen großen Raumes durchführen, wie es etwa in der Volksbücherei von Hørsholm, einem Vorort nördlich Kopenhagens, geschah. Dieses System hebt allzu starre Begrenzungen auf und ermöglicht die Aufsicht von einer zentralen Position aus. Die Bibliothek ist ein großer öffentlicher Raum und bietet zugleich private Bereiche. Der Entwurf der Hørsholmer Bibliothek ging davon aus, daß solche Aspekte wichtiger sind als eine Abgeschlossenheit, die den Leser sowieso erwartet, wenn er das Buch zu Hause liest. Es wurde also erkannt, daß sich eine öffentliche Bibliothek dieser Art von anderen Bibliotheken unterscheidet, bei denen die Kommunikation der Information innerhalb des Gebäudes stattfindet. So kommt also den vier Phasen des normalen Benutzungszyklus in den einzelnen Bibliotheken unterschiedliche Bedeutung zu, ein Faktor, der sich auch auf die Planung des Bauwerks auswirkt. Akzentverschiebungen im Benutzungszyklus sind für den Entwurf wichtiger als Größenunterschiede.

Eine öffentliche Bücherei gehört zu den Einrichtungen, die der ganzen Gemeinde zur Verfügung stehen sollen. Sie muß deshalb so einfach wie möglich zu benutzen sein. Wie beim Supermarkt hängt auch bei der Bibliothek der Erfolg weitgehend davon ab, daß sie leicht zugänglich ist. Deshalb spielt die Lage des Gebäudes eine außerordentlich wichtige Rolle, vorausgesetzt natürlich, daß der Leser zum Buch kommt und nicht das Buch zum Leser, wie in vielen ländlichen Gebieten, wo fahrbare Büchereien eingesetzt werden.

Die öffentliche Bücherei sollte in unmittelbarer Nähe der normalen Verkehrswege liegen, beispielsweise in einem von Fußgängern viel frequentierten Gebiet, damit sie ebenso leicht zu erreichen ist wie ein Kaufhaus. Sie sollte zudem so günstig placiert sein, daß sie nicht nur dem ständigen Besucher zur Verfügung steht, sondern auch potentielle Leser anzieht. Eine solche städtebauliche Situation ist keineswegs mit dem Bedürfnis nach Ruhe und der ebenso wichtigen Möglichkeit späterer Erweiterung unvereinbar. Beide Bedingungen lassen sich erfüllen, wenn der Entwurf sich Grundstückstiefe und mehrge-

like branch or village libraries since their gravitational pull may in any case be rather weak. The community library at Säynätsalo in central Finland (see page 170), for example, gains enormously by being part of Alvar Aalto's complex of town-hall and shops.

The shopping centre is in these terms in many ways the natural location for a branch library and particularly for its adult section. To neglect this area because of high land values is both an economic and a social mistake. The cost of a library service is largely determined by annual running charges – staff salaries, book and record purchases, periodicals subscriptions, lighting, heating, cleaning – and very little by capital expenditure. Some American figures give annual operating costs at from a quarter to half the cost of the building. It must be remembered moreover that these yearly outgoings do not vary a great deal with the amount of use a given library receives. It is clear, therefore, that the greater the use, the less the cost per book borrowed. An unfrequented library is thus a poor investment.

There is quite another aspect which also ought to determine location and which strongly suggests a high degree of accessibility. Branch libraries are in many places rather more than book-lending institutions; they become the gathering place of the old, of those living in cramped or unheated rooms, of the socially isolated looking for a public meeting place. This additional function ought to be accepted as desirable and catered for in spaces which can at other times perhaps become a lecture room, a meeting hall, a cinema. Local libraries are, especially in northern climates, the only covered and heated social gathering places with a permanent functional justification. Their ready availability over large periods of the day should be

schossige Bebauung zunutze macht. So nimmt zum Beispiel die Children's Library im Londoner Stadtteil Pimlico (Seite 172) zwei Fensterachsen innerhalb einer Reihe von Läden ein, die im Erdgeschoß eines siebengeschossigen Gebäudes an einer wichtigen Verkehrsstraße untergebracht sind. An der Südseite öffnet sich die Bücherei zu einem umschlossenen Garten, der den rückwärtigen Nebenräumen der Geschäfte auf beiden Seiten entspricht. Ein Stuhlmagazin, ein Raum für die Verwaltung, die Toiletten und der Eingang liegen an der Straßenseite und schirmen den inneren Bereich ab. Dieses Prinzip eines räumlichen Übergangs von der öffentlichen Funktion zur sozusagen privaten Tätigkeit des Bücherlesens läßt sich ebenso durch vertikale Gliederung verwirklichen, wie es zum Beispiel bei der Bibliothek für die dänische Minderheit Südschleswigs in Flensburg (Seite 172) geschah. Dort liegt das Erdgeschoßniveau des Gebäudes an der Straße, während Bücher und Lesebereiche auf einem höheren Niveau untergebracht sind, das sich auf einen Garten an der Rückseite des ansteigenden Geländes öffnet. Eine geschickte Raumorganisation ermöglicht also Isolierung ebenso wie Teilnahme am äußeren Geschehen.

Daß Bibliotheken mit anderen Funktionen, vor allem mit so alltäglichen wie Einkaufen oder Schulgang, verbunden werden, ist besonders wichtig für sehr kleine Institutionen wie Zweig- oder Dorfbüchereien, die im allgemeinen nur eine geringe Anziehungskraft besitzen. So profitiert zum Beispiel die Gemeindebücherei von Säynätsalo in Mittelfinnland (Seite 170) sehr davon, daß sie in das von Alvar Aalto errichtete Gemeindezentrum mit Rathaus und Läden einbezogen wurde.

In mancher Hinsicht ist deshalb das Einkaufszentrum der gegebene Ort für die Zweigstelle einer Bücherei, beson-

4, 5. Central Library, Akershus, Norway, 1961. Architects: Paul Cappelen and Torbjørn Rodahl. An elaboration of the basic plan divisions.

4, 5. Zentralbücherei, Akershus, Norwegen, 1961. Architekten: Paul Cappelen und Torbjørn Rodahl. Dieser Grundriß stellt eine Weiterentwicklung des Normalgrundrisses dar.

Plans of ground floor and basement floor / Grundrisse Erdgeschoß und Untergeschoß.

1 Entrance / Eingang
2 Lobby / Halle
3 Reading room for adults / Lesesaal für Erwachsene
4 Reading room for children / Lesesaal für Jugendliche
5 Receiving and packing / Anlieferung und Packraum
6 Offices / Büros
7 Garage
8 Garden court / Gartenhof
9 Caretaker's apartment / Hausmeisterwohnung
10 Study rooms / Studienräume
11 Archives / Archiv
12 Heating plant / Heizungsraum
13 Ventilation plant / Lüftungsanlage
14 Workroom and storage / Arbeitsraum und Lager
15 Tea kitchen / Teeküche

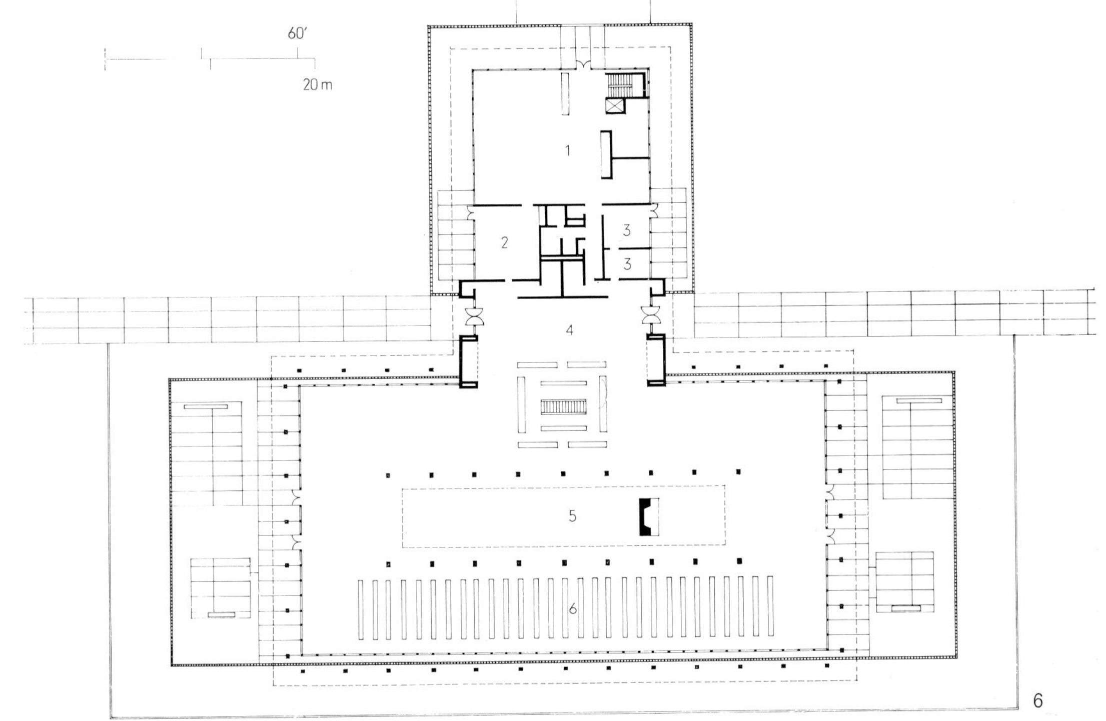


6. Main Library, Palo Alto, California, 1956. Architect: Edward Durell Stone. The service functions are separated from the main space which can seat 160 and hold 100,000 volumes.

6. Hauptbücherei, Palo Alto, Kalifornien, 1956. Architekt: Edward Durell Stone. Die Verwaltung ist vom Hauptraum getrennt, der Platz für 160 Besucher bietet und 100000 Bände aufnehmen kann.

Main floor plan / Grundriß Hauptgeschoß.
1 Workroom / Arbeitsraum
2 Lounge / Halle
3 Offices / Büros
4 Lobby / Vorraum
5 Reading room / Lesesaal
6 Stacks / Magazin

acknowledged, made use of and included in the design consideration; they ought, as Werner Mevissen has suggested, each have an enclosed "market place".
Problems of siting and general social service are of course also allied to the idea of enticement. What this in fact presupposes is that the public library is a very ordinary component in our pattern of life to be visited frequently, without special effort, perhaps even on sudden impulse because some item of interest has just come to our attention. There seems no reason, for instance, why libraries should not have some form of window display—the Baltimore Public Library already does this with great success—or why, in a completely different way, they should not include a bookshop like the Library of the Performing Arts, part of the New York Public Library at Lincoln Center, since buying is an almost more usual activity for an affluent society than taking something out on loan (other than money). It is such attitudes, allied to a design approach which accepts this kind of a view of the library in the community, which are likely to change the appearance and organization of the public library building.
This emphasis on certain aspects of the public library, especially of a high degree of accessibility to the casual user of both the building and of the contents within it, is not intended to deny that within certain public libraries there may be zones which have to do with the communication of the information and may therefore need seclusion. This is of course particularly true in the larger public library which has a reading room for research students or a sizeable reference section. These specialized areas have however a character which is much closer to that of a university or research library. The emphasis within the cycle of use moves from retrieval to communication.

ders, wenn sie sich an den erwachsenen Leser wendet. Eine solche Gegend zu meiden, weil dort die Grundstückskosten hoch sind, wäre ein wirtschaftlicher wie sozialer Fehler. Der Etat einer Bibliothek wird in erster Linie durch die jährlichen laufenden Kosten – Gehälter der Angestellten, Ankauf von Büchern und Schallplatten, Zeitschriftenabonnements, Licht, Heizung, Reinigung – und sehr viel weniger durch die einmaligen Grundstücks- und Baukosten belastet. Nach einer amerikanischen Berechnung betragen die jährlichen laufenden Kosten etwa 25 bis 50% der Baukosten. Im übrigen ändern sich die laufenden Ausgaben einer Bibliothek bei steigenden Benutzungsziffern nicht wesentlich. Die Kosten pro ausgeliehenes Buch sind daher um so geringer, je mehr die Bibliothek frequentiert wird. Eine wenig benutzte Bibliothek ist eine schlechte Kapitalanlage.
Noch ein weiterer Aspekt, der für leichte Zugänglichkeit spricht, sollte die Lage des Grundstücks bestimmen: Zweigstellen von Büchereien sind vielerorts mehr als nur Einrichtungen für die Buchausleihe; sie werden zu einem Treffpunkt der Alten, der Menschen, die in überfüllten oder ungeheizten Räumen leben, und der gesellschaftlich Isolierten, die einen Ort der Kontaktaufnahme suchen. Diese zusätzliche Funktion sollte als wünschenswert akzeptiert werden; sie läßt sich in Räumen erfüllen, die zu anderen Zeiten als Vortragssaal, Versammlungsraum oder Kino dienen. Örtliche Büchereien sind vor allem im nördlichen Klima die einzigen geschützten und geheizten Versammlungsorte, die von ihrer Funktion her gerechtfertigt sind. Die Tatsache, daß sie den größten Teil des Tages über zur Verfügung stehen, sollte ausgenutzt und bei der Planung berücksichtigt werden. Büchereien sollten, wie Werner Mevissen vorschlug, einen »Marktplatz« besitzen.
Auch das Prinzip der stimulierenden Wirkung hängt natürlich davon ab, wie günstig die Bibliothek liegt und in welchem Maße sie ihre sozialen Aufgaben erfüllen kann. Denn dieser »Aufforderungscharakter« setzt voraus, daß die öffentliche Bücherei einen Bestandteil unseres Alltags bildet, daß wir sie ohne besondere Umstände häufig aufsuchen können, vielleicht sogar aus einem Impuls heraus, weil uns plötzlich irgendeine Information interessant erscheint. Es ist beispielsweise nicht einzusehen, warum Bibliotheken nicht über eine Art Schaufensterauslage verfügen sollten – wie die Public Library in Baltimore, die damit große Erfolge erzielt – oder warum sie nicht wie die Library of the Performing Arts, die zur New York Public Library im Lincoln Center gehört, einen Buchladen betreiben sollten; denn das Kaufen ist einer Wohlstandsgesellschaft beinahe noch selbstverständlicher als das Leihen (es sei denn, es handle sich um Geld!). Eine solche Auffassung, die den Bibliotheken eine besondere Rolle innerhalb der Gemeinschaft zuweist und daraus Konsequenzen im Entwurf zieht, könnte zu einem Wandel in Erscheinung und Organisation des Bibliotheksgebäudes führen.
Wenn hier die leichte Zugänglichkeit des Gebäudes wie auch des Bücherbestandes als besonders wünschenswert hervorgehoben wird, so ist dabei natürlich nicht an jene Bibliotheken gedacht, in denen bestimmte Bereiche der unmittelbaren intensiven Beschäftigung mit dem Buch vorbehalten sind und deshalb isoliert werden müssen. Das gilt vor allem für die größere öffentliche Bibliothek, die über einen Lesesaal für wissenschaftlich arbeitende Studenten oder über einen umfangreichen bibliographischen Apparat verfügt. Diese Sonderzonen gehören freilich eher zu den Funktionen einer Universitätsbibliothek oder einer wissenschaftlichen Bibliothek; der Hauptakzent im Benutzungszyklus verlagert sich dann von der Beschaffung auf die Kommunikation.

**Public Library at Hørsholm, Denmark, 1956**

Architects: Jørgen Juul Møller and Holger Næsted

**Öffentliche Bücherei, Hørsholm, Dänemark, 1956**

Architekten: Jørgen Juul Møller und Holger Næsted

The library which was inaugurated in November 1956 is for the municipality of Hørsholm about 16 miles (25 km) north of Copenhagen. The sections of the library – loan and reference for adults, the children's library, periodicals – are separated by furniture. Only the offices are enclosed by floor to ceiling walls. Experience has shown that the level of disturbance is not too great.
The community had a population of 12,000 at the time the building was designed. The main floor holds 16,000 volumes – 10,000 for adults, 6,000 for children – and a further 5,000 can be stored in the stack on the lower floor. A lecture room for 100 people and three seminar rooms are also provided.

Die Bücherei für die Gemeinde Hørsholm, die 25 km nördlich Kopenhagens liegt, wurde im November 1956 eingeweiht. Die einzelnen Abteilungen – Leihbücherei und Handbibliothek für Erwachsene, Jugendbücherei und Zeitschriftenlesesaal – sind durch Einrichtungsgegenstände voneinander getrennt. Nur die Büros sind durch Wände abgeschlossen. Die Praxis hat gezeigt, daß Störungen sich in erträglichen Grenzen halten.
Hørsholm hatte 12000 Einwohner, als die Bibliothek geplant wurde. Die Bücherei verfügt über 16000 Bände, 10000 für Erwachsene und 6000 für Jugendliche. Weitere 5000 Bände können im Magazin des Untergeschosses untergebracht werden. Im Untergeschoß liegen außerdem Studienräume sowie ein Vortragssaal für 100 Personen.

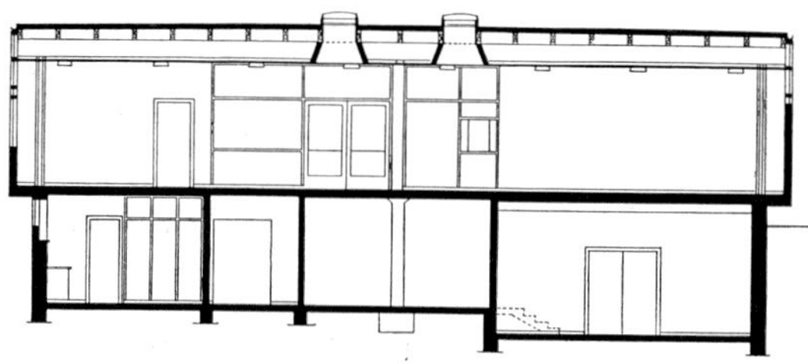

Cross section / Querschnitt.

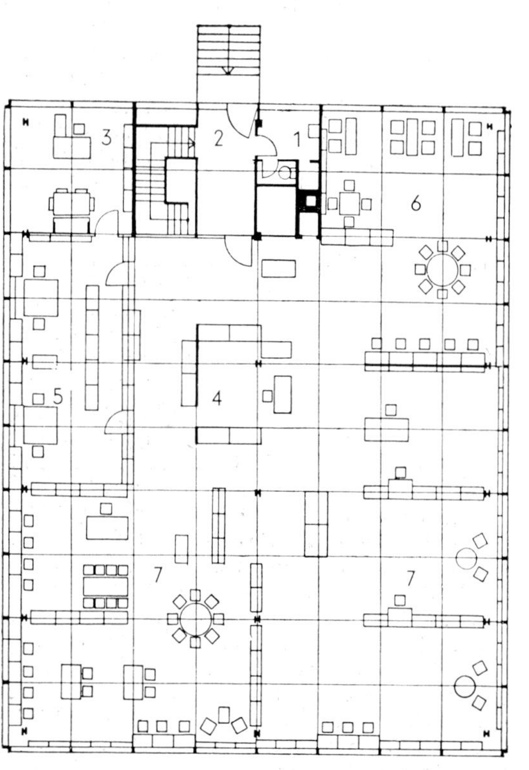


Main floor plan / Grundriß Hauptgeschoß.

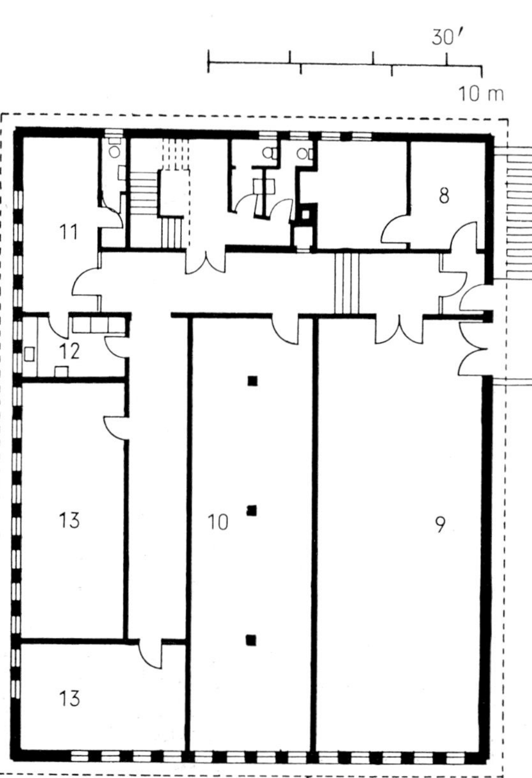


Basement floor plan / Grundriß Untergeschoß.

Key to plans / Legende zu den Plänen:
1 W.C.
2 Staircase / Treppe
3 Librarian / Bibliothekar
4 Reception / Empfang
5 Office / Büro
6 Periodical section / Zeitschriftenabteilung
7 Lending and reference section / Leihbücherei und Nachschlagewerke
8 Ventilation plant / Lüftungsanlage
9 Lecture room / Vortragssaal
10 Book store / Magazin
11 Staff room / Personal
12 Kitchen / Küche
13 Study rooms / Studienräume

1

1. The library is in a quiet suburban street but still near the community shopping places. An off-street parking area adjoins the building.
2. The central control desk is near the entrance but the librarian is also able to see almost all parts of the main room.
3. The periodicals section.
4. Furniture and shelving are in bright colours – blue, yellow, red, purple – and the internal columns of the building are brilliant lacquer red.

1. Die Bibliothek liegt in einer stillen Vorstadtstraße, aber nicht weit vom Einkaufszentrum entfernt. Ein Parkplatz neben der Straße schließt an das Gebäude an.
2. Empfang und Kontrolle liegen in Eingangsnähe, erlauben jedoch einen Überblick über den Lesesaal.
3. Blick in die Zeitschriftenabteilung.
4. Möbel und Regale sind in leuchtenden Farben – blau, gelb, rot und purpur – gestrichen. Die Innenstützen sind in leuchtendem Rot lackiert.

2

3

4

**Municipal Library at Horsens, Denmark, 1961**

Architects: Jørgen Juul Møller and Erik Laursen

This municipal library for Horsens in Jutland is an enlargement and development of the plan for Hørsholm. The same construction of steel columns and non-loadbearing partitions is used. In this instance however the total volume includes within it a paved courtyard. Except for offices and reference rooms the interior space is again only subdivided by bookshelves and counters; separation between parts is only suggested rather than enforced.
Both the plan and construction of the building could be considered as a prototype for a standard, industrially produced library building. This notion was present in the minds of the architects at the time of design.

**Stadtbücherei, Horsens, Dänemark, 1961**

Architekten: Jørgen Juul Møller und Erik Laursen

Bei dieser Bücherei in Jütland wurde der Grundriß von Hørsholm erweitert und weiterentwickelt. Außerdem wurde die gleiche Stahlkonstruktion mit nichttragenden Wänden verwandt, doch ist hier ein gepflasterter Hof in das Bauvolumen eingefügt. Mit Ausnahme der Büros und der Handbibliothek ist der Innenraum durch Regale und Tische gegliedert; die Unterteilung ist jedoch nur angedeutet.
Grundriß und Konstruktion des Gebäudes könnten durchaus als Grundlage für ein standardisiertes, industriell vorgefertigtes Gebäude dienen, wie es die Architekten bei ihrem Entwurf beabsichtigten.

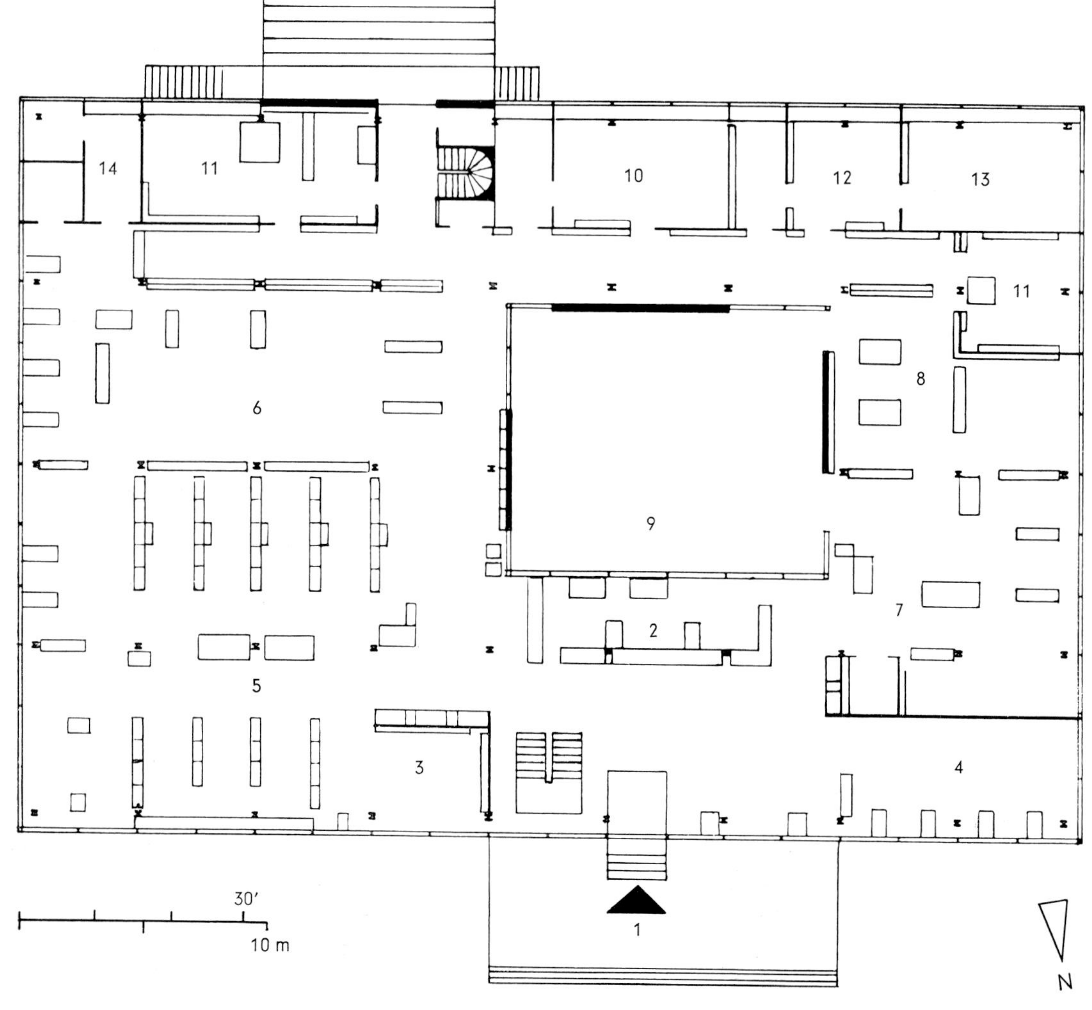


Ground floor plan / Grundriß Erdgeschoß.
1 Main entrance / Haupteingang
2 Lending counter / Ausleihe
3 Young people's section / Jugendbücherei
4 Periodicals reading room / Zeitschriftenlesesaal
5 Lending library for adults / Leihbücherei für Erwachsene
6 Reading room for adults / Lesesaal für Erwachsene
7 Lending library for children / Leihbücherei für Kinder
8 Reading room for children / Lesesaal für Kinder
9 Courtyard / Gartenhof
10 Librarian / Bibliothekar
11 Offices / Büros
12 Accessioning / Akzession
13 Cataloguing / Katalogisierung
14 Book storage / Magazin

1

1. The entrance to the library from a small new park.
2. The cobbled courtyard which is both a focus and a division between spaces.
3. Catalogue area and the issue desk beyond; the shelves are white, the supports black.
4. Ordinary, quite domestic furniture is used and this as well as the background is deliberately colourful; the atmosphere is only a slight intensification of the kind then current in a Danish house.

1. Der Eingang zur Bibliothek in dem neu angelegten kleinen Park.
2. Der gepflasterte Hof bildet den Mittelpunkt des Bauwerks und trennt zugleich die verschiedenen Zonen.
3. Der Katalogbereich mit der Ausgabe im Hintergrund; die Fächer sind weiß, die Gestelle schwarz gestrichen.
4. Für die Einrichtung wurden normale Möbel verwandt, die wie der ganze Raum betont farbig gehalten sind und die Atmosphäre eines dänischen Wohnhauses hervorrufen.

2

3

4

**Luigi Einaudi Memorial Library, Dogliani, Italy, 1963**

Architects: Studio A/Z (Vittorio Gigliotti, Antonio Di Carlo, Michele Pagano); Design consultant: Bruno Zevi

The "Luigi Einaudi" library was given to the town by Giulio Einaudi, a publisher, in memory of his father, the first President of the Italian Republic. The intention was to bring facilities to an area which at present lacked these and to place them so as to involve the community. The building is therefore positioned along a river-side walk and is prominent at night through its method of internal and external lighting. The reading area which is divided by bookshelves can be made into a small lecture room or meeting place by sliding away three sections of shelving which are suspended from a track in the ceiling.

**Luigi-Einaudi-Gedächtnisbibliothek, Dogliani, Italien, 1963**

Architekten: Studio A/Z (Vittorio Gigliotti, Antonio Di Carlo, Michele Pagano); Berater: Bruno Zevi

Diese Bibliothek, eine Stiftung des Verlegers Giulio Einaudi, ist dem Andenken an seinen Vater, den ersten Präsidenten der italienischen Republik, gewidmet. Um das Gemeindeleben zu aktivieren, wurden Einrichtungen einbezogen, über die der Ort bisher nicht verfügte. Außerdem liegt das Gebäude an einer vielbegangenen Uferpromenade und tritt abends durch seine Beleuchtungsakzente in Erscheinung. Der Lesesaal, der durch Regale unterteilt ist, läßt sich durch Verschiebung von drei Regaleinheiten in einen Vortrags- oder Versammlungsraum verwandeln. Die Regale sind an Deckenschienen befestigt.

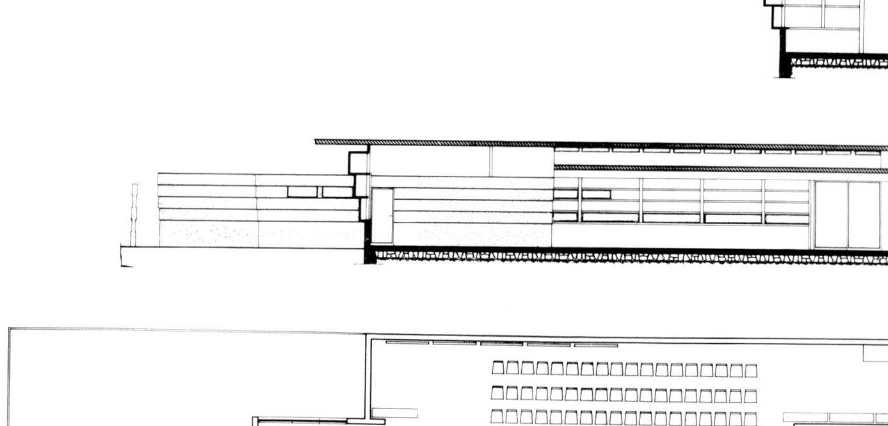

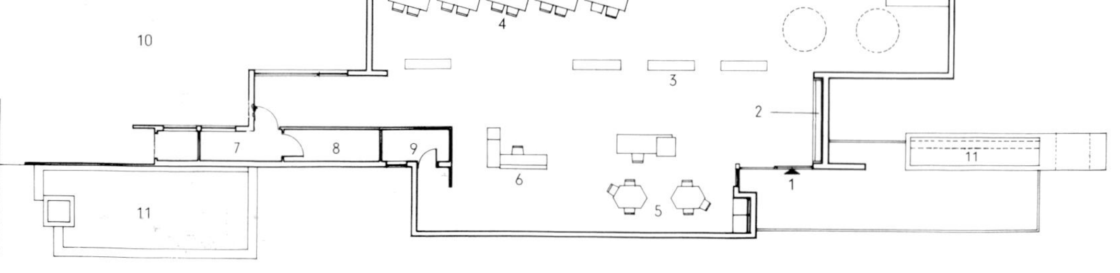


Cross section, longitudinal section and ground floor plan. The upper plan shows the main room arranged for a lecture, the lower plan shows the usual library arrangement.

Querschnitt, Längsschnitt und Grundriß Erdgeschoß. Im oberen Grundriß ist der Leseraum in einen Vortragssaal verwandelt, der untere Grundriß zeigt die normale Einrichtung der Bücherei.

1 Entrance / Eingang
2 Book exhibition / Buchausstellung
3 Movable shelves / Verschiebbare Regaleinheiten
4 Reading area for adults / Lesebereich für Erwachsene
5 Reading area for children / Lesebereich für Kinder
6 Catalogue / Katalog
7 Book store / Büchermagazin
8 Chair store / Stuhlmagazin
9 W.C.
10 Open-air reading area / Lesebereich im Freien
11 Flower-beds / Blumenbeete

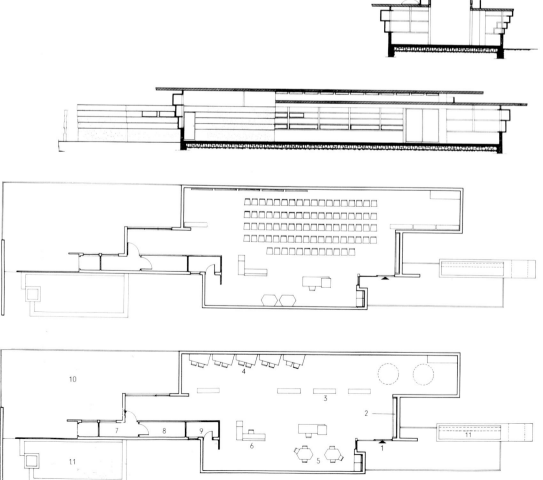

1. View of the south side; the paved area links directly with the town street pattern.
2. An oblique view of the entrance at night.

1. Blick auf die Südseite; der mit Steinen ausgelegte Vorplatz schließt direkt an die Straße an.
2. Nachtansicht der Eingangszone.

1

2

3

4

3. The adults' reading area; the sliding book sections are on the left.
4. The other end of the adults' area; the two tables in the corner include facilities for listening to music.

3. Blick in den Lesebereich für Erwachsene; links die verschiebbaren Regaleinheiten.
4. Die andere Seite des Lesebereichs für Erwachsene. Die beiden Tische in der Ecke sind mit Abhöranlagen für Schallplatten ausgestattet.

5

6

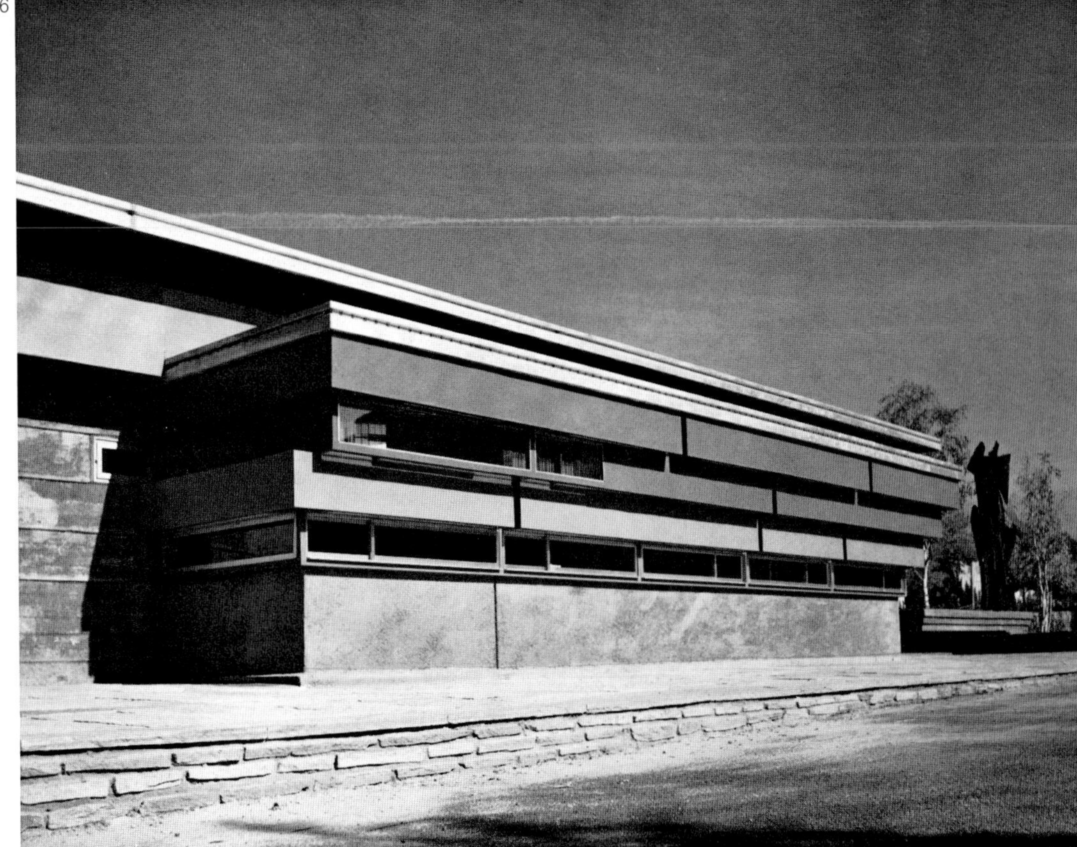

5. The children's reading corner near the entrance; the lit sloping shelves are for exhibiting new books which can be seen on entering.
6. Bookshelving, natural and artificial lighting and building enclosure have been considered together; in some instances this particular solution may, however, produce glare conditions inside.

5. Die Leseecke für Kinder in der Nähe des Eingangs. In den beleuchteten schräggestellten Fächern sind neue Bücher ausgelegt.
6. Gebäudeform, Regalanordnung und natürliche und künstliche Beleuchtung sind aufeinander abgestimmt. In einigen Fällen konnten dadurch Blendeffekte im Inneren nicht ganz vermieden werden.

## Grace A. Dow Memorial Library, Midland, Michigan, 1955

Architects: Alden B. Dow Associates, Inc.

The library service in the community had grown from 200 books, 25 members and a circulation of about 1400 books in 1900 to a collection of 17,000 books, 6,622 borrowers and a circulation of 142,248 in 1953. A new library building was endowed to deal with this expansion and was opened in 1955.

The total capacity of the open shelf library in the new building is 85,000 volumes. The design assumed that the building would be a general cultural centre and it therefore contains not only space for a public library, but also an auditorium to seat 266 equipped with a stage and a projection room, as well as an exhibition hall at lower level. The entire building is air-conditioned.

## Grace-A.-Dow-Gedächtnisbibliothek, Midland, Michigan, 1955

Architekten: Alden B. Dow Associates, Inc.

Von 200 Bänden, 25 Mitgliedern und einem Leihverkehr von 1400 Büchern im Jahre 1900 war die Gemeindebücherei auf 17000 Bücher, 6622 Ausleiher und einen Leihverkehr von 142248 Bänden im Jahre 1953 angewachsen. Das neue Gebäude ist eine Stiftung und soll der gestiegenen Nutzungsfrequenz Rechnung tragen.

Die Freihandbibliothek kann 85000 Bände aufnehmen. Bei der Planung gingen die Architekten davon aus, daß der Bau auch als Kulturzentrum dienen soll; so entstanden neben den Bibliotheksräumen ein Vortragssaal mit 266 Plätzen, der mit Bühne und Projektionsraum ausgestattet ist, sowie ein Ausstellungssaal im Untergeschoß. Das Gebäude ist vollklimatisiert.

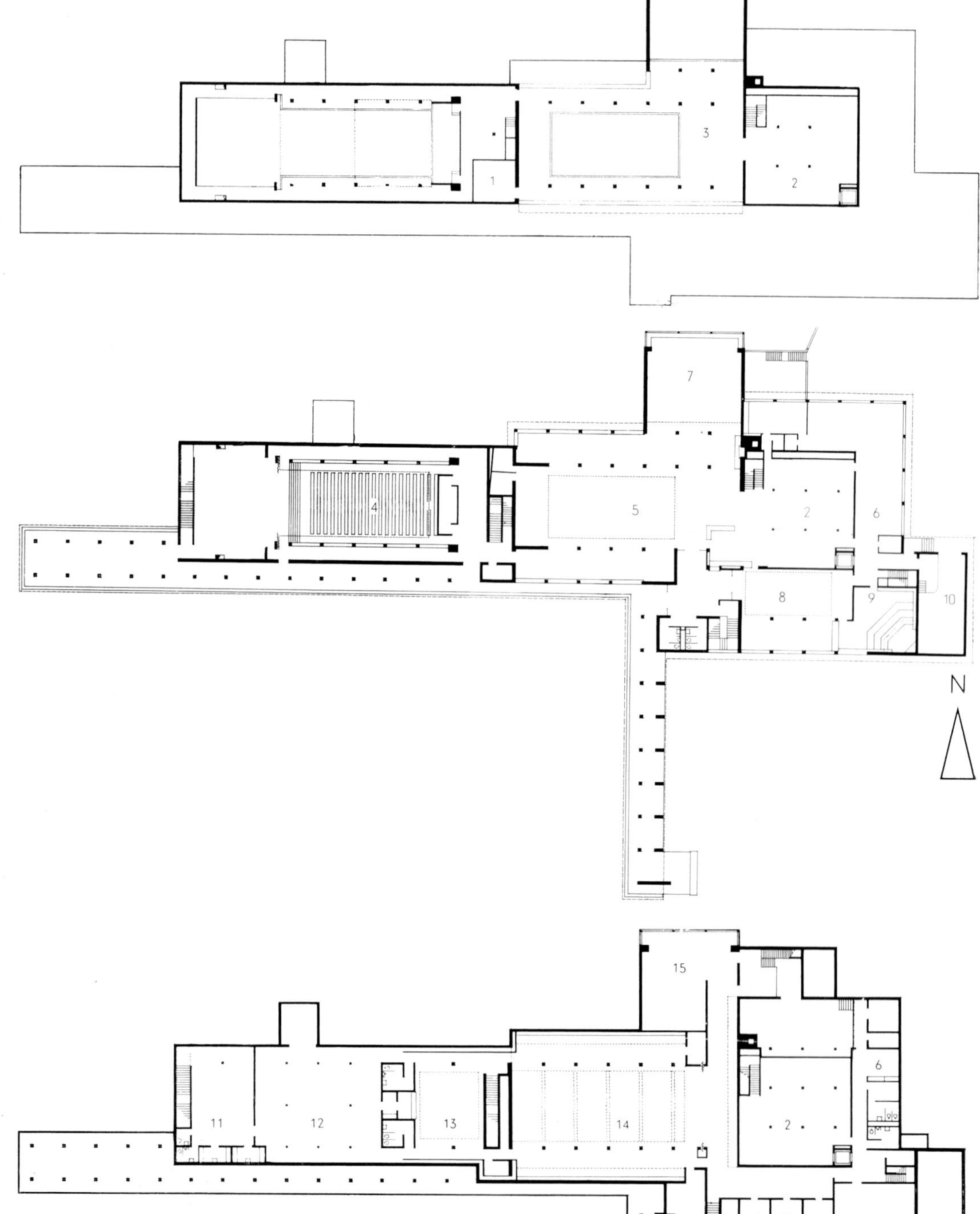


Plans of upper floor, first floor, and lower floor / Grundrisse Obergeschoß, Erdgeschoß und Untergeschoß.

1 Microfilm / Mikrofilme
2 Stack / Magazin
3 Balcony / Balkon
4 Auditorium / Vortragssaal
5 Reading reference / Katalog und Nachschlagewerke
6 Office / Büro
7 Young people / Jugendbücherei
8 Children / Kinderbücherei
9 Story-telling room / Vorleseraum
10 Garage
11 Workshop / Werkstatt
12 Machinery / Maschinenraum
13 Lounge / Halle
14 Exhibition hall / Ausstellungssaal
15 History / Geschichtliche Abteilung
16 Conference rooms / Konferenzräume

1. There is parking space for 100 cars; a provision almost on the scale of a small shopping centre.
2. The children's room; some of the tables have sloping tops to make it easier for small children to look at picture books.
3,4. In the general reading room there are different kinds of seating arrangements and there is space for the display and storage of 100 periodicals in the main central area; on either side there are bays near windows with further seats and low tables.

1. Der Parkplatz für 100 Wagen entspricht nahezu dem eines kleinen Einkaufszentrums.
2. Blick in den Leseraum für Kinder; einige Tischplatten sind geneigt, damit auch kleinere Kinder Bilderbücher betrachten können.
3, 4. Der große Lesesaal verfügt über verschiedene Sitzgruppen. In der Mitte des Raumes sind etwa 100 Zeitschriften ausgelegt. Auf beiden Seiten finden sich in Nischen an den Fenstern weitere Sitzplätze mit niedrigen Tischen.

1

2

3

4

**Public Library, Hansaviertel, Berlin, 1957**

Architect: Werner Düttmann

The library, built as part of the Interbau exhibition in 1957, is in the centre of a housing area and directly linked to the underground station which is the focal point of the local movement pattern. It is very much a building to be used almost casually as one comes back from work or goes out shopping. Different activities go on in the different wings of the four-sided single storey building which almost encloses a central courtyard.
The design is an example of the kind of modest branch library which it ought to be possible to build and successfully relate within almost any kind of housing group. Libraries such as these should be seen as something to be financed out of a total budget allocated to a project for the construction of houses, schools, drains, playgrounds and shops within a certain area. Only in this kind of a way is one likely to get communal facilities as part of the normal provision of services; services being considered not only in the form of electricity or sewage but also as clinics or libraries.

**Hansabücherei, Hansaviertel, Berlin, 1957**

Architekt: Werner Düttmann

Die Bücherei, die während der Interbau-Ausstellung errichtet wurde, liegt im Zentrum des Wohngebiets an der U-Bahnstation, die den Verkehrsmittelpunkt des Hansaviertels bildet. Das Gebäude ist also ohne viel Aufwand nach der Arbeit oder vor dem Einkaufen zu erreichen. Die um einen zentralen Innenhof angeordneten Flügel erfüllen unterschiedliche Funktionen.
Die Lösung ist beispielhaft für eine kleinere Zweigbücherei, wie sie sich in nahezu jeder Neubausiedlung einplanen ließe. Solche Büchereien sollten stets in den Gesamtfinanzierungsplan eines neuen Stadtgebietes einbezogen werden, der für den Bau von Wohnungen, Schulen, Kanalisationsanlagen, Spielplätzen und Läden entwickelt wird. Nur so ist es möglich, zu kommunalen Einrichtungen zu gelangen, die ebenso wie Elektrizität oder Kanalisation als normale Dienstleistungen jedem Bürger zur Verfügung stehen sollten.

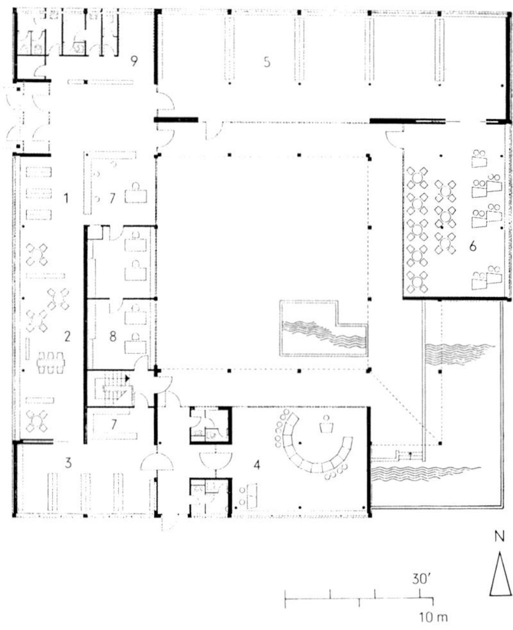


Main floor plan / Grundriß Hauptgeschoß.
1 Catalogue / Katalog
2 Periodicals reading room / Zeitschriftenlesesaal
3 Lending library for young people / Leihbücherei für Jugendliche
4 Reading room for young people / Lesesaal für Jugendliche
5 Lending library for adults / Leihbücherei für Erwachsene
6 Reading room / Lesesaal
7 Outgoing books / Ausleihe
8 Administration / Verwaltung
9 Cloakroom / Garderobe

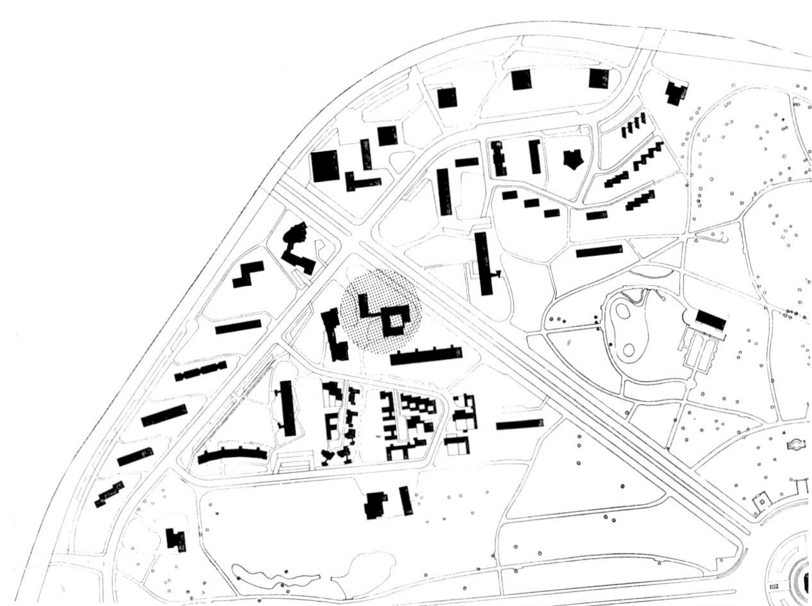

Site plan / Lageplan.

1

1. The covered way linking the underground station entrance with that of the library.

1. Der überdachte Gang verbindet die U-Bahnstation mit der Bücherei.

2

3

4

5

2. The building is set within a green area which runs between the blocks of flats of the Hansaviertel.
3, 4. The courtyard is seen from most of the internal spaces both during the day and night and has chairs for outdoor reading.
5. The adult lending library.

2. Das Gebäude wurde in die Grünanlagen einbezogen, die sich zwischen den Wohnblocks des Hansaviertels erstrecken.
3, 4. Fast alle Räume ermöglichen einen Blick in den Innenhof, in dem Stühle für die Lektüre im Freien aufgestellt sind.
5. Blick in die Leihbücherei für Erwachsene.

6

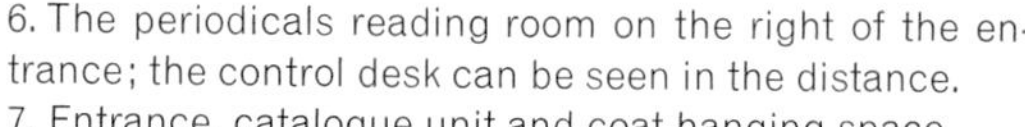

6. The periodicals reading room on the right of the entrance; the control desk can be seen in the distance.
7. Entrance, catalogue unit and coat hanging space.

6. Der Zeitschriftenbereich liegt rechts vom Eingang; im Hintergrund der Kontrolltisch.
7. Blick auf Eingang, Katalog und Garderobe im Hintergrund.

7

8

9

10

11

8. Adjustable shelving.
9. The adults' reading room provided with two different kinds of seating; there is a glass wall on the left facing the courtyard.
10. Trolleys used for the return of books; subsidiary catalogues can be seen at the ends of each run of shelving.
11. Movable magazine display in the reading room.

8. Die Regale sind leicht verstellbar.
9. Der Leseraum für Erwachsene ist mit zwei verschiedenen Stuhlmodellen ausgestattet. Eine Glaswand links ist zum Innenhof orientiert.
10. Die Bücherkarren für die Rückgabe; am Ende jeder Regalreihe sind Teilkataloge untergebracht.
11. Im Lesesaal sind auf fahrbaren Regalen Zeitschriften ausgestellt.

**Library, Växjö, Sweden, 1965**

Architect: Erik Uluots

The design won first prize in an open competition. Design work started in 1961 and the building was completed in 1965. The library is within a park in the centre of the town. The building consists of three floors, each different in character but each extremely flexible within itself. The basement floor is for mechanical equipment and book storage, some of it on compact shelving. Further compact shelving can be installed very easily since the rails for it have already been cast in the floor and are only temporarily covered with a steel section. The ground floor is an open glazed space with a square column grid containing the lending and reading departments. The first floor, enclosed on the outside but opening on to an inner central roof garden, has offices, work rooms, research rooms with microfilm readers and a lecture theatre for about 150 people with a stage which can become a story-telling room. The library has a capacity of about 500,000 volumes.

**Bücherei, Växjö, Schweden, 1965**

Architekt: Erik Uluots

Der Entwurf erhielt den ersten Preis in einem offenen Wettbewerb. Mit den Planungsarbeiten wurde 1961 begonnen; 1965 wurde der Bau fertiggestellt. Die Bücherei liegt in einem Park mitten in der Stadt. Das Gebäude hat drei Geschosse, die sich im Charakter voneinander unterscheiden, aber in sich äußerst flexibel sind. Im Untergeschoß sind die technischen Einrichtungen und das Magazin untergebracht, das zum Teil mit raumsparenden Regalen ausgestattet wurde. Weitere Kompaktregale sind leicht einzubauen, da die Laufschienen bereits in den Boden eingegossen wurden; sie sind vorläufig noch mit einem Stahlband abgedeckt. Das Erdgeschoß ist ein nach allen Seiten offener verglaster Raum mit quadratischer Stützenanordnung und enthält die Leihbücherei sowie die Leseräume. Das Obergeschoß ist geschlossen, öffnet sich aber nach innen auf einen Dachgarten. In diesem Geschoß liegen Büros, Studios mit Ablesegeräten für Mikrofilme und ein Saal mit ungefähr 150 Plätzen, dessen Bühne abgetrennt und in einen Vorleseraum verwandelt werden kann. Die Bücherei hat eine Kapazität von etwa 500000 Bänden.

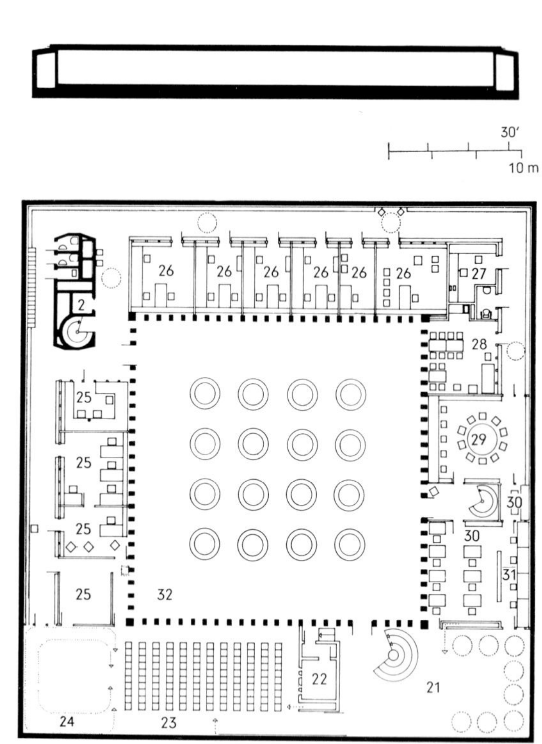

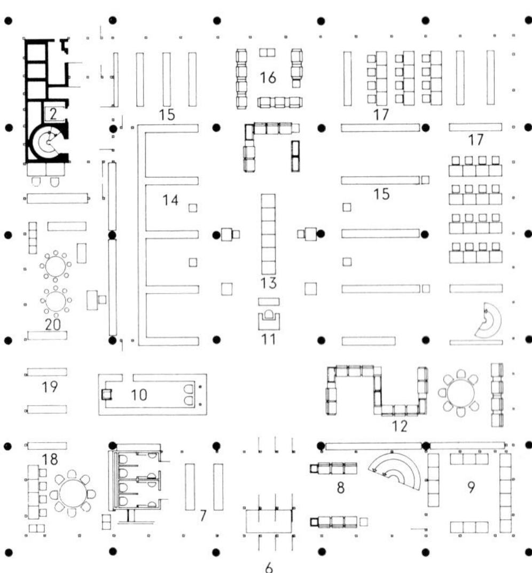

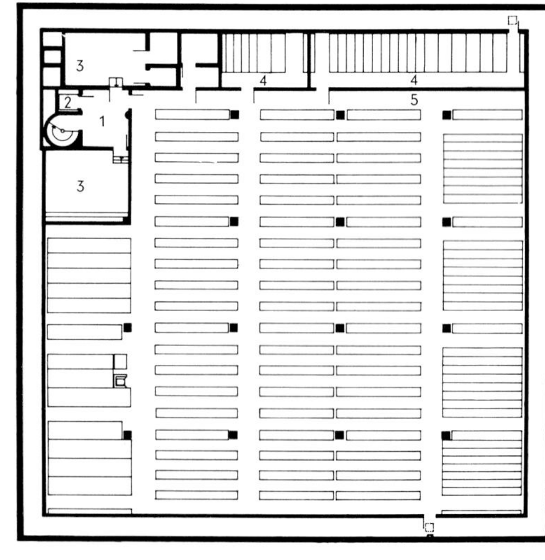

Section, plans of first floor, ground floor, and basement floor (from top to bottom).
Schnitt, Grundrisse Obergeschoß, Erdgeschoß und Untergeschoß (von oben nach unten).

1 Staircase hall / Treppenhaus
2 Lift / Aufzug
3 Machinery / Maschinenraum
4 Archives / Archiv
5 Book storage / Magazin
6 Main entrance / Haupteingang
7 Cloakroom / Garderobe
8 Daily newspapers / Tageszeitungen
9 Display room / Ausstellungsraum
10 Lending counter / Ausleihe
11 Information counter / Auskunft
12 Magazines / Zeitschriften
13 Catalogue / Katalog
14 Fiction / Belletristik
15 Non-fiction / Sachbücher
16 Music department (armchairs for listening to gramophone) / Musikabteilung (Sessel für Grammophonempfang)
17 Reading department / Lesebereich
18 Teenage department / Teenagerbücherei
19 Juvenile department / Jugendbücherei
20 Children's department / Kinderbücherei
21 Foyer and display hall / Foyer und Ausstellungshalle
22 Cinema machine-room / Projektionsraum
23 Lecture room / Vortragssaal
24 Stage and room for reading stories to small children / Bühne und Vorleseraum für kleine Kinder
25 Workroom and storage / Arbeitsraum und Lager
26 Librarian / Bibliothekar
27 Photo room / Fotolabor
28 Lunchroom for staff / Speiseraum für Bibliotheksangestellte
29 Småland-room / Småland-Raum
30 Offices / Büros
31 Microfilm readers / Ablesegeräte für Mikrofilme
32 Roof terrace for open-air reading / Dachterrasse für Lektüre im Freien

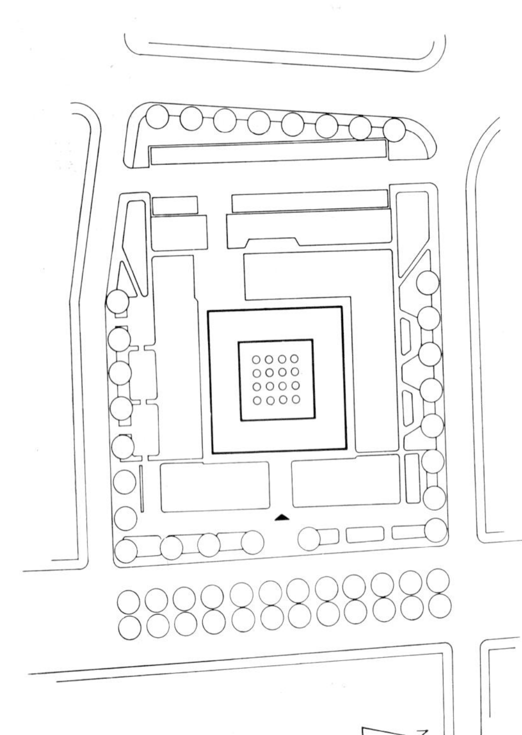

Site plan / Lageplan.

1. The library entrance seen from the park; the upper wall is white marble, the columns rendered with white marble particles, the glass is set in bronze frames.
2. 3'4" (1 m) high gilt letters on the main elevation; these are lit up from behind at night.

1. Blick vom Park auf den Eingang. Die Außenwände sind mit weißem Marmor verkleidet, die Stützen mit Putz, der mit weißen Marmorteilchen durchsetzt ist. Die Fenster haben Bronzerahmen.
2. Die 1 m hohen vergoldeten Buchstaben an der Eingangsseite werden nachts von hinten beleuchtet.

1

2

3

4

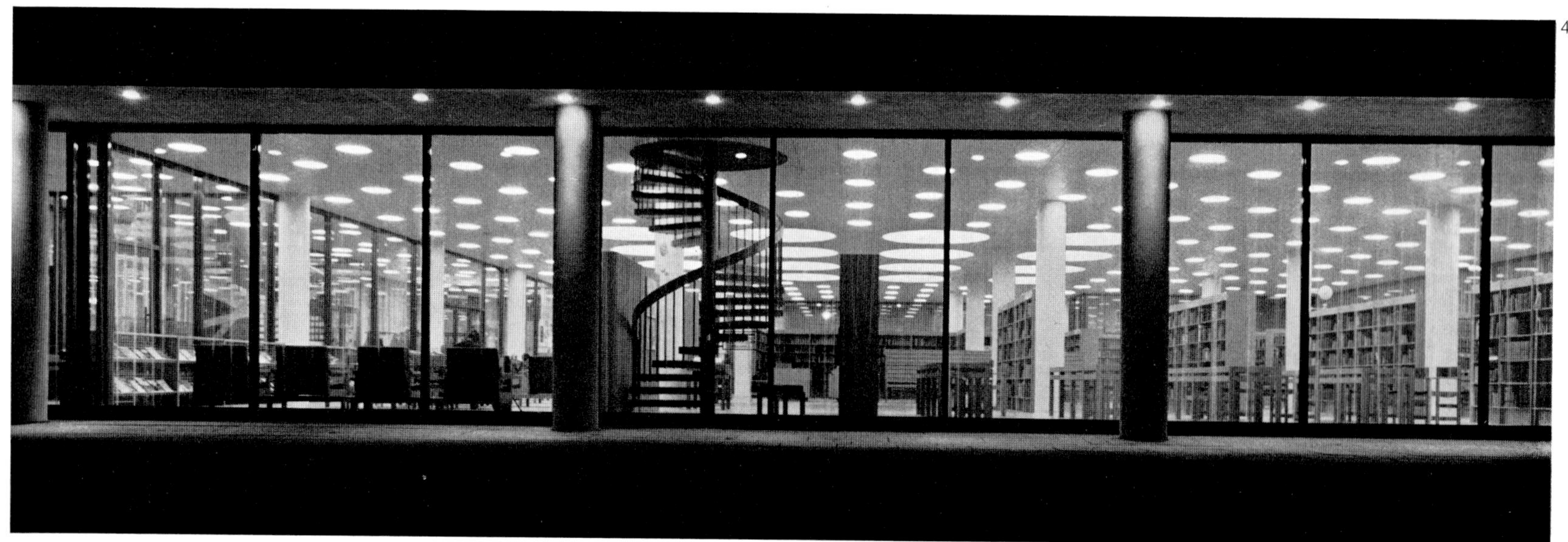

◁ 3. Part of the ground floor library space seen from the entrance; the information desk and the catalogue are straight ahead, the check-out desk is on the left with a plan of the library next to it against the glass wall.
4. The ground floor space revealed at night.

◁ 3. Blick vom Eingang in die Bücherei im Erdgeschoß. In der Mitte Auskunft und Katalog, links die Ausgangskontrolle. An der Glaswand links ist ein Grundriß der Bibliothek befestigt.
4. Nachtaufnahme des Erdgeschosses.

5

6

5, 6. Shelving and seating on the ground floor; the sections of shelving are movable and the shelves adjustable; furniture and shelving are in timber; columns and ceilings are white, the floor grey linoleum.

5, 6. Regale und Sitzgruppen im Erdgeschoß. Die Regaleinheiten sind beweglich und die Fächer verstellbar. Möbel und Regale sind aus Naturholz. Stützen und Decken sind weiß gestrichen, der Fußboden ist mit grauem Linoleum ausgelegt.

7

8

9

10

◁ 7. Gramophone playing equipment on the ground floor.
8. The children's section; the area for teenagers is on the other side of the book shelves.
9. Storage in the basement; movable compact shelving on the left, fixed steel shelving on the right.
10. Exhibition show cases; all the furniture and equipment were designed by the architect.

◁ 7. Die Abhöranlagen für Schallplatten im Erdgeschoß.
8. Blick in die Kinderabteilung. Die Jugendbücherei liegt auf der anderen Seite der Bücherregale.
9. Blick in das Magazin des Untergeschosses. Links die beweglichen raumsparenden Regale, auf der rechten Seite feste Stahlregale.
10. Die Vitrinen wurden wie alle anderen Möbel und Einrichtungsgegenstände vom Architekten entworfen.

11

12

11. The stage on the first floor which becomes a story-telling room.
12. The first floor roof terrace which becomes a central courtyard for reading and sitting out.

11. Die Bühne des Vortragssaales im Obergeschoß kann in einen Vorleseraum für Kinder verwandelt werden.
12. Die umschlossene Dachterrasse im Obergeschoß lädt zur Lektüre und zum Aufenthalt im Freien ein.

**Public Library, Hälsingborg, Sweden, 1965**

Arton, Consultant Architects

The site of the library, opened in April 1965, is a gently sloping piece of ground 130′ × 130′ (40 m × 40 m) in the municipal park within the town centre. The building is made of local brick which is also exposed inside.
The main library functions are on the ground floor with the adult sections on two sides of a courtyard, the young people's and children's sections on the other two. The first floor has the rather more secondary activities including a combined tea room and smoking room which can be reached by a staircase going directly up into it from the entrance hall. This room also becomes the crush space for a lecture theatre seating 170. The basement houses book storage.

**Öffentliche Bücherei, Hälsingborg, Schweden, 1965**

Arton, beratende Architekten

Die Bücherei, die im April 1965 eröffnet wurde, liegt auf einem sanft abfallenden Gelände (40 × 40 m) des Stadtparks mitten im Stadtzentrum. Das Gebäude ist in Backstein errichtet, der auch innen sichtbar gelassen wurde.
Im Erdgeschoß liegen die Bücherei für Erwachsene an zwei Seiten des Innenhofs und die Bücherei für Kinder und Jugendliche an den beiden anderen Seiten. Das Obergeschoß enthält die Nebenräume und einen Tee- und Rauchsalon mit direktem Zugang zur Eingangshalle. Dieser Raum wird auch als Foyer des Theatersaals benutzt, der über 170 Plätze verfügt. Im Untergeschoß befinden sich die Magazine.

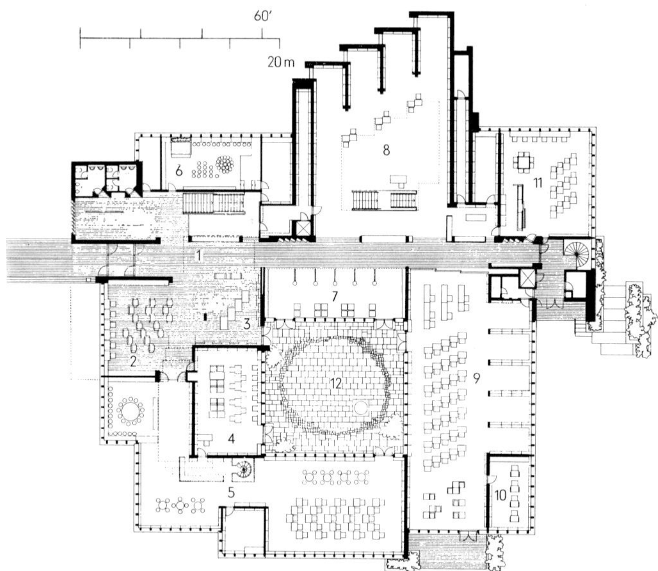


Ground floor plan / Grundriß Erdgeschoß.

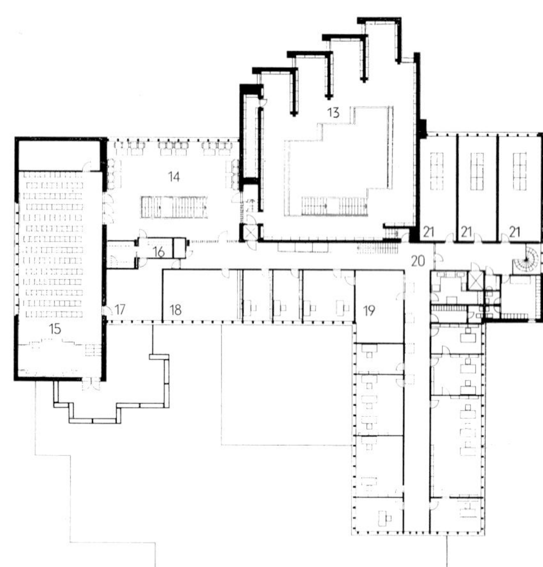


First floor plan / Grundriß Obergeschoß.

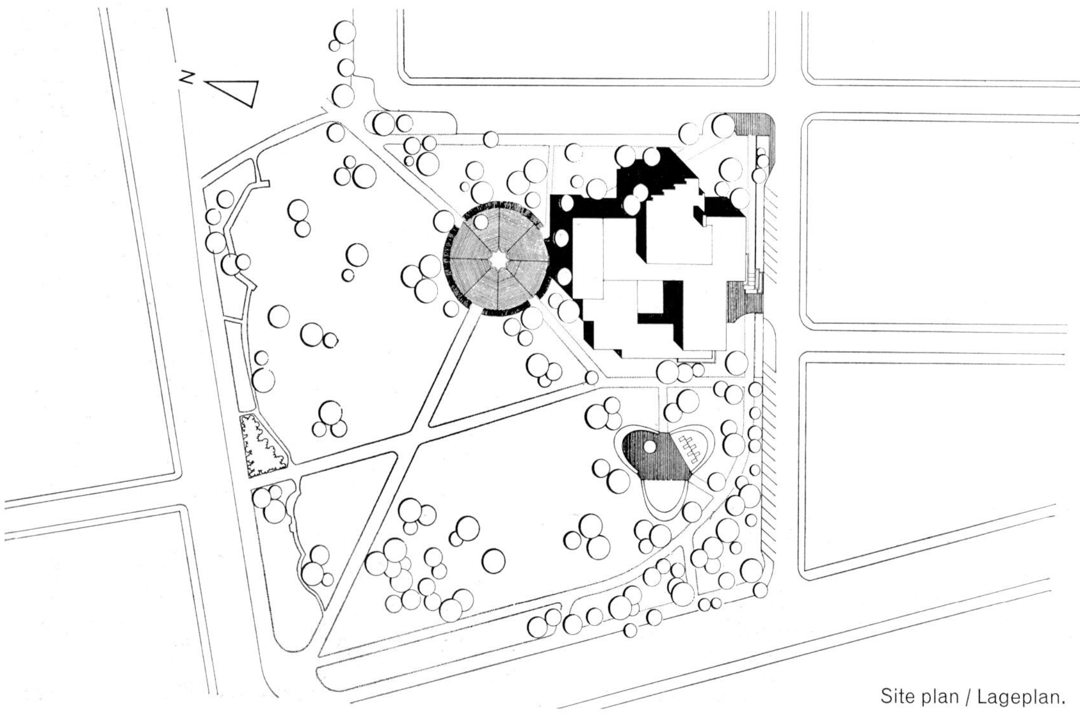


Site plan / Lageplan.

Key to plans / Legende zu den Plänen:
1 Vestibule with central lending counter / Vorhalle mit Ausleihe
2 Newspapers / Zeitungen
3 Changing displays / Wechselausstellungen
4 Young people's section / Jugendabteilung
5 Children's section / Kinderabteilung
6 Story-telling room and nursery / Vorleseraum und Kindergarten
7 Periodicals / Zeitschriften
8 Books / Bücher
9 Reading room for adults / Leseraum für Erwachsene
10 Study room / Studienraum
11 Music room / Musikraum
12 Patio / Innenhof
13 Books and gallery / Bücher und Galerie
14 Tea room and smoking room / Tee- und Rauchsalon
15 Lecture theatre / Vortrags- und Theatersaal
16 Tea kitchen / Teeküche
17 Staff luncheon room / Speiseraum des Personals
18 Librarian / Bibliothekar
19 Caretaker's office / Büro des Hausmeisters
20 Offices / Büros
21 Spare rooms / Reserveräume

1

2

1. Exterior of the two-storey high main room.
2. The west side; the small terrace links to the adults' reading room.
3. Exterior of the children's rooms; the main entrance is on the left.
4. The paved courtyard onto which four reading areas open.

1. Außenansicht des zweigeschossigen Hauptraums.
2. Blick auf die Westseite. Die kleine Terrasse liegt vor dem Leseraum für Erwachsene.
3. Außenansicht der Kinderbücherei, links im Hintergrund der Haupteingang.
4. Der gepflasterte Hof ist von vier Lesebereichen aus zugänglich.

3

4

5

5. The two-storey high lending library; each bay is lit by a window on the left.
6. The first floor hall which is acoustically balanced for chamber music; it can also be used for lectures, films, and since the chairs are movable, be arranged for exhibitions.

5. Blick in die zwei Geschosse hohe Leihbücherei; jede Nische erhält zusätzliches Tageslicht durch hohe schmale Fenster.
6. Der Saal im Obergeschoß bietet die akustischen Voraussetzungen für Kammermusikkonzerte. Hier finden auch Vorträge und Filmvorführungen sowie Ausstellungen statt, da die Stühle demontiert werden können.

6

7. The staircase joining the gallery of the main room to the ground floor; the balustrade frequently has a seat projecting from it so that it is possible to sit down while choosing books.
8. Coat hooks in the children's story-telling room.
9. Children's story-telling room; a small stage is on the right.

7. Blick auf die Verbindungstreppe zwischen Galerie und Erdgeschoß. Die Balustrade ist an mehreren Stellen mit vorkragenden Sitzen ausgestattet, so daß die Benutzer bei der Lektüre Platz nehmen können.
8. Die Kleiderhaken im Vorleseraum der Kinder.
9. Blick in den Vorleseraum mit einer kleinen Bühne auf der rechten Seite.

7

8

9

## Public Library, Solna, Sweden, 1964

Architect: Sture Frölén

Solna's new town centre contains commercial buildings, a hotel, restaurants as well as a 400 seat theatre. The library was added to this centre during 1963–64. It is a square six-storey building, two floors being below street level. It has been deliberately designed somewhat larger than was necessary for immediate needs so as to be able to deal with an increased book collection and more readers. In view of its position within the town centre—an isolated building with all four sides enclosing important urban spaces—expansion by building additional floor area was extremely difficult and probably in any case undesirable. A rather greater amount of spare space tnan normal seems therefore an extremely sensible precaution.

## Öffentliche Bücherei, Solna, Schweden, 1964

Architekt: Sture Frölén

Das neue Stadtzentrum von Solna umfaßt Geschäftsbauten, ein Hotel, Restaurants und ein Theater mit 400 Plätzen. Die Bücherei, ein sechsgeschossiges Gebäude (zwei Geschosse liegen unter Straßenniveau), wurde 1963–64 errichtet. Sie wurde bewußt größer geplant, als es für den augenblicklichen Bedarf notwendig ist, damit ein späterer Zuwachs an Büchern und Lesern aufgefangen werden kann. Im Hinblick auf die Lage im neuen Stadtzentrum – ein frei stehendes Gebäude, das auf allen vier Seiten wichtige städtische Bereiche umgrenzt – wäre eine Erweiterung äußerst schwierig und wahrscheinlich auch nicht wünschenswert. Deshalb war es eine gute Lösung, das Gebäude von vornherein für einen größeren Raumbedarf anzulegen.

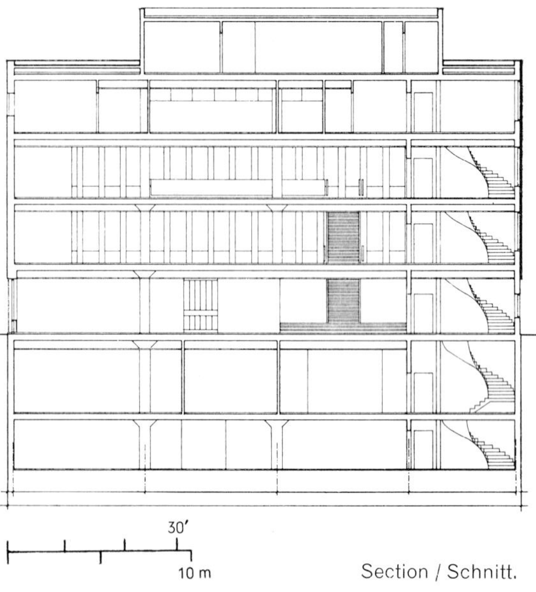


Section / Schnitt.

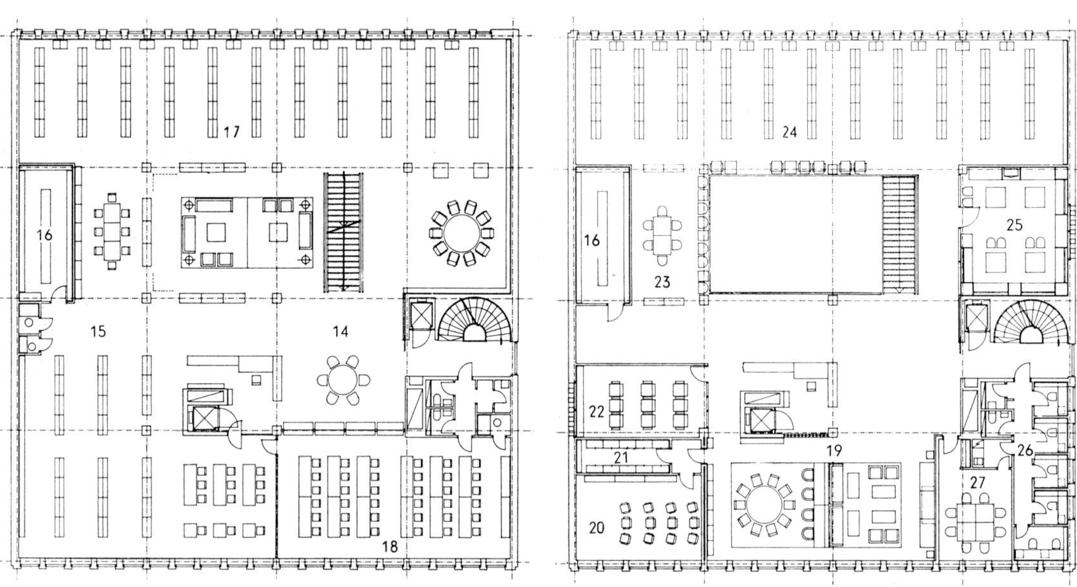


First floor plan / Grundriß erstes Obergeschoß.

Second floor plan / Grundriß zweites Obergeschoß.

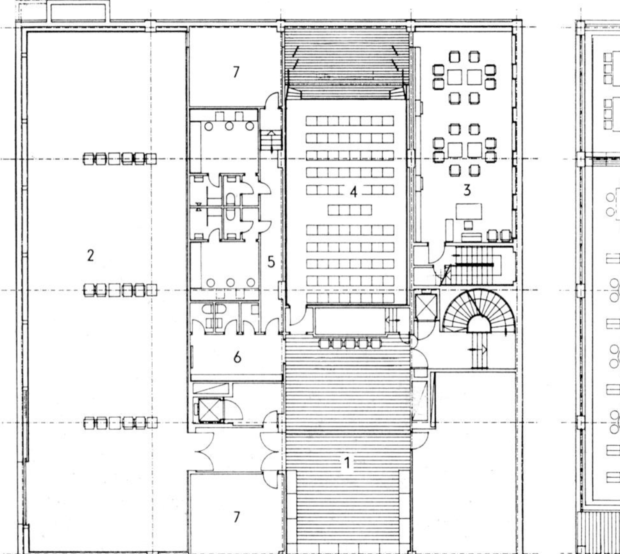

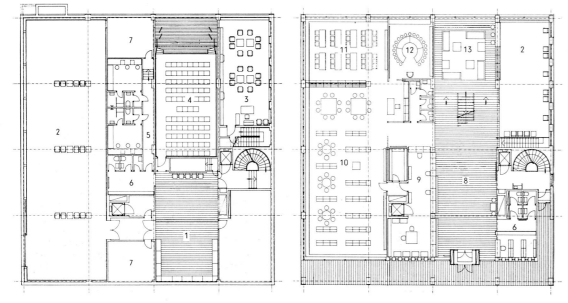

Upper basement floor plan/Grundriß erstes Untergeschoß.

Ground floor plan / Grundriß Erdgeschoß.

Key to plans / Legende zu den Plänen:

1 Foyer
2 Display / Ausstellung
3 Teenagers' reading room / Leseraum für Teenager
4 Lecture hall / Vortragssaal
5 Changing room / Umkleideraum
6 Cloakroom / Garderobe
7 Storage / Lager
8 Entrance hall / Eingangshalle
9 Lending counter / Ausleihe
10 Children and young people's department / Abteilung für Kinder und Jugendliche
11 Juvenile reading room / Leseraum für Jugendliche
12 Story-telling room / Vorleseraum für kleine Kinder
13 Newspapers / Zeitungen
14 Hall / Halle
15 Reference and reading room / Nachschlagewerke und Lesesaal
16 Stockroom / Lager
17 Non-fiction / Sachbücher
18 Students reading room / Lesesaal für Studenten
19 Lounge / Aufenthaltsraum
20 Stereo room / Stereo-Raum
21 Record library / Schallplatten
22 Music room / Musikraum
23 Solna room / Solna-Raum
24 Fiction / Belletristik
25 Smoking and TV room / Rauch- und Fernsehzimmer
26 Study rooms / Studienräume
27 Group room / Gruppenraum

1. The entrance side; the draught-lobby opens straight into a large entrance hall which has the newspaper room at the far end.
2. The west side with a sculpture of a "Water Carrier" by Bror Hjorth.

1. Blick auf die Eingangsseite. Der Windfang führt direkt in eine große Eingangshalle mit dem Zeitungsraum im Hintergrund.
2. Die Westseite mit der Skulptur eines »Wasserträgers« von Bror Hjorth.

1

2

3

4

3. The check-in and issue desks on the left of the entrance; the door behind the column is that of a lift linking all six floors; the ceiling has sound absorbent tiles.
4. A sitting area on the second floor with a fireplace on the left.

3. Die Eingangskontrolle und die Ausgabetische liegen links vom Eingang; die Tür hinter der Stütze gehört zum Aufzug, der alle sechs Geschosse verbindet. Die Decke ist mit schallschluckenden Platten verkleidet.
4. Der Aufenthaltsraum im zweiten Obergeschoß ist mit einem großen Kamin ausgestattet.

5

6

7

5–7. The periodicals reading area in the centre of the three storey high hall is a carpeted island within the bigger space; the floor immediately above has more bookstacks and a number of specialist and social rooms; the top floor houses the administrative offices.

5–7. Die Zeitschriftenabteilung im Zentrum der drei Geschosse hohen Halle bildet eine mit Teppich ausgelegte Insel. Im ersten Obergeschoß befinden sich weitere Magazine und die Sonder- und Gesellschaftsräume. Die Verwaltung ist im obersten Geschoß untergebracht.

**Public Library, Reuchlinhaus, Pforzheim, Germany, 1961**

Architect: Manfred Lehmbruck

The Reuchlinhaus, formally opened on 20th October 1961, is a complex of buildings within a town park containing an important jewellery museum, a folk museum, a temporary exhibition gallery, the town historical collection, the town archives, the rooms of the local Arts and Crafts Society, the workshops of two guilds as well as the public library. It is an important centre for a town of around 80,000, over 10% of whom were users of the library soon after its opening in the new building.
The size of the collection after the library had transferred to the Reuchlinhaus was 30,200 volumes. These were placed on open access and the number of loans increased in the first year of use by almost 65%.

**Öffentliche Bücherei, Reuchlinhaus, Pforzheim, 1961**

Architekt: Manfred Lehmbruck

Das Reuchlinhaus liegt in einem städtischen Park und umfaßt ein bedeutendes Schmuckmuseum, das Museum für Volkskunst, einen Bau für Ausstellungen, das Heimatmuseum, das Stadtarchiv, Räume für die städtischen Handwerker-Vereinigungen, Werkstätten für zwei Innungen sowie die öffentliche Bücherei. Es ist ein wichtiges kulturelles Zentrum für die 80000 Einwohner der Stadt, von denen bereits 10% kurz nach der Eröffnung die Bücherei benutzten.
Bei der Eröffnung verfügte die Bibliothek über 30200 Bände, die frei zugänglich sind; die Zahl der ausgeliehenen Bücher war bereits nach einem Jahr um fast 65% gestiegen.

Key to plans / Legende zu den Plänen:

1 Entrance hall / Eingangshalle
2 Courtyard / Skulpturenhof
3 Pool / Wasserbecken
4 Lecture room / Vortragssaal
5 Town historical collection / Stadtgeschichtliche Sammlung
6 Modern jewellery exhibition / Ausstellung von modernem Schmuck
7 Coats / Garderobe
8 W. C.
9 Kitchen / Teeküche
10 Boiler-room, mechanical equipment / Heizung und technische Anlagen
11 Workshop / Werkstatt
12 Restaurant / Kellerschenke
13 Guild room / Zunftraum
14 Storage / Magazin
15 Jewellery museum / Schmuckmuseum
16 Folk museum / Heimatmuseum
17 Library and reading rooms / Bibliothek und Leseräume
18 Main exhibition gallery / Großer Ausstellungssaal
19 Void over main exhibition gallery / Luftraum Ausstellungssaal
20 Caretaker's apartment / Hausmeisterwohnung
21 Discussion room / Diskussionsraum
22 Offices / Büros
23 Void over library / Luftraum Bibliothek
24 Town archives / Stadtarchiv

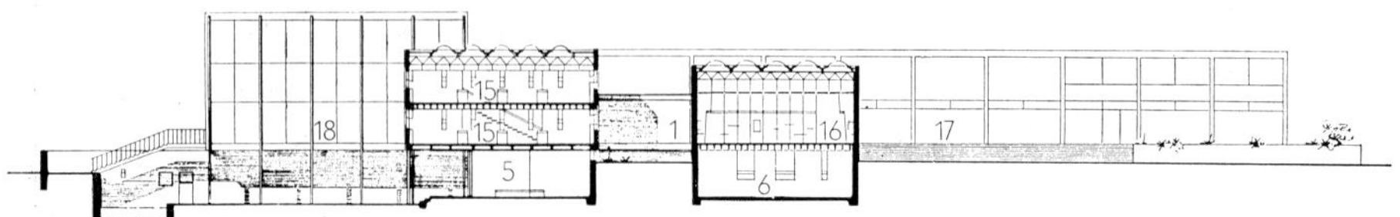

Longitudinal section / Längsschnitt.

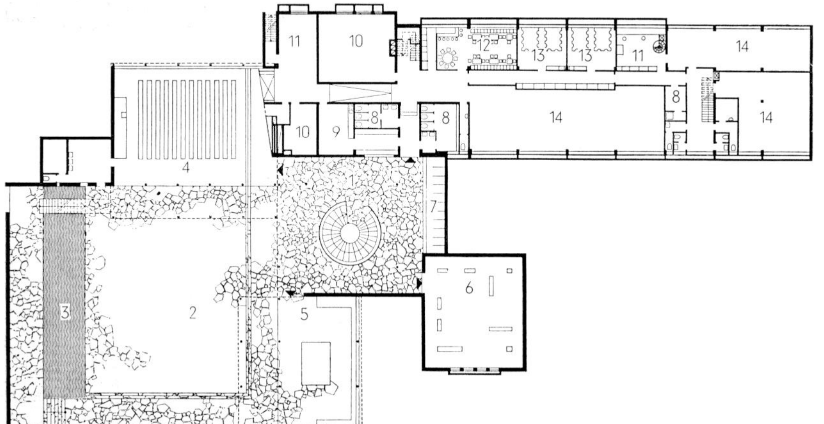

Plan of lower ground floor / Grundriß Untergeschoß.

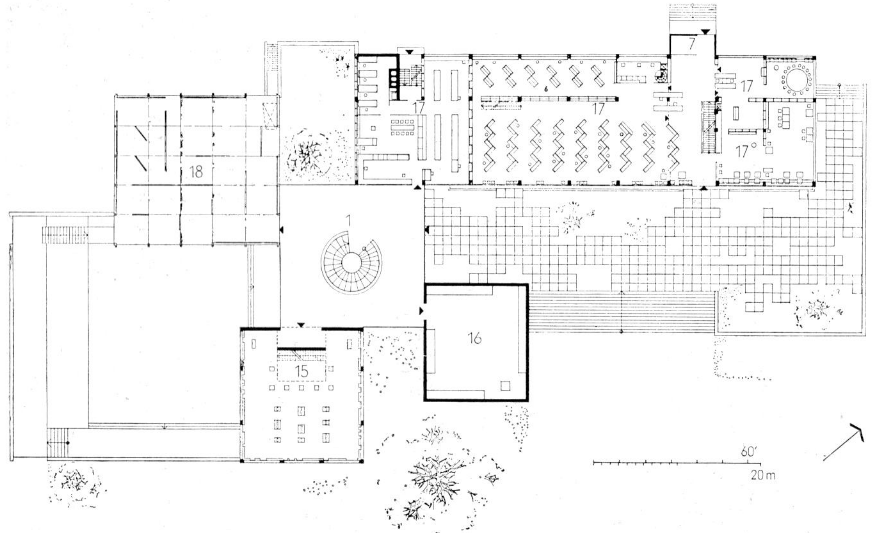

Ground floor plan / Grundriß Erdgeschoß.

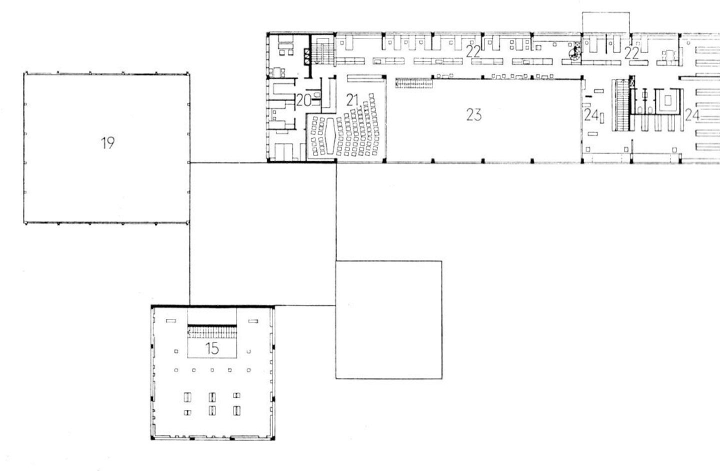

First floor plan / Grundriß Obergeschoß.

1

2

1. The library faces the main steps leading up to the terrace which links the different elements of the Reuchlinhaus.
2. The library is on the right; the entrance to the different parts of the museum is from the glass enclosed lobby straight ahead which however also has a door to the library; all sections are thus connected.

1. Die Bücherei liegt an der Haupttreppe zu der Terrasse, von der aus man zu den verschiedenen Gebäuden des Komplexes gelangt.
2. Die Bücherei liegt rechts; die verglaste Halle im Hintergrund führt zu den verschiedenen Abteilungen des Museums, gewährt aber auch Zugang zur Bücherei, so daß alle Räume miteinander verbunden sind.

3

3. The control desk just inside the main entrance to the library; the door on the left is the entrance from the north-west, while the main entrance is on the side of the terrace leading to the museums.
4. Newspaper reading area at the foot of the stairs.
5. The desk at the entrance to the lending library.

3. Blick in die Eingangshalle der Bücherei mit dem Kontrolltisch. Die Tür links im Bild bildet den Eingang von Nordwesten, während der Haupteingang von der Terrasse durch eine gegenüberliegende Tür führt.
4. Der Zeitungsleseraum am Fuß der Treppe.
5. Der Kontrolltisch am Eingang der Leihbücherei.

4

5

6

7

6. The main lending library seen from above.
7. The wooden free standing shelves are kept low and form small enclosures each clearly labelled.

6. Blick von oben in die große Leihbücherei.
7. Die frei stehenden Regale aus Holz sind niedrig gehalten; sie bilden Lesenischen, die übersichtlich bezeichnet sind.

8

9

8. A study area on the ground floor; spaces are subdivided by uprights which hold shelving or screens.
9. The children's room; the space above the last shelf or the top of the screen has here been glazed.

8. Blick auf einen Lese- und Arbeitsbereich im Erdgeschoß; die Räume sind nur durch Pfosten getrennt, an denen Regalfächer oder Platten befestigt sind.
9. Blick in die Kinderabteilung. Die Wände über den Regalen und Trennwänden sind verglast.

10. The lecture room under the main gallery; one side of the room looks out on to a sunk sculpture court.
11. A group of offices on the first floor; the upper part of the lending library is on the other side of the storage wall on the right.
12. The spiral staircase in the main entrance hall which acts as the node linking the library with the museums, the exhibition gallery and the lecture room.

10. Unter dem Ausstellungssaal liegt der Vortragssaal; die Fenster links gewähren einen Blick in den Skulpturenhof.
11. Blick in den Bürotrakt des Obergeschosses. Der obere Teil der Leihbücherei liegt rechts hinter der Wand.
12. Die Treppe der Haupteingangshalle schafft die Verbindung zwischen der Bibliothek und den Museen, dem Ausstellungssaal und dem Vortragssaal.

10

11

12

## Library, Teachers' Training College, Malmö, Sweden, 1962

Architect: Carl Nyrén

Two schools and a teachers' training college occupy a large corner site. Within this group the library in the Training College is also a branch of the Malmö City Library. This kind of combined use makes sense not only in terms of economics but also as a link between a potentially isolated group and the general community. Such multiple use could of course happen in most secondary schools, for example, and would probably make it possible to provide a much higher order of service. This may become particularly true at the time when communication equipment, other than books, is being introduced into libraries. The library, designed in 1961–62, is a single storey building on the street corner with long three-storey buildings behind it. The courtyard in the middle can be reached from the reading areas and becomes in the summer an outdoor reading room.

## Bücherei der Lehrerbildungsanstalt, Malmö, Schweden, 1962

Architekt: Carl Nyrén

Auf einem großen Eckgrundstück sind zwei Schulen und die Lehrerbildungsanstalt zusammengefaßt; die Bücherei in der Lehrerbildungsanstalt dient zugleich als Filiale der Stadtbücherei von Malmö. Diese kombinierte Nutzung hat nicht nur wirtschaftliche Gründe, sondern fördert auch die Kontakte zwischen den Studierenden und der Bevölkerung. Ähnliche Zusammenschlüsse ließen sich beispielsweise auch an vielen Oberschulen einführen; dadurch würden weitaus günstigere bibliothekstechnische Voraussetzungen geschaffen, wie sie vor allem für künftige Kommunikationsmittel erforderlich sind.
Die Bücherei, die 1961–62 errichtet wurde, ist eingeschossig und liegt an einer Straßenecke zwischen langgestreckten, dreigeschossigen Gebäuden. Der Hof in der Mitte ist von den Lesebereichen aus zugänglich und wird im Sommer zu einem Leseraum im Freien.

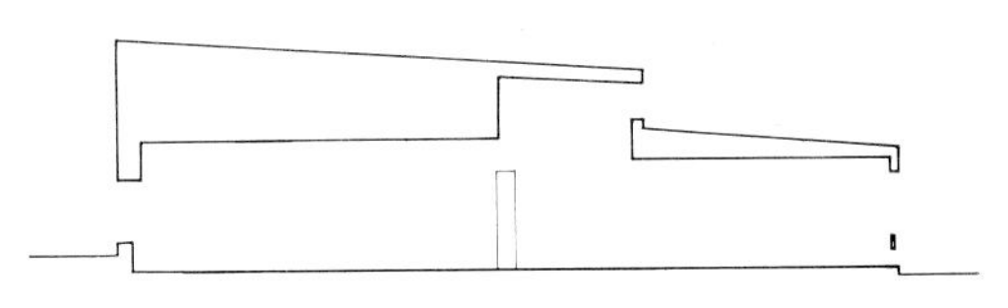

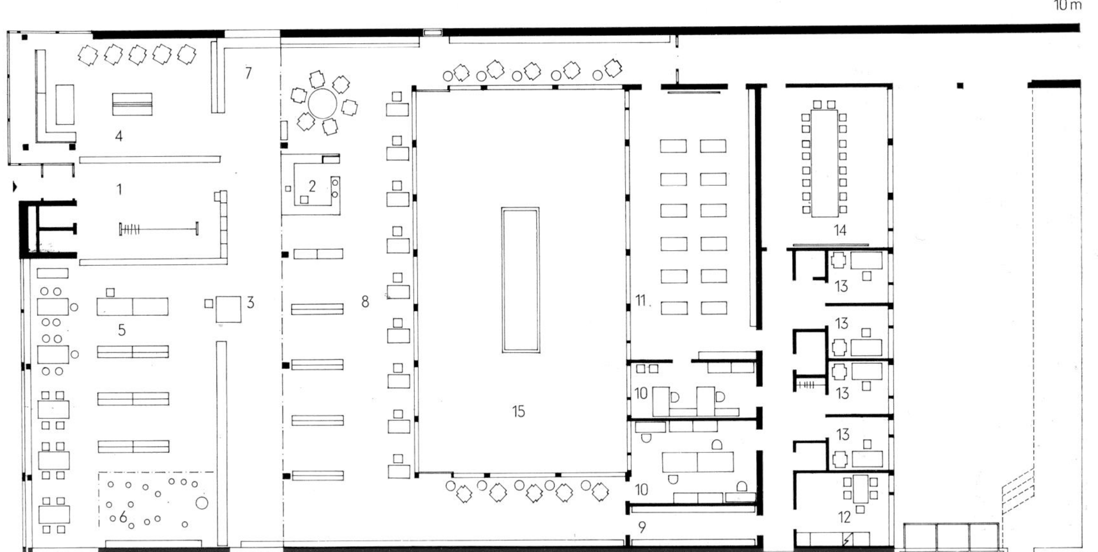


Section and ground floor plan / Schnitt und Grundriß Erdgeschoß.
1 Cloakroom / Garderobe
2 Control desk / Kontrolltisch
3 Information / Auskunft
4 Juvenile reading room / Leseraum für Jugendliche
5 Children's reading room / Leseraum für Kinder
6 Story-telling room / Vorleseraum für kleine Kinder
7 Periodicals / Zeitschriften
8 Reading room / Lesesaal
9 Stockroom / Lager
10 Librarian / Bibliothekar
11 School library / Schulbücherei
12 Kitchen / Küche
13 Study rooms / Studienräume
14 Group room / Gruppenraum
15 Courtyard / Innenhof

1

1. A seating area and a window garden to one side of the entrance and next to the control desk.

1. Neben dem Eingang und in der Nähe des Kontrolltisches wurde eine Sitzecke mit einem großen Blumenfenster eingerichtet.

3

2. Gramophone records are put on by the librarian at the control desk and there are some plug-in points next to the seats near-by for listening to music through ear phones.
3. The librarian's control desk overlooks the entrance and a large section of the library; there is overhead storage for reference material; returned books go into book boxes which when filled are put into book carts.

2. Schallplatten werden vom Bibliothekar am Kontrolltisch aufgelegt; Anschlüsse für Kopfhörer sind neben den Stühlen angebracht.
3. Von seinem Kontrolltisch aus überblickt der Bibliothekar den Eingang und einen großen Teil der Bücherei. Über dem Tisch sind Regale für Nachschlagewerke angebracht. Die zurückgegebenen Bücher kommen in Kästen, die gefüllt in Bücherkarren gestellt werden.

4. There is a separate section for children with its own librarian who can help them find books. ▷
5. Adjustable timber shelves on metal brackets and supports; furniture and shelves are all in natural birch, the floor yellow-grey linoleum.
6. The lending library, and the reading tables facing the central courtyard.

4. Blick in die Kinderabteilung, in der ständig ein Bibliothekar anwesend ist, der den Kindern behilflich sein kann. ▷
5. Die verstellbaren Holzfächer sind an Metallhaltern befestigt; Möbel und Regale sind aus Naturbirke, der Boden ist mit gelbgrauem Linoleum ausgelegt.
6. Blick in die Leihbücherei mit Leseplätzen, die zum Innenhof orientiert sind.

4

5

6

If the public library is in some ways analogous to a supermarket, the university and research library can in a similar way be likened to a warehouse and workshop: a great information store with which it is possible to work closely over long or short periods. The character of that work is however of a special kind and it is this character rather than the size of the stock which is critical.

Two aspects immediately stand out: the continuity of the interaction between the information store and the user, and the need for the communication of this information to the user to be as free as possible from interference. In other words, for it to be efficient. The first condition comes about from the fact that as the work proceeds, new sources of information may continually be needed and that perhaps to start with there is an almost random search through a particular part of the store in order to locate a relevant item. The second condition is the result of the nature of the information which may be complex, or in a foreign language, or require comparison with similar sources or for some reason or other demand a high level of concentration. Visual and aural interference as well as bodily discomfort may thus be serious distractions.

As far as the reader is concerned the research library must emphasize the first three operations of the library cycle: location, retrieval and communication. Each of these will have a bearing on the design of the building insofar as each needs a particular kind of area, while their relationship to each other under preferred conditions of use will affect the general organization of the building. The research library becomes a different architectural problem from the public library because of the special tasks to be performed within it.

Information location is partly a question of librarianship – of a comprehensive catalogue, of cross-referencing, of using an intelligible numbering system, of following definite catalogue rules – and partly of spatial design. It is the latter aspects which will be discussed here in a general way; the particular problems of this kind of area are described in a later section dealing specifically with location. Since the desire to locate a particular book or periodical is likely to occur at irregular and unpredictable intervals, and may occur several times during any one period of use, the space in which this task is done should be somewhere near the centre of gravity in terms of the distribution of users both in space and time, or should be provided at intervals throughout the building. As a normal large catalogue is a very expensive item to produce and keep up-to-date, it is very unlikely to be duplicated. Occasionally there may be one catalogue for readers and another for library staff and sometimes duplicate catalogues dealing with a department may be placed within that section. This situation will change when copies of catalogues

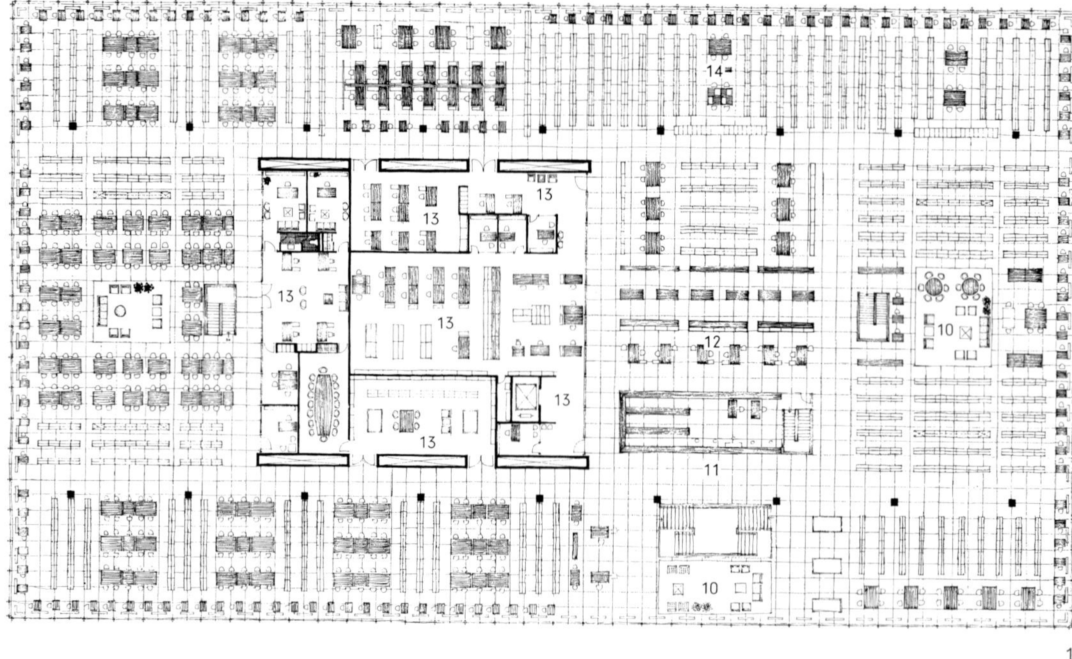

1

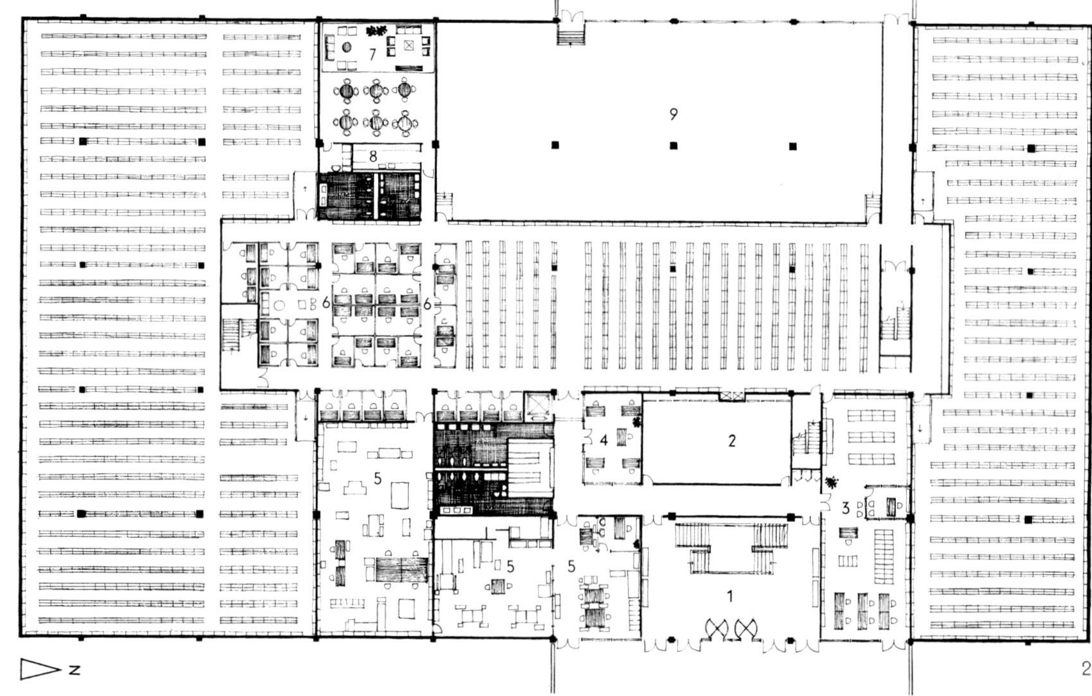

2

1–3. The John Crerar Library, Illinois Institute of Technology, Chicago, Illinois, 1962. Architects: Skidmore, Owings & Merrill. The library deals with science and technology. It has 150,000 volumes in open access stacks, 70,000 in limited access and 600,000 in closed stacks. There are places for 586 readers. Extension is possible to the south and this in fact accounts for the core of the building being off-centre.

1–3. John Crerar Library, Illinois Institute of Technology, Chicago, Illinois, 1962. Architekten: Skidmore, Owings & Merrill. Die Bibliothek ist auf Wissenschaft und Technik spezialisiert. Sie umfaßt 150000 frei zugängliche, 70000 beschränkt zugängliche und 600000 im geschlossenen Magazin untergebrachte Bände. Die technischen Einrichtungen liegen nicht im Mittelpunkt des Gebäudes, damit sich später eine Erweiterung nach Süden durchführen läßt.

Plans of second floor and first floor / Grundrisse zweites und erstes Obergeschoß.

1 Lobby / Eingangshalle
2 Conference room / Konferenzraum
3 Translation service / Übersetzungsdienst
4 Turn-tables and tape recorders / Raum für Tonbandgeräte
5 Workrooms for printing, binding, photographers / Arbeitsräume für Drucker, Buchbinder und Fotografen
6 Carrels
7 Staff lounge and dining room / Aufenthalts- und Speiseraum für Bibliotheksangestellte
8 Kitchen / Küche
9 Mechanical and technical equipment / Technische Einrichtungen
10 Lounge / Aufenthaltsraum
11 Circulation desk / Ausleihe und Rückgabe
12 Reference and catalogues / Auskunft und Kataloge
13 Library staff working area / Arbeitsbereich des Personals
14 Microfilm / Mikrofilme

Wenn die öffentliche Bücherei in mancher Hinsicht einem Supermarkt ähnelt, so lassen sich die Universitätsbibliothek und die wissenschaftliche Bibliothek einem Lagerhaus und einer Werkstatt vergleichen: Sie enthalten einen großen Vorrat an Information, mit dem der Benutzer über kürzere oder längere Zeit hinweg intensiv arbeiten kann. Diese Arbeit ist freilich besonderer Art, und ihre spezifische Qualität spielt eine wichtigere Rolle als die Quantität der magazinierten Bücher.

Zwei Aspekte sind hier von Bedeutung: Die ständige Wechselbeziehung zwischen Benutzer und gespeicherter Information muß gewährleistet sein, und die Kommunikation dieser Information an den Benutzer muß sich so störungsfrei wie möglich vollziehen. Die erste Voraussetzung ergibt sich daraus, daß im Laufe der Arbeit ständig neue Informationsquellen benötigt werden, während der Benutzer möglicherweise zu Beginn nahezu aufs Geratewohl eine bestimmte Abteilung des Magazins durchforscht, um ein für ihn wichtiges Faktum zu ermitteln. Die zweite Voraussetzung leitet sich aus der Art des Materials her, das sehr komplex sein kann oder in einer Fremdsprache geschrieben ist oder Vergleiche mit ähnlichen Quellen erfordert oder aber aus irgendeinem anderen Grund große Konzentration verlangt. Optische und akustische Störungen wie auch physische Unbequemlichkeit können sich hier äußerst nachteilig auswirken.

Vom Leser her gesehen sind bei der wissenschaftlichen Bibliothek die ersten drei Phasen des Benutzungszyklus die wichtigsten: Lokalisierung, Beschaffung und Kommunikation. Jede dieser Phasen beeinflußt die Planung des Gebäudes, da jede einen eigenen Bereich erfordert. Ihre wechselseitige Verbindung bei optimalen Benutzungsverhältnissen bestimmt die allgemeine Organisation des Gebäudes. Die wissenschaftliche Bibliothek stellt andere architektonische Probleme als die öffentliche Bücherei, weil sie andere Aufgaben zu erfüllen hat.

Die Lokalisierung der Information ist zum einen eine bibliothekstechnische Frage – umfassender Katalog, Querverweise, verständliches und von einheitlichen Regeln bestimmtes System der Signaturen – und zum anderen eine Frage der räumlichen Organisation. Die letzte Frage wird im folgenden kurz behandelt; die besonderen Probleme dieser Funktionszone sind in einem späteren Kapitel beschrieben, das sich mit der Lokalisierung der Information befaßt.

Da das Bedürfnis, ein bestimmtes Buch oder eine Zeitschrift zu lokalisieren, zu den verschiedensten Zeitpunkten und manchmal auch während eines Bibliotheksbesuches auftreten kann, sollte der Katalog in der Nähe des Gebäudezentrums aufgestellt werden, in dem sich die Wege der Benutzer schneiden, sofern er nicht in mehrfacher Ausführung existiert und über das Gebäude verteilt werden kann. Es ist freilich sehr kostspielig, einen normal großen Katalog herzustellen und auf dem laufenden zu halten, und deshalb besitzen die wenigsten Bibliotheken Duplikate. Nur gelegentlich gibt es einen Katalog für die Leser und einen für das Bibliothekspersonal; bisweilen werden Zweitkataloge mit den Titeln einer bestimmten Abteilung in dem jeweiligen Bereich aufgestellt. Das kann sich freilich ändern, wenn Kopien des Kataloges mechanisch von einem Computer hergestellt werden, in dem die Katalogdaten gespeichert sind, denn die eigentlichen Druckkosten machen nur einen relativ geringen Teil der Gesamtherstellungskosten aus.

Ob es aber nun einen einzigen zentralen Katalog gibt oder mehrere Kataloge, die über das Gebäude verteilt sind – sie beanspruchen einen Platz, an dem sie untergebracht werden, und genügend freien Raum, damit sie leicht zugänglich sind. Die meisten wissenschaftlichen Bibliotheken besitzen einen Katalogsaal, der im Mittel-

Key to plan / Legende zum Plan:
1 Lobby and exhibitions / Halle und Ausstellungen
2 Circulation desk / Ausleihe und Rückgabe
3 Check room and toilets / Garderobe und Toiletten
4 Public catalogues / Öffentliche Kataloge
5 Reference service / Nachschlagewerke
6 Periodicals / Zeitschriften
7 Catalogue / Katalog
8 Bibliography / Bibliographie
9 Pamphlets / Broschüren
10 Maps / Landkarten
11 Microfilm and microcard / Mikrofilme und Mikrokarten
12 Reading room / Lesesaal
13 Open stacks / Offenes Magazin
14 Study rooms / Studienräume
15 Rare books / Seltene Bücher
16 Reservation-information service / Reservierung und Auskunft
17 Administration / Verwaltung
18 Conference room / Konferenzraum
19 Limited access stacks / Geschlossenes Magazin
20 W. C.
21 Staff lounge / Aufenthaltsraum des Personals
22 Carrels
23 Catalogue department / Katalogabteilung
24 Acquisitions department / Neuerwerbungen
25 Printing and binding / Druckerei und Buchbinderei
26 Photo-duplication service / Fotoabteilung
27 Special library association / Bibliotheksgesellschaft
28 Maintenance / Werkstatt für Ausbesserungen
29 Shipping and receiving / Versand und Annahme
30 Mechanical equipment / Technische Einrichtungen

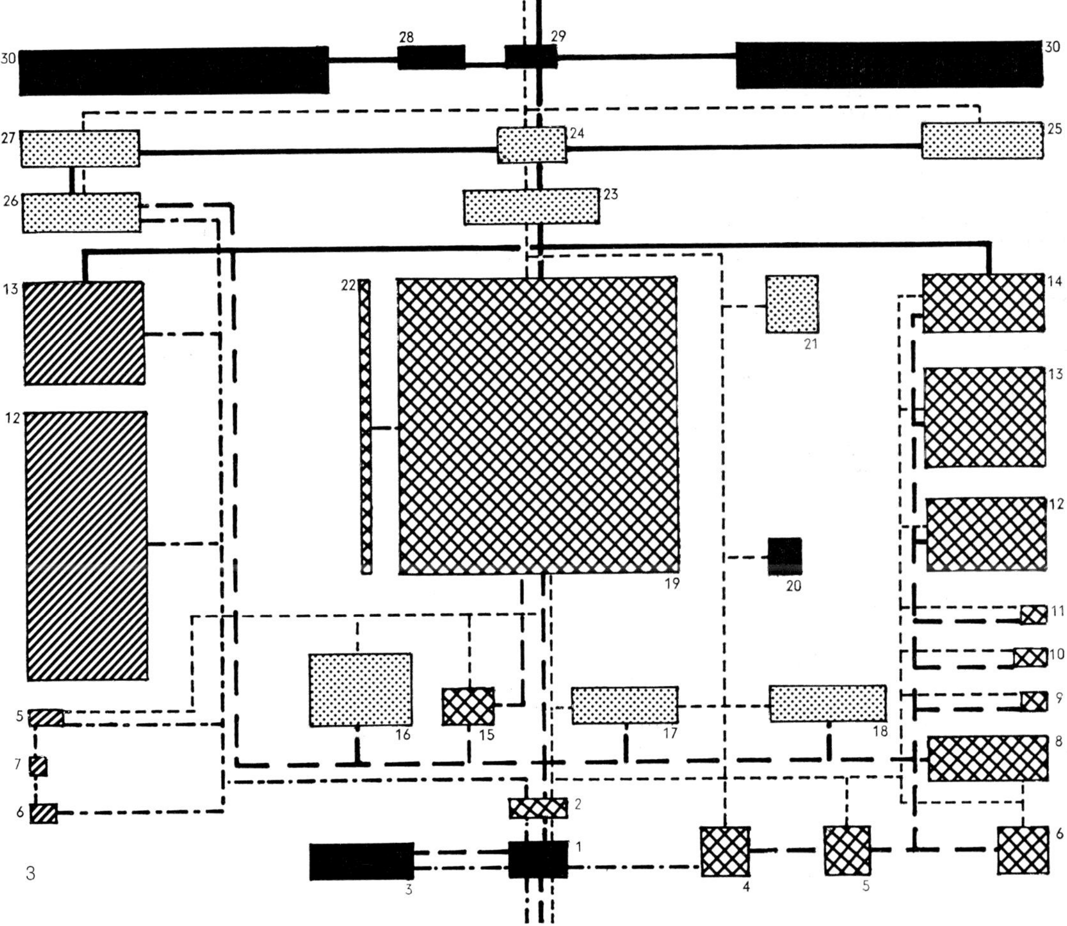


3

Flow diagram / Organisationsschema.

— — — — Research / Forschung
—— – —— – Students / Studenten
- - - - - - Staff / Personal
——— Ancillary and materials flow / Hilfsmaterial

are produced by mechanical print-out from a computer holding a catalogue on magnetic tape, since the cost of making the printed version is a relatively small fraction of the whole operation.
Whether there is a single central catalogue or whether there are several at nodal points in the building, there will be a demand for space to house this item and for space around it to allow people to use it effectively. Most academic research libraries provide this space in a catalogue hall placed fairly centrally in the building and near the entrance, partly because this conforms to a pattern of use by which at least some titles are located immediately on arrival, and partly because it is at the entrance that a number of staff activities are usually to be found which make it easy to get help with any bibliographical problems.
Retrieval is performed either by the staff or by the reader. The decision to use one or other method has considerable repercussions on planning and the layout of both the reading and stack spaces. This distinction between closed and open access to the stacks was not only a lively debating point among librarians in the recent past but is crucial in terms of the anatomy of the building. In the closed access plan the storage of books is in a zone separate from the reading area and the staff is responsible for bringing the book from the shelf to the reader's table. They may be helped in this by various mechanical devices so that these two spaces can be quite some distance apart. In the open access plan, the user has free access to the stacks and takes the book from the shelf to his reading place so that the spaces for storage and communication need to be grouped close to each other. The first system produces defined compartments, the second a meshed distribution of the two kinds of space in terms of use though not necessarily construction.
The choice between these systems in the design of a new library building is not a simple one but will very largely depend on the size of the stack and the space available for it. With an increase in the size of the book store it becomes progressively more difficult for a person to locate a given title and probably also more time-consuming. This is likely to happen since a large book collection may not necessarily have a large number of readers, so that the ratio of stack to reading area is probably of a kind which inevitably produces considerable journeys in order to find a book. Even if the areas were to be balanced, there can in any case be no certainty that a reader would not want a number of books from widely dispersed locations and therefore have to be involved in quite complex movement patterns. It has been suggested by Harold Holdsworth that "the average reader cannot usefully browse among a quarter of a million volumes or more". If the library is very clearly subdivided into certain sections which correspond to the major interests of its users, if there are almost sub-libraries within a single complex, that figure can probably be higher.
In the closed access system it is possible to plan a more space-saving stack layout. This can be done by using compact methods of storage such as shelving books by size or by having sliding stacks like "Compactus" which are moved sideways on rails in order to make a particular run of shelf accessible. Neither method is possible if the reader is to find his own book. As the number of people using the stacks is also very much smaller and they know their way about, narrower aisles can be planned. If trolleys are to be used these can then have a minimum width of 2'2". Such a layout will increase the storage capacity by about 16% compared to the more usual layout with aisles 3'0" wide, while "Compactus" shelving would increase it by nearly 85%. (See diagrams of stack layouts, pp. 134–135).

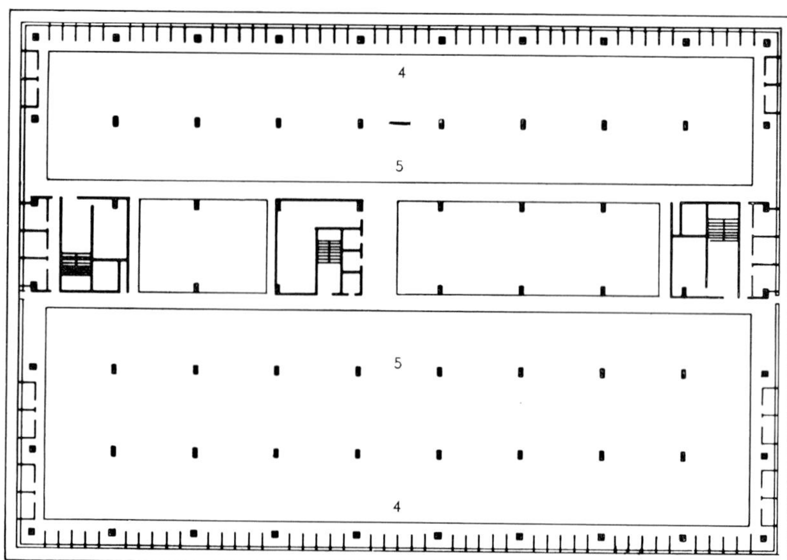

4

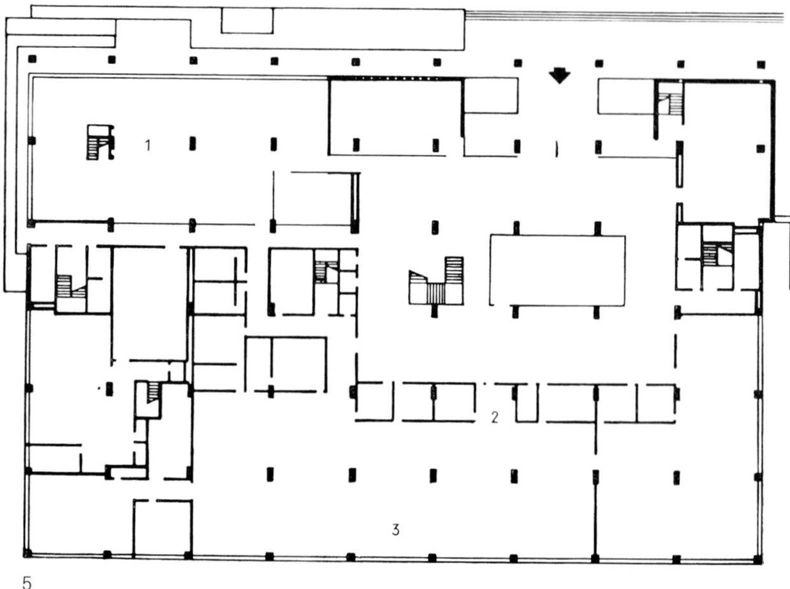

5

4, 5. Library, University of Edinburgh, 1966. Architects: Sir Basil Spence, Glover & Ferguson. A large multi-storey university library with space for 2,000,000 books and seating for 1,850 readers. The floors are extremely deep, about 170 ft. (52 m) from window to window and the entire building is air conditioned. A very large proportion of the total floor area can be used either for stack or reading.

4, 5. Bibliothek der Universität Edinburgh, 1966. Architekten: Sir Basil Spence, Glover & Ferguson. Die mehrgeschossige Universitätsbibliothek bietet Raum für 2000000 Bücher und 1850 Leser. Die Geschosse sind ungewöhnlich tief (etwa 52 m von Fenster zu Fenster). Das Gebäude ist vollklimatisiert. Die Geschoßflächen können zu einem großen Teil entweder für Magazine oder für Lesebereiche genutzt werden.

Plans of typical upper floor and ground floor / Grundrisse Normalgeschoß und Erdgeschoß.
1 Periodicals / Zeitschriften
2 Offices / Büros
3 Catalogues / Kataloge
4 Carrels
5 Stacks / Magazin

punkt des Gebäudes und zugleich nahe am Eingang liegt, einmal, weil auf diese Weise zumindest der Standort einiger Titel gleich nach dem Betreten der Bibliothek lokalisiert werden kann, und zum anderen, weil am Eingang gewöhnlich eine Reihe bibliothekarischer Verwaltungsstellen untergebracht sind, so daß es ohne weiteres möglich ist, bei bibliographischen Problemen Auskunft zu erhalten.

Für die Beschaffung sorgt entweder das Personal oder der Leser. Die Entscheidung für die eine oder andere Methode wirkt sich auf Planung und Grundrißgestaltung des Lese- wie auch des Magazinbereichs aus. Die Unterscheidung zwischen der Freihandaufstellung und der Magazinverwahrung war in der jüngsten Zeit eine Streitfrage unter Bibliothekaren und ist entscheidend für die Anatomie des Gebäudes. Bei einem System, das die Bücher den Benutzern nicht unmittelbar zugänglich macht, werden die Publikationen getrennt vom Lesebereich gespeichert, und das Bibliothekspersonal muß das Buch vom Regal zum Tisch des Lesers bringen. Verschiedene technische Hilfsmittel für den Büchertransport ermöglichen es, beide Zonen in einiger Entfernung voneinander anzuordnen. Bei der Freihandbibliothek dagegen hat der Benutzer freien Zugang zum Magazin. Er nimmt selbst das Buch aus dem Regal und trägt es an seinen Platz so daß die Räume für Lagerung und Kommunikation eng miteinander verbunden sein müssen. Das erste System führt zu gesonderten Abteilungen, das zweite zu einer Verklammerung der beiden Zonen von der Funktion her, wenn auch nicht unbedingt von der Konstruktion her.

Welches dieser Systeme bei der Planung einer neuen Bibliothek angewandt wird, hängt weitgehend von der Größe des Magazins und dem dafür verfügbaren Raum ab. Wenn die Zahl der Bücher wächst, wird es immer schwieriger und möglicherweise auch immer zeitraubender für den Leser, einen bestimmten Titel aufzufinden. Dieser Fall tritt beispielsweise ein, wenn eine große Büchersammlung eine vergleichsweise geringe Zahl von Lesern hat, so daß das Magazin sehr viel größer ist als der Lesebereich und der Leser infolgedessen lange Wege zurücklegen muß, um ein Buch zu finden. Selbst wenn sich die Bereiche ungefähr entsprechen, kann es geschehen, daß ein Leser Bücher von ganz verschiedenen Standorten benötigt und deshalb einem höchst komplizierten Bewegungsablauf unterworfen wird. Harold Holdsworth ist der Meinung, daß es »für den Durchschnittsleser sinnlos ist, unter einer Viertelmillion oder mehr Büchern zu stöbern«. Wenn die Bibliothek jedoch sehr klar in bestimmte Abteilungen gegliedert ist, die den Hauptinteressen ihrer Benutzer entsprechen, wenn sich also innerhalb eines Bibliothekskomplexes sozusagen mehrere Spezialbibliotheken befinden, dürften die Bestände auch einer Freihandbibliothek wahrscheinlich noch größer sein.

Bei unzugänglichem Magazin ist es möglich, raumsparende Methoden anzuwenden, also zum Beispiel die Bücher nach Formaten aufzustellen oder Regaltypen wie »Compactus« zu benutzen, die sich auf Schienen seitlich verschieben lassen, damit eine bestimmte Regaleinheit erreichbar wird. Wenn jedoch der Leser sein Buch selbst finden soll, kommt keines dieser Verfahren in Frage. Bei unzugänglichem Magazin können zudem die Gänge schmaler gehalten werden, da sie nur von einigen wenigen Bibliotheksangestellten benutzt werden, die ihren Weg kennen. Falls Wagen für den Transport der Bücher eingesetzt werden, müssen die Gänge mindestens 65 cm breit sein. Im Vergleich zu dem üblicheren Grundriß mit 90 cm breiten Gängen erhöht eine solche Raumorganisation die Kapazität des Magazins um ungefähr 16%, während »Compactus«-Regale zu einer Steigerung um nahezu

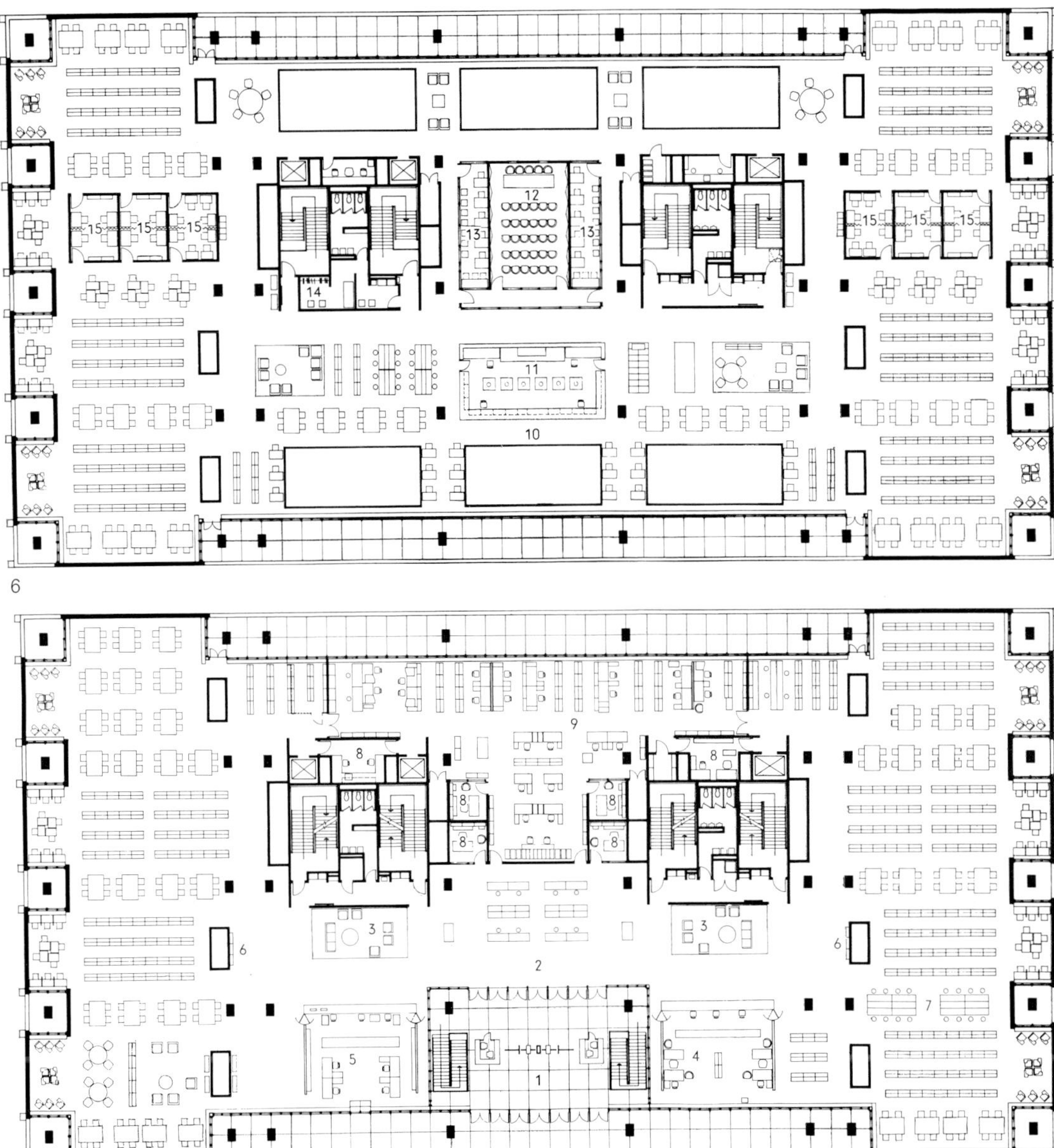

6, 7. Library, University of Illinois, Chicago Circle Campus, Chicago, Illinois, 1965. Architects: Skidmore, Owings & Merrill. The library building faces the central space of the new urban campus of the University of Illinois. It has open access and its column structure is used to define spaces for books and readers.

6, 7. Bibliothek der University of Illinois, Chicago Circle Campus, Chicago, Illinois, 1965. Architekten: Skidmore, Owings & Merrill. Die Bibliothek liegt im Zentrum des neuen Campus der University of Illinois. Das Magazin ist frei zugänglich und wird durch die Stützenkonstruktion in Regal- und Lesebereiche unterteilt.

Plans of fourth floor and second floor / Grundrisse viertes und zweites Obergeschoß.

1 Foyer
2 Catalogue / Katalog
3 Lounge / Aufenthaltsraum
4 General reference service / Auskunft und Nachschlagewerke
5 Circulation desk / Ausleihe und Rückgabe
6 New book display / Ausstellung von Neuerwerbungen
7 Periodical indices / Zeitschriftenkartei
8 Librarian / Bibliothekar
9 Library staff / Bibliothekspersonal
10 Service desk / Arbeitspult
11 Turn-tables and tape recorders / Raum für Tonbandgeräte
12 Listening room / Abhörstudio
13 Earphone listening / Räume für Kopfhörerempfang
14 Cloakroom / Garderobe
15 Carrels

In an open access library the reader can roam throughout the bulk of the storage area. Only very little used items and rare books, for instance, might be excluded. Ideally therefore his place for consulting the material he has himself collected is as near as it can be; in other words tables and chairs are grouped adjacent to or even within the stacks. This arrangement is now common, especially in the university libraries of the U.S. and the libraries of the new universities in Great Britain. Apart from making it possible for people to inspect material without the cumbersome procedure of filling in a card or dialling a code in order to demand a book and also to find sources casually because they have picked up a volume next to the one they were actually looking for, there are important and probably beneficial implications on the plan.

The space assigned to books and to people reading is so interwoven that in its basic form it is going to be very similar. As likely as not it is the same kind of space used in a different way and made appropriate to its particular use by local manipulations of light, furniture and its attachment to the routes of movement within the building. This means that the decision on how the space is to be used can be varied from time to time; the ratio of stack space to reading area need not remain fixed. There is thus a large measure of interchangeability including of course the drastic alternative of cutting off whole areas and making them closed access stacks.

There is moreover a further aspect of the open access plan which is of great importance in a research library. It is that the communication of the information is of a kind where two apparently conflicting demands should be satisfied: it should be easy to concentrate on the task of reading, yet it should be equally simple to replenish or change the information source at frequent and random intervals without disturbing other users. This conflict is

85% führen (vgl. Diagramme der Regalgrundrisse auf Seite 134–135).

In einer Freihandbibliothek ist das Magazin dem Leser zum größten Teil frei zugänglich. Nur sehr wenig verlangte Titel und seltene Bücher sind bisweilen gesondert untergebracht. Im Idealfall ist daher der Arbeitsplatz des Lesers, an dem er sich mit dem selbstbeschafften Material befaßt, so nahe wie möglich beim Magazin, das heißt, Tische und Stühle sind unmittelbar neben den Regalen oder sogar mitten im Regalbereich gruppiert. Diese Anordnung ist heute allgemein üblich, vor allem in den Universitätsbibliotheken der Vereinigten Staaten und den Bibliotheken der neuen Universitäten in Großbritannien. Sie ermöglicht es dem Leser, Material in Augenschein zu nehmen, ohne daß er umständlich eine Signatur ermitteln und einen Bestellschein ausfüllen muß, um ein Buch zu erhalten; zudem kann er zufällig auf unvermutete Informationsquellen stoßen, weil er etwa einen Band neben dem ursprünglich gewünschten herausgenommen hat. Doch darüber hinaus hat das System möglicherweise auch vorteilhafte Rückwirkungen auf die Grundrißgestaltung. Die Bereiche, die für die Bücher und für die Leser bestimmt sind, sind so eng miteinander verzahnt, daß sie sich in der Grundform sehr ähnlich sehen können. In vielen Fällen kann der gleiche Raumtyp in verschiedener Weise genutzt werden und seiner jeweiligen Funktion durch entsprechende Beleuchtung, Möblierung und Verbindung zu den Verkehrswegen innerhalb des Gebäudes angepaßt werden. Über die Nutzung des Raumes läßt sich dann von Fall zu Fall entscheiden; das Verhältnis von Magazinbereich zu Lesebereich braucht nicht ein für allemal festgelegt zu werden, so daß ein großes Maß an Flexibilität gegeben ist. Natürlich ist es auch möglich, nachträglich ganze Bereiche abzusondern und zum geschlossenen Magazin zu machen.

8, 9. Municipal and University Library, Frankfurt-on-Main, 1965. Architect: Ferdinand Kramer. The library as a complex warehouse; the service functions are separated out into a four storey block which makes it possible to subdivide the main building almost randomly between storage and reader space.

8. The west side of the main block sheathed in a curtain wall with additional vertical louvres where there are reading rooms.

9. The south side of the service building.

8, 9. Universitäts- und Stadtbibliothek, Frankfurt am Main, 1965. Architekt: Ferdinand Kramer. Die Bibliothek ähnelt einem umfangreichen Warenlager. Da die technischen Einrichtungen in einem vier Geschosse hohen Nebengebäude untergebracht sind, läßt sich das eigentliche Bibliotheksgebäude nahezu beliebig in Magazin- und Lesebereiche unterteilen.

8. Blick auf den Curtain Wall an der Westseite des Gebäudes. Vor den Leseräumen sind vertikale Lamellen angebracht.

9. Blick auf die Südseite des Nebengebäudes.

8

9

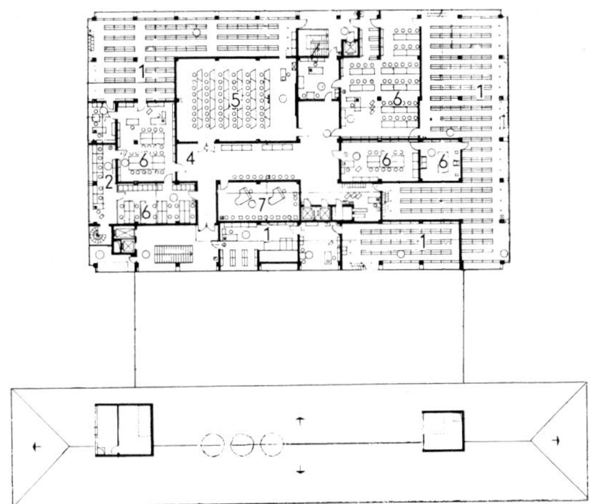

Third floor / Drittes Obergeschoß.

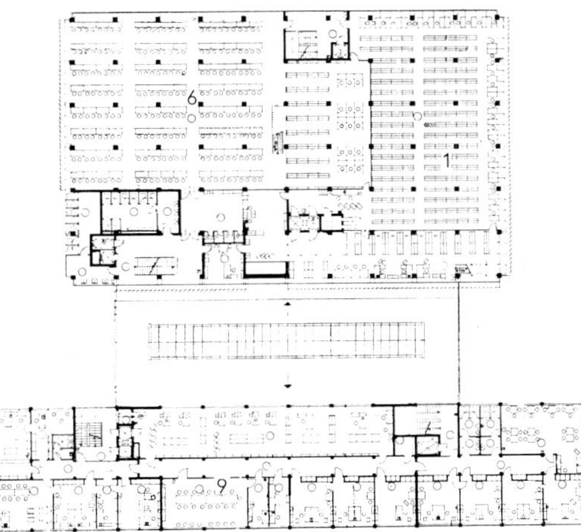

First floor / Erstes Obergeschoß.

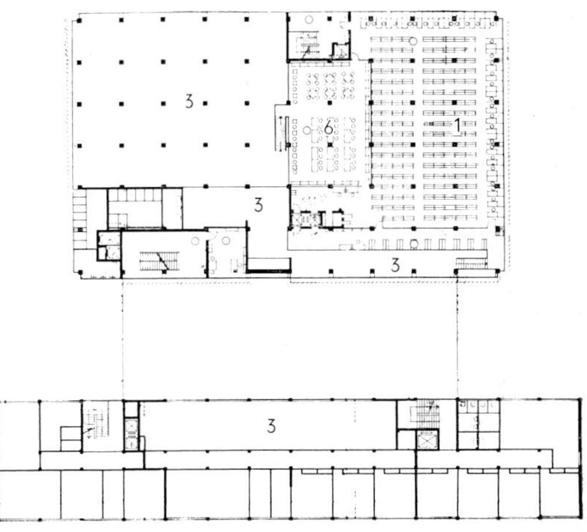

Mezzanine floor above first floor / Zwischengeschoß im ersten Obergeschoß.

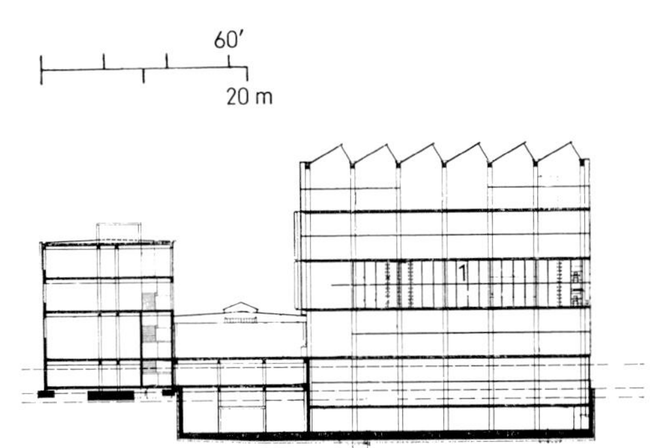


Section / Schnitt.

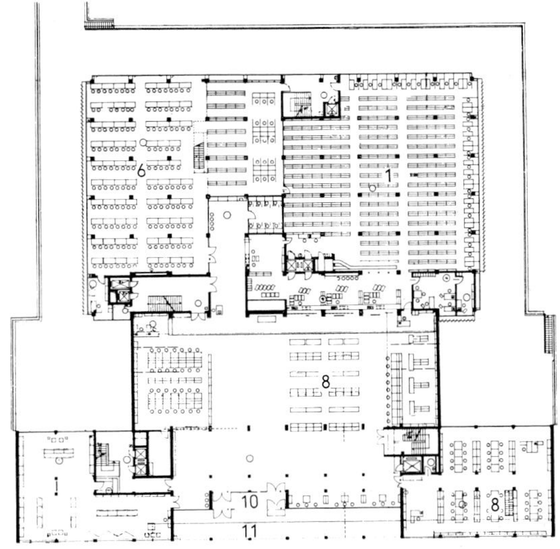

Ground floor / Erdgeschoß.

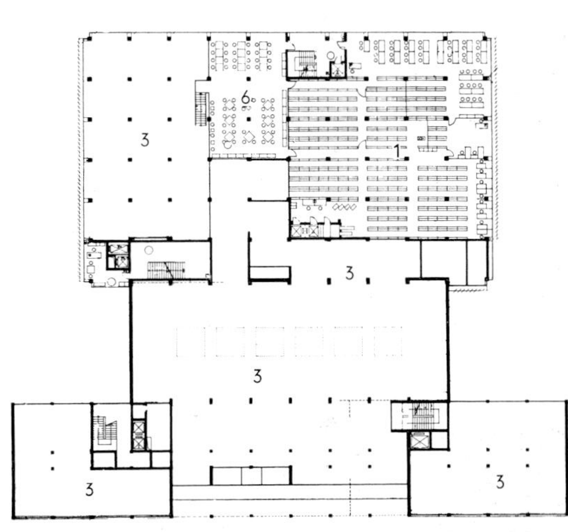

Mezzanine floor above ground floor / Zwischengeschoß im Erdgeschoß.

10–17. Municipal and University Library, Frankfurt-on-Main, 1965. Architect: Ferdinand Kramer. Floor plans and section.

10–17. Universitäts- und Stadtbibliothek, Frankfurt am Main, 1965. Architekt: Ferdinand Kramer. Grundrisse und Schnitt.

1 Stacks / Magazin
2 Audition booths / Abhörkabinen
3 Void / Luftraum
4 Foyer
5 Classroom / Unterrichtssaal
6 Reading rooms / Leseräume
7 Piano room / Flügelzimmer
8 Catalogue / Katalog
9 Conference room / Konferenzraum
10 Information / Auskunft
11 Entrance / Eingang
12 Lounge / Aufenthaltsraum
13 Bookbinding, stores, staff rooms / Buchbinderei, Lager, Personalräume
14 Librarian's school / Bibliothekarlehranstalt
15 Technical installations / Technische Einrichtungen

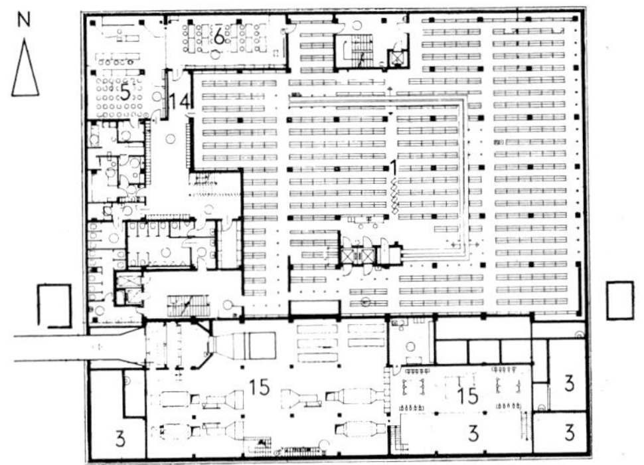


Main basement floor / Untergeschoß.

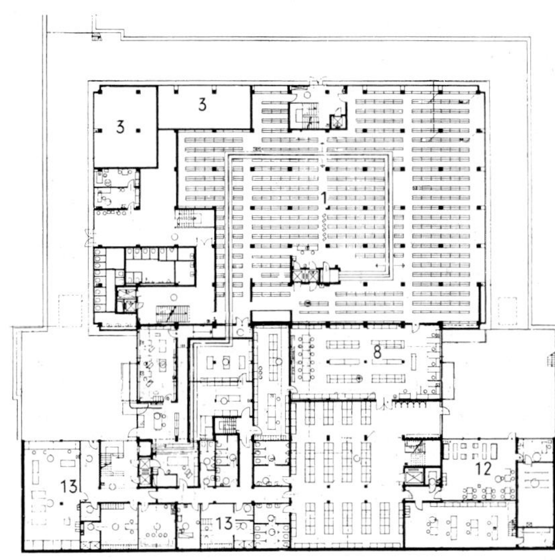

Mezzanine floor above basement level / Zwischengeschoß im Untergeschoß.

very much easier to resolve when books are close to readers and when the book stacks in fact provide a good deal of the screening of one user or group of users from another. The spatial organisation which results from an open access system appears to be particularly appropriate to the way in which a research library can be used most effectively.

It also seems appropriate to the critical problem of increase in size. Metcalf has shown that a collection will expand from 50% to 85% of full capacity in just over 13 years if growth is at a compound rate of 4% and under 5 years if at a compound rate of 10%. At the design stage all book shelving should be calculated on the assumption that at the opening of the library at most only half its capacity will be filled. This allows for the first increase of books during a number of years until 75% to 85% capacity is reached. Shelves should not be fuller than this if books are not to be damaged and if they are to be easily handled. Thereafter the amount of shelving will have to be increased.

The warehousing of information becomes thus an increasingly acute problem. This has almost frightening implications on the degree of flexibility needed in planning and the amount of space to be allocated at the outset for expansion. This in turn may affect the position of the library within the university. There are very strong arguments for putting it at the centre of gravity and certainly near the main paths of student movement. The building ought to be placed in such a way, for example, that it is accessible from both the academic and the residential areas (where these exist as specific entities), for university libraries are used during the day, often between classes and again in the evening. Most of the libraries of the newly-planned British universities have such a position. Space in such a location may well however be restricted and thus limit future expansion. It is important therefore to devise library plan forms which make expansion possible even within a restricted area.

Die Freihandaufstellung hat im übrigen noch einen weiteren Vorteil, der bei einer wissenschaftlichen Bibliothek eine wichtige Rolle spielt. Um die Kommunikation der Information zu gewährleisten, müssen nämlich hier zwei scheinbar widersprüchliche Forderungen erfüllt werden: Der Leser muß sich auf seine Lektüre konzentrieren können, zugleich aber in der Lage sein, das Material nach Belieben zu vervollständigen oder auszutauschen, ohne daß dadurch andere Besucher gestört werden. Dieses Problem läßt sich sehr viel leichter lösen, wenn die Bücher in der Nähe der Leser aufbewahrt werden und wenn die Regale die einzelnen Benutzergruppen gegeneinander abschirmen. Die räumliche Organisation eines Freihandbereichs ist also besonders geeignet, die Arbeit in einer wissenschaftlichen Bibliothek zu erleichtern.

Sie scheint auch für das schwierige Problem des wachsenden Bücherbestandes eine Lösung zu bieten. Metcalf hat nachgewiesen, daß eine Sammlung in etwas mehr als 13 Jahren um 50% bis 85% der vollen Kapazität zunimmt, wenn die jährliche Zuwachsrate 4% beträgt, und in knapp fünf Jahren, wenn die Zuwachsrate bei 10% liegt. Im Entwurfsstadium sollte die Berechnung des Regalraums davon ausgehen, daß bei Eröffnung der Bibliothek höchstens die Hälfte der Kapazität ausgenutzt ist. Damit wird der Zunahme des Bestandes über eine Reihe von Jahren Rechnung getragen, bis 75% oder 85% der Kapazität erreicht sind. Voller sollten die Regale nicht werden, damit die Bücher leicht herausgenommen werden können und Beschädigungen vermieden werden. Danach müssen die Regalflächen vergrößert werden.

Die Speicherung der Bücher wird daher ein immer brennenderes Problem. Es hat nahezu erschreckende Auswirkungen auf die Planung, weil ein immer höheres Maß an Flexibilität gefordert wird und die Erweiterungsflächen immer großzügiger bemessen werden müssen. Diese Tatsache könnte wiederum die Situation der Bibliothek innerhalb der Universität beeinträchtigen. Zwar sprechen starke Argumente dafür, sie in den Mittelpunkt zu stellen,

20–22. Francis A. Countway Library of Medicine, Harvard Medical School, Boston, Massachusetts. Architects: Hugh Stubbins & Associates. This is a medical research library in which the place chosen for storing information is dependent on the frequency with which it is likely to be consulted. The floor immediately below the entrance level deals with current periodicals and the issues of the preceding nine years of the same periodicals in bound volumes; the level above the entrance houses books published in the last ten years. Floors further away have material older than this. ▷

20–22. Francis A. Countway Library of Medicine, Harvard Medical School, Boston, Massachusetts. Architekten: Hugh Stubbins & Associates. In dieser medizinischen Forschungsbibliothek entspricht der Aufbewahrungsort des Informationsmaterials jeweils der wahrscheinlichen Benutzungsfrequenz. Das Geschoß unter dem Eingangsniveau enthält laufende Zeitschriftennummern sowie Jahresbände derselben Zeitschriften aus den letzten neun Jahren; das Geschoß über dem Eingangsniveau nimmt Bücher auf, die in den vergangenen zehn Jahren veröffentlicht worden sind. Älteres Material ist in Geschossen untergebracht, die weiter vom Eingang entfernt liegen. ▷

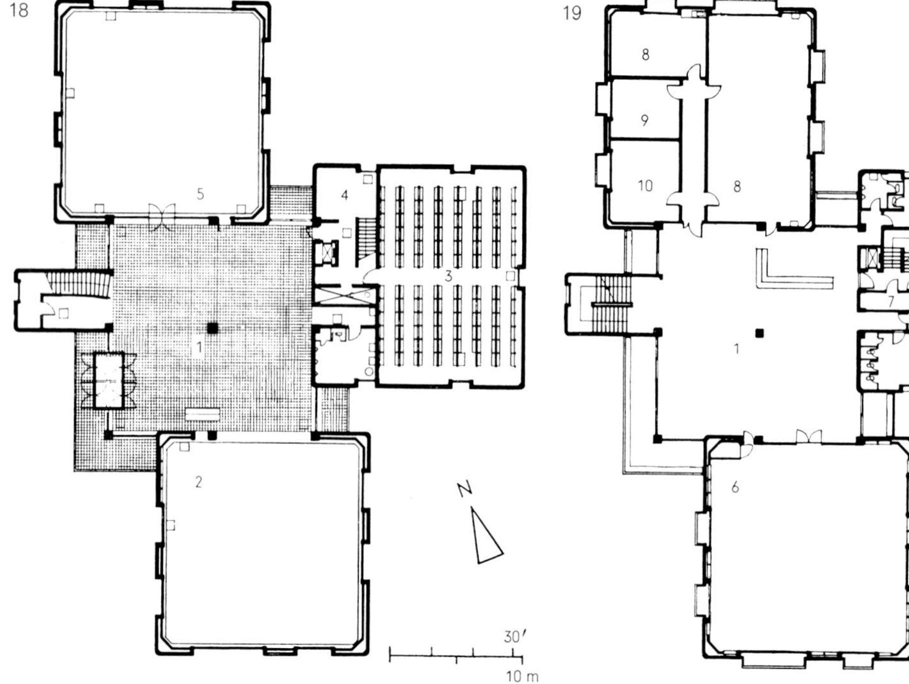


18, 19. Library, Gakushuin University, Tokyo, 1963. Architects: Kunio Mayekawa & Associates. Library zoning arranged vertically in separate but linked pavilions. The defined organization of spaces in relation to the outer envelope and to the internal fixed elements such as stairs and lavatories, makes changes in use difficult to handle.

18, 19. Bibliothek der Gakushuin-Universität, Tokio, 1963. Architekten: Kunio Mayekawa & Associates. Die Bibliotheksfunktionen sind in gesonderten, aber miteinander verbundenen Pavillons vertikal gegliedert. Die Organisation der Räume, die sowohl im Verhältnis zur Außenform wie zu den inneren Festpunkten (Treppen und sanitäre Installationen) festgelegt ist, macht eine flexible Nutzung schwierig.

Plans of ground floor and upper floor / Grundrisse Erdgeschoß und Obergeschoß.

1 Lobby / Halle
2 Reading room / Lesesaal
3 Book stacks / Magazin
4 Entrance from the Faculty building / Eingang vom Fakultätsgebäude
5 Study hall / Studienraum
6 Reference library / Handbibliothek
7 Store / Lager
8 Office / Büro
9 Librarian / Bibliothekar
10 Conference room / Konferenzraum

20

Pictorial section / Perspektivischer Schnitt.

Key to plans / Legende zu den Plänen:

1 Information / Auskunft
2 Catalogues and reference / Katalog und Nachschlagewerke
3 Reference staff / Bibliothekspersonal (Handbibliothek)
4 Librarian / Bibliothekar
5 Circulation staff / Bibliothekspersonal (Leihverkehr)
6 Circulation service / Leihverkehr
7 Reserve books / Präsenzbücherei
8 Reserve reading room / Leseraum der Präsenzbücherei
9 Workroom / Arbeitsraum
10 Cataloguing department / Katalogabteilung
11 Acquisition / Neuerwerbungen
12 Balcony / Balkon
13 Carrels
14 Main hall (void above) / Haupthalle (darüber Luftraum)
15 Older books / Ältere Bücher

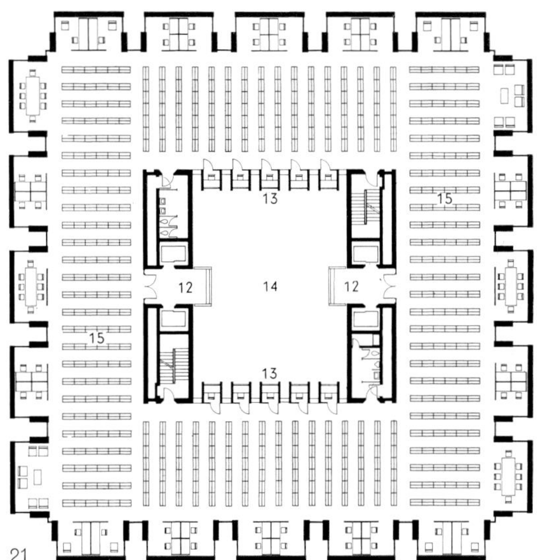


21

Plan of third and fourth floor / Grundriß drittes und viertes Obergeschoß.

The kind of increase which occurs in libraries also poses problems of magnitude, namely that an increase in size may not only be a simple quantitative enlargement but may also demand changes in organization which are likely to alter the anatomy of the building. It may for instance be decided to divide the collection into an undergraduate library which would have a stock of perhaps 100,000 titles associated with a large number of reading spaces and a very much more sizeable research stock with, proportionately, a relatively small number of users. It is probable that such changes are easier to achieve in a building in which a number of the typical library operations can be done in characteristically the same kind of space. There are thus strong architectural reasons for designing university libraries on the basis that they will be used on an open access system even if that decision should at some time be reversed. To switch from open to closed access is a good deal easier than the other way round.

auf jeden Fall aber in die Nähe der wichtigsten Zirkulationswege. Das Gebäude sollte beispielsweise sowohl von den Instituten und Hörsälen wie auch von den akademischen Wohnbereichen (sofern sie eine gesonderte Gruppe bilden) leicht zugänglich sein, denn Universitätsbibliotheken werden tagsüber, häufig zwischen den Vorlesungen, und auch am Abend benutzt. Die meisten Bibliotheken der neu geplanten englischen Universitäten nehmen eine solche Lage ein. Der Nachteil dabei ist jedoch, daß häufig nur eine beschränkte Grundstücksfläche zur Verfügung steht, so daß eine spätere Erweiterung erschwert wird. Deshalb müssen Grundrißformen entworfen werden, die Erweiterung auch innerhalb eines begrenzten Raumes ermöglichen.
Der wachsende Bücherbestand der Bibliotheken stellt auch Probleme der Größenordnung, da er nicht nur die Quantität betrifft, sondern auch zu Änderungen der Organisation führen kann, die wiederum die Anatomie des Gebäudes beeinflussen. Es ist zum Beispiel denkbar, daß eine Sammlung in eine Bibliothek für Studenten mit etwa 100000 Titeln und zahlreichen Lesebereichen und in eine sehr viel umfangreichere Bibliothek für wissenschaftliche Zwecke mit einer relativ geringen Zahl von Benutzern unterteilt wird. Solche Veränderungen sind wahrscheinlich leichter in einem Gebäude durchzuführen, in dem verschiedenartige Funktionen der Bibliothek in grundsätzlich verwandten Raumtypen abgewickelt werden. Gewichtige Gründe sprechen also dafür, Universitätsbibliotheken so zu planen, daß sie auf dem Prinzip der Freihandaufstellung basieren, auch wenn die Entscheidung möglicherweise später rückgängig gemacht wird. Die Umstellung vom offenen auf das geschlossene System ist sehr viel einfacher als umgekehrt.

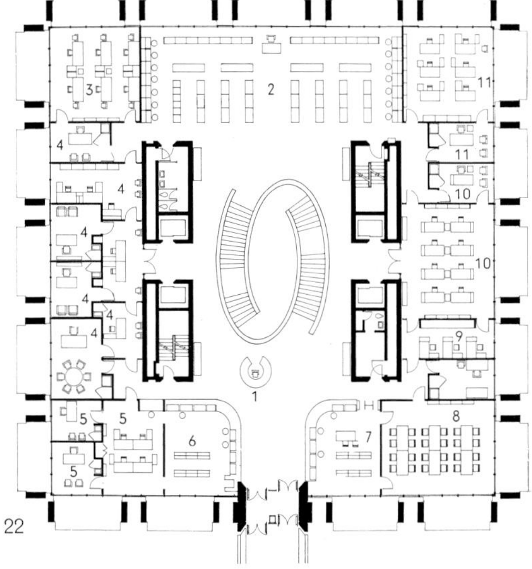


22

Plan of entrance floor / Grundriß Eingangsgeschoß.

**Edward Clark Crossett Library, Bennington College, Bennington, Vermont, 1959**

Architects: Carl Koch & Associates and Pietro Belluschi

The small campus of Bennington, a New England women's college, was built in 1932 in the colonial tradition of white painted timber. In 1957 it was decided to build a new library which would represent modern architecture but which, placed next to the central college quadrangle, would nevertheless not conflict with the existing and by then well established character of the place. A white, partly sunk, timber-clad building with a brick-walled garden court was the answer.
The library has a capacity of 75,000 volumes. These are distributed on three floors and associated with different kinds of reading spaces, one of which opens out onto a brick-paved and brick-walled court. The sloping ground makes it possible to enter the building at its middle floor and to go only one flight up or down from the entrance level.
The consultant for this undergraduate library was Keyes D. Metcalf, at one time librarian to Harvard College.

**Edward Clark Crossett Library, Bennington College, Bennington, Vermont, 1959**

Architekten: Carl Koch & Associates mit Pietro Belluschi

Die Bauten des Bennington College für Mädchen in New England wurden 1932 im Kolonialstil aus weiß gestrichenem Holz errichtet. 1957 entschloß man sich, als Beispiel zeitgenössischer Architektur eine neue Bibliothek zu bauen, die zugleich mit den bereits bestehenden Gebäuden harmonisieren sollte. Ein weißer, teilweise vertieft liegender, holzverkleideter Bau mit einem von Backsteinmauern umschlossenen Gartenhof war die adäquate Lösung.
Die Bücherei hat 75000 Bände, die auf drei Geschosse verteilt sind; jedes Geschoß verfügt über einen Lesebereich. Der Lesesaal im Erdgeschoß hat Zugang zum Gartenhof. Da das Gelände abfällt, kann der Besucher das Gebäude im mittleren Geschoß betreten und braucht dann vom Eingangsniveau aus nur ein Geschoß nach oben oder nach unten zu gehen.
Der Berater für die Planung dieser Bibliothek war Keyes D. Metcalf, ehemals Bibliothekar am Harvard College.

Key to plans / Legende zu den Plänen:
1 Ground floor / Erdgeschoß
2 Entrance floor / Eingangsgeschoß
3 Upper floor / Obergeschoß
4 Garden court / Gartenhof
5 Reading area / Lesebereich
6 Utility room / Materialraum
7 Storage / Lager
8 W. C.
9 Main entrance / Haupteingang
10 Coats / Garderobe
11 Foyer
12 Lobby / Halle
13 Control desk / Kontrolle
14 Periodicals / Zeitschriften
15 Reference / Nachschlagewerke
16 Microfilm / Mikrofilme
17 Catalogue, bibliography / Katalog, Bibliographie
18 Cataloguing room / Katalogisierung
19 Librarian, secretary / Bibliothekar, Sekretariat
20 Storage and delivery / Lager und Versand
21 Folios / Folianten
22 Listening room / Abhörstudio
23 Typing room / Schreibraum
24 Seminar room / Seminarraum
25 Staff lounge / Aufenthaltsraum des Personals

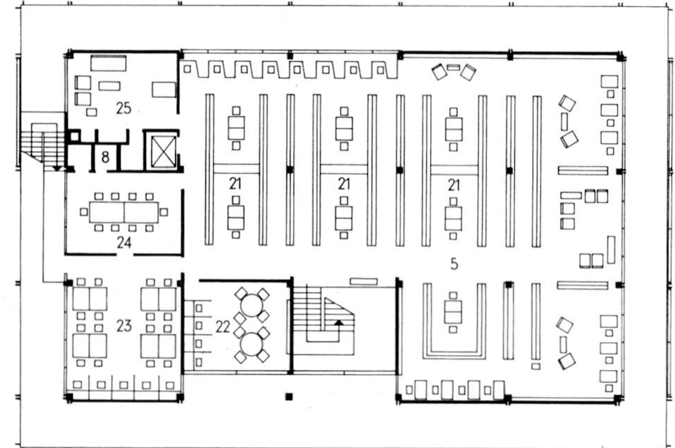


Upper floor plan / Grundriß Obergeschoß.

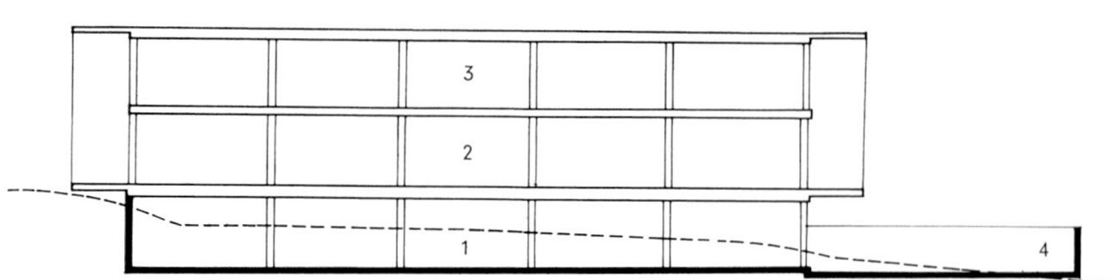


Longitudinal section / Längsschnitt.

30'
10 m

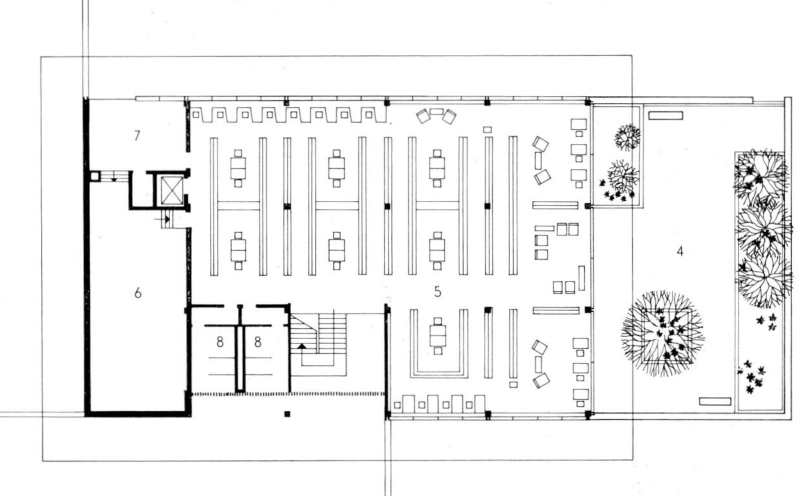


Ground floor plan / Grundriß Erdgeschoß.

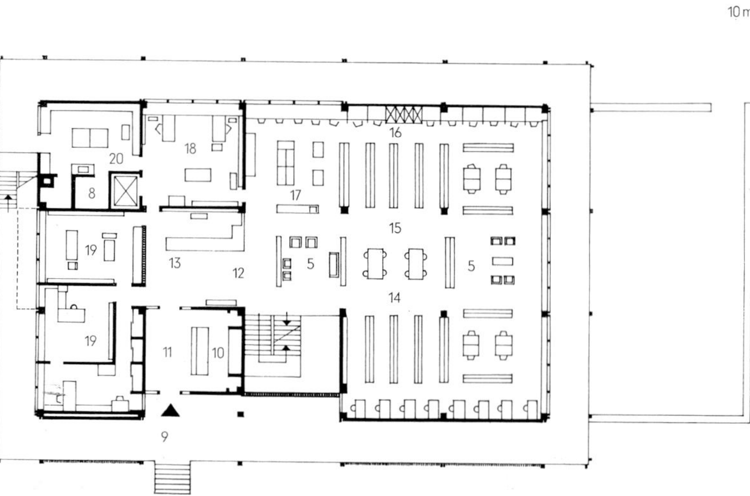


Entrance floor plan / Grundriß Eingangsgeschoß.

1

2

1. The entrance side on the corner of the main college quadrangle; the terrace and columns which surround the building give it a kind of American Colonial portico.
2. The inner door at the end of the draught lobby; the control desk faces the door.

1. Die Eingangsseite liegt an der Ecke des Hauptplatzes. Terrasse und Stützen, die das Gebäude umgeben, erinnern an einen Porticus der amerikanischen Kolonialzeit.
2. Blick auf die innere Tür am Ende des Windfangs; der Kontrolltisch steht der Tür gegenüber.

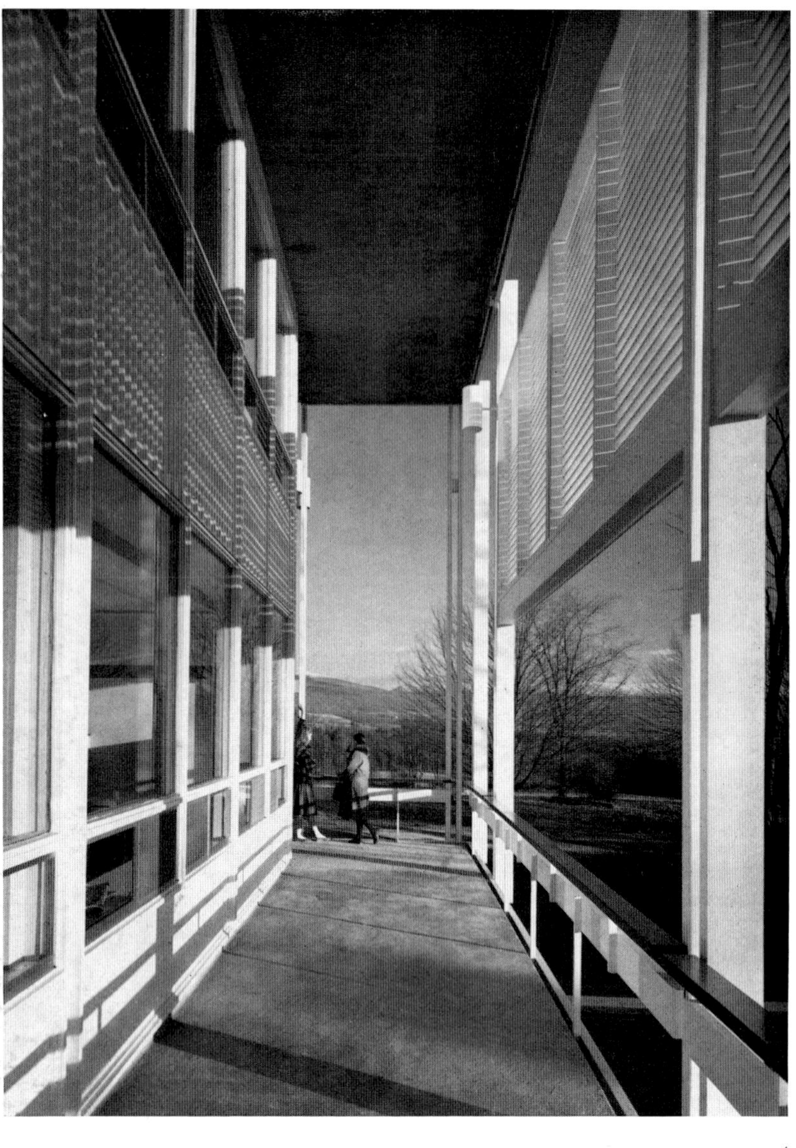

3

3. The raised terrace which goes right round the building; the overhang and the wooden slats help to shade the building and so reduce the load on its air-conditioning plant.
4. A study area on the middle floor; alcoves are made by the arrangement of the shelving and these are furnished in different ways.
5. Staircase, entrance on the right and the control des kon the main floor; beyond the wooden screen there are librarians' offices, a catalogue room and a shipping room linked by a goods lift to the ground level.

3. Die erhöhte Terrasse geht um das ganze Gebäude herum. Das vorkragende Dach und die Holzlamellen gewähren Sonnenschutz und verringern dadurch die Belastung der Klimaanlage.
4. Blick in einen Studiensaal des mittleren Geschosses. Durch die Anordnung der Regale entstanden abgesonderte Bereiche, die unterschiedlich möbliert sind.
5. Blick in das Hauptgeschoß mit der nach oben und unten führenden Treppe, rechts der Eingang mit dem Kontrolltisch. Hinter der hölzernen Trennwand liegen die Büros der Bibliothekare; ein Katalograum und der Versandraum sind durch einen Bücheraufzug mit dem Erdgeschoß verbunden.

4

5

6. Small booths lined with sound absorbent material occur throughout the library; to mask the worrying intermittent noises the air-conditioning system has been designed so that it is allowed to emit a continuous low hum.
7. The three floors of the library seen at night from the garden court; the entire building is lit by a suspended luminous ceiling of corrugated plastic which also acts as a sound absorber.
8. The garden court extends the bottom floor reading area to the outside; low bookcases subdivide the indoor spaces.

6. Kleine, mit schalldämmenden Platten verkleidete Kabinen sind überall in der Bibliothek zu finden; um Störung durch wechselnde Geräusche zu vermeiden, wurde die Klimaanlage so konstruiert, daß sie einen ständigen leisen Summton von sich gibt.
7. Nachtansicht vom Gartenhof. Das Gebäude wird durch eine abgehängte Leuchtdecke aus gewelltem Kunststoff belichtet, die gleichzeitig schalldämmend wirkt.
8. Der Gartenhof erweitert den Leseraum im Erdgeschoß nach außen; niedrige Bücherregale gliedern hier den Innenraum.

6

7

8

**Library, C. Thurston Chase Learning Center, Eaglebrook School, Deerfield, Massachusetts**

Architects: The Architects Collaborative and Campbell, Aldrich & Nulty

The library is the focus of this group of classrooms, laboratories and meeting hall. The programme for the centre and its design were worked by the architects with the Stanford Research Institute, the Educational Facilities Laboratories and other consultants. The intention is to create a place where the emphasis is on learning rather than teaching and where, as a result, school children find out a great many things by themselves. A good many of their information sources will be in the library and it is appropriate, therefore, that this should be both symbolically and physically the central and most important space.
The library is a two-storey high volume. The lower floor contains study areas, book stacks as well as a librarian's office, a conference room and five departmental rooms each large enough for six members of the teaching staff. On the mezzanine floor above there are ten small rooms fitted out with television and language laboratory facilities, two larger rooms for groups of four or five, seventeen individual reading tables, some of which are for members of staff, and a small informal sitting space. There is storage for books, records and microfilm.

**Bücherei des C.-Thurston-Chase-Lernzentrums, Eaglebrook School, Deerfield, Massachusetts**

Architekten: The Architects Collaborative und Campbell, Aldrich & Nulty

Die Bücherei bildet den Mittelpunkt eines Komplexes von Klassenzimmern, Laboratorien und einem großen Versammlungsraum. Programm und Planung dieses Zentrums wurden von den Architekten in Zusammenarbeit mit dem Stanford-Forschungsinstitut, den Educational Facilities Laboratories und anderen Beratern entwickelt. Es ging dabei vor allem darum, eine Stätte zu schaffen, wo das Lernen eine wichtigere Rolle spielt als das Lehren und wo die Schüler in vielen Fällen selbst die Lösungen finden. Eine wichtige Informationsquelle ist für sie die Bücherei, die deshalb der symbolische und architektonische Mittelpunkt wurde.
Die Bücherei ist zweigeschossig. Im Erdgeschoß liegen Studienräume, Büchermagazine und ein Bibliothekarsbüro, ein Konferenzzimmer und fünf Räume für je sechs Lehrer. Das Zwischengeschoß enthält zehn kleinere Räume, die alle mit Fernsehgeräten und Sprachlaboratorien ausgestattet sind, zwei größere Räume für vier oder fünf Schüler, siebzehn Arbeitsplätze, von denen einige für Lehrer reserviert sind, und eine kleine Sitzgruppe. Außerdem sind hier die Schallplatten und Mikrofilme untergebracht.

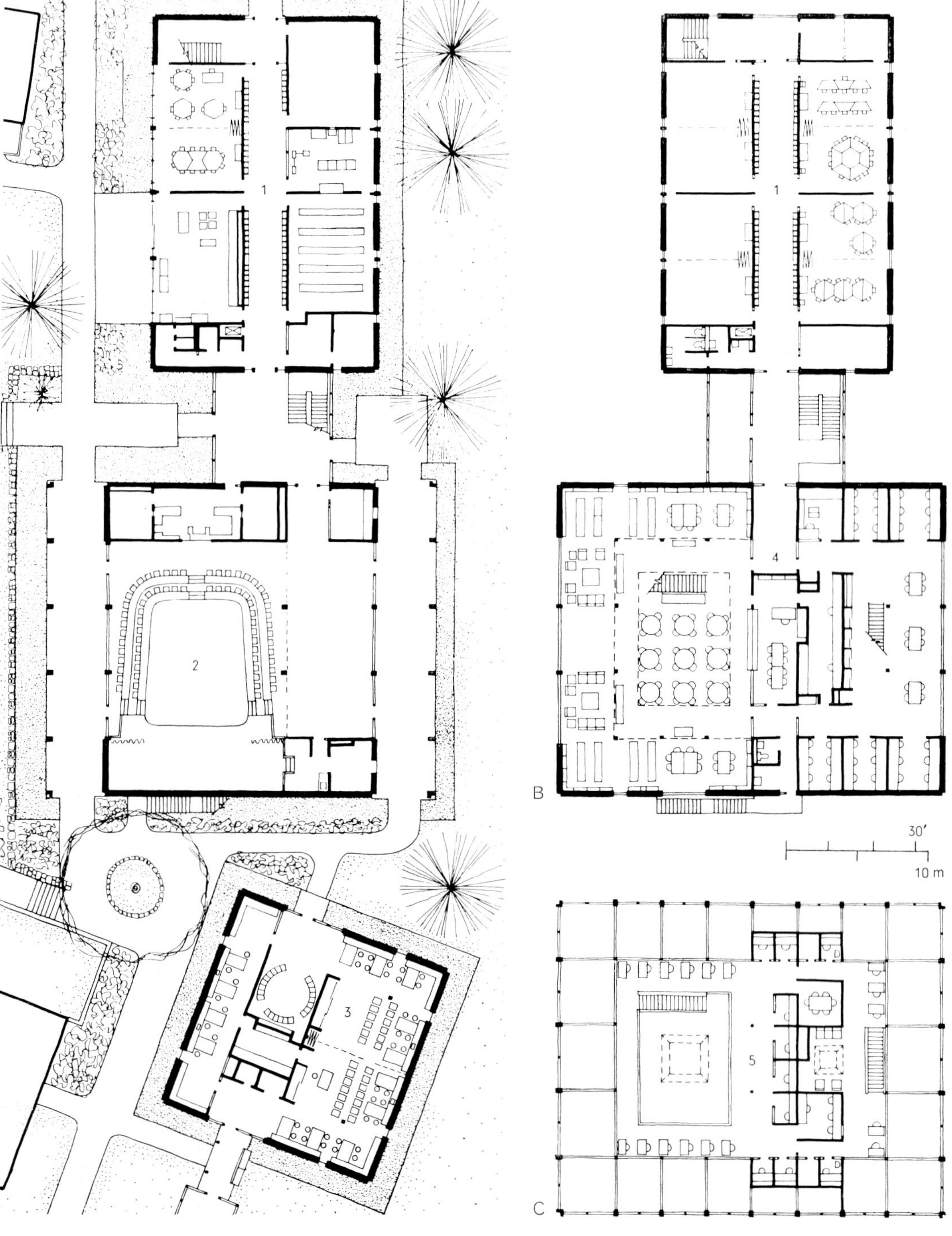


Plans of ground floor (A), first floor (B), and mezzanine floor (C) / Grundrisse Erdgeschoß (A), Obergeschoß (B) und Zwischengeschoß (C).
1 Classroom block / Klassenzimmer
2 Auditorium / Versammlungsraum
3 Science block / Studienbereich
4 Library / Bücherei
5 Library mezzanine / Zwischengeschoß der Bücherei

1

2

3

4

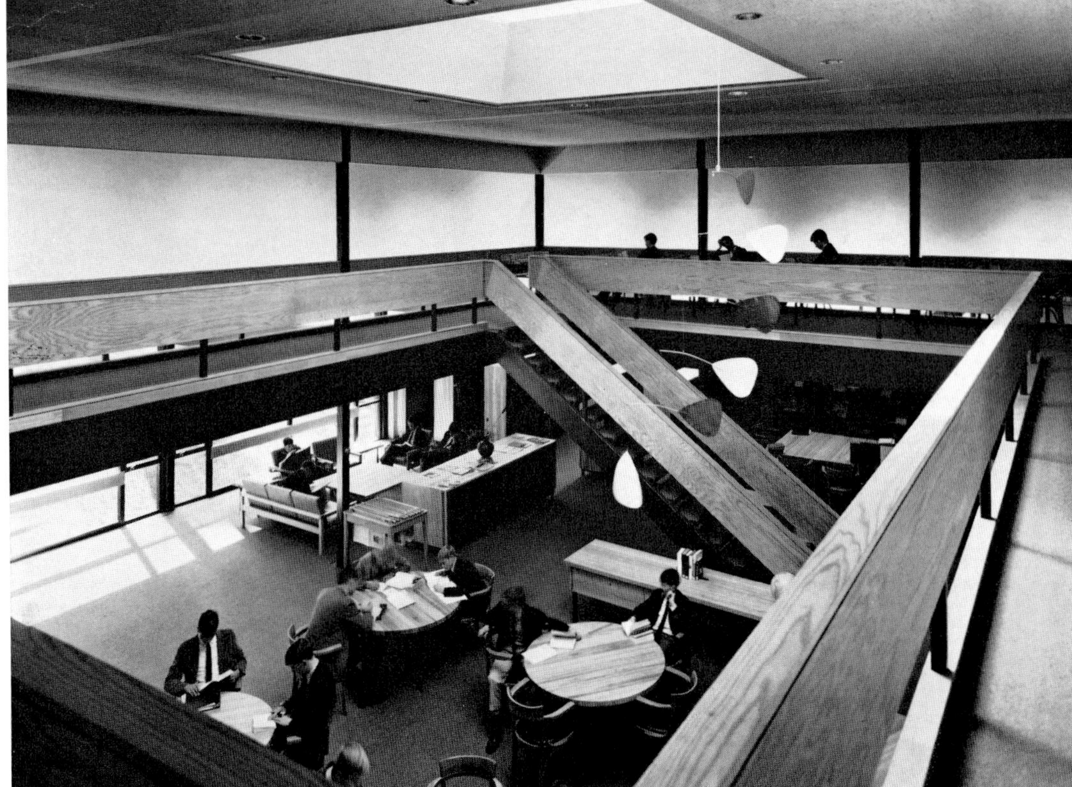

5

1. The library and meeting hall building seen at night.
2. Some of the individual work spaces at mezzanine level.
3. Two of the study spaces allocated to staff on the main floor.
4, 5. The central top lit reading space which can also be used for team teaching projects. The entire library is carpeted.

1. Nachtansicht der Bibliothek und des Versammlungsraumes.
2. Blick auf die Arbeitsplätze im Zwischengeschoß.
3. Blick auf zwei Studienbereiche für Lehrer im Erdgeschoß.
4, 5. Der zentrale Leseraum erhält Oberlicht. Er wird auch für Gruppenunterricht benutzt. Die gesamte Bücherei ist mit Teppichen ausgelegt.

**Library, Theological College, Eichstätt, Germany, 1964**

Architect: Karljosef Schattner

**Bücherei der Theologischen Hochschule, Eichstätt, 1964**

Architekt: Karljosef Schattner

A library with a capacity of 400,000 volumes had to be placed near the Bishop's Palace in Eichstätt and it was felt important to provide a solution which would be in sympathy with the existing complex. The five-storey stack has been surrounded by single storey reading rooms, offices and a caretaker's flat. The effect of its bulk has thus been reduced. The stack, about 55′ × 64′ (16,80 × 19,50 m) on plan, with 7′8″ (2,20 m) high floors is a self-supporting steel structure carrying the loads of the books and of the 2¾″ (7 cm) thick concrete floors to the foundations on a 4′8″ × 3′8″ (1,40 × 1,10 m) grid of uprights. Assuming that the books had to be placed in a multi-storey separate stack such an arrangement produces the minimum total height for a given number of floors or alternatively will allow the greatest number of floors to be fitted within a given height.

Die Bücherei, die 400000 Bände umfaßt, sollte in der Nähe der Bischofsresidenz liegen und sich gleichzeitig in den bereits bestehenden Komplex einfügen. Das fünfgeschossige Magazingebäude ist von eingeschossigen Lesesälen, Büros und der Hausmeisterwohnung umgeben, so daß das Volumen des Magazins optisch weniger stark in Erscheinung tritt. Das Büchermagazin (Grundfläche 16,80 × 19,50 m, Geschoßhöhe 2,20 m) ist eine selbsttragende Stahlkonstruktion, die die Last der Bücher und der 7 cm starken Betondecken in die Fundamente leitet. Der Stützenraster hat die Maße 1,40 × 1,10 m. Wenn die Bücher in einem mehrgeschossigen, freistehenden Magazingebäude untergebracht werden müssen, ist mit dieser Konstruktion die geringste Höhe bei gegebener Zahl der Geschosse oder umgekehrt die größte Zahl von Geschossen innerhalb einer gegebenen Höhe zu erzielen.

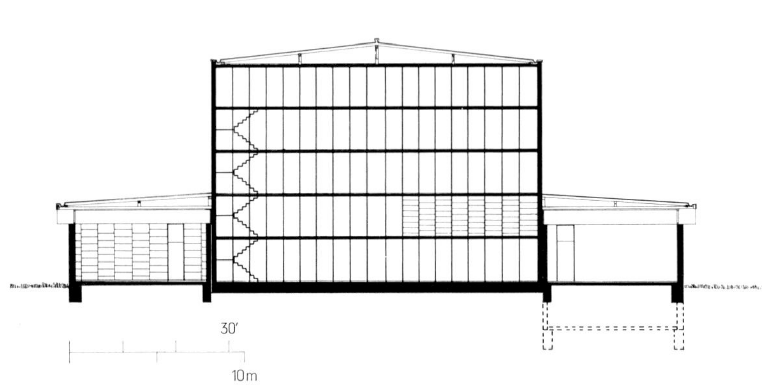


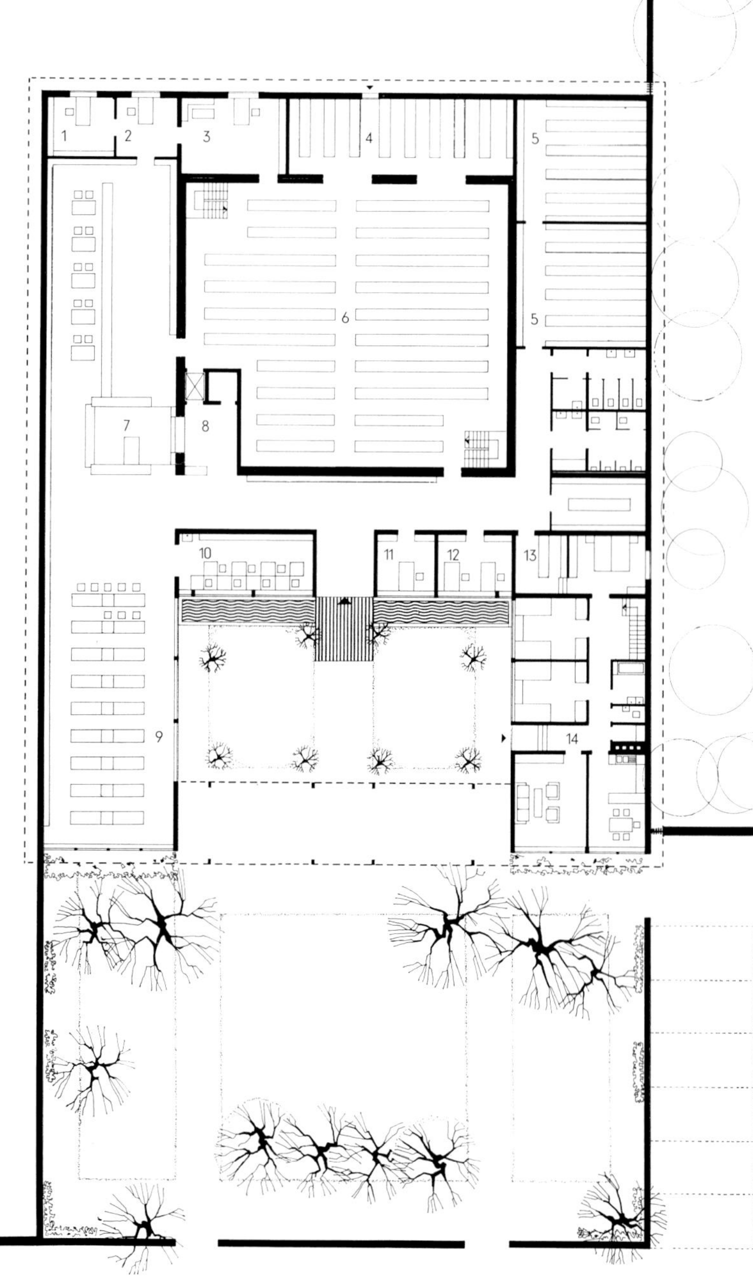


Cross section and ground floor plan / Querschnitt und Grundriß Erdgeschoß.

1 Librarian / Bibliothekar
2 Secretary / Sekretariat
3 Office / Büro
4 Stacks / Magazin
5 Archives / Archiv
6 Five-storey stack / Fünfgeschossiges Magazin
7 Issue desk / Ausleihe
8 Waiting room / Wartezimmer
9 Reading room / Lesesaal
10 Professors / Professoren
11 Director / Direktor
12 Office / Büro
13 Cloakroom / Garderobe
14 Caretaker's apartment / Hausmeisterwohnung

1

1. The view from the south which suggests the placement of the library within a walled garden of the Bishop's Palace.
2. The courtyard and one of the glass walls of the reading room.
3. The main entrance.

1. Ansicht von Süden. Die Bibliothek liegt in dem mit Mauern umschlossenen Park der Bischofsresidenz.
2. Die Leseräume sind vom Innenhof nur durch eine Glaswand getrennt.
3. Blick auf den Haupteingang.

2

3

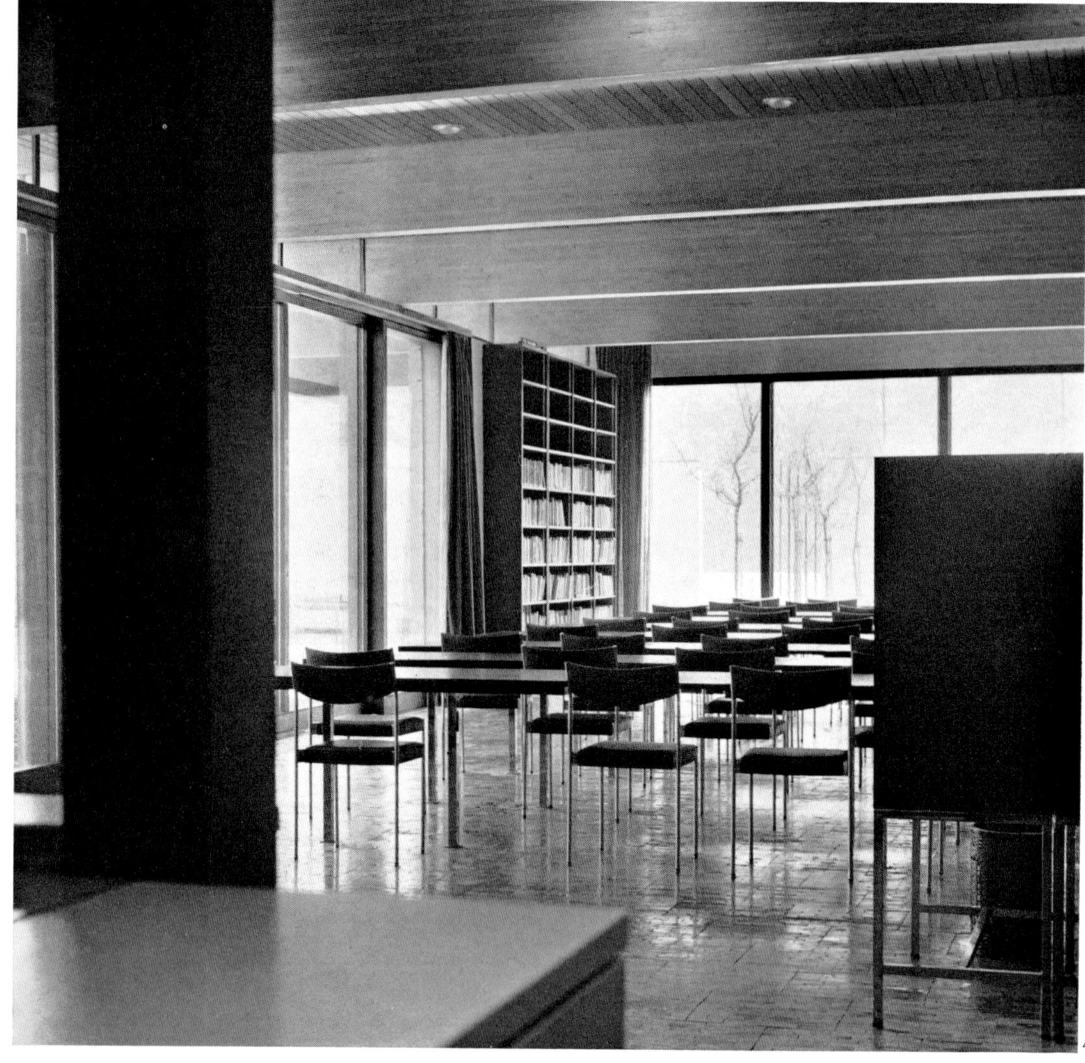

4

5

4. The reading room; curtains can be drawn across the glass to cut down glare.
5. View from the courtyard into the reading room.

4. Blick in den Lesesaal. Bei zu starker Sonneneinstrahlung können die Vorhänge zugezogen werden.
5. Blick vom Innenhof in den Lesesaal.

6

7

6. Showcases in the entrance; it ought to be possible for librarians to put their new acquisitions or special treasures on display and to change these exhibits simply and frequently.
7. One of the reading areas and the issue desk; shielded roof lights provide top lighting of the tables.

6. In den Vitrinen am Eingang können die Bibliothekare Neuerwerbungen oder besonders wertvolle Bücher ausstellen und ohne viel Aufwand häufig auswechseln.
7. Blick in einen Lesesaal, im Vordergrund die Ausleihe. Die Arbeitstische erhalten Oberlicht.

**James F. Lincoln Library, Lake Erie College, Painesville, Ohio, 1966**

Architects: Victor Christ-Janer & Associates

Lake Erie is a small college started shortly after the American Civil War as a seminary for women which recently expanded to about 550 students. A plan for the college was established in 1954 and a library in the centre of the site was completed in 1966.
The library building consists of a number of areas partly defined by cube-like enclosures visible from the outside. These cubes are sheathed in aluminium panels which project beyond the edge of the sill-line creating a ring of horizontal glass. This band of shielded glass together with very deep roof-lights allows some daylight to enter the interior although the building has been principally thought of as winter's evening experience, the time of its main use.
Apart from offices and staff working areas which have doors, all other spaces open uninterruptedly into each other both vertically and horizontally. The floors are carpeted and the ceilings have sound absorbent tiles so that most of the noise is muffled at source. Study areas which occur in amongst the stacks are further shielded by high walls.
The fragmented nature of the plan and the gaps left between the elements should make it possible to follow a process of accretion by which the building expands in perhaps two or three directions when the need arises.

**James F. Lincoln Library, Lake Erie College, Painesville, Ohio, 1966**

Architekten: Victor Christ-Janer & Associates

Lake Erie ist ein kleines College für Mädchen, das nach dem amerikanischen Bürgerkrieg gegründet und kürzlich auf etwa 550 Studienplätze erweitert wurde. Im Jahre 1954 wurde ein Bebauungsplan für das Collegegelände aufgestellt; 1966 wurde die Bibliothek im Mittelpunkt des Campus vollendet.
Das Bibliotheksgebäude besteht aus verschiedenen Bereichen, die teilweise nach außen hin durch die Aufgliederung der Baumasse in kubische Einzelformen definiert sind. Die Kuben sind mit Aluminiumplatten verkleidet, die über die Fensterbrüstungen herunterreichen und nur einen umlaufenden horizontal gelegten Glasstreifen freilassen. Durch dieses Fensterband und durch die tiefen Oberlichter fällt Tageslicht in das Innere, obwohl das Gebäude vor allem für die Benutzung an Winterabenden konzipiert wurde, an denen die höchsten Besucherzahlen zu verzeichnen sind.
Abgesehen von den Büros und den Arbeitsräumen des Personals, die mit Türen versehen sind, gehen alle Bereiche sowohl vertikal wie horizontal ineinander über. Die Böden sind mit Teppichen ausgelegt, die Decken mit schalldämmenden Platten verkleidet, so daß Geräusche größtenteils schon an der Quelle absorbiert werden. Die Arbeitsplätze im Magazin sind außerdem durch hohe Wände abgeschirmt.
Der aufgebrochene Grundriß und die Zäsuren zwischen den einzelnen Elementen lassen die Möglichkeit offen, das Gebäude je nach Bedarf nach zwei oder drei Richtungen hin zu erweitern.

1. The west side of the library; the whole of the upper part of the wall rising out from the concrete base is in aluminum, a design which won the building the 1967 R.S. Reynolds Memorial Award.

1. Die Westseite der Bibliothek. Die oberen Teile des Gebäudes, die sich über der Betonkonstruktion erheben, sind aus Aluminium, ein Entwurf, für den die Architekten 1967 den Reynolds Memorial Award erhielten.

1

2

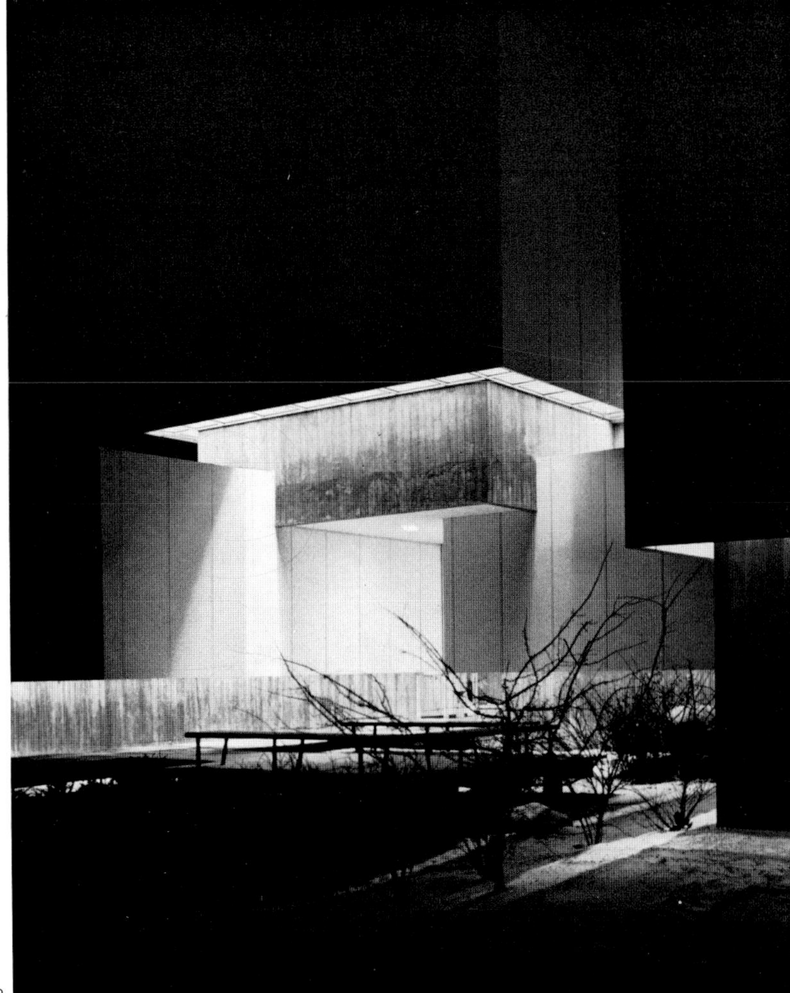

3

2, 3. One of the outdoor reading areas which jut out from the building as wooden platforms.

2, 3. Eine der hölzernen Plattformen, die aus dem Gebäude herausführen und einen Lesebereich im Freien bilden.

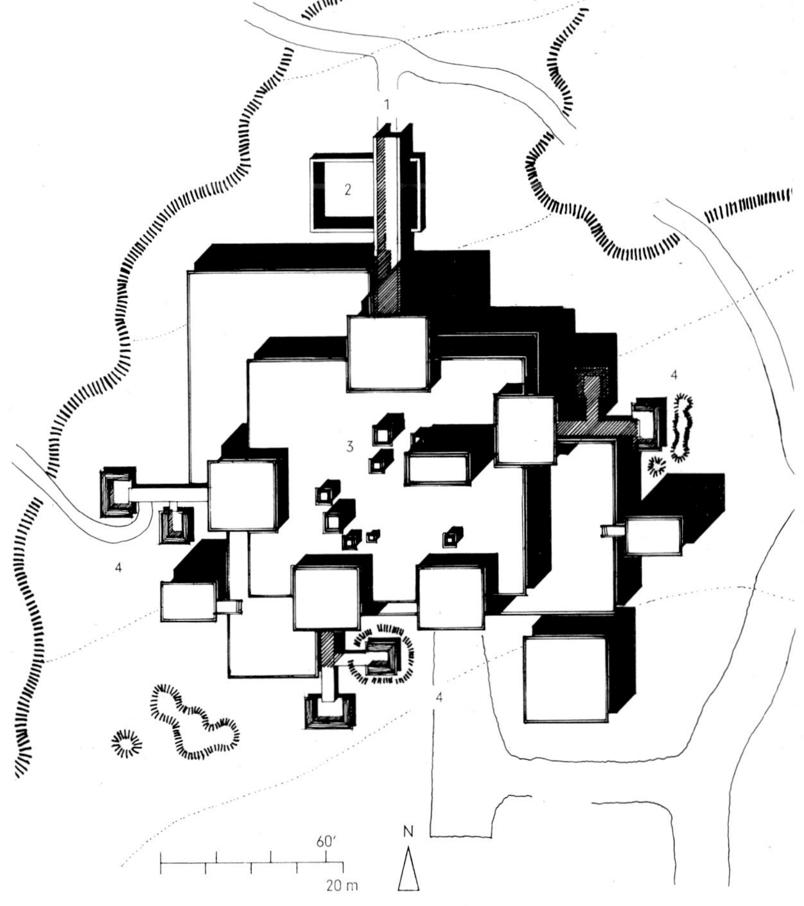


Site Plan. The library is at the centre of the college campus with both classrooms and residential buildings near it.

Lageplan. Die Bibliothek liegt in der Nähe der Wohn- und Vorlesungsgebäude im Zentrum des Collegegeländes.

1 Main entrance / Haupteingang
2 Fountain / Wasserbecken
3 Skylight / Oberlichter
4 Outdoor reading area / Lesebereich im Freien

Key to plans / Legende zu den Plänen:

1 Main entrance / Haupteingang
2 Main control / Hauptkontrolle
3 Catalogue / Katalog
4 Periodicals / Zeitschriften
5 Technical services / Bibliothekstechnische Einrichtungen
6 Reference / Nachschlagewerke
7 Double-tier main stack / Doppelgeschossiges Magazin
8 Elevator / Aufzug
9 Office / Büro
10 Secretary / Sekretariat
11 Rest room / Ruheraum
12 W.C.
13 Service entrance / Nebeneingang
14 Exit stair / Treppe
15 Mechanical equipment / Technische Einrichtungen
16 Chapel / Kapelle
17 Upper part of chapel / Luftraum der Kapelle
18 Informal study area / Studienraum
19 Skylights above / Oberlichter
20 Void to floor below / Luftraum
21 Stack area / Magazin
22 Study area / Studienbereich
23 Mechanical equipment / Technische Einrichtungen
24 Roof / Dach
25 Skylight / Oberlicht

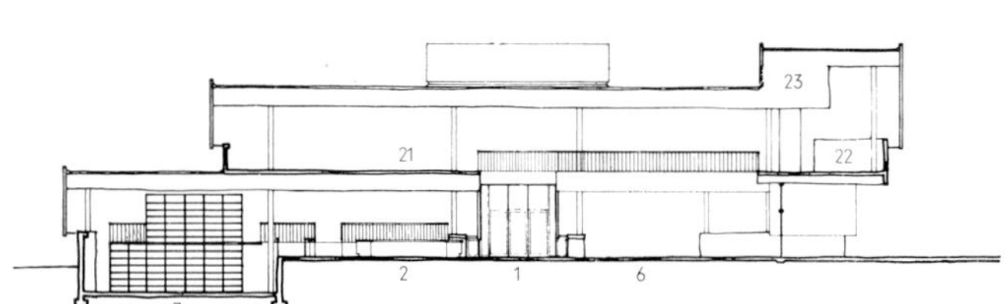


Section A–A / Schnitt A–A.

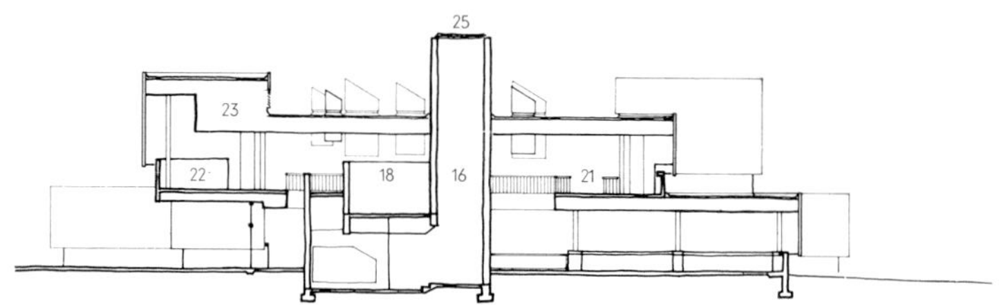


Section B–B / Schnitt B–B.

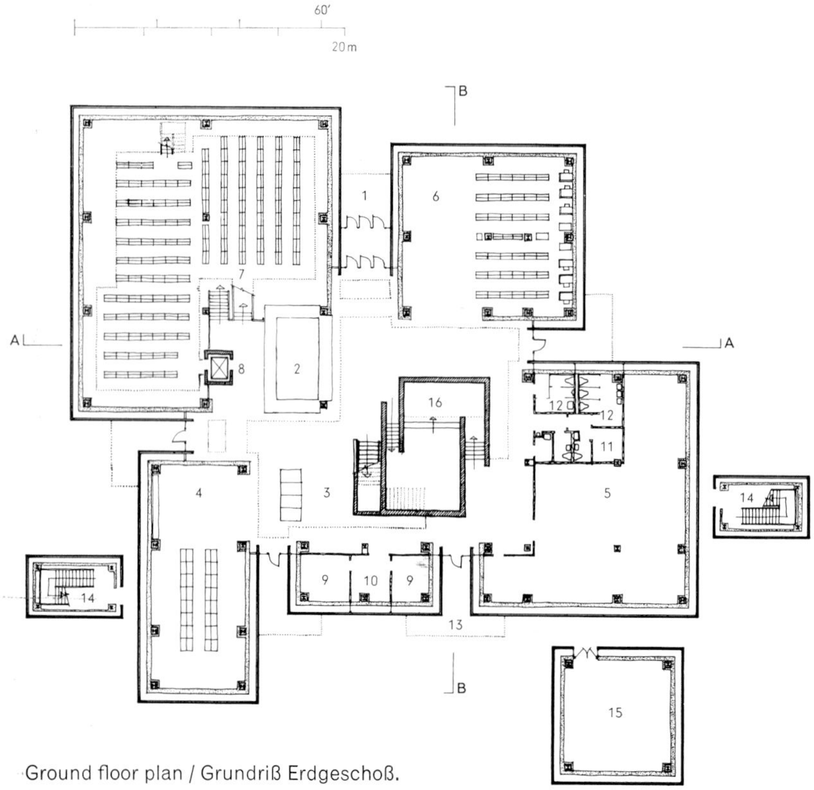

Ground floor plan / Grundriß Erdgeschoß.

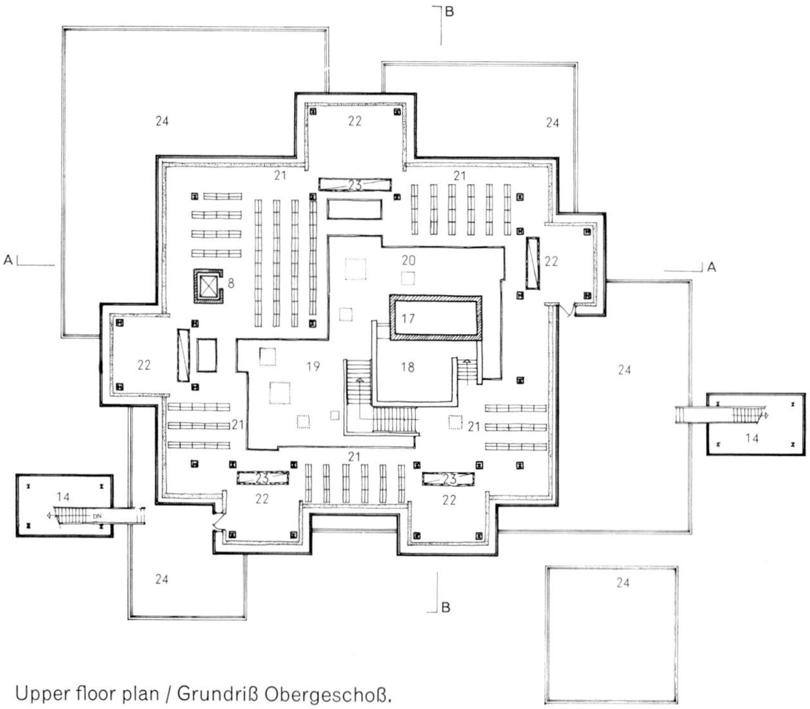

Upper floor plan / Grundriß Obergeschoß.

4

5

6

4. The catalogue adjacent to the main desk; on the far side to the left is the beginning of the periodicals room, on the right a double-tier stack with its lower level below ground.
5, 6. The catalogue area seen from above showing also the deep skylights which pierce the ceiling of the central space.

4. Der Katalog in der Nähe der Hauptkontrolle. Hinten links der Zeitschriftenraum, rechts ein doppelgeschossiges Magazin, dessen unterer Teil unter dem Geschoßniveau liegt.
5, 6. Blick von oben auf den Katalog. An der Decke die tiefreichenden Oberlichter, die den Zentralbereich mit Tageslicht versorgen.

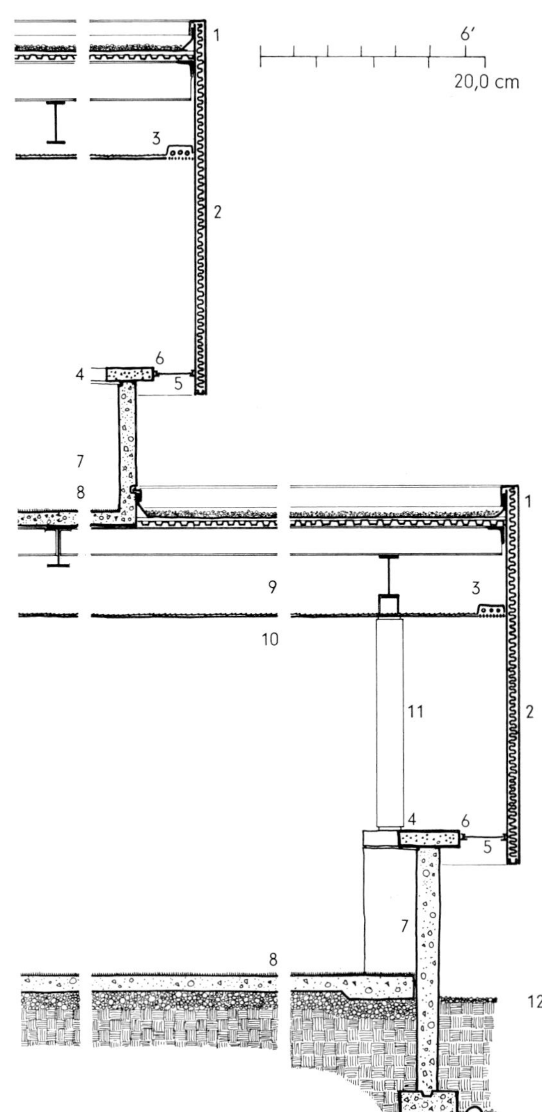


7

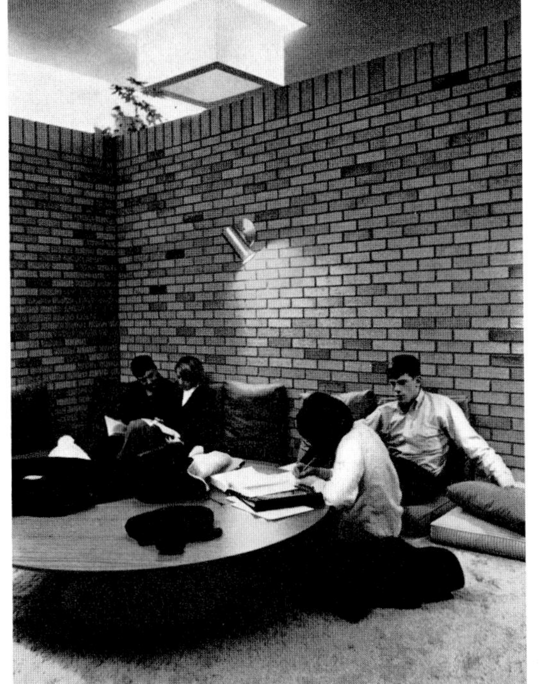

7. The informal study room which is at the head of the stairs in the middle of the library.

7. Blick in den unkonventionell eingerichteten Studienraum, der oberhalb der Treppe in der Mitte der Bibliothek liegt.

Wall section detail / Wandschnitt (Detail).
1 Integral cap flashing / Dachschürze
2 Aluminum insulated wall panel / Wandtafel aus isolierendem Aluminium
3 Lighting / Beleuchtung
4 Precast terrazzo sill / Vorgefertigte Fensterbank aus Terrazzo
5 Glass / Glas
6 Outrigger / Seitenstütze
7 Concrete base wall / Wandbrüstung aus Beton
8 Floor slab / Deckenplatte
9 Mechanical plenum / Klimaanlage
10 Ceiling diffusion / Zwischendecke
11 Column / Stütze
12 Grade / Bodenniveau

**Library, University of Sussex, Falmer, Sussex, 1964**

Architects: Sir Basil Spence, Bonnington & Collins

Sussex is the first of a group of seven new universities which were started in England in the early 1960s. The planning of their libraries has been an opportunity to experiment in design, and at each of the universities the library has been an important building which was started as early as possible within the university building programme. It was recognized that no institution of higher education could function properly without an adequate library.
The first discussions on the design of this building took place at the end of 1960 by which time the university librarian had also been appointed so that he could participate in the design from the start. Like all the librarians at the new university libraries which were to follow Sussex, he strongly advocated open access and a variety of reading areas closely connected with the book stacks. This continued the practice current in the United States.
The first portion of the library which can be extended on the side opposite the entrance facing the central "Great Court" of the university, has shelf space for 250,000 volumes and seats for about 900 readers. It was opened in the autumn of 1964.

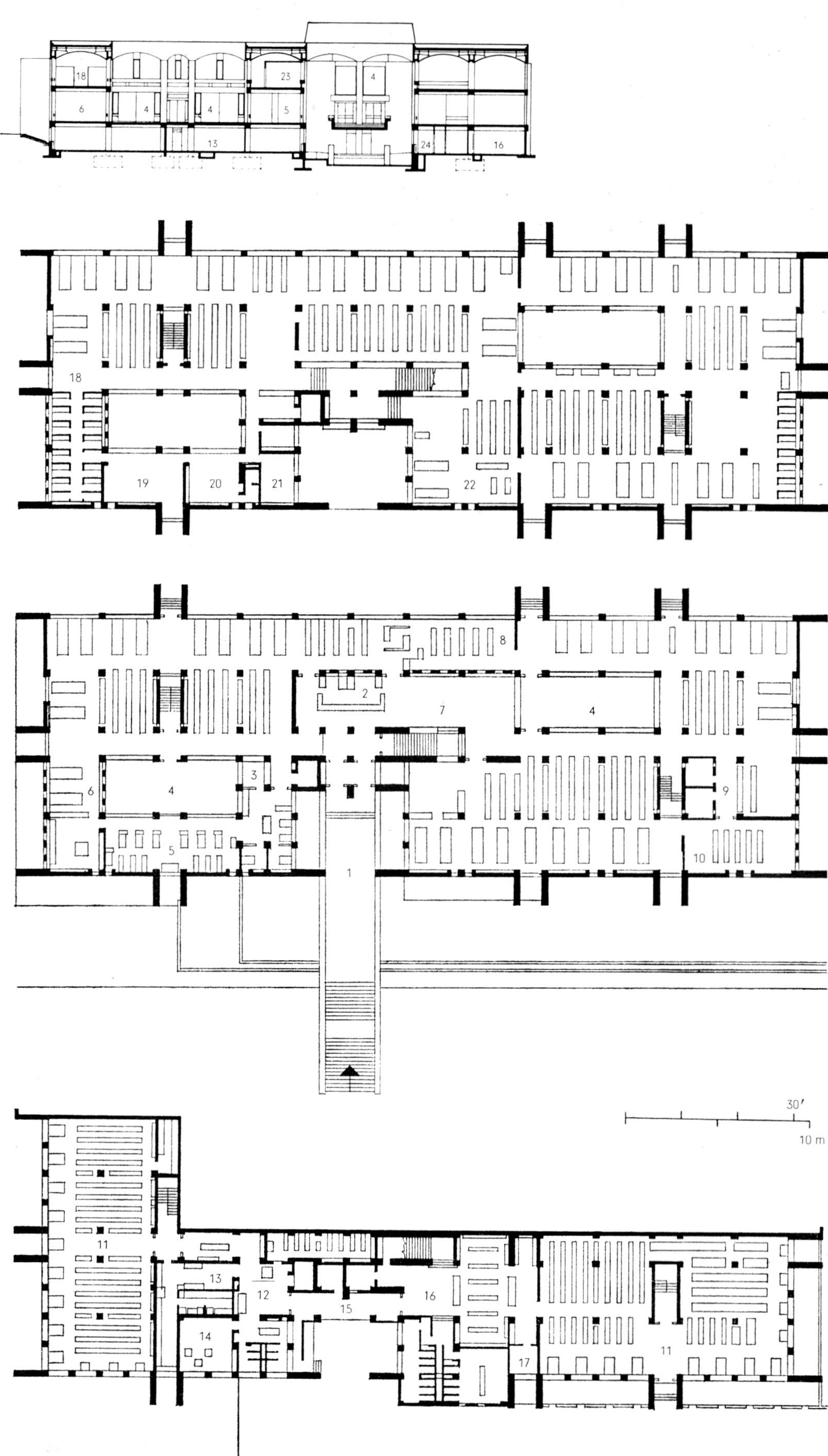


Part of longitudinal section / Teil des Längsschnitts.
First floor plan / Grundriß Obergeschoß.
Ground floor plan / Grundriß Erdgeschoß.
Basement floor plan / Grundriß Untergeschoß.
(From top to bottom / Von oben nach unten)

Key to plans / Legende zu den Plänen:
1 Entrance hall / Eingangshalle
2 Control / Kontrolle
3 Enquiries / Auskunft
4 Court / Hof
5 Administration / Verwaltung
6 Staff reading room / Leseraum für Universitätsangestellte
7 Catalogue hall / Katalogsaal
8 Delta collection / Delta-Sammlung
9 Recorded speech section / Schallplatten und Tonbandaufnahmen
10 Lecture room / Vortragsraum
11 Stack / Magazin
12 Workroom / Arbeitsraum
13 Photographic unit / Fotoabteilung
14 Staff common room / Personalraum
15 Loading bay / Laderampe
16 Locker rooms / Raum für Schließfächer
17 Rest room / Ruheraum
18 Studies / Studienbereiche
19 Seminar room / Seminarraum
20 Librarian / Bibliothekar
21 Secretary / Sekretariat
22 Periodicals / Zeitschriften
23 Office / Büro
24 W. C.

**Bibliothek der University of Sussex, Falmer, Sussex, 1964**

Architekten: Sir Basil Spence, Bonnington & Collins

Sussex war die erste von sieben neuen englischen Universitäten, mit deren Bau in den frühen sechziger Jahren begonnen wurde. Die Planung der Universitätsbibliotheken war ein gegebener Anlaß für die Entwicklung neuer Ideen. In jeder der sieben Universitäten spielte die Bibliothek eine wichtige Rolle, und die Errichtung der Gebäude wurde innerhalb der Gesamtplanung so früh wie möglich in Angriff genommen, denn man ging davon aus, daß eine akademische Bildungsstätte ohne Bibliothek nicht funktionsfähig ist.
Die ersten Planungsbesprechungen fanden Ende 1960 statt. Zu diesem Zeitpunkt war der Bibliothekar bereits berufen, so daß er an den Diskussionen von Anfang an teilnehmen konnte. Wie alle Bibliothekare an den neuen Universitätsbibliotheken setzte er sich für die Freihandaufstellung und für die Einrichtung von Leseplätzen in der Nähe der Bücherregale ein. Man folgte somit der in den USA üblichen Praxis.
Der Eingang der Bibliothek liegt am »Großen Platz« der Universität. Der erste Bauabschnitt, der im Herbst 1964 fertiggestellt wurde, bietet Raum für 250000 Bände und 900 Leser. Die Bibliothek kann auf der dem »Großen Platz« abgewandten Seite erweitert werden.

1

2

1. The library seen on the left through the arch covering the main route into the university which passes under the central social building.
2. The entrance side.
3. Brick piers occur at 10′ and 20′ centres (3 m and 6 m).
4. The entrance bridge passes over the loading bay on the floor below.

1. Blick durch den Bogen des Hauptzugangs zur Universität, der unter dem Gemeinschaftsgebäude hindurchführt. Die Bibliothek liegt links oben.
2. Blick auf die Eingangsseite.
3. Backsteinpfeiler im Abstand von 3 und 6 m gliedern die Fassade.
4. Die Eingangsbrücke führt über die Laderampe des Untergeschosses.

3

4

5

6

7

8

5. Individual reading spaces with their own artificial light sources; there is an electrical distribution system in the floor into which these can be plugged.
6. Books and readers in close proximity; the floor has been designed for a loading of 180 lbs/sq.ft. (900 kg/sq.m.) so that the bookshelves can be positioned anywhere; the stacks carry their own lighting.
7. The carrel-like furniture is just high enough to separate groups.
8. The staircase to the top floor starts in the catalogue hall.

5. Die Leseplätze haben ihre eigenen künstlichen Lichtquellen; elektrische Anschlüsse sind über den ganzen Fußboden verteilt.
6. Bücher und Leser sind nahe beieinander. Der Fußboden trägt eine Last von 900 kg/qm, so daß die Regale mit ihrer unabhängigen Beleuchtung überall aufgestellt werden können.
7. Die Arbeitsplätze sind durch Trennwände unterteilt, so daß sie jeweils einen abgeschlossenen Bereich bilden.
8. Die Treppe führt vom Katalograum ins Obergeschoß.

9. Floors in most reading areas are carpeted and the ceiling is lined with a sound-absorbent board; windows facing south and west have venetian blinds.
10, 11. A small sitting space with armchairs on one side of the staircase which overlooks the entrance bridge.

9. Die Fußböden sind in den meisten Leseräumen mit Teppichen ausgelegt; die Decke ist mit schalldämmenden Platten verkleidet. Die nach Süden und Westen liegenden Fenster haben Lamellenstores.
10, 11. Von den Sitzgruppen neben der Treppe überblickt man die Eingangsbrücke.

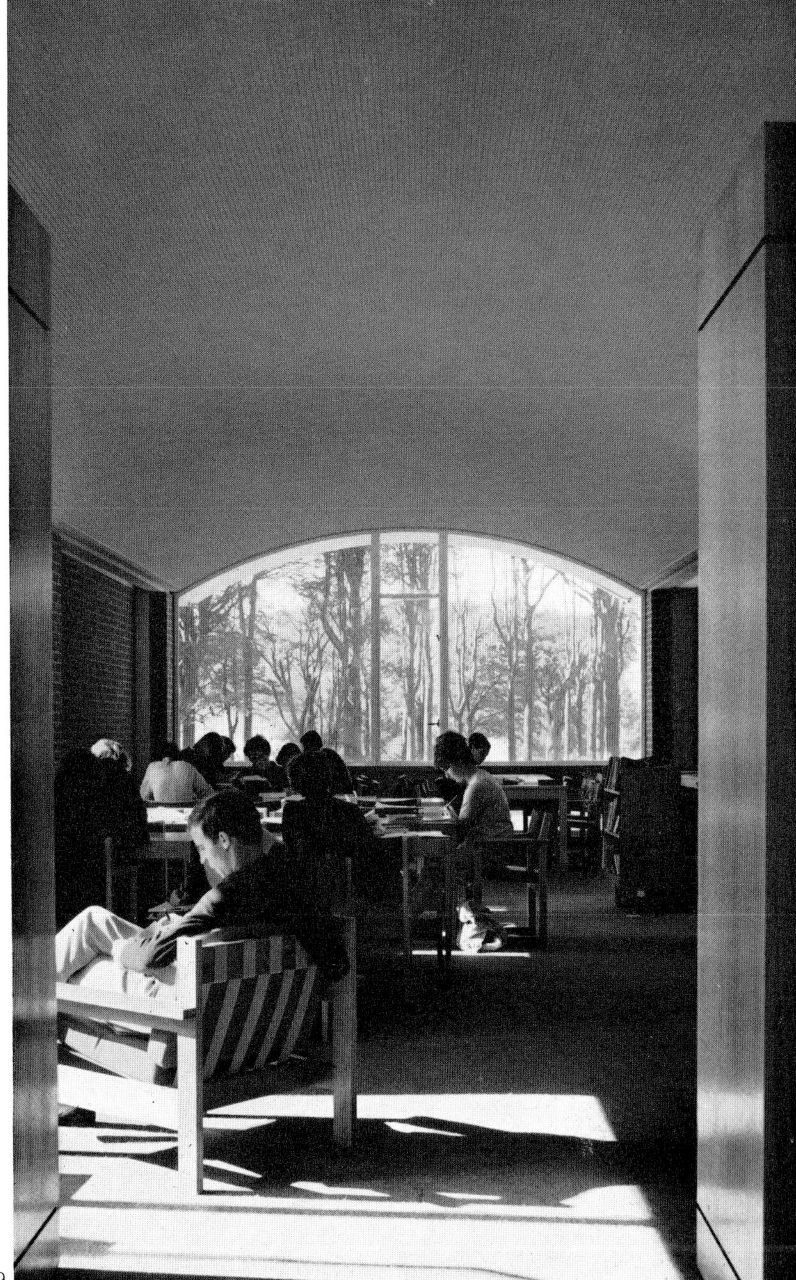

9

10

11

## J. B. Morrell Library, University of York, 1966

Architects: Robert Matthew, Johnson-Marshall & Partners

York is the second in the series of seven new British universities and its library was completed in the summer of 1966. It is linked to the remainder of the university through a system of covered ways and bridges which connects the clusters of buildings forming colleges and teaching groups. The entrance level of the library has a bookshop, a small coffee shop and various service and cloakroom facilities. Space for books and readers does not start until the first floor where the circulation desk faces the stairs from the entrance floor. These stairs and a lift rise in an open well in the middle of the building.
The library has been designed for a university student population of 3,300 and has a capacity of 250,000 volumes. There are 680 places for readers and space for 45 members of the library staff.

## J. B. Morrell Library, University of York, 1966

Architekten: Robert Matthew, Johnson-Marshall & Partners

York war die zweite der sieben neuen englischen Universitäten, die zu Beginn der sechziger Jahre geplant wurden. Die Bücherei ist mit dem Universitätskomplex, der verschiedene Colleges und Fakultätsgebäude umfaßt, durch gedeckte Brücken und Wege verbunden. Im Eingangsgeschoß sind eine Buchhandlung, eine kleine Kaffeebar, die Garderobe und Nebenräume untergebracht. Die eigentlichen Bibliotheksräume beginnen erst im ersten Obergeschoß; die Leihstelle liegt gegenüber der Treppe, die vom Eingangsgeschoß heraufführt. Treppe und Aufzug befinden sich in einem Lichthof im Zentrum des Gebäudes.
Die Bücherei wurde für eine Universität mit 3300 Studenten geplant. Ihre Kapazität beträgt 250000 Bände. Es sind 680 Leseplätze und Räume für 45 Bibliotheksangestellte vorhanden.

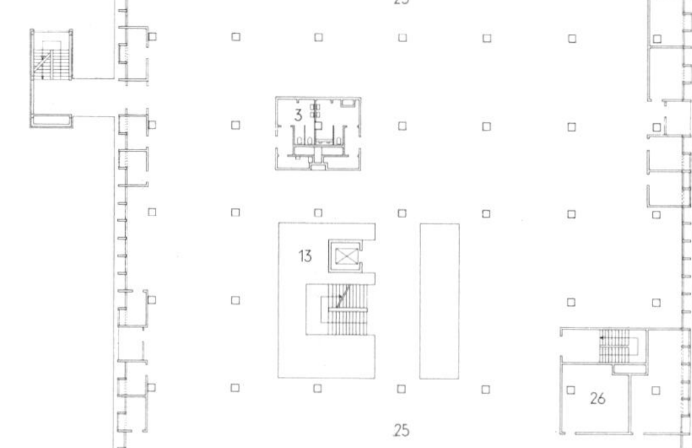

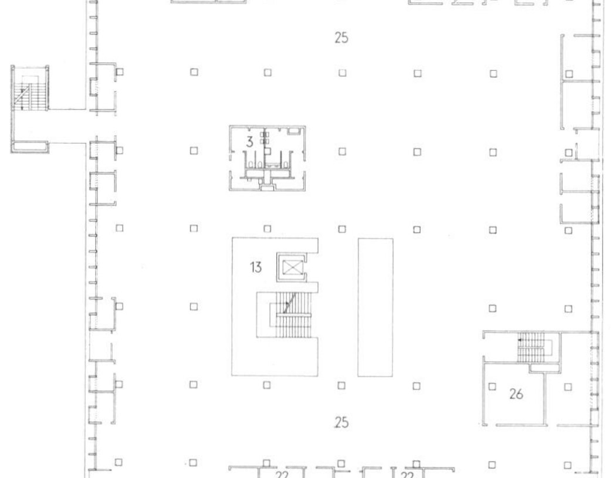

Second floor plan / Grundriß zweites Obergeschoß.

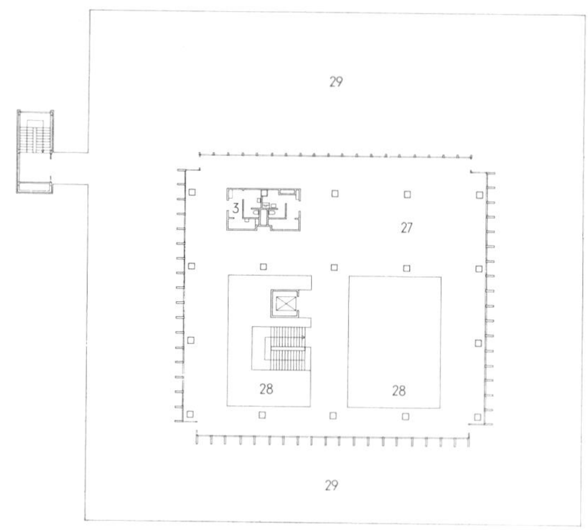

Third floor plan / Grundriß drittes Obergeschoß.

Key to plans / Legende zu den Plänen:

1 Cafeteria
2 Cloakroom / Garderobe
3 W. C.
4 Staff room / Personalraum
5 Bookshop / Buchhandlung
6 Photographic department / Fotoabteilung
7 Bindery / Buchbinderei
8 Store / Lager
9 Mechanical equipment / Technische Einrichtungen
10 Cycles / Fahrräder
11 Reception / Annahme
12 Issue / Ausleihe
13 Void / Luftraum
14 Catalogue / Katalog
15 Librarian / Bibliothekar
16 Offices / Büros
17 Cataloguing / Katalogisierung
18 Accessioning / Akzession
19 Dispatch / Versand
20 Periodicals / Zeitschriften
21 Special collections, maps / Spezialsammlungen, Landkarten
22 Carrels
23 Seminar room / Seminarraum
24 Audio-visual / Hör- und Lesegeräte
25 Bookstacks, reading area / Magazin, Lesebereich
26 Microfilm / Mikrofilme
27 Informal reading area / Leseraum
28 Lightwell / Lichtschacht
29 Roof terrace / Dachterrasse

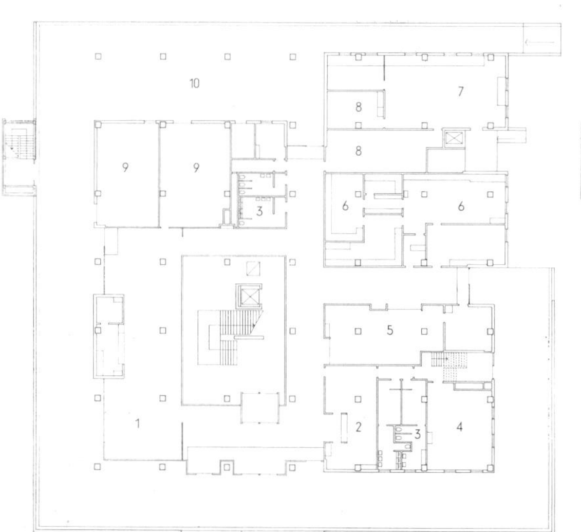

Ground floor plan / Grundriß Erdgeschoß.

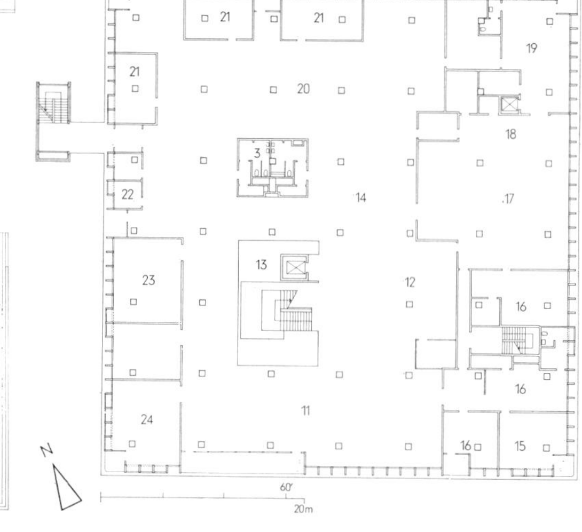

First floor plan / Grundriß erstes Obergeschoß.

1

2

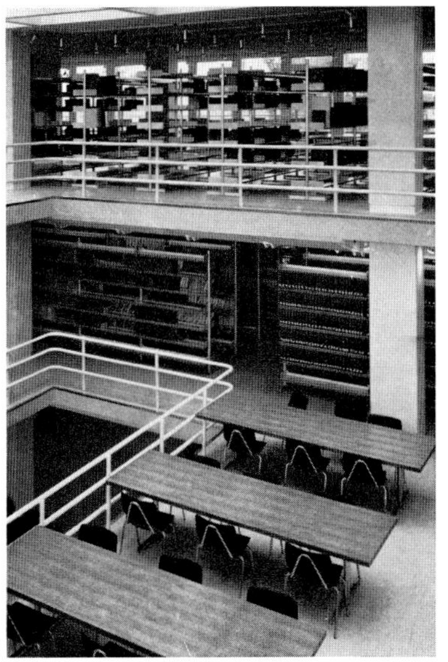
3

4

1. The library is on a slope above the road and looks out on colleges grouped around a lake.
2–4. The three floors of the library proper have as their focus a large top-lit void which has within it an open stair and the lift shaft; the degree to which the spaces interconnect both horizontally and vertically goes somewhat counter to the notion of an individual's aural and visual seclusion being one of the principal characteristics of the planning of academic and research libraries.

1. Die Bücherei liegt auf leicht abfallendem Gelände über der Straße; von hier überblickt man die an einem See liegenden College-Bauten.
2–4. Die drei Geschosse der Bücherei sind um einen Lichthof angeordnet, in dem sich Treppen und Fahrstuhlschacht befinden. Die horizontale und vertikale Verklammerung der Räume entspricht nicht den Planungsvorstellungen für Universitäts- und Forschungsbibliotheken, die als wichtiges Charakteristikum akustisch und visuell abgeschlossene Bereiche für den einzelnen Leser vorsehen.

**Library, History Faculty, University of Cambridge, 1968**

Architect: James Stirling

**Bibliothek des Historischen Instituts, University of Cambridge, 1968**

Architekt: James Stirling

The library is one element of a general teaching building designed for the History Department as part of the development of the University on the west side of the river. Other new buildings are already next to it and further construction is intended in this area. The History Building was completed in 1968 and should be seen as a pavilion within a growing campus, a campus quite different in character to the earlier web of courtyards and paths on the other side of the river.
The reading room with space for 300 readers and 12,000 linear ft. of shelving is a quarter of a circle held between the two wings of an L-shaped six-storey teaching building. The plan is directly descended from that of the British Museum and its 19th century progeny based on strict ideas of supervision. This sense of being overlooked is further enhanced by placing the control desk four feet above the level of the reading room and leaving the corridors of the upper floors glazed so as to encourage continuous views downwards.
Every reader is exposed and the furniture (not installed at the time the photographs were taken) does nothing to provide any shielding. The library produces an environment radically different from the carpeted broken-up and variable spaces of other recent solutions. It instead reinterprets the tradition of the great reading room as the focal space. This may to some extent be due to the fact that when a design was being selected as a result of a limited competition in the latter part of 1963, the Faculty Library had suffered a good many losses through theft.
Although it is thought unlikely that the library will expand in the future, it is assumed that it could do so by taking over seminar rooms at the library level.
The interior spaces of the building are, when not glass, covered in soft, sound-deadening materials; cork flooring, slotted sound absorbent walls and ceilings. The exterior surfaces, on the other hand, are hard, reflective and smooth: glass, tile and engineering brick. At night the continuous cascading glass surfaces glow brilliantly.

Die Bibliothek bildet einen Teil des Institutsgebäudes, das im Rahmen der Universitätserweiterung westlich des Flusses Cam für die Historische Abteilung geplant wurde. In der Nachbarschaft dieses Gebäudes sind bereits neue Universitätsbauten entstanden, und weitere Bauten sind vorgesehen. Das Institutsgebäude stellt also eine Art Pavillon innerhalb eines wachsenden Universitätsbereiches dar. Der neue Campus unterscheidet sich deutlich von dem System miteinander verflochtener Wege und Höfe auf der anderen Seite des Flusses.
Der Lesesaal, der Raum für 300 Leser bietet und rund 3600 laufende Meter Regalfläche enthält, bildet einen Viertelkreis zwischen den beiden Flügeln des L-förmigen sechsgeschossigen Institutsgebäudes. Der Grundriß ist von dem des British Museum hergeleitet; wie bei den Bibliotheksplanungen des 19. Jahrhunderts wurde auch hier großer Wert auf die Kontrolle aller Bereiche gelegt. Zudem liegt der Aufsichtsplatz 1,20 m über dem Niveau des Lesesaals. Der Eindruck, überwacht zu werden, wird noch dadurch verstärkt, daß die Korridore der oberen Geschosse verglast sind und ständige Beobachtung von oben her ermöglichen.
Der Leser ist also exponiert, und auch die Einrichtungsgegenstände (die noch nicht vorhanden waren, als die Aufnahmen gemacht wurden) tragen keineswegs zu einem Gefühl der Abgeschlossenheit bei. In dieser Hinsicht unterscheidet sich die Bibliothek deutlich von anderen neueren Bauten mit ihren teppichbelegten, vielfach gegliederten und variablen Räumen. Die Tradition des großen Lesesaals als Zentralbereich wurde hier wieder aufgegriffen. Diese Lösung mag auch darauf zurückzuführen sein, daß die Bibliothek des Instituts gerade in jenen Jahren beträchtliche Verluste durch Diebstahl erlitten hatte, als der Entwurf den ersten Preis in einem beschränkten Wettbewerb erhielt (Ende 1963).
Obgleich nicht mit einer Erweiterung gerechnet wird, besteht die Möglichkeit, später Seminarräume in den Bibliotheksbereich einzubeziehen.
Die Innenräume des Gebäudes sind, soweit sie nicht verglast sind, mit weichen, schalldämmenden Materialien verkleidet: Korkböden, mit Schlitzen versehene schallabsorbierende Platten an Decken und Wänden. Die Außenflächen dagegen sind hart, glatt und spiegelnd: Glas und Ingenieurziegel. Bei künstlicher Beleuchtung senden die übereinandergestaffelten Glasflächen einen strahlenden Glanz aus.

Key to plans / Legende zu den Plänen:
1 Secretary / Sekretariat
2 Enquiries / Auskunft
3 Library offices / Bibliotheksverwaltung
4 Typing room / Schreibraum
5 Lecture room (can become expansion space for reading room) / Vorlesungssaal (kann zur Erweiterung des Lesesaals herangezogen werden)
6 Seminar rooms / Seminarräume
7 Reading area / Lesebereich
8 Stacks / Magazin
9 Staff entrance / Eingang für Bibliothekspersonal
10 Staff cloakrooms / Garderobe für Bibliothekspersonal
11 Student common room / Gemeinschaftsraum der Studenten
12 Tea counter / Teeausschank
13 Microfilm / Mikrofilme
14 Research room / Raum für Wissenschaftler
15 Faculty boardroom / Aufenthaltsraum für Fakultätsmitglieder
16 Student meeting room / Aufenthaltsraum für Studenten
17 Upper level stacks / Magazin (oberes Geschoß)
18 Staff common room / Gemeinschaftsraum des Personals
19 Tea counter / Teeausschank
20 Terrace to staff common room / Terrasse vor dem Gemeinschaftsraum des Personals
21 Seminar rooms / Seminarräume
22 Staff rooms / Arbeitsräume
23 Control desk including a console for the adjustment of heating, lighting and ventilation / Aufsichtsplatz mit Einrichtung für die Regulierung von Heizung, Lüftung und Beleuchtung
24 Catalogue / Katalog
25 Floor of reading room / Fußboden des Lesesaals
26 Bookstacks on two levels / Zweigeschossiges Magazin
27 Book lift / Bücheraufzug

1

1. West elevation; the top floors have small staff rooms and the building steps outwards away from the reading room on its lower floors to accommodate progressively bigger spaces; the solid surfaces are red brick and tile, behind the glass there are silver coloured venetian blinds.

1. Ansicht von Westen. In den Obergeschossen sind kleine Arbeitsräume untergebracht. In den unteren Geschossen vor dem Lesesaal verbreitert sich das Gebäude, so daß die Räume nach unten zu an Tiefe zunehmen. Die geschlossenen Flächen bestehen aus rotem Ziegel; hinter der Verglasung sind silbrige Lamellenstores angebracht.

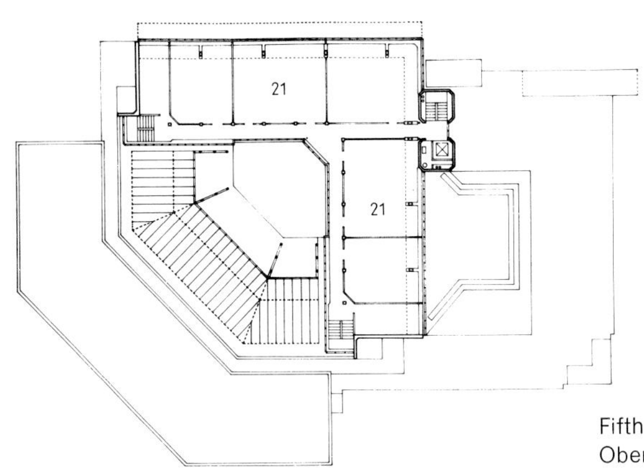


Third floor plan / Grundriß drittes Obergeschoß.

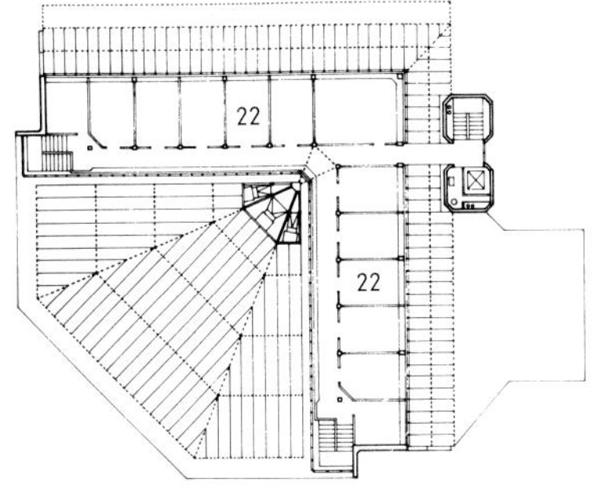


Fifth and sixth floor plan / Grundriß fünftes und sechstes Obergeschoß.

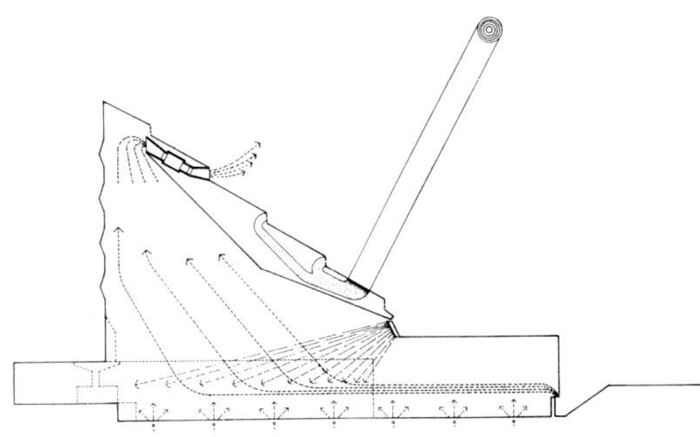

East-west section showing the heating and ventilating controls for the reading room; heating coils are embedded in the floor and radiator panels are placed at the junction of the glass roof with the ceiling over the book stacks; the space between the two skins of the glazed roof is naturally ventilated through adjustable glass louvres, the reading room is mechanically ventilated by three extract fans fitted with silencers and suspended in the apex of the roof.

Ost-West-Schnitt mit Heizungs- und Lüftungsschema des Lesesaals. In den Boden sind Heizspiralen eingelassen, und am Anschluß des Glasdaches mit der Decke des Magazins sind Radiatoren angebracht. Der Raum zwischen Innen- und Außenhaut des verglasten Daches wird durch verstellbare Glaslamellen natürlich belüftet. Für die Lüftung des Lesesaals sorgen drei geräuscharme Ventilatoren, die im Scheitelpunkt des Daches aufgehängt sind.

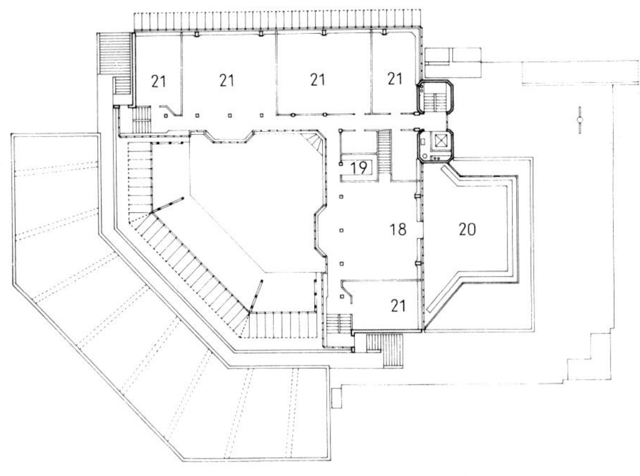


Second floor plan / Grundriß zweites Obergeschoß.

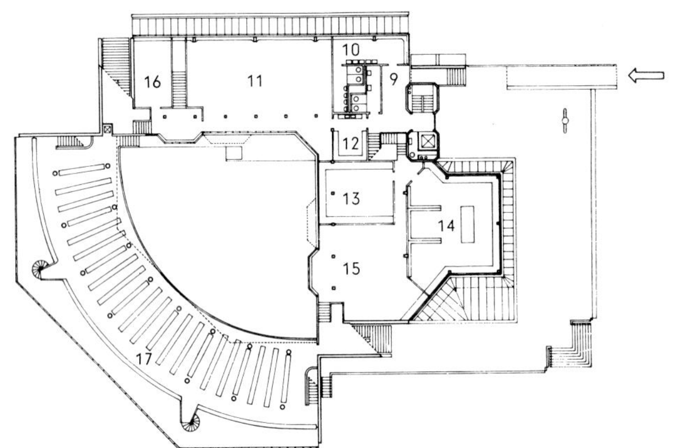


First floor plan / Grundriß erstes Obergeschoß.

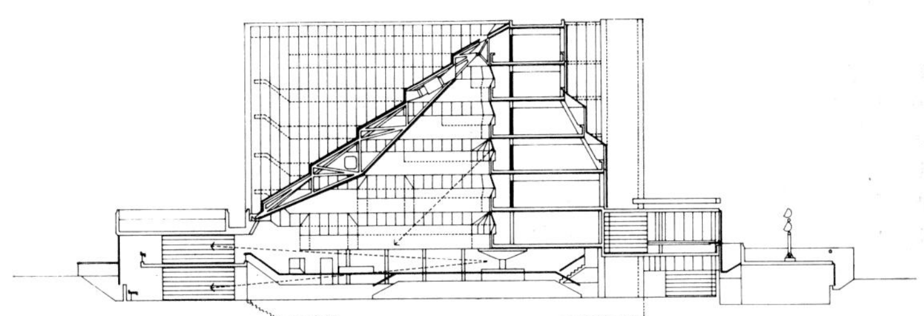

North-south section / Nord-Süd-Schnitt.

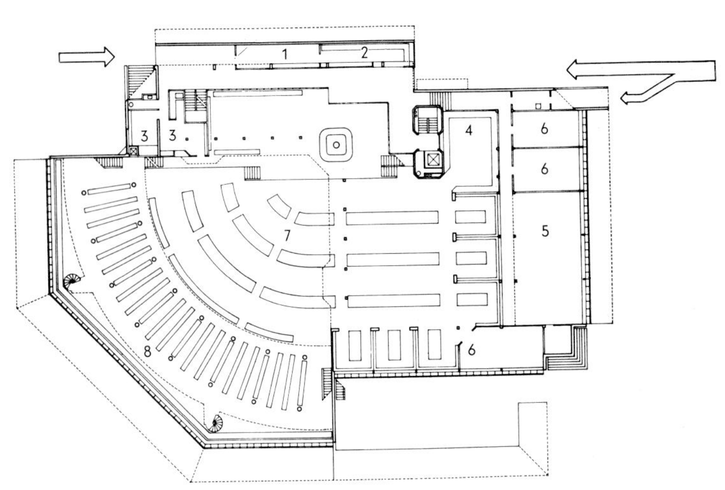


Ground floor plan / Grundriß Erdgeschoß.

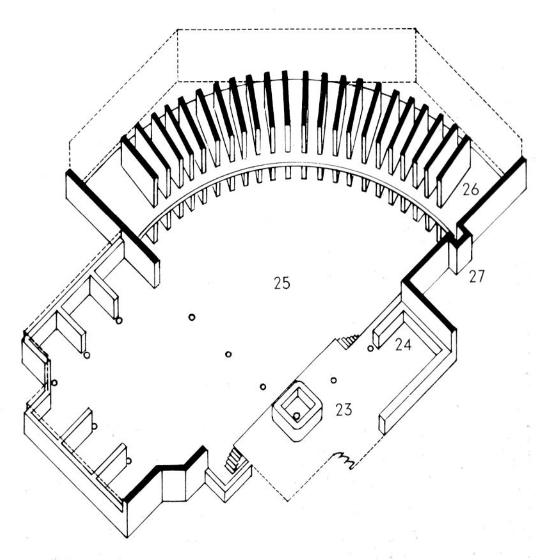


Axonometric of the reading room / Isometrie des Lesesaals.

2

2. East elevation; the two-storey book stacks are in the projecting portion on the left; the sloping glazed roof of the reading room rises behind between the two wings of seminar and staff rooms; the sloping concrete paving in the foreground screens a bicycle enclosure.

2. Ansicht von Osten. Das zwei Geschosse hohe Magazin ist in dem vorspringenden Teil links untergebracht. Das schräg auskragende Glasdach des Lesesaals erhebt sich dahinter zwischen den beiden Flügeln mit Seminar- und Arbeitsräumen. Die angeböschte, mit Betonplatten abgedeckte Fläche im Vordergrund schirmt einen Fahrradunterstand ab.

3. The control desk, catalogue and entrance area at ground floor level which is four feet (1,20 m) above the reading room floor; the projecting window in the middle distance at first floor level belongs to the Librarian's office.
4. The two inner walls of the reading room are formed by the glazed corridors leading to teaching and staff rooms, the projecting windows being small lay-bys off those corridors for students waiting to go into seminars; the walls are structural upstands covered in panels of fibrous plaster with glass quilt behind the slots.

3. Aufsicht, Katalog und Eingangsbereich auf Erdgeschoß-Niveau, das 1,20 m über dem des Lesesaals liegt. Das auskragende Fenster im Hintergrund oben gehört zum Büro des Bibliothekars im ersten Obergeschoß.
4. Verglaste Korridore, die zu Seminar- und Arbeitsräumen führen, bilden die beiden Wände des Lesesaals. Die auskragenden Fenster sind Nischen an den Korridoren, in denen die Studenten auf den Beginn des Seminars warten können. Die Brüstungen vor den tragenden Stützen sind mit Gipsfaserplatten verkleidet und mit Glaswolle hinter den Schlitzen isoliert.

3

4

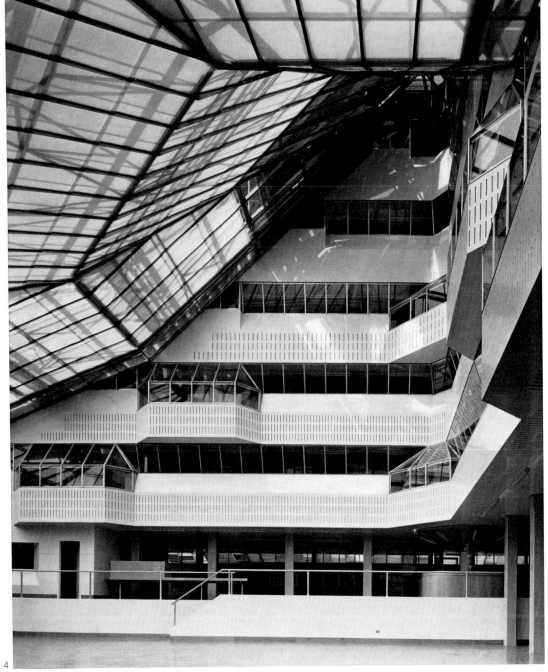

5. The reading room and the two floors of radial bookstacks; the steel roof structure has an outer and an inner skin and catwalks exist between these allowing cleaning and maintenance, particularly of the fluorescent tubes fixed to the underside of the major trusses; the layer of vinyl between glass skins acts as a diffuser to both natural and artificial light.
6. There are three axial flow fans in the top of the roof extracting air from the reading room; the fans are painted red, blue and yellow.

5. Der Lesesaal und das zwei Geschosse hohe radial angeordnete Magazin. Zwischen der inneren und der äußeren Haut der stählernen Dachkonstruktion liegen Laufstege, die Reinigung und Reparatur vor allem der Leuchtröhren ermöglichen, die an der Unterseite der Hauptträger befestigt sind. Die Vinylzwischenschicht der Glasdecke wirkt sowohl bei Tageslicht wie bei künstlicher Beleuchtung lichtstreuend.
6. Drei Axialventilatoren auf dem Dach, die rot, blau und gelb angestrichen sind, sorgen für die Entlüftung des Lesesaals.

5

6

**Library Group, University of Oxford, 1964**

Architects: Sir Leslie Martin in association with Colin St. John Wilson

This building, completed in 1964, brings together three university libraries and their associated rooms which are also able to share certain facilities. Each section has as its node a square double height and top-lit reading room clearly recognizable from the outside. The largest of the three sections is the Bodleian Law Library which is an open access reference collection of about 450,000 volumes. Next in size is the English Library which has a reference and loan collection of 84,000 volumes with a closed stack of 10,000 volumes. The smallest is the Institute of Statistics which is mainly a research organization with a loan and reference collection of only 50,000 volumes. The amount of ancillary space which is attached to each of these libraries varies a good deal.

Although the three libraries and their attached spaces form a single building of interlocked spaces, each of the three sections can be entered separately from a large external staircase. Though connected internally, each library can thus have its own front door. Within each library, the first plan for this group tried to establish a clear relationship between books, different kinds of readers, natural lighting and the routes needed for movement by using a grid of alternating small and large bays. Within each large bay 21 feet (6.30 m) square, there would have been an island of bookcases or tables for 25 undergraduate readers. This arrangement was related, in the case of the Law Library, to a catalogue and control area intermediate in level between the readers and the first floor of stacks and carrels. This would have made the catalogues equally accessible from the two main floors and would have separated the movement and disturbance which occurs around the catalogue and control zone from that given over to communication. As this is not a lending library the problem of trolleys manoeuvring half levels did not exist. This proposal would also, as the architects have since written, have had the advantage that "this segregation by structural groups, changes in floor-level and light control would establish a scale reduction sympathetic to the individual reader". The design was abandoned on the insistence of the librarian because it was thought that the view from the control desk was too obstructed for proper supervision. This conflict between the interests of the readers and those of the administrative staff of a library is often real and poses serious difficulties to the architect whose contact is as a rule only with half the people involved in the use of a library.

**Bibliothekskomplex der University of Oxford, 1964**

Architekten: Sir Leslie Martin in Zusammenarbeit mit Colin St. John Wilson

Dieses 1964 fertiggestellte Gebäude faßt drei Universitätsbibliotheken und die damit verbundenen Räume zusammen; somit können verschiedene Einrichtungen auch gemeinsam benutzt werden. Jede Abteilung hat als Kernzone einen quadratischen, zweigeschossigen Lesesaal mit Oberlicht, der sich von außen klar artikuliert. Die größte der drei Abteilungen ist die juristische Bodleian-Bibliothek, eine Präsenzbücherei mit etwa 450000 Bänden. Die zweitgrößte ist die English Library mit einer Präsenz- und Leihbücherei von 84000 Bänden; 10000 Bände befinden sich in einem geschlossenen Magazin. Die Bücherei des Instituts für Statistik, die in erster Linie zu Forschungsarbeiten dient, umfaßt lediglich 50000 Bände. Der Anteil an Nebenräumen variiert entsprechend.

Zwar bilden die drei Bibliotheken mit ihren zugeordneten Räumen ein einziges Gebäude mit ineinandergreifenden Räumen, doch hat jede Bücherei einen separaten Eingang, der an der großen Freitreppe liegt. So sind sie wohl im Inneren verbunden, haben aber doch ihren eigenen Zugang. Schon im ersten Entwurf für diesen Komplex wurde versucht, durch einen Wechsel kleiner und großer Raumeinheiten eine klare Beziehung zwischen den Büchern, den verschiedenen Gruppen von Lesern, einer natürlichen Beleuchtung und den notwendigen Verkehrswegen zu schaffen. In jeder großen Raumeinheit (6,30 × 6,30 m) sollte mit Regalen oder Tischen ein abgeschlossener Bereich für 25 Studierende der unteren Semester gebildet werden. Bei der juristischen Bücherei war zwischen dem Leseraum und dem ersten Geschoß mit Magazin und *carrels* noch ein Zwischengeschoß mit Katalogen und Kontrolle vorgesehen; damit wären die Kataloge von den beiden Hauptgeschossen gleicherweise zugänglich gewesen, und die im Kontroll- und Katalogbereich auftretenden Störungen hätten sich nicht auf die Lesezone ausgewirkt. Da es sich nicht um eine Leihbücherei handelte, wäre es zudem nicht notwendig gewesen, Bücherkarren ein halbes Geschoß nach oben oder unten zu transportieren.

Wie die Architekten inzwischen schrieben, hätte dieser Vorschlag im übrigen den Vorteil mit sich gebracht, daß »die Gliederung durch konstruktive Einheiten, Niveauwechsel und Lichtführung zu einer Reduzierung des Maßstabs geführt hätte, die für den einzelnen Leser nur angenehm wäre«. Auf den Einspruch des Bibliothekars hin wurde dieser Entwurf aufgegeben, da man annahm, daß Aufsicht und Kontrolle durch zu starke Sichtbehinderung erschwert würden. Ein solcher Konflikt zwischen den Interessen der Leser und denen der Bibliotheksverwaltung tritt häufig auf und stellt den Architekten, der in der Regel nur mit einer der beiden Gruppen in Berührung kommt, vor große Schwierigkeiten.

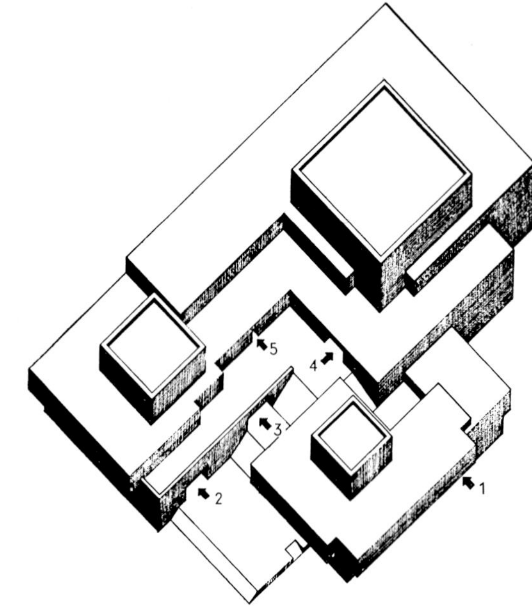


Axonometric showing the entrances to the various units.
Isometrie mit den Eingängen zu den verschiedenen Abteilungen.

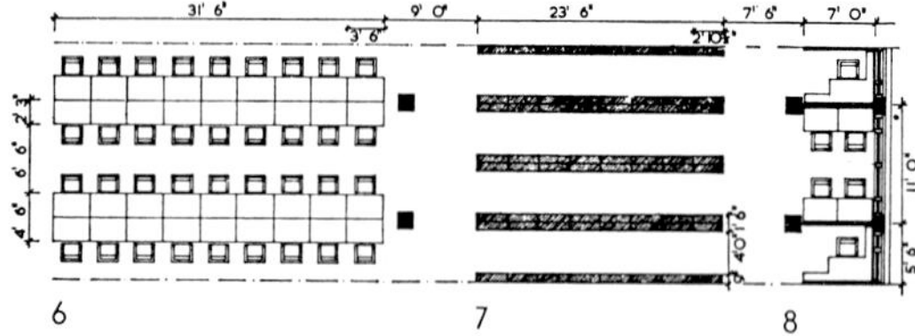


Basic diagram of readers, stacks and study carrels, and sizes on which the scheme was based.
Grundrißschema der Leseplätze, Regale und *carrels* mit den dem Entwurf zugrunde liegenden Maßeinheiten.

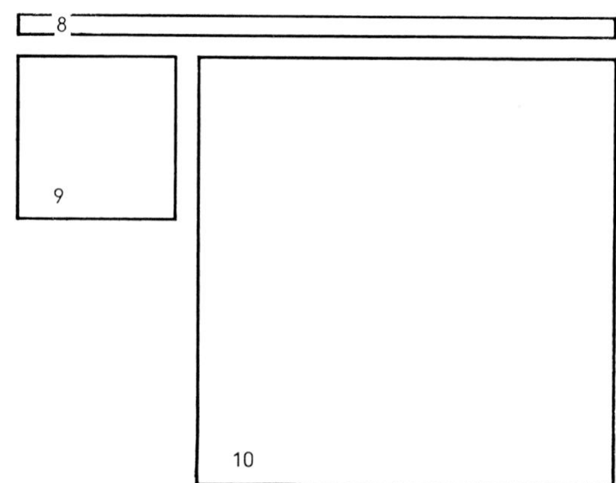


Diagram showing the relative areas of accommodation in the Law Library.
Schematische Darstellung des relativen Flächenbedarfs der einzelnen Bereiche in der juristischen Bibliothek.

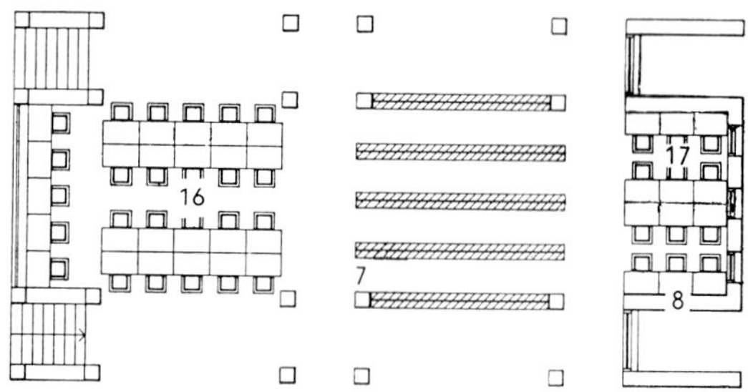


Diagram of the relationship of the reading bays to the open stacks and the study carrels. (Original proposal.)
Schematische Darstellung des Verhältnisses von Lesebereichen zum offenen Magazin und den *carrels*.

Section through the Law Library, showing the position of the elements, and the number of books stacked in the various levels. (Original proposal.)
Schnitt durch die juristische Bibliothek mit den Magazinen und der Zahl der Bücher, die in den verschiedenen Geschossen untergebracht sind. (Erster Entwurf.)

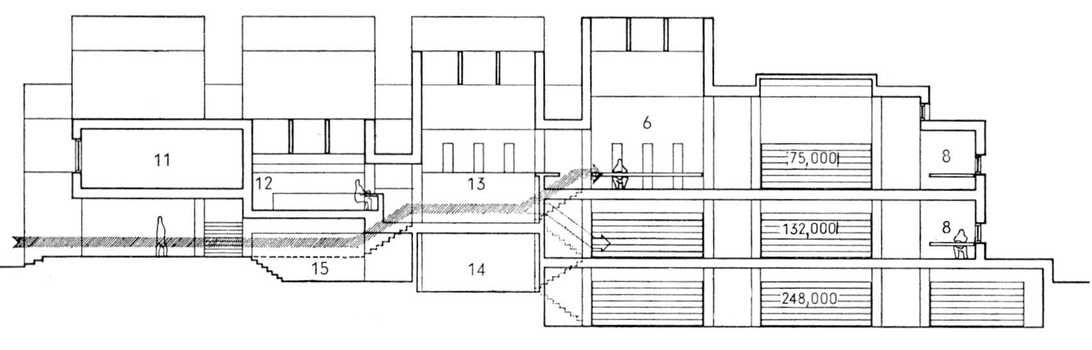

Page / Seite 104
Key to plans / Legende zu den Plänen:

1 Institute of Statistics / Institut für Statistik
2 English Library
3 Lecture hall / Vortragssaal
4 Law Library / Juristische Bibliothek
5 Common rooms / Gemeinschaftsräume
6 Readers / Leser
7 Stacks / Magazin
8 Carrels
9 Reading room, control, catalogue (80′ × 80′) / Leseraum, Kontrolle, Katalog (24 × 24 m)
10 Open stacks (200′ × 200′) / Offenes Magazin (60 × 60 m)
11 Librarian / Bibliothekar
12 Control / Kontrolle
13 Catalogue / Katalog
14 Seminar / Seminarraum
15 Cloaks / Garderobe
16 Undergraduate readers / Lesebereich für Studenten
17 Postgraduate readers / Lesebereich für Wissenschaftler

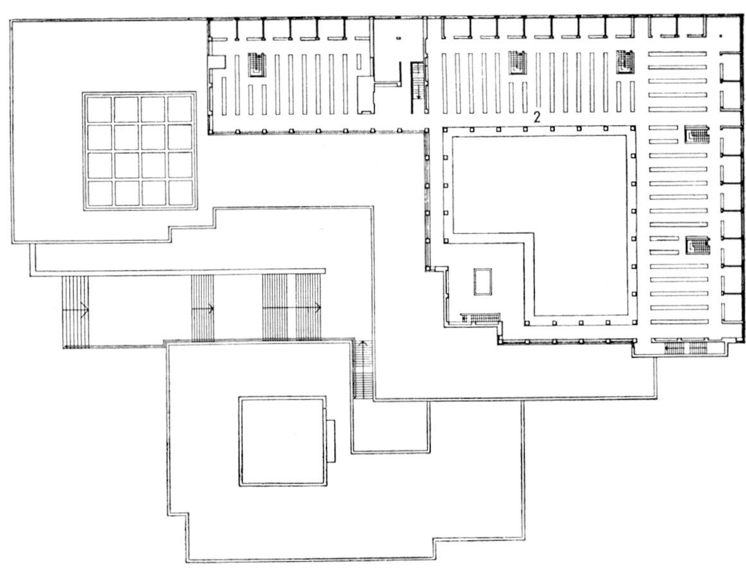

Third floor plan / Grundriß drittes Obergeschoß.

Page / Seite 105
Key to plans / Legende zu den Plänen:

1 Carrels
2 Law Library gallery / Galerie der juristischen Bibliothek
3 English Library gallery / Galerie der English Library
4 Stack / Magazin
5 Junior common room / Gemeinschaftsraum für Studenten
6 Kitchen / Küche
7 Senior common room / Gemeinschaftsraum für Lehrer
8 Workspace / Arbeitsraum
9 Microfilm / Mikrofilme
10 Law Library stack / Magazin der juristischen Bibliothek
11 Secretary / Sekretariat
12 Librarian / Bibliothekar
13 Entrance hall / Eingangshalle
14 Study / Studienraum
15 Seminar / Seminarraum
16 Cataloguing / Katalogabteilung
17 Reading room / Lesesaal
18 W.C.
19 Staff common room / Personalraum
20 Binding / Buchbinderei
21 Porter / Hausmeister
22 Statistics Library gallery / Galerie des Instituts für Statistik
23 Research room / Raum für wissenschaftliche Arbeiten
24 Courtyard / Hof
25 Director / Direktor
26 Office / Büro
27 Punched card / Lochkarten
28 Computing room / Computerraum
29 Lecture theatre / Vortragssaal
30 Lecture room / Vortragsraum
31 Plant room / Maschinenraum
32 Receiving and packing / Versand
33 Coffee / Kaffeebar
34 Statistics Library reading room / Leseraum des Instituts für Statistic
35 Janitor's flat / Hausmeisterwohnung

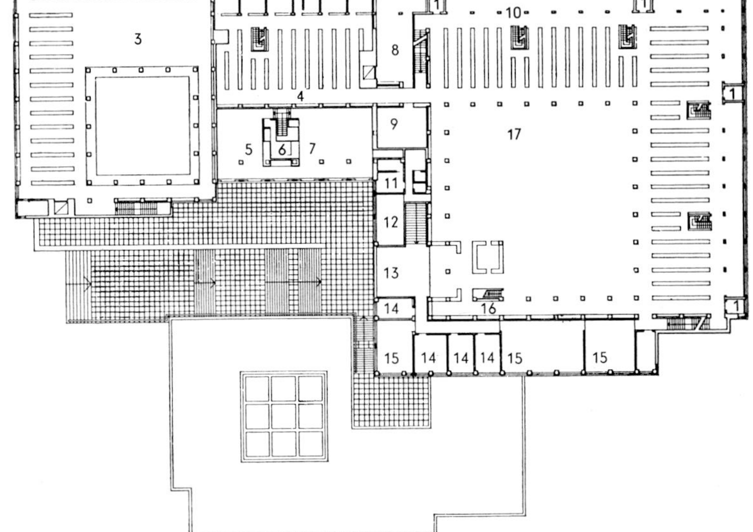

Second floor plan / Grundriß zweites Obergeschoß.

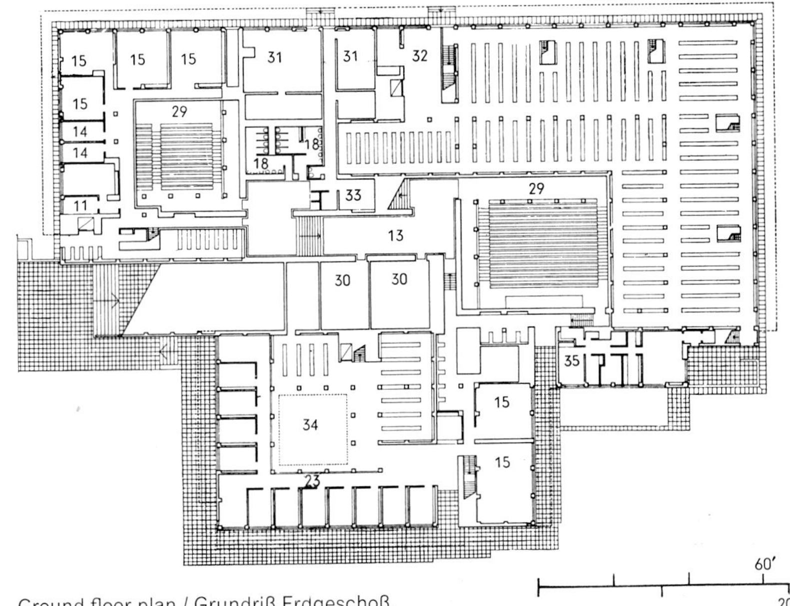


Ground floor plan / Grundriß Erdgeschoß.

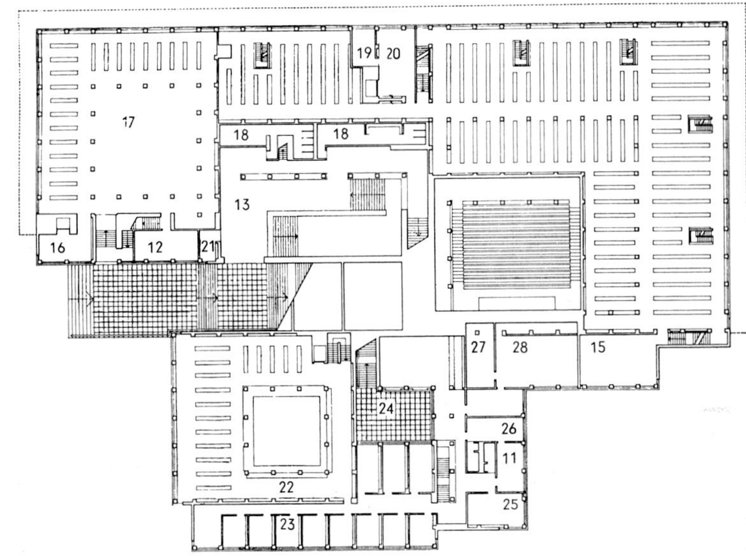

First floor plan / Grundriß erstes Obergeschoß.

1

1. The main staircase leading to the libraries, the lecture-hall and common rooms.
2. View from half-way up the stair across to the centre of Oxford.
3. The staircase seen from the side, with the entrance to the English Library from the first landing.
4. The reading room of the Statistics Library seen from the gallery.

1. Die Haupttreppe führt zu den Bibliotheken, dem Vortragssaal und den Gemeinschaftsräumen.
2. Blick von der Treppe auf das Zentrum von Oxford im Hintergrund.
3. Seitenansicht der Treppe. Der Eingang zur English Library liegt auf dem ersten Absatz.
4. Blick von der Galerie in den Lesesaal des Instituts für Statistik.

2

5. The reading room of the Law Library; a deep coffered roof diffuses natural lighting. ▷
6. Walnut reading tables and continuous brass light fittings given by a donor, and designed by the architects.
7. Catalogues in the Law Library; most of the furniture and panelling is in beech, the floor is cork tile.
8. Carrels in the Law Library shown with their doors open.

5. Der Lesesaal der juristischen Bibliothek. Die tiefe Kassettendecke streut das einfallende Tageslicht. ▷
6. Die Lesetische aus Walnuß und die durchgehenden Beleuchtungskörper aus Messing sind eine Stiftung und wurden von den Architekten entworfen.
7. Der Katalog der juristischen Abteilung. Einrichtungsgegenstände und Wandverkleidung sind aus Buche, der Boden ist mit Korkplatten belegt.
8. Blick durch die offenstehende Tür in einen *carrel* der juristischen Bibliothek.

3

4

5

6

7

8

## Library, Trinity College, Dublin, 1967

Architects: Ahrends, Burton & Koralek

The design of the library is the result of an international competition held in 1961. It continues the tradition of making quadrangles and starts to define a new set of spaces to the south of the 250 year-old library and the museum built in 1850. The existing library will continue to be used as a book store and to display the Book of Kells in its Long Room. It is linked to the new building below ground level. The roof of this link is made into a slightly raised forecourt which also visually joins the two old buildings with the new.

The basement of the library under the forecourt and the whole of the library is a 14 feet (4.20 m) high space which makes it possible to have a two tier stack. The area used at present for books has a capacity of 272,500 volumes and also includes tables for 70 readers. The remainder is temporarily taken over by lecture halls, study rooms and an exhibition hall. Ultimately the whole space will be able to take 829,000 volumes.

The ground floor has public rooms on the west side, administrative offices and staff rooms on the east side. The catalogue and bibliography area beyond the enquiry counter has a card catalogue with a capacity of 2,160,000 cards, shelves for 7,000–8,000 reference volumes and tables for 34 readers. Members of the general public also have access to this room.

The two top floors of the building are thought of as a set of linked double-height spaces lit by large sloping skylights. Within this volume there are rows of free standing tables, mainly under the two main groups of top lights and against the windows, and clusters of individual seating spaces which grow out of the concrete structure and appear part of it. The library as a whole has 469 reading places. The collection serves not only the university but is also one of three libraries in the British Isles which is entitled by statute to receive a free copy of every publication put out in the United Kingdom and in Eire. It is thus an important research centre.

## Bibliothek des Trinity College, Dublin, 1967

Architekten: Ahrends, Burton & Koralek

Der Entwurf für diese Bibliothek ging aus einem internationalen Wettbewerb im Jahre 1961 hervor. Er setzt die Tradition der Platzanlagen fort und schafft einen neuen architektonischen Schwerpunkt im Süden der 250 Jahre alten Bücherei und des Museums aus dem Jahre 1850. Die frühere Bibliothek wird jetzt als Buchhandlung benutzt und enthält einen Ausstellungsraum für das »Book of Kells«. Sie ist mit der neuen Bibliothek durch einen unterirdischen Gang verbunden. Die Decke dieses Verbindungsweges bildet einen leicht erhöhten Vorhof, der auch optisch die alten Bauten mit den neuen verbindet.

Das Untergeschoß unter dem Vorhof und die Obergeschosse sind 4,20 m hoch, so daß in den Magazinen doppelt hohe Regaleinheiten untergebracht werden können. Der augenblicklich als Magazin dienende Bereich bietet Platz für 272500 Bände und für 70 Leser. Der übrige Raum wird zur Zeit für Vortragssäle, Studienräume und einen Ausstellungssaal genutzt. Das Gebäude wird später insgesamt 829000 Bände aufnehmen können.

Auf der Westseite des Erdgeschosses liegen die Publikumsräume, auf der Ostseite die Verwaltung und die Personalräume. Im Katalog und der bibliographischen Abteilung hinter der Auskunft können 2160000 Karteikarten, Regale für 7000–8000 Nachschlagewerke und Tische für 34 Leser untergebracht werden. Diese Zone ist auch dem Publikum zugänglich.

Die zwei oberen Geschosse sind als zusammenhängende doppelgeschossige Bereiche konzipiert, die durch große, schräg gestellte Oberlichter belichtet werden. In diesen Räumen sind neben den Fenstern und unter den Oberlichtern frei stehende Tische angeordnet; die Einzelplätze sind in die Betonwände einbezogen und scheinen einen Teil der Konstruktion zu bilden. Die Bibliothek hat insgesamt 469 Plätze. Sie dient nicht nur als Universitätsbibliothek, sondern gehört auch zu den drei Bibliotheken auf den britischen Inseln, die einen gesetzlichen Anspruch auf ein Exemplar von jedem in England und Irland erscheinenden Buch haben. So ist sie zugleich ein bedeutendes Forschungszentrum.

1. The north side and the raised entrance forecourt.

1. Blick auf die Nordseite mit dem erhöhten Eingangshof.

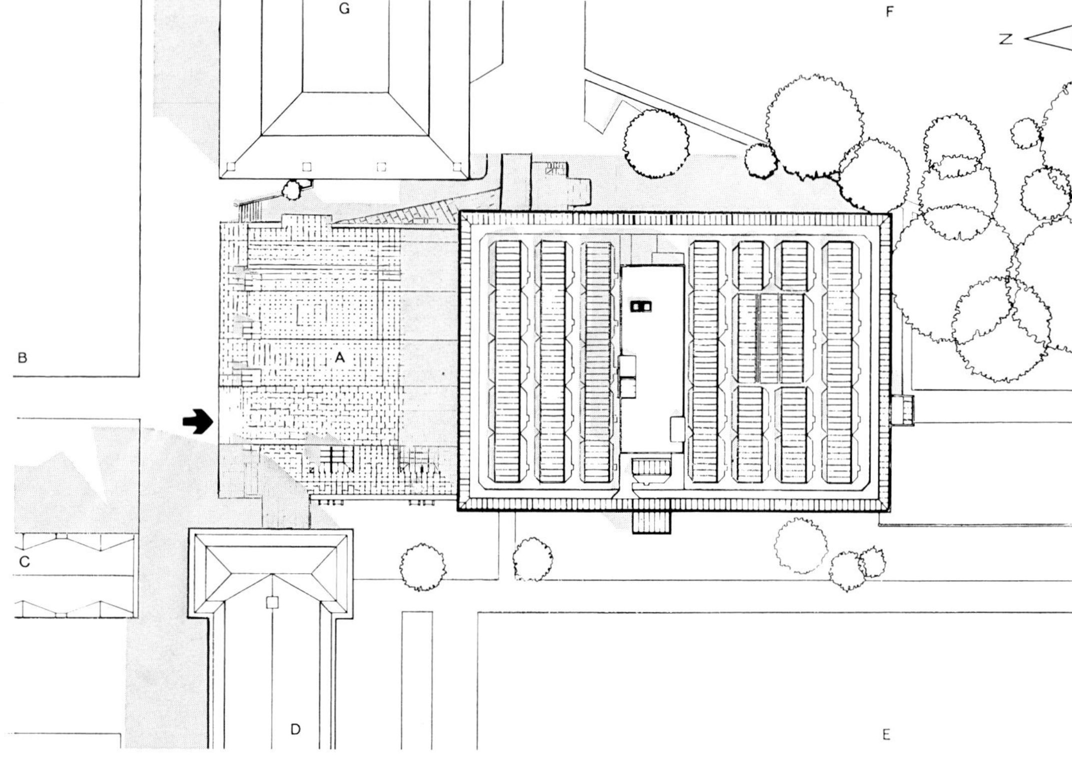


Site plan / Lageplan.
A Forecourt / Vorhof
B New square / Neuer Platz
C Rubrics / Registratur
D Old library / Frühere Bibliothek
E Fellows' garden / Garten für Dozenten
F College park / Park des College
G Museum

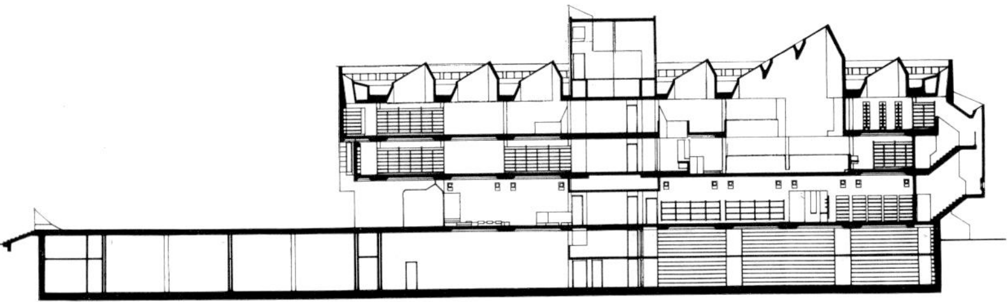

Longitudinal section / Längsschnitt.

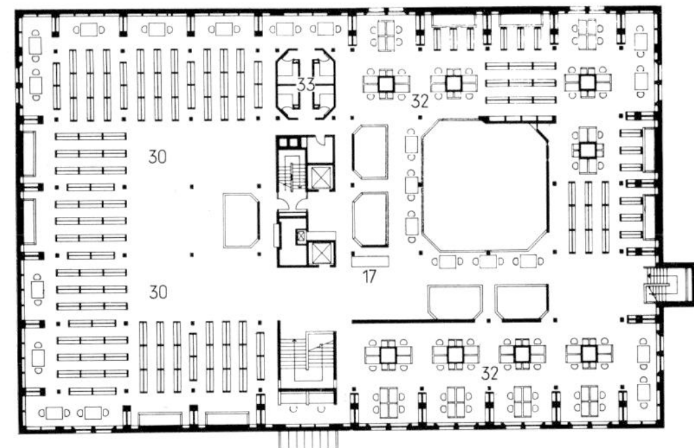

Second floor plan / Grundriß zweites Obergeschoß.

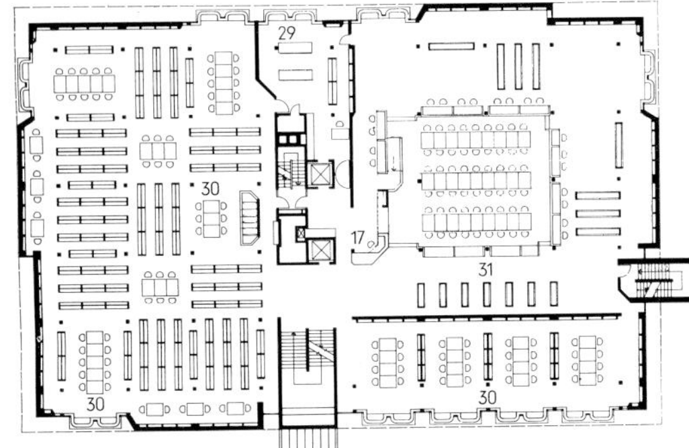

First floor plan / Grundriß erstes Obergeschoß.

Key to plans / Legende zu den Plänen:

1 Lecture rooms / Vortragssäle
2 Seminar rooms / Seminarräume
3 Teaching rooms / Unterrichtsräume
4 W.C.
5 Photographic department / Fotoabteilung
6 Banned book room / Raum für Bücher unter Verschluß
7–11 Heating, ventilation, electricity / Heizung, Lüftung, Strom
12 Oil tank / Öltank
13 Stacks / Magazin
14 Exhibition hall / Ausstellungshalle
15 Lecture rooms – void above / Lufträume über den Vortragssälen
16 Gallery / Galerie
17 Control desk / Kontrolle
18 Librarian / Bibliothekar
19 Conference room / Konferenzraum
20 Offices / Büros
21 Catalogue staff / Personal der Katalogabteilung
22 Catalogue and bibliography / Katalog und Bibliographie
23 Book arrival / Eingehende Bücher
24 Staff common room / Gemeinschaftsraum des Personals
25 Entrance hall / Eingangshalle
26 Dining room / Speiseraum
27 Kitchen / Küche
28 Coat room / Garderobe
29 Periodical binding room / Buchbinderei für Zeitschriften
30 Specialized reading areas / Lesebereiche für Spezialgebiete
31 Periodicals and general reading room / Allgemeiner Lesesaal und Zeitschriftenlesesaal
32 Carrels
33 Microtext cubicle / Kabinett für Mikrofilme

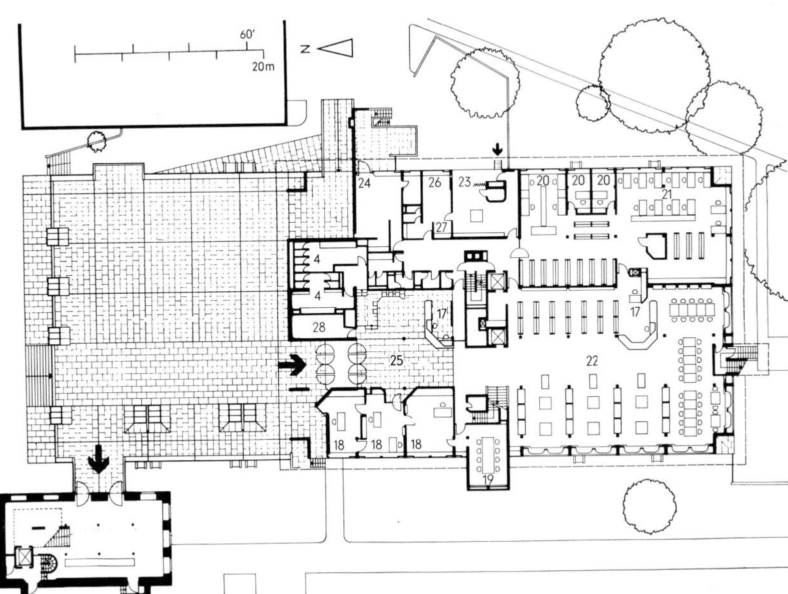



Ground floor plan / Grundriß Erdgeschoß.

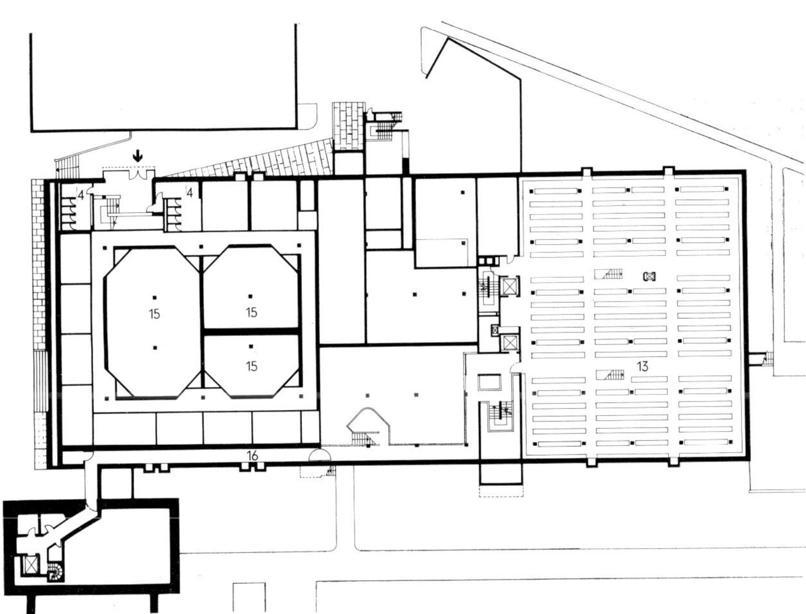

Upper basement floor plan / Grundriß erstes Untergeschoß.

Lower basement floor plan / Grundriß zweites Untergeschoß.

2

3

2. Curved plate glass windows; on the first floor, the projecting part becomes a window seat inside.
3. The west side; the upper part of the building is sheathed in bush-hammered slabs of grey Wicklow Granite.
4. The main entrance with a sculpture by Henry Moore; the lanterns light the basement stack.
5. The entrance hall and control desk; the grilles in the wall are the extract of the artificial ventilation system which has filtration and humidity control.

2. Die Fenster sind aus gebogenem Glas; im Obergeschoß bilden die Nischen im Inneren Fensterplätze.
3. Blick auf die Westseite. Der obere Teil des Gebäudes ist mit grauen Granitplatten verkleidet.
4. Der Haupteingang mit einer Plastik von Henry Moore; die Oberlichter belichten das Magazin im Untergeschoß.
5. Blick in die Eingangshalle mit dem Kontrolltisch. Die Wandauslässe gehören zu dem Belüftungssystem, das die Luft filtert und die Luftfeuchtigkeit kontrolliert.

4

5

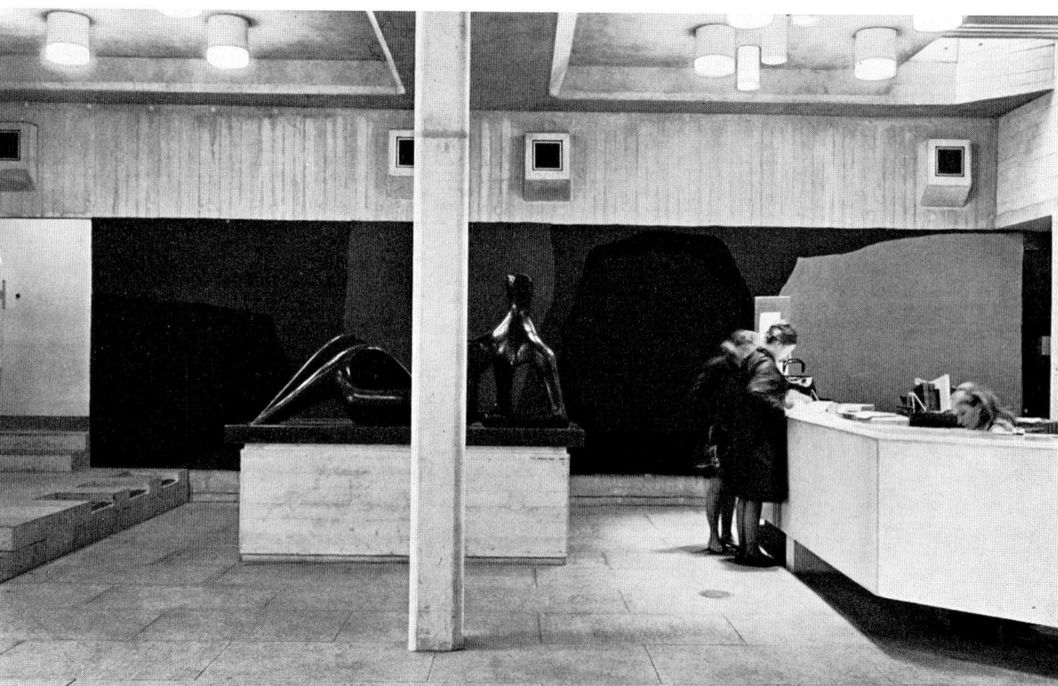

6

7

6. An individual reading space on the second floor consisting of shelf, desk, light and chair with the support and screen of the desk made as part of one of the permanent building elements; a similar sense of enclosure and indeed of permanence could have been obtained by treating the whole of the interior as a moulded and varied lining of an outer shell.
7. Reading tables and chairs in the main reading room; the tables are supported on a chromium plated steel framework which also carries individually switched fluorescent fittings; the floor is carpeted.
8. A reading area on the second floor separated from its adjacent space by a row of bookshelves.
9. Part of the main reading room which is a slightly sunk central area on the first floor.
10. Stacks and readers on the second floor; the stacks carry their own lights cantilevered from the top; the floor is ribbed rubber.

6. Ein Einzelplatz im zweiten Obergeschoß, der aus Regal, Tisch und Lampe besteht. Die Tischsockel und die Trennwände sind als zum Gebäude gehörende Elemente aufgefaßt und in die Betonwände einbezogen. Eine ähnliche Wirkung der Abgeschlossenheit wäre erreicht worden, wenn die Architekten den ganzen Innenraum als plastische Variation einer äußeren Hülle behandelt hätten.
7. Lesetische und Stühle im Hauptlesesaal; die Tische haben verchromte Untergestelle, an denen auch die Halterungen der Leuchtröhren befestigt sind. Der Fußboden ist mit Teppichen ausgelegt.
8. Ein Lesebereich im zweiten Obergeschoß, der durch Bücherregale von den anschließenden Räumen abgetrennt ist.
9. Blick in den tiefer liegenden Hauptlesesaal im Zentrum des ersten Obergeschosses.
10. Magazin und Lesebereich im zweiten Obergeschoß; die Regale erhalten künstliches Licht durch auskragende Leuchtröhren über den obersten Fächern. Der Fußboden ist mit geripptem Gummi ausgelegt.

8

9

10

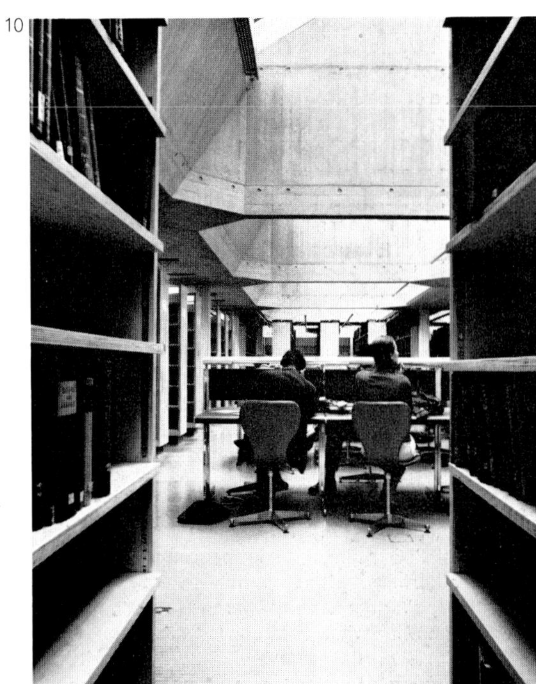

These are the great warehouses of any library system; though they are normally the apex of a national system, libraries of this kind may also be the central institution of a large university. Their attempt at comprehensiveness produces phenomenally large stocks: the Lenin library in Moscow had 23,000,000 units in 1966 and was acquiring approximately 1,100,000 further units each year, the Library of Congress in Washington had in the same year 43,500,000 items in the system as a whole, including manuscripts, maps, music, micro-films, prints, posters, etc., out of which about 7,000,000 books were housed in two buildings on Capitol Hill. Although other national and all university collections are smaller—the Bibliothèque Nationale in Paris and the Harvard library system each have over 6,000,000 books, for instance—they still deal with formidable numbers. The problems and crucial design considerations of these institutions arise from the size of the information store and its continuous expansion.

The location of a title from this accumulated store becomes a considerable undertaking dependent in the first instance on an efficient inventory system of the items available. National libraries are therefore greatly preoccupied with the preparation of usable and complete catalogues and the ability to keep these up-to-date. The size of such an undertaking can perhaps be gauged from the fact that the printed version of the British Museum General Catalogue of Printed Books which only lists part of the total collection, leaving out manuscripts, maps, periodicals, a great deal of oriental material etc., takes up 263 volumes.

Because of the complexity of this operation a good deal of work is under way to try and simplify as well as speed up this process by using some of the electronic technology now available. This may also reduce the cost of a very expensive task being done simultaneously in a large number of libraries. Frederick G. Kilgour of the Sterling Memorial Library at Yale University speaking at the Brasenose Conference on the Automation of Libraries in 1966 suggested that "the cost of cataloguing and reproducing bibliographic information in the United States today, some of it duplicate cataloguing, is very high. My particular estimate couldn't be got down below the bracket of 50 to 70 million dollars a year". Any moves in this direction might have serious repercussions on the kind of space needed for what is obviously one of the highly important operations in the cycle of use of a national library.

At present a card catalogue or a book catalogue as in the British Museum is consulted in order to find the call number of the item which is wanted. This number and title is transferred to a printed form which is given to a member of the staff, who then sends it to the appropriate section of the stack where another member of staff retrieves the book and despatches it to a central issue position from which the reader collects it or from which a messenger takes it to the reader's table. This process may take anything from twenty minutes to over one hour, and may in any case result only in a message saying the book is already out, is being bound or is for some other reason not available.

The procedure of location and retrieval is obviously cumbersome and time-consuming. There are mechanical means for speeding up certain sections of the process—sending the printed form with the call number to the stacks by pneumatic tube, delivering the book to the central issue desk by paternoster—which are analyzed on pages 128–146. Though they mechanize and speed up laborious movements otherwise having to be done by people, they do not radically alter the nature of the service. There is still no way of knowing whether a book is on the shelf or not, for example. Nor is the process of discovering which information source to look for by any means foolproof; even



National- und Universitätsbibliotheken sind die großen Lagerhäuser eines jeden Bibliothekssystems. Obwohl Bibliotheken dieses Umfangs gewöhnlich an der Spitze einer nationalen Hierarchie stehen, können sie auch die zentrale Institution einer großen Universität bilden. Ihr Bemühen um Vollständigkeit führt dazu, daß sie über riesige Bestände verfügen: Die Lenin-Bibliothek in Moskau besaß im Jahre 1966 etwa 23000000 Titel und erwirbt jedes Jahr 1100000 hinzu. Im gleichen Jahr hatte die Library of Congress in Washington insgesamt 43500000 Einheiten einschließlich Manuskripten, Landkarten, Noten, Mikrofilmen, Drucken, Plakaten und so weiter; etwa 7000000 Bücher sind in zwei Gebäuden am Capitol Hill untergebracht. Andere Nationalbibliotheken und alle Universitätssammlungen besitzen weniger Titel – die Bibliothèque Nationale in Paris und die Harvard-Bibliotheken verfügen über je 6000000 Bände –, doch handelt es sich immer noch um sehr ansehnliche Zahlen. So ergeben sich die organisatorischen und architektonischen Probleme dieser Institutionen aus der Menge der gespeicherten Information und ihrer ständigen Zunahme.

Die Ermittlung eines Titels aus diesem gespeicherten Vorrat wird zu einem schwierigen Unternehmen, dessen Erfolg in erster Linie davon abhängt, daß die verfügbaren Werke übersichtlich katalogisiert sind. Nationalbibliotheken verwenden deshalb große Mühe darauf, brauchbare und vollständige Kataloge herzustellen und sie auf dem laufenden zu halten. Wie umfangreich diese Aufgabe ist, mag die Tatsache beweisen, daß die gedruckte Ausgabe des General Catalogue of Printed Books im British Museum, die nur einen Teil der gesamten Sammlung aufführt und zum Beispiel Manuskripte, Landkarten, Zeitschriften oder orientalisches Material nicht berücksichtigt, 263 Bände umfaßt.

Um dieses komplizierte Verfahren zu vereinfachen und zu beschleunigen, werden Versuche unternommen, die heute verfügbaren elektronischen Hilfsmittel heranzuziehen. Dadurch lassen sich möglicherweise auch die hohen Kosten der Katalogisierungsarbeiten senken, die in vielen Bibliotheken gleichzeitig anfallen. Frederick G. Kilgour von der Sterling Memorial Library der Yale University sagte 1966 auf der Tagung über die Automation der Bibliotheken in Brasenose, daß »die Kosten für die Herstellung eines Katalogs, der manchmal sogar in doppelter Ausführung existiert, und für die Vervielfältigung bibliographischer Information in den Vereinigten Staaten heute außerordentlich hoch liegen. Ich kann meine eigene Schätzung nicht niedriger ansetzen als 50 bis 70 Millionen Dollar jährlich«. Jeder Fortschritt auf diesem Gebiet würde sich auch auf die architektonische Gestaltung des Katalogbereichs auswirken, des Bereichs also, in dem sich eine besonders wichtige Phase des Benutzungszyklus einer Nationalbibliothek abspielt.

Heute konsultiert der Leser einen Katalog in Kartei- oder in Buchform wie den des British Museum, um die Signatur des gewünschten Werkes ausfindig zu machen. Signatur und Titel überträgt er auf ein gedrucktes Formular, das er einem Bibliotheksangestellten überreicht; dieser schickt den Schein an die entsprechende Abteilung des Magazins; dort nimmt ein weiterer Bibliotheksangestellter das Buch aus dem Regal und sendet es an eine zentrale Ausgabestelle, wo der Leser es abholt, wenn nicht ein Bote es an seinen Tisch bringt. Dieses Verfahren nimmt mindestens zwanzig Minuten, meist aber mehr als eine Stunde in Anspruch, wobei das Ergebnis manchmal nur in der Mitteilung besteht, das Buch sei bereits ausgeliehen, befinde sich beim Buchbinder oder sei aus einem anderen Grunde nicht verfügbar.

Das Verfahren der Lokalisierung und Beschaffung ist jedenfalls höchst mühsam und zeitraubend. Zwar gibt es

if the title and author are known, one is after all trying to pick out one item among several million. Much more frequently in any case the title is not known and one is looking for an item of information rather than a specific and identified source in which it is known to exist. The use of electronic systems may change the nature of this process and lead to a simplification and certainly a greater chance of success in locating the source.

If computers to cope with this task are introduced to the library, they are likely to need specialized places in which it is possible to make a large number of electrical connections, either in a false floor or overhead, between the computer and its memory banks and possibly between a central computer and a number of separate consoles which present the information. Such a space will need to be air-conditioned and will thus be a highly serviced zone quite different from the catalogue hall found in most very large libraries.

Because of the size of the stacks in such buildings, these are as a rule of the closed access kind with only occasional permission granted to special users to roam freely. Reading areas are therefore separate from the storage, and the problem of providing an appropriate environment in which communication is to take place has to be solved without the aid of bookshelving acting as a screening device. All of this communication is likely to be within the building; it is very rare for books to go out on loan. Some of these very large libraries are however considering the possibility of having an open access arrangement for the most used part of their collection—perhaps as many as 500,000 volumes out of their total of seven or eight million—in which case reading areas rather like those in a research library could be planned. A decision on the relationship of warehouse to workshop areas of books and readers, and their ratio within the total plan is critical to the organization of the building and the mechanized movement systems within it. The efficiency of the vertical and horizontal mechanical book transporters in the design for the new library of the British Museum depends for example on a specific geometric arrangement of reading rooms placed over stacks and on the assumption that practically all readers will be in this upper zone.

In libraries of this size books are supplied on demand so that there is a more or less continuous one way movement from the stacks to the reading rooms. The return of the material is however usually made in bulk at the end of the day and may even be done by a separate system such as a motorized trolley. Despite the size of the store, the last cycle in the sequence of library operations is thus not a major problem. It is the first two, location and retrieval, which loom largest.

technische Hilfsmittel (vgl. Seiten 128–146), die einzelne Phasen des Vorgangs beschleunigen: Der Bestellzettel mit der Signatur wird per Rohrpost ins Magazin geschickt, oder das Buch wird mit dem Paternoster zur Ausgabestelle befördert. Aber wenn solche Installationen auch einige Aufgaben übernehmen, die sonst vom Personal erfüllt werden müssen, führen sie doch keine grundlegende Änderung herbei. Es gibt zum Beispiel noch keine technische Einrichtung, mit deren Hilfe sich feststellen ließe, ob sich ein Buch im Regal befindet oder nicht. Auch die Lokalisierung der Informationsquelle im Katalog ist keineswegs narrensicher; selbst wenn Titel und Autor bekannt sind, muß der Leser immerhin einen Titel unter mehreren Millionen herausfinden. Häufig ist ihm nicht einmal ein Titel bekannt, weil er sich über einen Sachzusammenhang informieren möchte und nicht nach einer bestimmten Quelle sucht, in der die von ihm benötigten Informationen enthalten sind. Hier können freilich elektronische Systeme das Verfahren vereinfachen und die Quellenermittlung erleichtern.

Wenn Computer in die Bibliothek eingeführt werden, brauchen sie Standorte, die dank doppelter Böden oder eingezogener Zwischendecken eine große Zahl elektrischer Kontakte zwischen dem Computer und seinen Informationsspeichern und möglicherweise zwischen einem zentralen Computer und einer Reihe gesonderter Informationszapfstellen erlauben. Ein solcher Bereich, der außerdem eine Klimaanlage benötigt, wäre eher eine mit differenzierten Installationen versehene technische Zone und gliche kaum noch dem traditionellen Katalogsaal der meisten großen Bibliotheken.

Der Umfang der Magazine in den National- und Universitätsbibliotheken bringt es mit sich, daß der Magazinbereich im allgemeinen nicht zugänglich ist und daß nur gelegentlich ein Benutzer die Erlaubnis erhält, sich dort umzusehen. Die Lesebereiche sind also vom Magazin getrennt. Es muß daher eine angemessene Umgebung für die Kommunikation geschaffen werden, ohne daß hier die Bücherregale als Trennelemente herangezogen werden können. Die Kommunikation findet in der Regel innerhalb des Gebäudes statt; nur selten werden Bücher ausgeliehen. Einige dieser großen Bibliotheken erwägen jedoch die Möglichkeit, den meistbenutzten Teil ihrer Sammlung in einer Freihandbücherei zugänglich zu machen – vielleicht etwa 500000 Bände aus ihrem Gesamtbestand von sieben oder acht Millionen Titeln. In diesem Fall könnten Lesebereiche geplant werden, die denen der kleinen wissenschaftlichen Bibliothek entsprechen. Für die Organisation des Gebäudes und die mechanischen Transportsysteme sind die Relationen zwischen Magazin und Lesebereichen und ihr Anteil an der Gesamtfläche ausschlaggebend. So hängt zum Beispiel die Funktionsfähigkeit der vertikalen und horizontalen Transportanlagen in dem Entwurf für die neue Bibliothek des British Museum von einer bestimmten geometrischen Anordnung der Lesesäle ab, die über dem Magazin liegen; Voraussetzung ist zugleich, daß praktisch alle Leser sich in dieser oberen Zone aufhalten.

In Bibliotheken dieser Größe werden Bücher auf Anforderung beschafft, so daß die Bücher mehr oder weniger kontinuierlich in einer Richtung vom Magazin zu den Leseräumen befördert werden. Die Rückgabe des Materials erfolgt gewöhnlich am Ende des Tages; in manchen Bibliotheken ist sogar ein eigenes Verkehrssystem – zum Beispiel motorisierte Förderwagen – für den Rücktransport ins Magazin vorgesehen. Trotz der Größe des Magazins stellt deshalb die letzte Phase im Benutzungszyklus kein besonderes Problem dar. Die eigentlichen Schwierigkeiten liegen in den beiden ersten Phasen, Lokalisierung und Beschaffung.

**New State Library, Berlin, begun 1967**

Architect: Hans Scharoun

The construction of the new State Library was started in the summer of 1967 and it can therefore still only be understood as a project rather than as a working library. Some of the assumptions behind the design are given in the following description by Edgar Wisniewski who has been associated with Professor Scharoun on the planning of this building.
The library is placed in what, due to the division of Berlin, now still seems a kind of no-man's-land peripheral to both centres. It is directly opposite the new National Gallery and close to the Philharmonic which it in some ways resembles both internally and externally. Whether the extreme fluidity of internal spaces which is so appropriate to the movement of concert-goers from entrance door to auditorium will be equally valid for the more static functions of reading and book storage still remains to be seen.

1

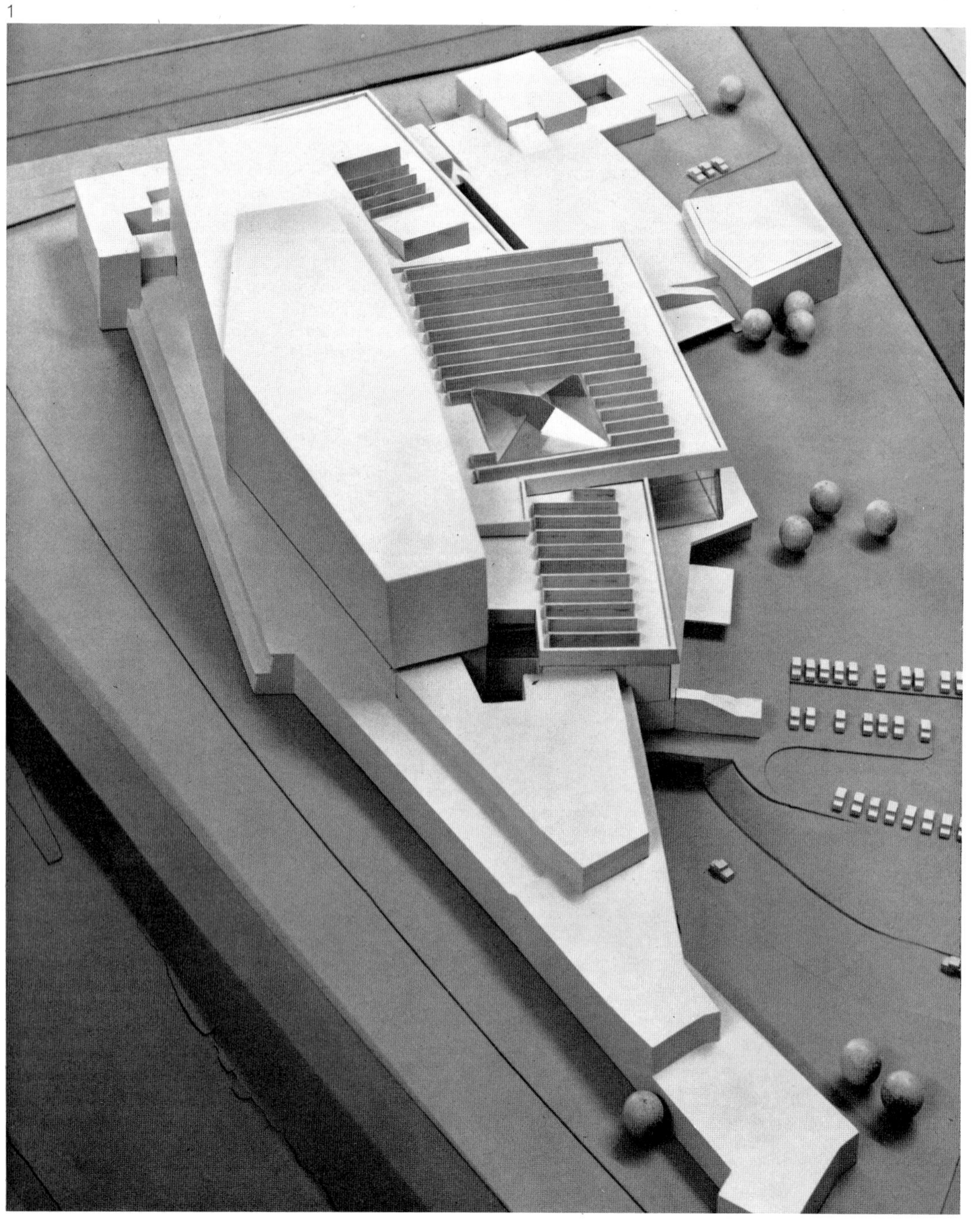

**The State Library**
by Edgar Wisniewski (from *Bauwelt* 41, Berlin 1967)

In common with the National Library in Paris and the Library of the British Museum, London, the State Library in Berlin is among the most important European libraries of national standing. Apart from the great number of new acquisitions, the particular value of such libraries lies in their old books, special collections and manuscripts. Because of the extensive number of books, these must be stored consecutively as they are acquired so that the stacks cannot be used by the reader. In selecting books, the reader must exclusively rely on catalogues, so that the proposed introduction of data processing equipment for library use should greatly facilitate the work. As far as information is concerned, printed and bound catalogues will be available, as it is ultimately intended to address title requests directly to the computer. But even the introduction of the printed catalogue is extremely costly and complicated, as it is first of all necessary to prepare the old books for computer storage.
The development, already discernible especially in America, towards an "open depository" applies to university or institutional libraries but is hardly suitable for the complicated structure of a national or state library. The State Library in Berlin is, for the time being, planned for a capacity of 4 million books. An extension to accommodate another 4 million books is envisaged and may already be needed within a foreseeable future. In contrast to the national libraries in Paris and London which are exclusively reference libraries, the Berlin State Library has to deal with numerous local and mail-despatch lending transactions.
The needs of the library and the urban setting gave rise to a linear layout plan. A core zone with the conveyor installations, lending counters, toilets and technical premises is flanked on either side by a traffic artery, leading to the librarians' working rooms on the east side and to the reading rooms on the west side. The traffic arteries are connected by the three staircases which are extended as main access corridors into the reading rooms. The vertical structure is formed by a core zone with conveyor installations which connect the six upper depositories and the two extensive underground depositories.

Premises open to the public

The State Library is linked with Berlin's traffic and transport network by the proposed West-Tangential Motorway and a new underground railway. Main access for road vehicles is from the new Potsdamer Strasse. A ramp leads to the delivery bays and to a deep-level garage which is connected with the entrance hall and the administrative section by stairs and lifts. Visitors, coming from the Potsdamer Strasse, enter the ground floor vestibule which contains the cloakrooms, a room for book displays, and the user catalogue. The local lending counter is placed in the core zone in the centre line of the building. For functional reasons, the mail-despatch lending office is also placed here. All the local lending transactions are handled on the ground floor near the check points. Included in the catalogue zone is the small bibliographical section with 5,000 volumes. For specific bibliographical questions, a larger collection with 25,000 volumes is available in the section not normally open to the public. For specialized questions, visitors are also able to see the subject librarians whose offices are situated on the west side of the first floor and which can be reached from the catalogue zone. The ground floor vestibule is also connected with the Ibero-American Institute and with a lecture room for 500 people.
After passing the check points, visitors reach the reading rooms by way of broad, ramp-like stairs which lead to the first floor concourse where three further stairs rise to the line of reading rooms. This concourse also serves as a recreation room where outstanding new acquisitions as well as daily papers are displayed. The concourse is also connected with a smoking lounge for 150 people, a milk bar, and a loggia on the east side of the building.
The stairs lead to the reading room concourse which gives

1. The model seen from the north; the Institute for Library Technology is in the foreground.

1. Modellansicht von Norden; im Vordergrund das Institut für Bibliothekstechnik.

## Neue Staatsbibliothek, Berlin, begonnen 1967

Architekt: Hans Scharoun

Mit dem Bau der neuen Staatsbibliothek wurde im Sommer 1967 begonnen. Über die Entwurfsvorstellungen berichtet im folgenden Edgar Wisniewski, der mit Hans Scharoun an der Planung der Bibliothek beteiligt war. Das Bibliotheksgebäude liegt in einer Art Niemandsland, das durch die Teilung Berlins zu beiden Seiten der Mauer entstanden ist, gegenüber der Neuen Nationalgalerie und in der Nähe der Philharmonie. Mit der Philharmonie hat es im Inneren wie im Äußeren eine gewisse Verwandtschaft. Ob allerdings die fließenden Raumfolgen, die den Konzertbesucher vom Eingang zum Konzertsaal leiten, sich auch bei den statischeren Funktionen des Lesens und der Aufbewahrung von Büchern bewähren, bleibt noch abzuwarten.

### Die Staatsbibliothek

von Edgar Wisniewski (aus *Bauwelt* 41, Berlin 1967)

Die Staatsbibliothek in Berlin gehört neben der Nationalbibliothek in Paris und der Bibliothek des Britischen Museums, London, zu den bedeutendsten europäischen Bibliotheken im Range einer Nationalbibliothek. Von besonderem Wert ist bei derartigen Bibliotheken neben der hohen Zahl der Neuerwerbungen der Altbestand, die Sondersammlungen und Handschriften. Der umfangreiche Gesamtbestand an Büchern zwingt zur Buchaufstellung nach dem Numerus currens (nach dem Zugang); die Magazine sind daher für den Leser nicht benutzbar. Da der Leser in der Auswahl der Bücher allein auf die Kataloge angewiesen ist, dürfte die geplante Einbeziehung der datenverarbeitenden Maschinen in den Bibliotheksbetrieb zu wesentlichen Erleichterungen führen. Im informativen Bereich werden gedruckte, gebundene Kataloge zur Verfügung stehen; das Endziel liegt in der direkten Titelanfrage an den Computer. Aber schon der Weg zum gedruckten Katalog ist äußerst kostspielig und kompliziert, da der Altbestand für den Computer erst speicherbar gemacht werden muß.
Die besonders in Amerika ablesbare Entwicklung zum »offenen Magazin« gilt für Universitäts- oder Institutsbibliotheken und ist für die komplizierte bibliothekarische Struktur der National- oder Staatsbibliothek kaum anwendbar. Die Staatsbibliothek in Berlin ist zunächst mit einer Kapazität von 4 Millionen Büchern geplant. Eine Erweiterung um weitere 4 Millionen Bücher ist vorgesehen und wird schon in absehbarer Zeit erforderlich werden. Im Gegensatz zu den Nationalbibliotheken in Paris und London, die reine Präsenzbibliotheken sind, hat die Staatsbibliothek in Berlin einen umfangreichen Orts- und Fernleihverkehr.
Die Aufgaben der Bibliothek und die städtebaulichen Gegebenheiten führten zu einer bandartigen Gebäudestruktur. Um die Kernzone mit den Fördereinrichtungen, Leihstellen, Toilettenanlagen und technischen Räumen ist beidseitig ein Verkehrsband gelegt, an das sich nach Osten die bibliothekarischen Arbeitsräume und nach Westen das Band der Lesesäle legen. Die Verkehrsbänder sind durch drei Treppenaufgänge miteinander verbunden, die sich als Erschließungsachsen in die Lesesäle fortsetzen. Die Vertikalstruktur entsteht wiederum durch die Kernzone, deren Fördereinrichtungen die sechs oberen Magazine und die zwei ausgedehnten unterirdischen Magazine verbinden.

#### Der öffentliche Bereich

Durch die geplante Westtangente und eine neue Untergrundbahnlinie wird die Staatsbibliothek an das Verkehrsnetz Berlins angeschlossen. Das Gebäude ist für den Kraftfahrzeugverkehr hauptsächlich von der neuen Potsdamer Straße erschlossen. Eine Rampenanlage führt zum Anlieferungsbereich und in die Tiefgarage, die durch eine Treppenanlage und Aufzüge mit der Eingangshalle und dem Verwaltungsteil verbunden wird. Die Besucher gelangen von der Potsdamer Straße in die Erdgeschoßhalle, in der sich die Garderoben, ein Raum für Buchausstellungen und der Benutzerkatalog befinden. An der Mittelachse des Hauses, der Kernzone, liegt die Ortsleihe und aus funktionellen Gründen auch die Fernleihe. Der gesamte Ortsleihverkehr wird im Erdgeschoß vor den Kontrollen abgewickelt. Zu dem Katalogbereich gehört der kleine bibliographische Apparat mit 5000 Bänden. Für spezielle bibliothekarische Fragen steht der große bibliographische Apparat mit 25000 Bänden im internen Bereich zur Verfügung. Auch sind die Sachreferenten, deren Räume an der Westseite im ersten Obergeschoß der Halle liegen, vom Katalogbereich aus für den Benutzer in speziellen Fragen erreichbar. Das Ibero-Amerikanische Institut und ein Vortragssaal mit 500 Plätzen haben mit der Erdgeschoßhalle Verbindung.
Der Besucher der Lesesäle gelangt nach Passieren der Kontrolle über breite rampenartige Treppen in das im ersten Obergeschoß liegende Umgangsfoyer, von dem drei Treppenanlagen zu dem Lesesaalband hinaufführen. Das Foyer dient außerdem als Raum der Muße zum Entspannen; hier liegen die wichtigsten Neuzugänge sowie Tageszeitungen aus. Ein Raucherraum mit 150 Plätzen und eine Milchbar sind vom Foyer aus erreichbar, und schließlich steht eine Loggia an der Ostseite des Gebäudes den Besuchern zur Verfügung.
Die Treppenanlagen führen auf den Lesesaalverteiler, von dem die Zugänge zu den verschiedenen Abteilungen der Lesesäle abzweigen. Die Abgänge zu den im Untergeschoß dem Lesesaal zugeordneten Räumen mit Schallplatten-Abhörkabinen und Mikrolese-Nischen sowie die Aufgänge zu den oberen Lesesaalplateaus beginnen an diesem etwa 140 m langen Lesesaalverteiler. Der Verteiler liegt direkt an der Kernzone mit den Aufzügen, Toiletten und Leihstellen; eine Gruppe Salons für Ausstellungen aus den Sammlungen der Staatsbibliothek oder aus bedeutenden Nachlässen ist ebenfalls nah am Verteilerweg vorgesehen. Über der Salongruppe liegt ein zentrales Aussichtsplateau mit weiteren Ausstellungsmöglichkeiten.
Die Mitte des Lesesaalbandes bildet der Allgemeine Lesesaal (600 Plätze), nördlich schließt der Zeitschriftenlesesaal (200 Plätze) mit der angrenzenden Zeitschriftenablage und südlich die Sonderlesesaalgruppe (ca. 300 Plätze) an. Der Allgemeine Lesesaal umfaßt die Abteilungen: Allgemeine Nachschlagewerke (80 Plätze), Geisteswissenschaften (150 Plätze) und Rechts- und Staatswissenschaften (170 Plätze), auf dem ersten der oberen Plateaus die Abteilung Medizin und Landwirtschaft (100 Plätze) und auf dem zweiten Plateau die Abteilung Technik (100 Plätze).
Das Hauptgeschoß des Allgemeinen Lesesaales ist durch kleine Niveauunterschiede, die den Größen der Abteilungen entsprechen, voneinander abgehoben und gegeneinander durch flache Brüstungen (Zuführungen der klimatisierten Luft), auf denen Pflanzen und Plastiken stehen können, gegliedert. Jeder Gruppe ist die entsprechende Präsenz (insgesamt 160000 Bände) und ein Ausgabepult für Bücher aus den Magazinen zugeordnet. Der Transport zu den Ausgabepulten erfolgt durch einen Strang der Kastenförderanlage, die unter dem Lesesaalboden entlang führt. Auch für die Abteilungen auf den Plateaus ist die entsprechende Präsenz und je eine Station der Kastenförderanlage vorgesehen. 36 Arbeits- und Diktaträume sind dem Allgemeinen Lesesaal auf verschiedenen Ebenen zugeordnet; vierzehn hängen unter dem Lesesaalboden raumgliedernd in den Katalogsaal hinein und sind durch Treppen vom Lesesaal zugängig. Wegen der großen Raumtiefe der Lesesäle (Allgemeiner Lesesaal 60 × 45 m) wurde für die Belichtung eine nach Norden gerichtete Sheddachkonstruktion gewählt. Unter den Sheds – eingebunden in die optische Decke – hängen kugelförmige Kunststoffkörper (Achsmaß 3,50 m), durch die das Tageslicht fällt oder durch die – bei Bedarf – Kunstlicht zugegeben werden kann. Die Decken der Lesesäle sind annähernd horizontal und entsprechen der ablesbaren einfachen Außenform; lediglich über den Plateaus kulminiert die Decke in gläsernen Pyramiden. Die Plateaus des Allgemeinen Lesesaales sind versetzt angeordnet, dadurch kann das Tageslicht von der gläsernen Pyramide durch große Ausschnitte in den Decks bis in die Buchausstellung im Erdgeschoß fallen.
Die Gesamtschau der Disziplinen und ein Maximum von Kommunikation liegen der Idee des Lesesaalbandes zugrunde; das ist im Räumlichen nachvollzogen. Natürlich muß in diesem 150 m langen Gesamtraum die Raumgliederung durch Gruppenbildung oder das individuelle Zurückziehen in Studierzellen möglich sein.
Die Information durch die Zeitschrift ist heute für die wissenschaftlich-technischen Gebiete von primärer Bedeutung, daher wurde besonderer Wert auf die unmittelbare Verbindung des Allgemeinen Lesesaales mit dem Zeitschriftenlesesaal gelegt: das Plateau mit der Abteilung Medizin und Landwirtschaft ist daher auch mit der Galerie des Zeitschriftenlesesaales direkt verbunden. Der südliche Abschnitt des Lesesaalbandes faßt die Sonderabteilungen Ost-, Südosteuropa, Orient, Ostasien, Musik und auf den zwei Plateaus die Karten- und Handschriftenabteilungen zusammen. Die Idee der »universitas literarum« drückt sich wohl besonders deutlich durch die Einbeziehung der Sonderlesesäle in das Lesesaalband aus. Nicht die Abgeschiedenheit in Kabinette und Säle, aber auch nicht die Zentralform eines kuppelgekrönten großen Lesesaales wird versucht, sondern die gleichberechtigte, im gegenseitigen Wechsel wirkende, einer Landschaft ähnelnde Lesesaalstruktur. In diesem 150 m langen fließenden Raum ist genügend Variabilität enthalten, wenn sich die Aufgaben der Bibliothek im Laufe der Zeit verändern. Das oberste Plateau des Allgemeinen Lesesaals ist mit dem ersten der sechs oberen Magazingeschosse räumlich verbunden. Es ist so die Möglichkeit für eine Lesesaalerweiterung, ein offenes Magazin oder für neue bibliothekarische Aufgaben gegeben.

#### Der interne Bereich

Das Band der bibliothekarischen Räume liegt vorwiegend auf der östlichen Seite der Kernzone. Die im Erdgeschoß befindlichen Abteilungen bearbeiten die Neuzugänge; es ist mit etwa 500 Neuzugängen (Monographien und Zeitschriften) pro Tag zu rechnen. Daher wurden großraumähnliche Raumzusammenhänge konzipiert. Die Reihenfolge der Räume entspricht dem Bearbeitungsvorgang; das Buch durchläuft die Räume von Nord nach Süd und gelangt schließlich – nach einer Kehre – über die Buchpaternoster in die Magazine. Der »Weg des Buches« beginnt in der unterirdischen Anlieferung, er führt weiter zur Poststelle im Erdgeschoß mit der Zugangssortierung, durchläuft die Akzessionen und den anschließenden Großraum der Katalogisierung. Das neu erworbene Buch wird von hier zur Einbandstelle und in die Hausbuchbinderei und schließlich nach der Schlußkontrolle in die Magazine befördert. Der zentrale Raum für die bibliothekarische Arbeit ist der etwa 100 m lange Katalogisierungsgroßraum, in dem der Verwaltungskatalog und der große bibliographische Apparat stehen; die Benutzungsabteilung und der Signierdienst befinden sich daher ebenfalls

2

access to the different reading room sections, to the associated record-listening and microfilm reading cabins on the lower level, and to the upper reading room levels. This concourse is about 140 metres long and directly adjacent to the core zone with the lifts, toilets and lending counters. Close-by are also a number of rooms for special displays from the library collections or from important bequests. Above this group of rooms is a central orientation platform with facilities for further displays.
The centre of the suite of reading rooms is formed by the general reading room (600 seats) which is flanked on the north side by the periodicals reading room (200 seats) and the adjacent periodicals depository and, on the south side, by a group of special reading rooms with approximately 300 seats.
The general reading room comprises the section for general reference books (80 seats), philosophy (150 seats) and juridical and political sciences (170 seats). On the first of the upper levels are the medical and agricultural sections (100 seats) and on the second level the technological section (100 seats).
The main floor of the general reading room is terraced by steps so that the individual sections are on slightly different levels, separated by low balustrades which also serve as air-conditioning ducts and as podia for plants and sculptures. Each section has its own reference collection (covering 160,000 volumes in all) and a desk for handing out books from the depositories. The books are conveyed to these desks by a branch of the box conveyor installation which runs along under the reading room floor. The sections on the upper levels are similarly equipped with a stock of reference books and a station of the box conveyor installation. Associated with the general reading room are 36 carrels for study and dictation, placed on different levels. Fourteen of them are suspended from the reading room floor, protruding into the void of the catalogue room below but accessible by stairs from the reading room. As the reading rooms have a great depth (the general reading room covers an area of 60 × 45 metres), a north-light roof structure has been chosen. Below this structure, flush with the false ceiling, globular plastic fittings are suspended at 3.50 metres intervals, admitting daylight or, alternatively, additional electric light. The reading room ceilings are approximately horizontal, in keeping with the simple, easily discernible outer shape. It is only above the upper levels that the ceiling culminates in glass pyramids. The upper levels of the general reading room are staggered so that the daylight entering through the glass pyramid can pass through large openings in the ceiling right down to the book display room on the ground floor. The concept of the suite of reading rooms, displaying all the disciplines and permitting a maximum of communications, is also reflected in the physical layout. But the very size of the 150 metres long hall calls for sectionalization and for the provision of small carrels for research workers.
Information disseminated by periodicals is today of primary importance to science and technology. That is why a special point has been made of providing direct connections between the general reading room and the periodicals reading room. For the same reason, the upper level with the medical and agricultural sections also has a direct connection with the gallery of the periodicals reading room. The special reading rooms at the southern end combine the specialized sections for Eastern Europe, South-East Europe, the Middle East and East Asia as well as the music section and, on the two upper levels, the maps and manuscripts sections. The inclusion of these special reading rooms in the suite of reading rooms is a particularly clear reflection of the concept of "universitas literarum". What is attempted is neither a fragmentation into small cabinets and library rooms nor, on the other hand, the concentration of all the facilities in a single, domed reading room, but rather a juxtaposition of equivalent, interacting sections in a kind of reading room landscape. This open-plan room of 150 metres length has sufficient flexibility to cope with any foreseeable changes of emphasis in the tasks of the library. The upper level of the general reading room is physically connected with the first of the six upper depository floors. In this way, the possibility of extending the reading room, providing an "open depository" or catering for new tasks has been kept open.

Premises not open to the public
The librarians' rooms are mainly concentrated on the east side of the core zone. The ground floor sections deal with new acquisitions which are expected to amount to some 500 items per day (including periodicals). This formidable task has led to the adoption of an "open plan". The premises are arranged to suit the handling of books which pass through the rooms from north to south and finally, after describing a U-turn, to the paternoster hoists leading to the depositories. The "way of the book" begins at the underground delivery bays, continues to the office for incoming mail on the ground floor where the new acquisitions are sorted, and passes through the accession section and the adjacent large cataloguing room. From here, the newly acquired book is taken to the bindery and finally, after a last check, to the depositories. The centre of all these activities is the cataloguing room of about 100 metres length which also contains the administrative catalogue and the large bibliographical section; the user and the marking sections are also placed here. The books are taken by three branches of the conveyor installation from the accession to the cataloguing zone which is composed of ten sub-sections, each headed by a specialized librarian. On the first floor is the accession section for periodicals with the comprehensive catalogue of foreign journals and periodicals. The depositories for the journals and periodicals extend over two storeys; the upper level is directly connected with the periodicals reading room.
Adjacent to the concourse are the rooms for special catalogues (location catalogues, comprehensive catalogues of foreign literature) which can also be reached from the public zone. In the south wing are the book restoring section, the Berlin Section and the workrooms of the music section. The core zone on the first floor contains the centre of the box conveyor installation. All the books intended for local or mail-despatch lending or for the five reading room counters pass through the sign-out point at this centre or are, on return, re-assigned to approximately 40 stations in the depositories.
On the second and third floor of the south wing, the offices and librarians' rooms of the special sections are adjacent to the reading room. The offices on the east side contain the sections for official publications and for the international exchange of publications as well as the documentation section; on the north side are the general offices.

Institutes
The Ibero-American Institute on the south-west side is affiliated to the State Library as a self-contained library with reading rooms and studies and with its own administration. This building is mainly confined to one storey and is terraced by steps which form a transition to the terracing of the State Library. A terrace with sculptures in front of this building is on the same level as the plinth of Mies van der Rohe's new National Gallery across the road. The Ibero-American Institute and the main complex of the State Library are separated by a patio which is surrounded by the Institute of Library Science where librarians are trained for further and advanced duties. The two storeys of this Institute provide accommodation for 180 students. Four lecture rooms as well as seminar rooms and work rooms are placed along the two-storey concourse; the lecture room of the State Library serves as the main hall. The north wing contains the Institute for Library Technology which is likewise affiliated to the State Library. This two-storey wing is designed to accommodate a large data processing plant which is mainly intended to be used for library functions and for the lending transactions of the State Library.

Depositories
The functional structure of the State Library calls for a horizontal rather than vertical spread of the depositories. As a first-stage programme, storage accommodation for

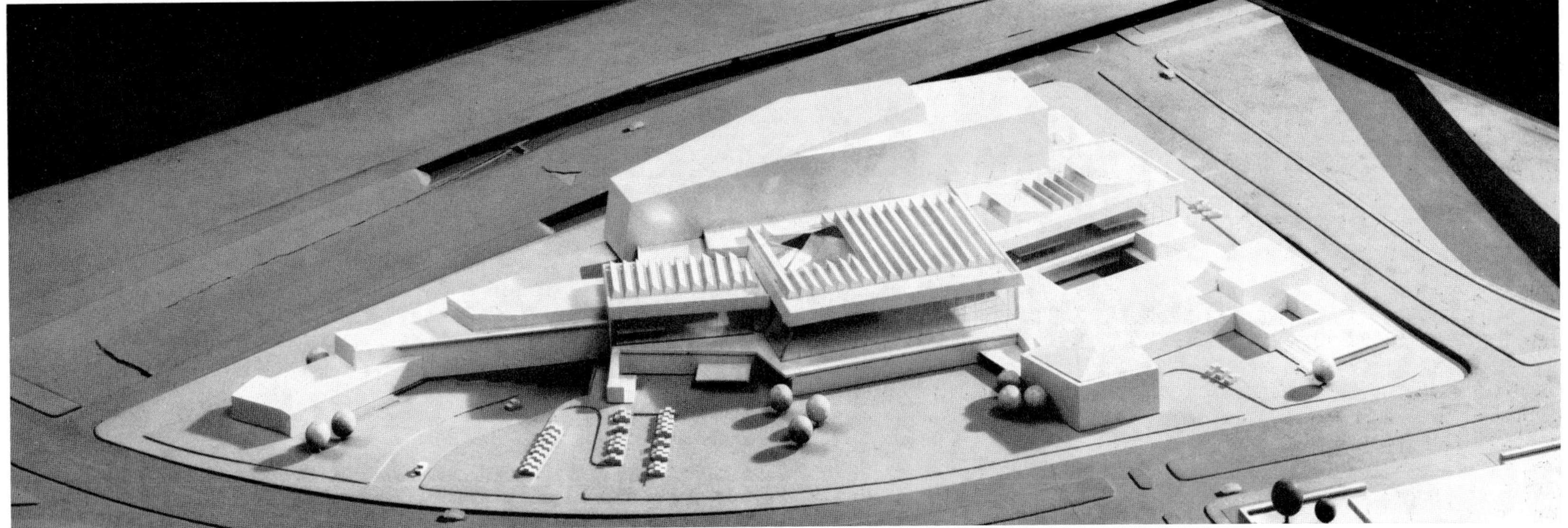

3

in dem Großraum. Drei Stränge der Kastenförderanlage führen die Bücher von der Akzession in den Katalogisierungsbereich, der sich aus zehn Arbeitsgruppen mit den vorgelagerten Sachreferenten-Arbeitsplätzen bildet. Im ersten Obergeschoß befinden sich die Räume der Zeitschriften-Akzession mit dem GAZS (Gesamtkatalog ausländischer Zeitschriften und Serien) und die auf zwei Geschosse verteilte Zeitschriften- und Serienablage, deren oberer Teil mit dem Zeitschriftenlesesaal in unmittelbarer Verbindung steht.
Neben dem Umgangsfoyer ist ein Raum für Spezialkataloge (Standortkataloge, Gesamtkatalog ausländischer Literatur) vom öffentlichen Bereich aus erreichbar. Der Südtrakt enthält die Buchrestaurierungsstelle, die Berlin-Abteilung und die Arbeitsräume der Musikabteilung.
In der Kernzone des ersten Obergeschosses liegt die Zentrale der Kastenförderanlage. Alle Bücher für die Orts- und Fernleihe oder die fünf Lesesaalausgaben passieren die Absignierstelle in der Zentrale oder werden beim Rücklauf von hier zu den etwa 40 Stationen der Magazine geleitet.
Im Südtrakt des zweiten und dritten Obergeschosses sind die Büros und bibliothekarischen Räume der Sonderabteilungen dem Lesesaal benachbart zugeordnet. Das Büroband an der Ostseite nimmt die Abteilungen Amtliche Druckschriften und Internationaler Schriftentausch sowie die Dokumentation auf; nach Norden schließt die Generalverwaltung an.

Die Institute
Das Ibero-Amerikanische Institut im Südwesten ist als selbständige Bibliothek mit Lese- und Studierräumen sowie einer eigenen bibliothekarischen Verwaltung der Staatsbibliothek zugeordnet. Das Gebäude ist vorwiegend eingeschossig und leitet stufenartig zu der Terrassierung der Staatsbibliothek über. Eine vorgelagerte Skulpturenterrasse nimmt die Sockelhöhe der jenseits der Straße liegenden Neuen Nationalgalerie von Mies van der Rohe auf.
Zwischen dem Ibero-Amerikanischen Institut und dem Komplex der Staatsbibliothek ist um einen Innengarten das bibliothekarische Lehrinstitut, zur Ausbildung des gehobenen und höheren bibliothekarischen Dienstes, gelegt. Es bietet in seiner zweigeschossigen Anlage für die Ausbildung von 180 Studierenden Platz. Vier Hörsäle sowie Seminar- und Arbeitsräume liegen an der zweigeschossigen Pausenhalle; als Auditorium Maximum kann der Vortragssaal der Staatsbibliothek benutzt werden. Im Nordbauteil ist das Institut für Bibliothekstechnik der Staatsbibliothek angegliedert. Das zweigeschossige Institut wird mit einer umfangreichen datenverarbeitenden Anlage geplant, die hauptsächlich für die bibliothekarischen Aufgaben und den Leihverkehr arbeiten soll.

Die Magazine
Für die bibliothekarische Struktur der Staatsbibliothek ist die Anordnung von Flächenmagazinen (im Gegensatz zum Magazinturm) die günstigste Lösung. Im ersten Bauabschnitt werden 25000 qm Magazinfläche für 4 Millionen Bände errichtet, von denen 18000 cbm in den oberen Magazingeschossen (4. bis 9. Obergeschoß) untergebracht werden; die restlichen Flächen sind in zwei Tiefgeschossen vorgesehen. Große Teile des 2. Bauabschnittes – mit nochmals 25000 qm Magazinfläche – werden zunächst provisorisch als Tiefgarage genutzt. Entsprechend dem Anwachsen der Bestände wird die Tiefgarage nach Einziehen einer Stahlzwischendecke zu einer zweigeschossigen Magazinerweiterung umgewandelt; die endgültige Tiefgarage wird dann außerhalb des Gebäudes liegen. Für die Konstruktion des oberen Magazintraktes ist eine deckentragende Regalkonstruktion vorgesehen.

Das Fördersystem
Neben einigen Buchaufzügen für Großformate ist eine umfangreiche Kastenförderanlage für den gesamten bibliothekarischen Betrieb projektiert. Die Möglichkeiten derartiger Anlagen haben revolutionär im Bibliothekswesen gewirkt, da die Zusammenlegung der Orts-, Saal- und Fernleihe, wie sie aus der Arbeitsweise der Flachförderbänder oder Aufzüge entstand, nicht mehr erforderlich ist. In großen Bibliotheken muß die Zusammenfassung der drei Leihen zu funktionellen Schwierigkeiten und in den anschließenden Lesesälen zu räumlichen Kompromissen führen. Die vorgesehene Anlage ermöglicht durch die Zieleinstellung am Kasten, alle 64 Stationen in der Staatsbibliothek miteinander korrespondieren zu lassen. Die kilometerlangen Bandstrecken sind durch drei Paternoster und andere automatische Hubvorrichtungen miteinander verbunden.
Eine Rohrpostanlage wird zunächst besonders für die Übermittlung der Leihscheine in die Magazine benötigt. Nach Einführung der Elektronik in den Bibliotheksbetrieb kann das Rohrpostnetz von diesen Aufgaben weitgehend entlastet werden.

Konstruktion und Bauausführung
Die Wahl der Konstruktion wird für das umfangreiche und vielgestaltige Bauwerk sehr unterschiedlich sein. Der hohe Grundwasserstand erfordert umfangreiche Wannengründungen für die unterirdischen Magazine. Aus dieser Wanne wachsen die plastisch gestalteten Treppentürme der Kernzone empor. Über diese Stahlbetonbauteile wird ein brückenartiges Konstruktionsgeschoß in etwa 20 m Höhe als Stahlbetonkonstruktion gestellt, an dem teilweise bis zu drei Geschosse aufgehängt sind. Von dem Brückengeschoß wird auch das Stahlbetonskelett der oberen Magazinhülle getragen, deren Deckeneinbauten als selbsttragende Regalkonstruktionen konstruiert sind. Auch im Bereich des Lesesaalbandes werden die Konstruktionen den funktionellen und architektonischen Intentionen entsprechen und gestaltgebend sein. So wird die Stahlbetonkonstruktion der Eingangs- und Kataloghalle die Terrassierung des Lesesaalbodens nachzeichnen und die Decke der Erdgeschoßhalle gliedern. Für die Decks in den Lesesälen, unter denen die Handbibliothek aufgestellt wird, werden flache Stahlkonstruktionen entwickelt. Die Sheddächer der Lesesäle sind als Spannbetonkonstruktion auf versetzbarer Schalung vorgesehen. Die Lasten werden über pylonartige Stützen abgetragen. Der Bau wird von Norden nach Süden ausgeführt; fertiggestellte Bauteile sollen baldmöglichst ausgebaut und der Nutzung zugeführt werden. Der umbaute Raum des gesamten Bauwerks ohne die zukünftige unterirdische Magazin- und Garagenerweiterung beträgt etwa 370000 cbm. Die Bauzeit ist mit vier bis fünf Jahren vorgesehen.

2, 3. The model from across the Potsdamer Strasse; Mies van der Rohe's National Gallery is on the right, the Tiergarten on the left; the new western tangential motorway is behind the library and rising at this point, a movement paralleled by the slope of the library roof.

2, 3. Ansicht des Modells von der anderen Seite der Potsdamer Straße; rechts Mies van der Rohes Nationalgalerie, links der Tiergarten. Die neue Westtangente ist hinter der Bibliothek höher gelegt, eine Bewegung, die von der Dachneigung des Gebäudes aufgenommen wird.

Site plan / Lageplan.
A State Library / Staatsbibliothek
B New National Gallery / Neue Nationalgalerie (Mies van der Rohe)
C Guest house / Gästehaus
D St. Matthew's Church / Matthäikirche
E West-Tangential Motorway / Westtangente
F Canal / Landwehrkanal
G Philharmonic Hall / Philharmonie (Hans Scharoun)
H Proposed Chamber Music Hall / Geplanter Kammermusiksaal
I Site of proposed museums / Standort der geplanten Museen
K Tiergarten

Ground floor plan / Grundriß Erdgeschoß.

4 million volumes, totalling 25,000 square metres, is being provided. Of these, 18,000 square metres are located on the upper depository floors (4th to 9th floor); the remainder are spread over two basements. Major parts of the proposed future depositories, designed to provide another 25,000 square metres of storage accommodation, are provisionally used as a deep-level garage. As the number of volumes grows, the deep-level garage will gradually be converted into a two-storey depository after insertion of an intermediate steel deck, and will eventually be replaced by one outside the building. The shelves of the upper depository floors are load-bearing.

Conveyor installation

In addition to some hoists for outsize books, the plans provide for an extensive box conveyor installation serving all the library sections. The facilities offered by such installations have had a revolutionary effect on library technology. In contrast to libraries relying on conveyor belts or on hoists, it is no longer necessary to combine the counters for local lending with those for reading room lending and mail despatch. In large libraries, the combination of these three types of lending points is bound to give rise to functional difficulties which lead, in the adjacent reading rooms, to the adoption of compromise layouts. With the installation here envisaged, it is possible to despatch boxes with books to any of the 64 stations in the State Library simply by setting a destination knob on the box. The conveyor sections extend over several kilometres and are interconnected by three paternoster hoists and other automatic lifting devices.
A pneumatic tube installation will, for the time being, mainly be needed for the conveyance of lending slips to the depositories. After the introduction of an electronic communication system, pneumatic tubes will become largely obsolete.

Engineering design and construction

The extensive and greatly varied building will call for a variety of structural designs. The high ground-water level necessitates tanked foundations for the underground depositories. Rising from these are the sculpturally treated staircases of the core zone. These reinforced concrete structures will be bridged at a level of about 20 meters by a steel floor from which up to three storeys are suspended. The steel bridge will also carry the steel structure for the outer walls of the upper floor depositories where the intermediate floors are designed as self-supporting shelf structures. The structure of the reading room suites will be similarly governed by functional and architectural considerations and will, in its turn, have an important bearing on the appearance. For instance, the reinforced concrete structure of the entrance and catalogue hall will match the terracing of the reading room floor and, at the same time, divide the void of the ground floor hall below. The reading room levels above the reference library consist of specially designed, flat steel structures. The north-light roofs of the reading room are pre-stressed concrete cast with movable formwork. The loads are transmitted through pylon-like columns.
The construction of the building is progressing from north to south and those parts already completed are to be equipped and used as soon as possible. The total enclosed space of the entire building, excluding the future underground extensions of depositories and garage, amounts to about 370,000 cubic metres. Construction will take four to five years.

Section A–A / Schnitt A–A.

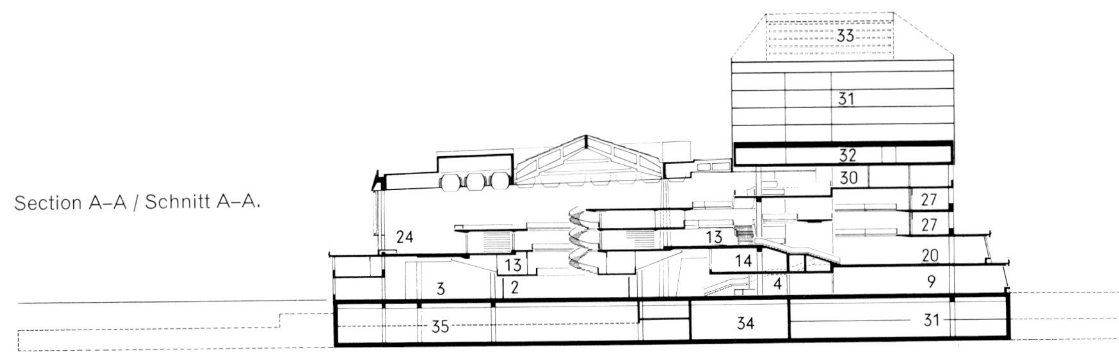


Key to plans / Legende zu den Plänen:

1 Main entrance / Haupteingang
2 Book display / Buchausstellung
3 Catalogue hall / Kataloghalle
4 Local and mail-despatch lending / Orts- und Fernleihe
5 Lecture room / Vortragssaal
6 Ibero-American Institute / Ibero-Amerikanisches Institut
7 Institute of Library Science / Bibliothekarisches Lehrinstitut
8 Binding / Buchbinderei
9 Cataloguing room and bibliographical section / Großraum für Katalogisierung und Signierdienst
10 Accession / Akzession
11 Incoming mail / Poststelle
12 Institute for Library Technology with data processing plant / Institut für Bibliothekstechnik mit datenverarbeitenden Anlagen
13 Research and dictation / Arbeits- und Diktaträume
14 Central station of book conveyor installation / Zentrale der Buchförderanlage
15 Specialized librarians / Referentenräume
16 Void above catalogue hall / Luftraum Kataloghalle
17 Microfilm reading / Raum für Mikrolesegeräte
18 Special sections / Sonderabteilungen
19 Special catalogue / Spezialkatalog
20 Foyer
21 Smoking lounge / Aufenthaltsraum für Raucher
22 Periodicals depository / Zeitschriftenablage
23 Periodicals reading room / Zeitschriftenlesesaal
24 General reading room / Allgemeiner Lesesaal
25 Reading room of special sections / Lesesaal der Sonderabteilungen
26 International exchange of publications / Internationaler Schriftenaustausch
27 Documentation / Dokumentation
28 General administration / Generalverwaltung
29 Display gallery / Ausstellungsempore
30 Rapid-access depository / Handmagazin
31 Stacks / Magazin
32 Manuscript stacks / Handschriftenmagazin
33 Ventilation fans / Lüfterzentrale
34 Air-conditioning plant / Klimazentrale
35 Deep-level garage / Tiefgarage

Fourth floor plan / Grundriß viertes Obergeschoß.

9 First floor plan / Grundriß erstes Obergeschoß.

Second floor plan / Grundriß zweites Obergeschoß.

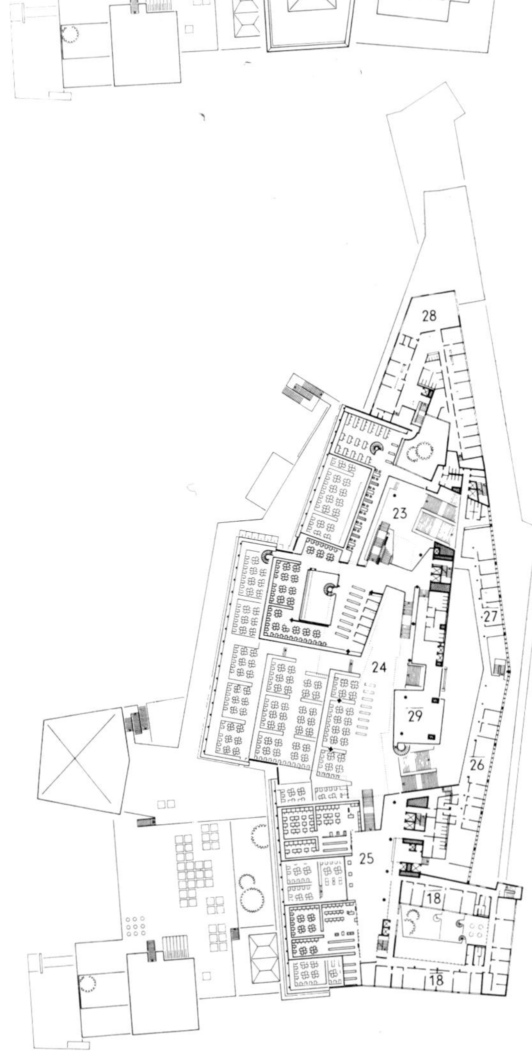

Third floor plan / Grundriß drittes Obergeschoß.

## The British Museum Library, London

Architects: Sir Leslie Martin, Colin St. John Wilson

The British Museum library is in all but official designation the National Library of Great Britain. The bulk of its space is at present in the central area of the British Museum complex occupying what was in fact a courtyard until Sydney Smirke, Sir Robert Smirke's younger brother, inserted the circular reading room and its adjacent stacks between 1854–56. The library consists of 4 museum departments: Printed Books, Manuscripts, Oriental Printed Books and Manuscripts, and Prints and Drawings. Among these Printed Books is by far the largest.
Like all libraries, that of the British Museum is growing rapidly and needs a great deal of space if it is to function efficiently in the foreseeable future. In order to discover its likely space needs and to find a possible organization for these, the Trustees of the Museum commissioned a study in 1962. The result of this study which is not a design for a building, but only an indication of a possible disposition, is illustrated here.
The site is immediately to the south of the present Museum and had been allocated for such a use in the County of London Plan of 1951. The plan was approved by the government in 1955 and the proposals for the library had governmental approval in principle in 1964. Since then, however, a subsequent government has decided to withdraw its agreement to the use of the site and the problem of the future function of a National Library is being studied by a government-appointed committee.
The organization of the library is based on a vertical division between four upper levels of reading area and seven lower levels of stack, four of these being below ground level. It is thus possible to arrange each sub-library and its bookstorage area as a vertical sequence of floors linked to its own offices on the perimeter wall above ground level. The Department of Printed Books and the General Reading Room are square on plan and are surrounded on two sides by the departmental libraries, each containing its own control and information point, reading room, stacks, offices and service rooms. Although this individuality of the departments exists on section, each floor level contains roughly similar activities so that horizontal linkages are simple and obvious.
This is particularly important at the main floor level where the catalogue hall, facing the entrance and in one corner of the General Reading Room is also near the entrances to the departmental reading rooms. This floor is reached by two banks of escalators from ground level. Directly related to this entrance, and accessible without going through any control point, is a public reference library taking up a square in the corner of the two L-shaped wings surrounding the main reading space.
Each of the seven reading rooms is made up of a principal reading area at the main floor level, level 111.00, and reading terraces above this floor stepping back to reveal a glazed roof straddling the whole of the upper space. Personal isolation would be achieved, as in the present British Museum Reading Room, by the creation of defined spaces made by furniture within a very large enclosure.
The building would have room for about 2,500 readers, half a million volumes on open access and 2,000,000 linear feet (609,000 m) of ordinary shelving in the stacks. If compact storage were to be used throughout in the latter area, 3,600,000 linear feet (1,100,000 m) of shelving could be provided. This would give a capacity of 25,200,000 standard volumes, or about 54,000,000 volumes of the kind normally coming to the British Museum Library. This represents more than seven times the present size of the collection. The book retrieval system would be fully mechanized and would use an adaptation of the Delft Bibliofoon (see pp. 142–144 for a description of the system) linked to a computer which would also immediately signal whether or not the title was available. There would be no abortive retrieval journeys by the library staff in the stacks.
The organization of the building is fully capable of dealing with the possible conversion of some of the information to microcopy or the eventual issue of material in microcopy form as the original method of publication. Such a change would naturally increase the storage capacity of the stack floors which however would still be capable of dealing with the present collection of books and those certainly to be published in the future and which, under legal arrangements, require to be deposited by their publishers and kept by the British Museum.
The assumption has also been made that the catalogue is extremely likely to take a form which would be dealt with by a computer, and that this would considerably affect the book retrieval system as well as the whole basis of recording accessions, issues and the possibility of preparing bibliographies. It is not thought likely that electronic data processing methods will, in the foreseeable future, deal with the whole of the past current information store and that even if these methods were to cope with part of the future store, the need to house a large and still continually increasing number of printed publications in their original form will remain.

## Bibliothek des British Museum, London

Architekten: Sir Leslie Martin, Colin St. John Wilson

Die Bibliothek des British Museum ist die inoffizielle Nationalbibliothek Großbritanniens. Sie ist zur Zeit noch überwiegend im Gebäudekomplex des British Museum untergebracht, wo Sydney Smirke, der jüngere Bruder Sir Robert Smirkes, 1854–56 in einem Hof des Museums den kreisförmigen Lesesaal und die Magazine errichtete. Die Bibliothek umfaßt vier Abteilungen: Bücher (die bei weitem umfangreichste Abteilung), Handschriften, orientalische Bücher und Handschriften sowie Druckgraphik und Zeichnungen.
Wie in allen Bibliotheken wächst auch in der des British Museum der Bücherbestand rapide und erfordert immer mehr Magazinflächen, wenn der Bibliotheksbetrieb in der nächsten Zukunft reibungslos funktionieren soll. Um den mutmaßlichen Raumbedarf festzustellen und gleichzeitig eine sinnvolle organisatorische Lösung zu finden, gab das British Museum 1962 eine Untersuchung in Auftrag. Das Ergebnis dieser Untersuchung, das nicht in einem Entwurf für ein Gebäude besteht, sondern nur dessen mögliche Disposition aufzeigt, wird hier dargestellt.
Das Bibliotheksgelände schließt unmittelbar südlich an das British Museum an und wurde im Bebauungsplan des County of London schon 1951 für diesen Zweck ausgewiesen. Der Plan wurde 1955 von der Regierung genehmigt, und die Vorschläge für die Bibliothek fanden 1964 die grundsätzliche Billigung des Parlaments. Nach dem Regierungswechsel wurde jedoch die Genehmigung für das vorgesehene Grundstück zurückgezogen, und zur Zeit ist ein von der Regierung ernannter Ausschuß damit beschäftigt, einen geeigneten Bauplatz für eine Nationalbibliothek zu suchen.
Die Organisation der Bibliothek beruht auf einer vertikalen Gliederung in vier obere Niveaus mit Lesebereichen und sieben untere Niveaus mit Magazinen, von denen vier unterhalb des Bodenniveaus liegen. Auf diese Weise läßt sich jede Abteilung und ihr dazugehöriges Magazin als vertikale Raumfolge anordnen, die mit den entsprechenden außenliegenden Büros über dem Erdgeschoßniveau in Verbindung steht. Die Abteilung für Bücher und der allgemeine Lesesaal sind im Grundriß quadratisch und grenzen auf zwei Seiten an die anderen Abteilungen, die jeweils Kontrolle und Auskunft, Lesesaal, Magazin, Büros und Nebenräume umfassen. Obwohl also die einzelnen Abteilungen in der vertikalen Gliederung ihre Individualität bewahren, nimmt jede Geschoßebene annähernd entsprechende Einrichtungen auf, so daß sich horizontale Verbindungen einfach und selbstverständlich herstellen. Das ist besonders im Hauptgeschoß von Bedeutung, wo der Katalogsaal in einer ausgesparten Ecke vor dem Eingang des allgemeinen Lesesaals und zugleich nahe bei den Eingängen zu den Lesesälen der einzelnen Abteilungen liegt. Dieses Geschoß ist vom Erdgeschoßniveau durch zwei Gruppen von Rolltreppen zu erreichen. In unmittelbarer Verbindung zum Eingang des allgemeinen Lesesaals ist im Winkel der beiden Flügel, die den Hauptbereich L-förmig umgeben, eine öffentliche, ohne Kontrolle zugängliche Handbibliothek untergebracht.
Jeder der sieben Lesesäle besteht aus einem Lesebereich auf dem Niveau des Hauptgeschosses (Niveau 111,00) und Leseterrassen oberhalb dieses Geschosses, die zurücktreten und den Blick auf das verglaste Dach freigeben, das den gesamten oberen Raumteil überspannt. Wie im jetzigen Lesesaal des British Museum sollen durch die Möblierung des riesigen Gesamtraumes abgeschlossene Arbeitszonen geschaffen werden.
Das Gebäude bietet Raum für ungefähr 2500 Leser, 500000 frei zugängliche Bände und 609000 m Regalfläche im Magazin. Wenn in den Magazinen raumsparende Regalsysteme verwendet werden, können sogar 1100000 m Regalfläche untergebracht werden. Damit wäre eine Kapazität von 25200000 Standardbänden oder etwa 54000000 Bänden des Formats, wie sie üblicherweise im British Museum eingehen, zu erzielen, so daß insgesamt mehr als siebenmal soviel Bücher Platz fänden als in der jetzigen Bibliothek. Die Ausleihe soll vollautomatisch vor sich gehen und mit einer dem Delfter Bibliofoon (vgl. Seiten 142–144) ähnlichen Einrichtung ausgestattet werden, die mit einem Computer gekoppelt ist und dem Benutzer mitteilt, ob ein Titel verfügbar ist oder nicht.
Die Organisation der Bibliothek ermöglicht außerdem die Umwandlung eines Teils der Information in Mikrokopien oder auch eine spätere Originalpublikation in Form von Mikrokopien. Dadurch würde natürlich die Kapazität der Magazine gesteigert, so daß die Bibliothek außer dem gegenwärtigen Bestand auch die Bücher aufnehmen könnte, die in Zukunft veröffentlicht werden und von denen die Verleger den gesetzlichen Vorschriften entsprechend dem British Museum Pflichtexemplare zur Verfügung stellen müssen.
Im übrigen gingen die Architekten davon aus, daß der Katalog künftig von Computern bearbeitet wird und daß sich dadurch das System der Ausleihe ebenso ändert wie die Registrierung von Neuerwerbungen und die Vorbereitung von Bibliographien. Es gilt jedoch nicht als wahrscheinlich, daß die gesamte gespeicherte Information in der nächsten Zeit mit Hilfe der elektronischen Datenverarbeitung erfaßt werden kann. Selbst wenn ein Teil des künftigen Materials durch solche Verfahren bearbeitet werden kann, ist es nach wie vor notwendig, eine ständig wachsende Zahl gedruckter Publikationen in ihrer Originalform aufzubewahren.

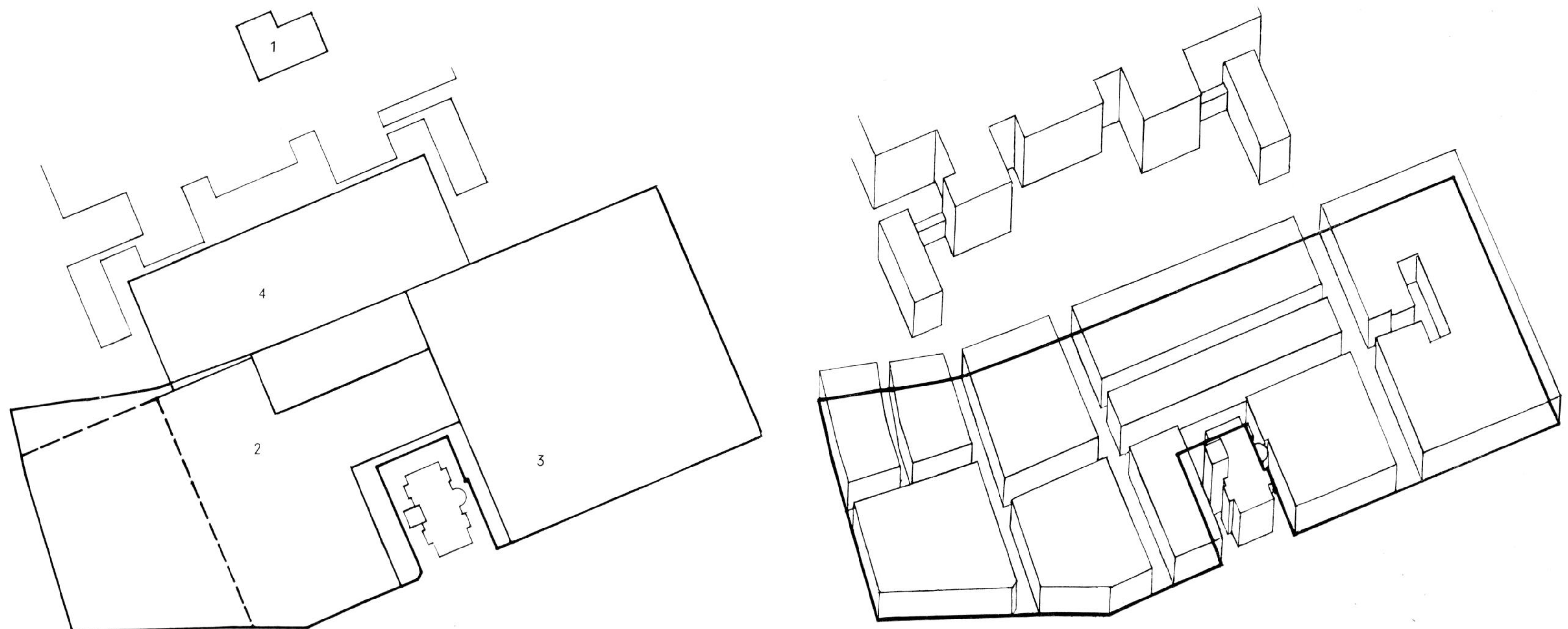


Site plan (numbers refer to sequence of building) / Lageplan (die Ziffern beziehen sich auf die Reihenfolge der Bauabschnitte).

Perspective site plan / Perspektivischer Lageplan.

Cross-section looking south towards the existing church of St. George; the underground car parking level links the two new elements of the Museum with the existing buildings to the north.

Querschnitt mit Blick nach Süden auf die Kirche St. George. Das unterirdische Parkgeschoß verbindet die beiden neuen Gebäude des Museumskomplexes mit den vorhandenen Bauten im Norden.

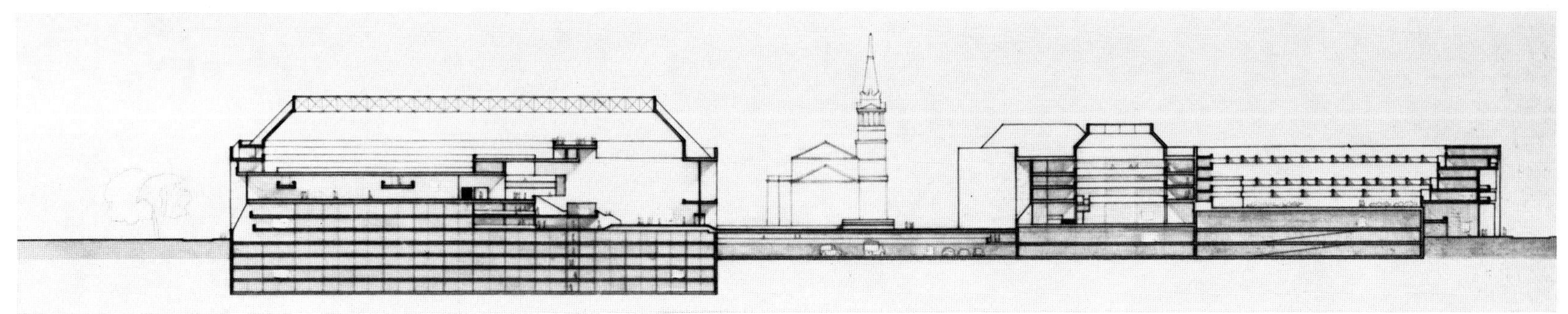

Cross-section looking north with housing and the Department of Prints and Drawings on the left and the Department of Printed Books on the right; the original portico by Sir Robert Smirke can be seen through the gap.

Querschnitt mit Blick nach Norden; links Wohnungen und die Abteilung für Graphik, rechts die Abteilung für Bücher. Zwischen den beiden Bauten ist der alte Portikus des Museums von Sir Robert Smirke zu erkennen.

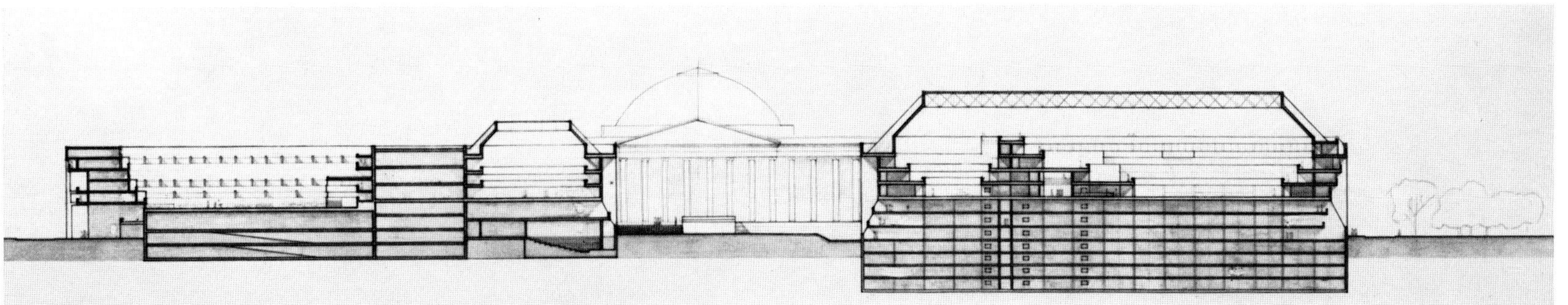

Key to plans / Legende zu den Plänen:

1 Departmental stack / Abteilungsmagazin
2 General stack / Allgemeines Magazin
3 Staff and material link to Museum / Verbindungsgang zum Museum für Angestellte und Materialtransporte
4 Car park / Tiefgarage
5 Departmental storage / Abteilungslager
6 Bus park / Tiefgarage für Autobusse
7 Service area / Anlieferung
8 Heating chamber / Heizung
9 Storage / Lager
10 Kitchen service / Nebenräume der Küche
11 Bindery storage / Lager der Buchbinderei
12 Lecture and conference room / Vortrags- und Konferenzraum
13 Copyright office / Büro für Copyright-Angelegenheiten
14 Central administration / Hauptverwaltung
15 Departmental administration / Verwaltung der Abteilungen
16 Cataloguers / Katalogbearbeitung
17 Pedestrian walkway / Fußgängerüberweg
18 Bindery / Buchbinderei
19 Cataloguers (Printed Books) / Katalogbearbeitung (Bücher)
20 Cloaks public / Öffentliche Garderobe
21 Toilets public / Öffentliches W. C.
22 Exhibition / Ausstellung
23 Staff conference room / Konferenzraum für Bibliotheksangestellte
24 Information centre / Auskunft
25 Shops / Läden
26 Shops service area / Anlieferung (Läden)
27 Entrance / Eingang
28 Information and bibliographical reference / Auskunft und Bibliographie
29 Restaurant
30 Canteen staff / Kantinenpersonal
31 Kitchen / Küche
32 Catalogue / Katalog
33 Public reference room / Handbibliothek
34 General reading room / Allgemeiner Lesesaal
35 Department of Manuscripts / Handschriften-Abteilung
36 Music room / Musikraum
37 Periodicals reading room / Zeitschriftenlesesaal
38 State paper room / Raum für Staatsakten
39 Map room / Raum für Landkarten
40 Department of Oriental Printed Books and Manuscripts / Abteilung für orientalische Bücher und Handschriften
41 Department of Prints and Drawings / Abteilung für Druckgraphik und Zeichnungen
42 Housing / Wohnungen
43 Special subject reading room / Leseräume für besondere Zwecke
44 State paper reading room / Leseraum für Staatsakten
45 Department of Manuscripts / Handschriften-Abteilung
46 Rare Books reading room / Leseraum für seltene Bücher

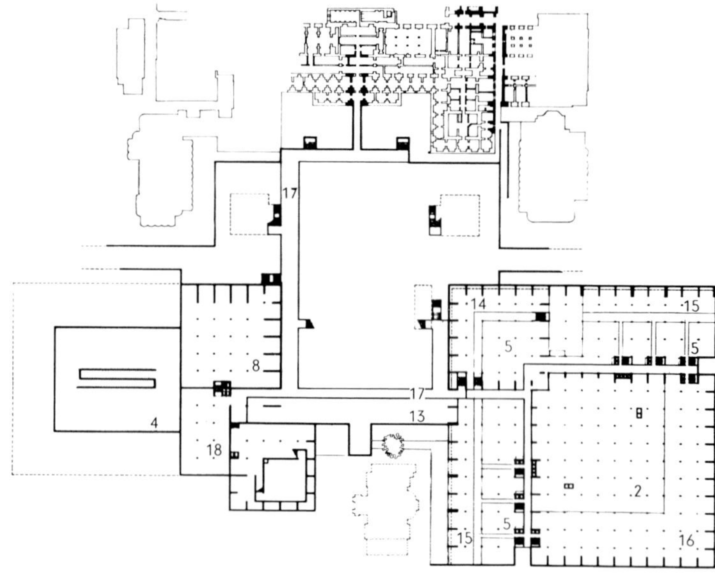

First basement floor plan / Grundriß erstes Untergeschoß.

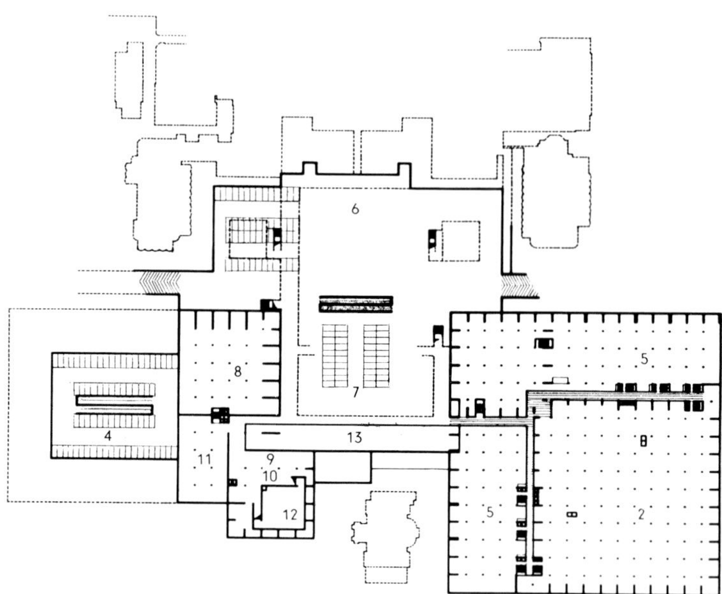

Second basement floor plan / Grundriß zweites Untergeschoß.

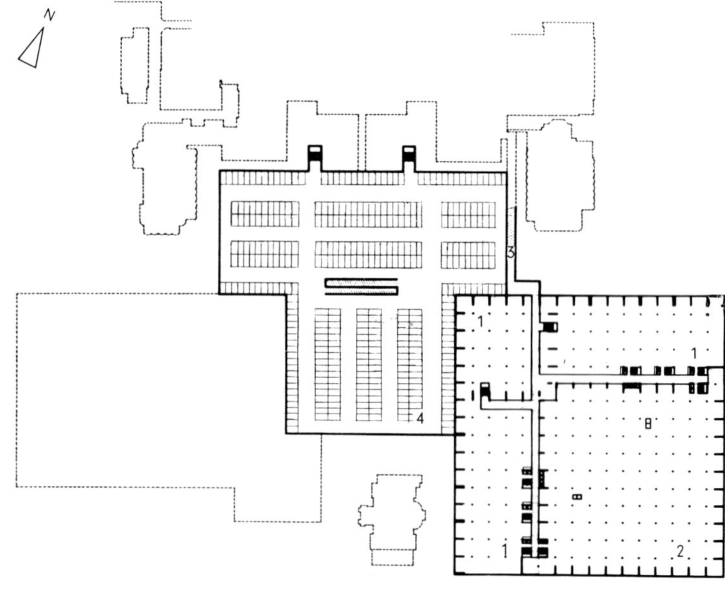

Third basement floor plan / Grundriß drittes Untergeschoß.

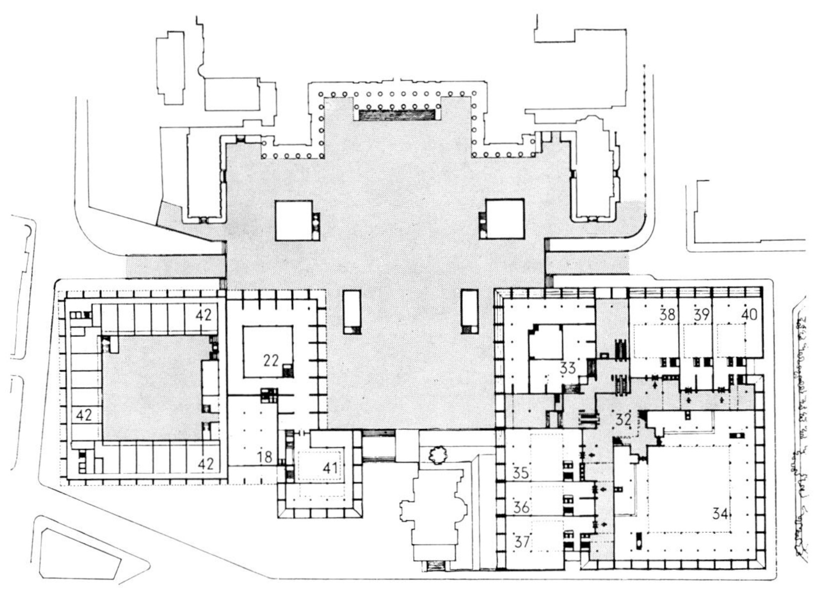


Second floor plan / Grundriß zweites Obergeschoß.

Fifth floor plan / Grundriß fünftes Obergeschoß.

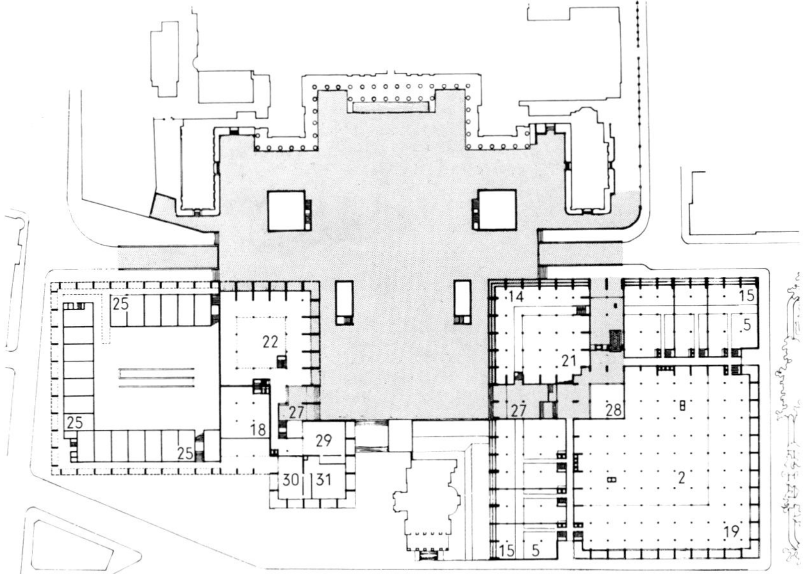


First floor plan / Grundriß erstes Obergeschoß.

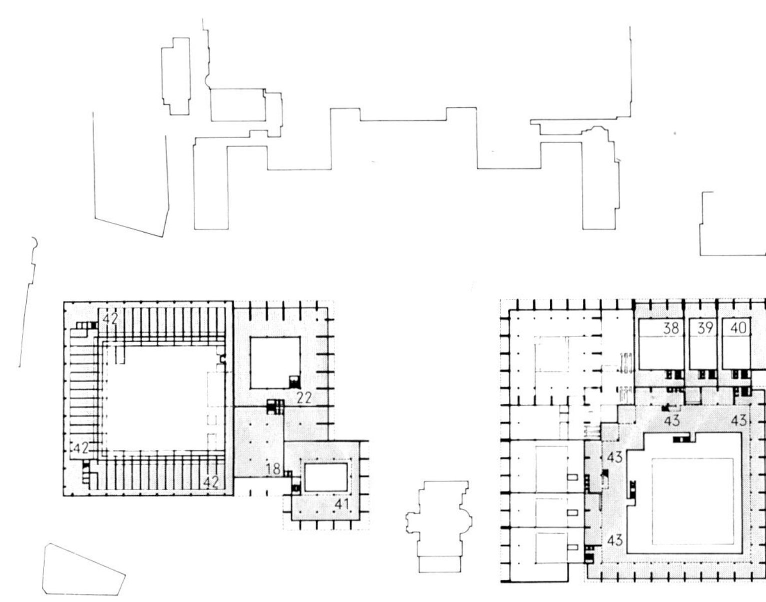


Fourth floor plan / Grundriß viertes Obergeschoß.

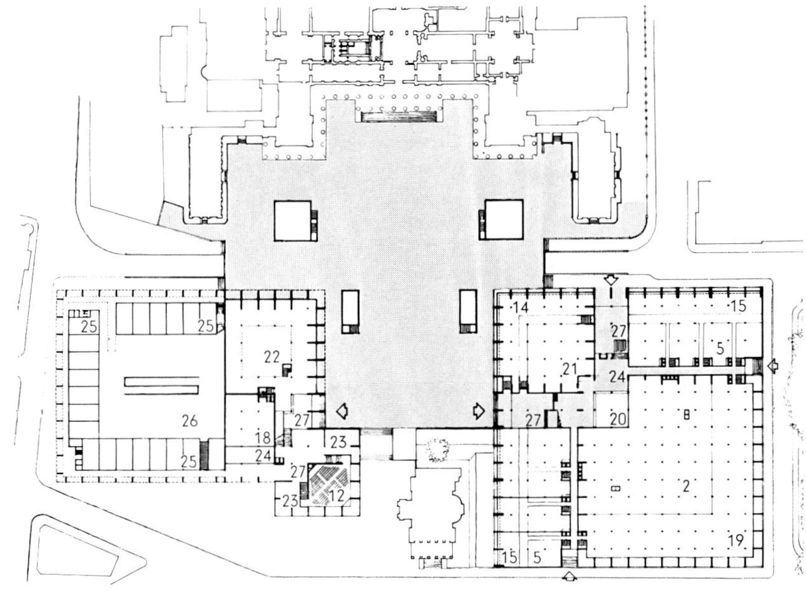


Ground floor plan / Grundriß Erdgeschoß.

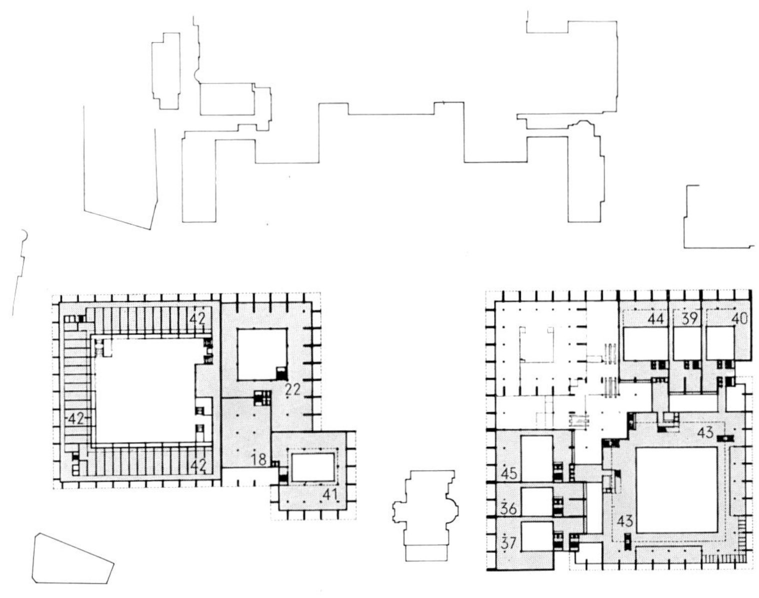


Third floor plan / Grundriß drittes Obergeschoß.

1. A view of the model from the south-east showing the whole museum complex with a new urban square in the centre.
2. An aerial view of the model.

1. Ansicht des Modells von Südosten mit dem gesamten Museumskomplex, in dessen Zentrum ein neuer Platz vorgesehen ist.
2. Luftansicht des Modells.

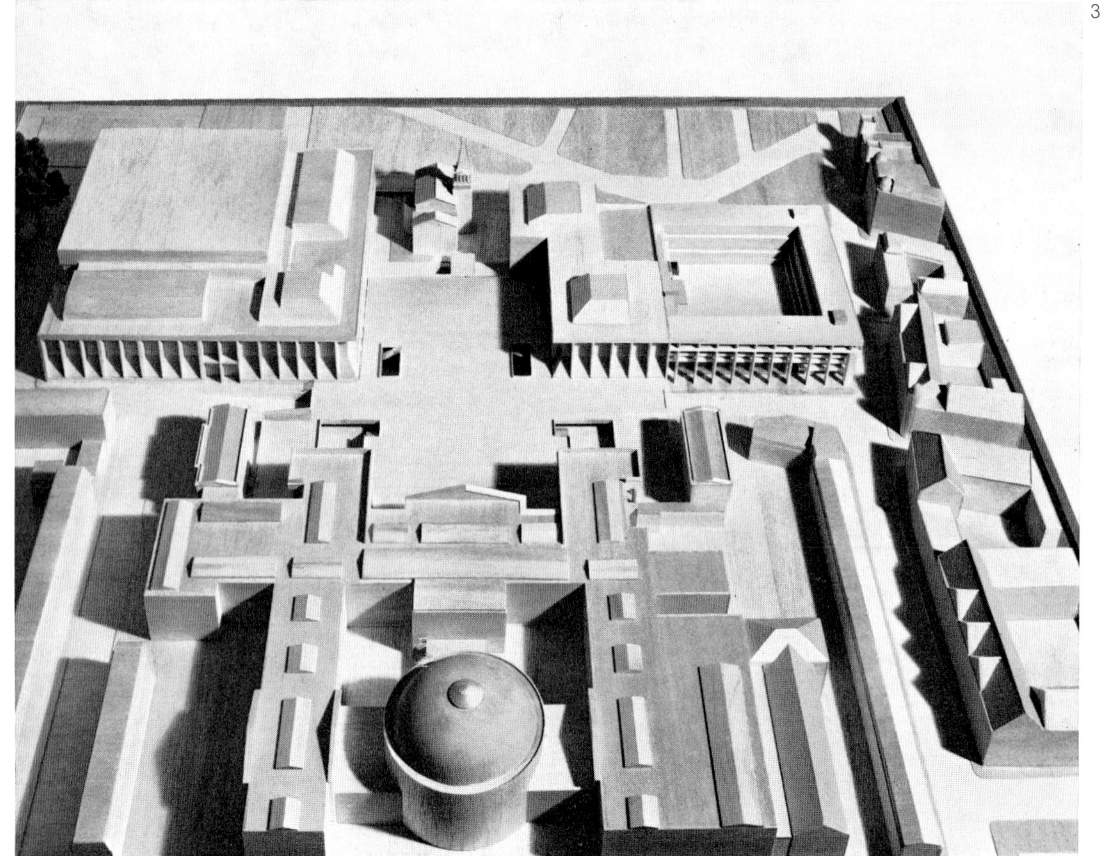

3. The model seen from the north with the existing reading room in the foreground; although certain forms are suggested by the model, the study is only intended to demonstrate basic ideas of organization rather than a specific architectural form.

3. Ansicht des Modells von Norden; im Vordergrund der jetzige Lesesaal. Obwohl das Modell Bauformen andeutet, soll die Studie nicht die endgültige architektonische Form, sondern grundsätzliche organisatorische Vorstellungen demonstrieren.

A selection from the schedule of furniture required for a university library. The importance of furniture as the element making the immediate environment in a library building cannot be overemphasized. Library furniture of the University of Guelph, Ontario, Canada. Design: Hancock, Little, Calvert & Associates.

Eine Auswahl aus dem Möbelprogramm, das für eine Universitätsbibliothek erforderlich ist. Da die Möblierung einen großen Einfluß auf die Atmosphäre einer Bibliothek ausübt, kann ihre Bedeutung kaum zu hoch eingeschätzt werden. Bibliothekseinrichtung der University of Guelph, Ontario, Kanada. Entwurf: Hancock, Little, Calvert & Associates.

1 7′ stack / Regal (2,10 m hoch)
2 Map case / Mappenschrank
3 Card catalogue file / Kartenkatalog
4 Information desk / Auskunftstisch
5 4′ half stack / Halbe Regaleinheit (1,20 m hoch)
6 Catalogue reference table / Arbeitsplatz im Katalog
7 Coffee vending table / Kaffeeausschank
8 7′ periodical stack / Zeitschriftenregal (2,10 m hoch)
9 Newspaper rack / Zeitungsständer
10 Dictionary stand / Halter für Nachschlagewerke
11 Study chair / Arbeitsstuhl
12 4′ display stack / Ausstellungsregal (1,20 m hoch)
13 Lounge chair / Sessel
14 Typist chair / Stuhl für Schreibkräfte
15 General purpose desk / Mehrzwecktisch
16 Library table / Bibliothekstisch
17 Book truck / Bücherwagen
18 4′ open coat storage / Offene Garderobe (1,20 m hoch)
19 Secretarial desk / Schreibtisch für Sekretärinnen
20 Conference table / Konferenztisch
21 Periodical shelf / Zeitschriftenhalter
22 Desk file case / Aktenschrank
23 Horizontal display / Ausstellungstisch
24 Ash tray / Aschenbecher
25 Waste basket / Papierkorb
26 Graduate storage / Schrankeinheit für Wissenschaftler
27 Graduate carrel / *Carrel* für Wissenschaftler
28 Display panel / Anschlagtafel
29 Subject area office / Umschlossener Bürobereich

## THE COMPONENTS OF THE LIBRARY

The last three sections dealt with certain library characteristics in so far as they affect the design of the building as a whole. Each of the three sections carried a descriptive label derived from the most typical library of that particular group. It could be seen moreover that the planning of any library was greatly dependent on the relative importance within it of the various functions and that this to some extent also depended on who was to perform them.

If we take, for instance, a library in which most of the reading is to be done elsewhere, those spaces which have to do with the communication of the information can be very unimportant or even non-existent. Location, retrieval and return will be the dominant operations. Such a library could be a small branch library from which a community borrows books or a central science information service which sends periodicals, abstracts and books out on loan to research workers. In both cases the staff will be dealing with the return of the information to storage; in the first case, however, location and retrieval is likely to be by the users, in the second, by the staff. This will significantly modify the plan of the building as would obviously a shift toward, a form of use in which communication happened within the building. These organizational differences can be discerned from the various building plans which were illustrated.

The next five sections will deal not with buildings as a whole, but with each of the four principal library operations and the service of these by staff and mechanical equipment, in order to attempt to define their particularities. Each section is again illustrated by recent architectural solutions showing the nature of the space most often assigned to each function; these show the components isolated for analysis, not the total organization.

## DIE ELEMENTE DER BIBLIOTHEK

Die letzten drei Abschnitte befaßten sich mit bestimmten Funktionen der Bibliothek, soweit sie sich auf die Planung des gesamten Gebäudes auswirken. Jeder Abschnitt trug ein beschreibendes Etikett, das sich von dem häufigsten Bibliothekstyp der jeweiligen Gruppe herleitete. Es erwies sich, daß die Planung eines Bibliotheksgebäudes weitgehend davon abhängt, welche Rolle den einzelnen Funktionen zukommt, und die unterschiedliche Bedeutung der Funktionen richtet sich wiederum nach den Benutzerschichten der Bibliotheken.

In einer Bibliothek, in der wenig oder keine Kommunikation stattfindet, sind zum Beispiel die Bereiche, die der Vermittlung der Information dienen, wenig wichtig oder gar nicht vorhanden. Hier sind Lokalisierung, Beschaffung und Rückgabe die vorherrschenden Vorgänge. Beispiele sind die kleine Zweigbücherei, die ein ländliches Gebiet versorgt, oder der zentrale wissenschaftliche Informationsdienst, der Zeitschriften, Abstracts oder Bücher an auswärtige Wissenschaftler verleiht. Für den Rücktransport der Materialien in das Magazin sorgt beide Male das Bibliothekspersonal, doch werden im ersten Fall Lokalisierung und Beschaffung zumeist von den Benutzern vorgenommen, im zweiten von den Angestellten der Bibliothek. Dadurch wird natürlich der Plan des Gebäudes beeinflußt, wie es auch der Fall wäre, wenn eine andere Benutzungsform gewählt würde, in der die Kommunikation innerhalb des Gebäudes stattfände. Diese Unterschiede in der Organisation lassen sich von den Grundrissen ablesen, die die vorhergehenden Abschnitte illustrieren.

Die nächsten fünf Abschnitte des Buches behandeln nicht das Gebäude als Ganzes, sondern die vier wichtigsten bibliothekstechnischen Vorgänge sowie die personelle und technische Ausrüstung, die sie jeweils erfordern. Auch hier ist wieder jeder Abschnitt mit neueren architektonischen Beispielen für die Raumformen illustriert, die den einzelnen Funktionen am häufigsten zugeordnet werden; die Beispiele zeigen nicht die Gesamtorganisation, sondern Ausschnitte, da es darum geht, die Eigenart der jeweiligen Funktionen zu definieren.

## Information Location

Two clearly definable aspects belong to this activity: the first has to do with discovering the source which is likely to contain the information, the second with locating that source within the library store so that retrieval, the next operation, can take place. The first of these needs, though seemingly largely a question of bibliographical organization, has nevertheless architectural implications.

In the first instance there will be a considerable difference between tracing a source manually or electronically. Manual tracing will take place in a bibliographical index, a card catalogue or a catalogue printed or written out in book form. In each of these cases the search takes place in the space which houses these listings, and this space has therefore to be large enough to accommodate both the catalogue and the readers and the advisory bibliographical staff. The size of this space has obviously a direct relationship to the size of the library stock and its complexity in terms of the amount of cross-reference required.

Using the figures given in Table 1 for 10 tray high card cabinets with trays 15" deep and using the layout shown in fig. 4, 100,000 cards and their associated tables will take up about 45 sq. ft. On the assumption that $2^{1}/_{2}$ cards are required for each volume, this space would be needed for every 40,000 volumes in the library stock or, very approximately, a little over 1 sq. ft. per 1,000 volumes. If 4 cards are needed for each volume, this space allocation would only deal with 25,000 volumes, representing a ratio of 1.8 sq. ft. per 1,000 volumes.

If the information source is to be traced electronically, this makes it possible to separate the space containing the listing from that housing the users, in other words a console placed in some zone accessible to readers is able to communicate with a computer placed elsewhere, not necessarily even within the library building. In addition to this, these consoles do not have to be within a single space like the traditional catalogue hall but can be distributed through the area open to readers if that should be an advantage. If the need to centralize catalogue facilities is no longer strong with an electronic system – the provision of several duplicate catalogues with manual tracing is prohibitively expensive – the movement system within the library may not need to be organized in relation to this powerful gravitational pull.

Once the information source has been identified, it has now to be located within the book holding spaces of the library. The catalogue entry will normally carry a description of the book as well as giving its position. This locational reference may be related to some system of information classification such as UDC in the sense that the content of the book determines its shelf position or books may be stored by accession, by size, or in alphabetical order within broad groupings – fiction, travel, hobbies, science – devised to suit the contents and the usage of the library in question.

If the library allows the reader to retrieve the book, this locational reference has then somehow also to indicate a recognizable place. The translation of such an abstract code into a message which in effect prescribes a route of movement to a particular shelf is far from simple and causes frequent difficulties in existing libraries. It does, of course, depend to some extent on organizing the movement system within the library in a comprehensible manner and, in particular, laying out the stack so that the sequence of book arrangement is coherent. Methods of achieving this are discussed in the next section under information storage.

If the book is retrieved by a member of the library staff, the reader has to pass the identification code to a staff member. This can be done in a number of ways, like handing over a filled-in form or dialling a series of numbers on an

## Lokalisierung der Information

Diese erste Phase des Benutzungszyklus weist zwei klar zu definierende Aspekte auf: Zum einen muß die Quelle gefunden werden, die wahrscheinlich die Information enthält, und zum anderen muß diese Quelle innerhalb des Bibliotheksbestandes lokalisiert werden, damit die Beschaffung, der darauffolgende Vorgang, eingeleitet werden kann. Der erste Aspekt scheint zwar weitgehend in den Bereich der bibliographischen Organisation zu gehören, hat aber nichtsdestoweniger Auswirkungen auf die Architektur.

Zunächst einmal ist es von großer Bedeutung, ob die Quelle von Hand oder elektronisch ermittelt wird. Wird sie von Hand aufgesucht, so sind ein bibliographischer Index, ein Katalog in Karteiform oder ein gedruckter oder geschriebener Katalog in Buchform erforderlich. In jedem Falle findet die Suche in dem Raum statt, der diese Verzeichnisse beherbergt, so daß der Bereich genug Fläche für Katalog, Leser und Auskunftspersonal bieten muß. Die Größe dieses Bereichs ist im übrigen auch vom Umfang des Bibliotheksbestandes und von der Anzahl der notwendigen Querverweise abhängig.

Entsprechend den in Tabelle 1 angegebenen Zahlen für Karteischränke mit einer Höhe von zehn Fächern und einer Fachtiefe von je 38 cm und entsprechend der in Abb. 4 dargestellten Anordnung nehmen 100000 Karteikarten und die dazugehörigen Arbeitsflächen etwas über 4 qm ein. Geht man davon aus, daß jeder Band $2^{1}/_{2}$ Karten erfordert, so würde dieser Raum für je 40000 Bände des Bibliotheksbestandes benötigt, also ungefähr 0,10 qm pro 1000 Bände. Wenn für jeden Band 4 Karteikarten nötig sind, können auf dem gleichen Raum nur 25000 Bände erfaßt werden, was einem Durchschnitt von etwa 0,16 qm pro 1000 Bände entspricht.

Wird die Informationsquelle elektronisch aufgesucht, so läßt sich der Bereich mit dem bibliographischen Apparat von dem der Benutzer trennen: Ein Pult, das an einem beliebigen für den Leser zugänglichen Ort aufgestellt ist, steht mit einem Computer in Verbindung, der an anderer Stelle – nicht einmal unbedingt innerhalb des Bibliotheksgebäudes – untergebracht ist. Diese Pulte müssen sich im übrigen nicht in einem einzigen Raum wie dem traditionellen Katalogsaal befinden, sondern können, falls sich diese Anordnung als Vorteil erweist, über die Publikumsräume verteilt werden. Da es bei einem elektronischen System nicht mehr notwendig ist, die Katalogeinrichtungen zu zentralisieren – die Aufstellung mehrerer Duplikatkataloge für manuelle Lokalisierung ist kostenmäßig zumeist nicht tragbar –, braucht das Zirkulationssystem innerhalb der Bibliothek nicht auf diesen Schwerpunkt hin organisiert zu werden.

Sobald die Informationsquelle identifiziert ist, muß sie im Magazin der Bibliothek lokalisiert werden. Der Katalogeintrag enthält normalerweise eine Beschreibung des Buches sowie die Angabe seines Standortes. Der Standort wird häufig durch ein Klassifizierungssystem wie etwa das UDC bestimmt, bei dem sich die Magazinierung des Buches nach seinem Inhalt richtet; Bücher können aber auch in der Reihenfolge der Anschaffung, nach Format oder nach dem Alphabet innerhalb größerer Sachgruppen – Roman, Reisen, Hobbies – geordnet werden, wobei die Wahl der Kategorien jeweils dem Bestand und der Zweckbestimmung der Bibliothek entspricht.

Wenn die Bibliothek es dem Leser erlaubt, sich sein Buch selbst zu beschaffen, so muß die Signatur auch einen verständlichen Hinweis auf den Standort des Buches enthalten. Die Übersetzung eines solchen abstrakten Code in eine Botschaft, die den Weg zu einem bestimmten Regal vorschreibt, ist alles andere als einfach und verursacht in manchen Bibliotheken große Schwierigkeiten. Hier hängt viel davon ab, ob die Verkehrswege innerhalb der Biblio-

1

2

3

Table 1

*Card Capacity for Standard Card Cabinets six trays wide*

| Trays high | Tray length 15″ | 17″ | 19″ |
|---|---|---|---|
| 10 | 51,000 | 60,000 | 69,000 |
| 12 | 61,200 | 72,000 | 82,800 |
| 14 | 71,400 | 84,000 | 96,600 |
| 16 | 81,600 | 96,000 | 110,400 |

Cabinets six trays wide occupy approximately 40 in. in width. Five-tray-wide cabinets occupy approximately 33¹/₃ in. in width and can be placed in a standard 3-ft-wide stack section. They will probably cost more per tray, but they may fit into the available space to advantage, sometimes combined with the wider units.

A 15-in. tray is estimated to provide 12 in. of net filing space, which, if filled to 71 per cent of capacity, will house comfortably approximately 850 cards which average 1/100 in. in thickness.

A 17-in. tray is estimated to provide 14 in. of net filing space, which, if filled to 72 per cent of capacity, will house comfortably approximately 1,000 cards which average 1/100 in. in thickness.

A 19-in. tray is estimated to provide 16 in. of net filing space, which, if filled to 73 per cent of capacity, will house comfortably approximately 1,150 cards which average 1/100 in. in thickness. These trays may be uncomfortably heavy when filled to capacity.

(Table taken from Keyes D. Metcalf, *Planning Academic and Research Library Buildings,* New York 1965.)

Tabelle 1

*Kapazität von Karteikartenschränken mit sechs Schubfächern Breite*

| Zahl der Schubfächer (vertikal) | Länge der Schubfächer 38 cm | 43 cm | 48 cm |
|---|---|---|---|
| 10 | 51 000 | 60 000 | 69 000 |
| 12 | 61 200 | 72 000 | 82 800 |
| 14 | 71 400 | 84 000 | 96 600 |
| 16 | 81 600 | 96 000 | 110 400 |

Schränke mit einer Breite von sechs Schubfächern sind ungefähr 1 m breit. Bei fünf Schubfächern nehmen sie etwa 80 cm ein und können in einer Regaleinheit mit der Standardbreite von 90 cm untergebracht werden. Die Kosten pro Schubfach sind dann möglicherweise höher, doch lassen sich solche Schränke sehr gut in den verfügbaren Raum einpassen und können auch mit breiteren Einheiten kombiniert werden.

Ein 38 cm langes Schubfach bietet schätzungsweise 30 cm Tiefe netto für die Unterbringung von Karteikarten. Wenn es zu 71% der Kapazität gefüllt ist, kann es ungefähr 850 Karteikarten mit einer durchschnittlichen Dicke von 0,25 mm aufnehmen.

Ein 43 cm langes Schubfach bietet schätzungsweise 35 cm Tiefe netto für die Unterbringung von Karteikarten. Wenn es zu 72% der Kapazität gefüllt ist, kann es ungefähr 1 000 Karteikarten mit einer durchschnittlichen Dicke von 0,25 mm aufnehmen.

Ein 48 cm langes Schubfach bietet schätzungsweise 40 cm Tiefe netto für die Unterbringung von Karteikarten. Wenn es zu 73% der Kapazität gefüllt ist, kann es ungefähr 1 150 Karteikarten mit einer durchschnittlichen Dicke von 0,25 mm aufnehmen. Schubfächer dieser Größe sind bei voller Kapazitätsausnutzung wegen ihres Gewichts sehr unhandlich.

(Nach Keyes D. Metcalf, *Planning Academic and Research Library Buildings,* New York 1965.)

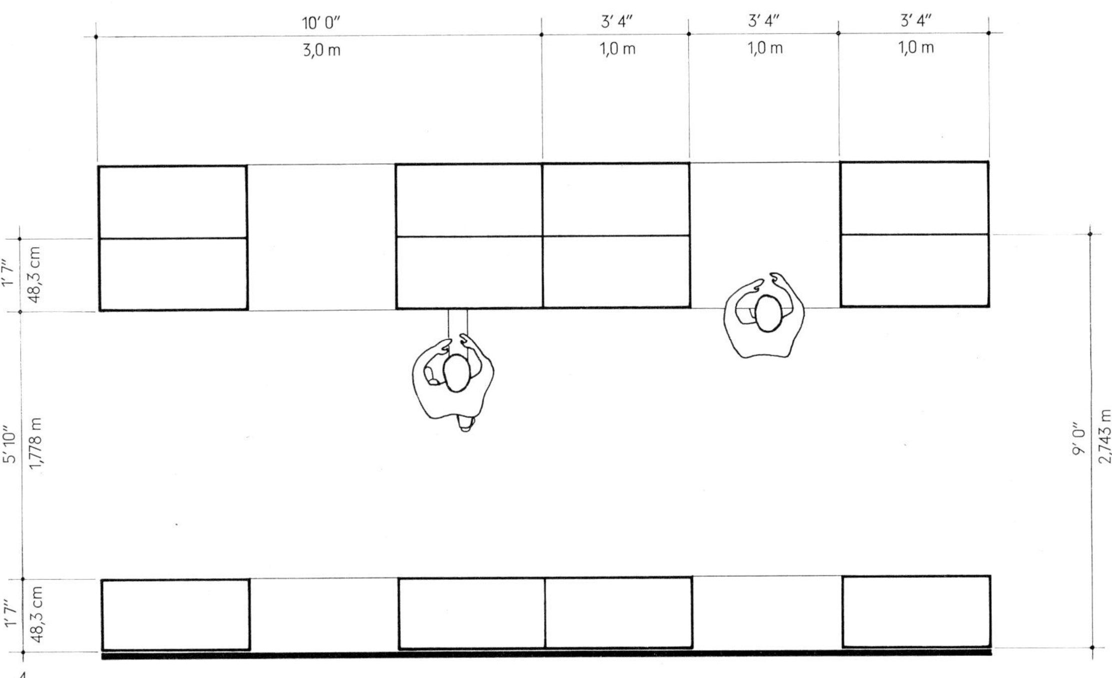


1–3. Card catalogue stands are made of timber or steel; the drawers contain cards which are usually pierced by a metal rod to prevent their removal. It is extremely useful to have some adjacent shelf space in order to make notes or compile a list. The library catalogue can also be in book form, as at the British Museum, and may increasingly take that shape when it becomes a print-out from a computer stored catalogue.

1. Brunswick Corporation, Kalamazoo, Michigan.
2. Library, Växjö, Sweden. Architect: Erik Uluots.
3. Beatley Library, Simmons College, Boston, Massachusetts. Architects: Campbell, Aldrich & Nulty.

4. Plan of catalogue area.

5. The main library catalogue of a large collection should have near it other bibliographical information and should be positioned so that it is easy for staff to give help. Catalogue Hall, Library, Sheffield University. Architects: Gollins, Melvin, Ward & Partners.

1–3. Kartenkatalogschränke werden in Holz oder Stahl hergestellt; die Schubfächer enthalten Karten, die gewöhnlich auf einen Metallstab aufgezogen sind, damit sie nicht entfernt werden können. Sehr nützlich sind Arbeitsflächen in der Nähe des Katalogs, die es dem Leser ermöglichen, Listen aufzustellen oder Notizen zu machen. Der Bibliothekskatalog kann auch, wie beim British Museum, in Buchform angelegt werden. Diese Form wird sich vor allem in Zukunft anbieten, wenn Katalogdaten in Computern gespeichert werden.

1. Brunswick Corporation, Kalamazoo, Michigan.
2. Bibliothek in Växjö, Schweden. Architekt: Erik Uluots.
3. Beatley Library, Simmons College, Boston, Massachusetts. Architekten: Campbell, Aldrich & Nulty.

4. Grundriß eines Katalogbereiches.

5. Der Hauptkatalog einer großen Sammlung sollte so gelegen sein, daß in der Nähe bibliographische Nachschlagewerke aufgestellt werden können und daß Bibliothekspersonal für Auskünfte zur Verfügung steht. Katalogsaal in der Bibliothek der Sheffield University. Architekten: Gollins, Melvin, Ward & Partners.

5

instrument rather like a telephone, which are described as part of the next sequence.
A great deal of the speed and efficiency with which information will be located will depend on non-architectural aspects. It is important therefore that any steps which are taken in speeding the process of book retrieval, such as mechanical means of handling, are matched by a similarly effective method of information location. The principal problem here is not one of actually looking up a card in a catalogue, but of discovering which card or similar catalogue entry is likely to carry the title of the work with the greatest possibility of containing the information which is wanted. This is very much a sifting process of selecting items with given characteristics from a random store. Such a process is eminently suitable for electronic data processing. Naturally the greater the amount of description of the contents that is contained in the catalogue entry, the more effective will be the sifting. The description must, however, (if it is to be electronically processed), be in a form which can be read by a machine. This problem of transcription is currently being investigated in studies such as Project MARC (Machine-Readable Cataloguing) in the USA and was discussed at the Brasenose Conference on the Automation of Libraries in 1966. It is in this operation of locating the likely source of information for the user that the greatest attempts at using electronic processes are being made and where they are also likely to be at the moment most fruitful. They are being made necessary, of course, by the very large and continually increasing knowledge store.

7. Tall catalogue, units demand that people should stand, but as a search may be quite prolonged it is helpful if they can be kept low and chairs are provided. Library, Örsted Institute, University of Copenhagen. Architects: Eva and Nils Koppel.

7. Bei großen Katalogeinheiten muß der Benutzer stehen; da aber die Suche längere Zeit in Anspruch nehmen kann, ist es sehr zweckmäßig, wenn die Einheiten niedrig gehalten werden und Stühle vorgesehen sind. Bibliothek des Örsted-Instituts, Universität Kopenhagen. Architekten: Eva und Nils Koppel.

thek in verständlicher Weise organisiert sind und ob vor allem die Anordnung der Regale es erlaubt, die Bücher in logischer Folge aufzustellen. Wie sich das erreichen läßt, wird im nächsten Abschnitt beschrieben.
Wird das Buch vom Bibliothekspersonal beschafft, so muß der Leser einem Angestellten der Bibliothek die Signatur mitteilen, indem er beispielsweise einen ausgefüllten Bestellzettel einreicht oder auf einem telefonähnlichen Instrument eine Reihe von Nummern wählt. Von den verschiedenen Verfahren wird ebenfalls im nächsten Abschnitt die Rede sein.
Wie schnell und wie leicht sich das Informationsmaterial lokalisieren läßt, hängt weitgehend von Faktoren ab, die nicht durch die Architektur bedingt sind. Es ist deshalb wichtig, daß zugleich mit allen Maßnahmen zur Beschleunigung der Buchbeschaffung, wie zum Beispiel technischen Hilfsmitteln, auch ähnlich wirksame Methoden für die Lokalisierung der Information eingesetzt werden. Dabei geht es weniger darum, eine Karteikarte in einem Katalog zu finden, als vielmehr festzustellen, welche Karte oder welcher entsprechende Katalogeintrag den Titel des Werkes enthält, das mit der größten Wahrscheinlichkeit die gewünschte Information bietet. Es handelt sich also um einen Prozeß der Auswahl bestimmter Daten mit gegebenen Eigenschaften aus einem großen Bestand anderer Daten. Für ein solches Auswahlverfahren eignet sich die elektronische Datenverarbeitung hervorragend. Natürlich läßt sich die Auswahl um so leichter treffen, je mehr beschreibende Angaben über den Inhalt des Buches im Katalogeintrag enthalten sind. Die Beschreibung muß jedoch, wenn sie elektronisch verarbeitet werden soll, in einer für Maschinen lesbaren Form gehalten sein. Dieses Problem der Transkription wird zur Zeit in Studien wie dem Projekt MARC (Machine-Readable Cataloguing) in den Vereinigten Staaten untersucht und wurde im Jahre 1966 auch auf der Tagung über die Automation der Bibliotheken in Brasenose diskutiert. Gerade auf dem Gebiet der Informationslokalisierung werden zur Zeit die meisten Versuche mit elektronischer Datenverarbeitung unternommen. Hier versprechen sie auch den größten Nutzen, denn der ständig wachsende Wissensstoff macht es dem Leser immer schwerer, die wahrscheinliche Informationsquelle zu ermitteln.

6

6. Catalogues are frequently divided between a subject list and an author-title list; here these are back to back on one side of the lending library. Public Library, Eskilstuna, Sweden. Architect: Gustaf Lettström.
8. It is a great help if duplicate catalogues of individual sections can be provided near the books. Public Library, Hansaviertel, Berlin. Architect: Werner Düttmann.

6. Der alphabetische und der systematische Katalog stehen hier Rücken an Rücken auf einer Seite der Bibliothek. Öffentliche Bücherei, Eskilstuna, Schweden. Architekt: Gustaf Lettström.
8. Wenn möglich, sollten Katalogduplikate einzelner Bereiche in der Nähe der Bücher angeordnet werden. Hansabücherei, Berlin. Architekt: Werner Düttmann.

7

8

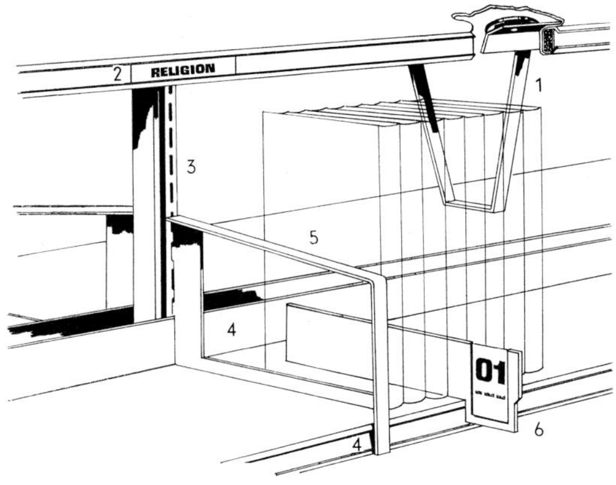


1. A bookshelf system and its accessories; book storage requires in addition to shelving (4), movable in this case on a metal support slotted at 1 inch centres (3) and held by shelf brackets which should project sufficiently to eliminate page damage when replacing books (5), some method of book support (1) and means of identification like the shelf label sprung into a groove (2) and the projecting section marker (6). Reska Equipment, Birkerød, Denmark.

1. Regalsystem. Die Fachböden (4), die hier in Metallpfosten mit Schlitzen in 2,5 cm Abstand (3) eingehängt sind, werden von Halterungen getragen, die weit genug vorstehen müssen, damit die Bücher beim Herausnehmen nicht beschädigt werden (5). Erforderlich sind außerdem Buchstützen (1) und Vorrichtungen zur Identifizierung wie das in einer Rille laufende Schild (2) und die überstehende Zahlenmarkierung (6). Reska, Birkerød, Dänemark.

Table 2
*Measurement of books*

| | |
|---|---|
| 5 × 8″ (or less) | 25% |
| 6 × 9″ | 29% |
| 7 × 10″ | 25% |
| 8 × 11″ | 11% |
| 9 × 12″ | 4% |
| 10 × 13″ | 3% |
| over 10 × 13″ | 3% |
| | 100% |

(Table from Keyes D. Metcalf, *Planning Academic and Research Library Buildings,* using data from Fremont Rider's *Compact Book Storage,* New York 1949.)

Tabelle 2
*Buchformate*

| | |
|---|---|
| 12,7 × 20,3 cm (oder weniger) | 25% |
| 15,2 × 22,9 cm | 29% |
| 17,8 × 25,4 cm | 25% |
| 20,3 × 27,9 cm | 11% |
| 22,9 × 30,5 cm | 4% |
| 25,4 × 33,0 cm | 3% |
| mehr als 25,4 × 33,0 cm | 3% |
| | 100% |

(Tabelle nach Keyes D. Metcalf, *Planning Academic and Research Library Buildings,* unter Benutzung von Angaben aus Fremont Riders *Compact Book Storage,* New York 1949.)

The connection between these two library operations is direct and obvious. The information cannot be communicated as long as it is in store: we cannot read a book while it is on the shelf or scan a tape in its container. Nor, conversely, are we able to store the enormous amount of available information in such a manner that communication can take place immediately without the intervention of the subsidiary role of retrieval. Even when not miniaturized, the information has, of necessity, been packaged and warehoused – this is implied by the concept of both book and library – in such a way that direct communication is not possible.
There is a further connection in the sense that the method of retrieval is dependent on the size of the store. A small public library is able to have its store open to the reader who carries out retrieval by himself; a large national library which has arranged its stack by accession and size, must carry out the retrieval process using its staff and mechanical means of handling. The problem of retrieval is in fact directly proportional to the size and complexity of the stack.
The arrangement of the stack and the kind of equipment which it is possible to install will moreover depend on whether or not retrieval is done by the reader or the staff. There are thus three clearly linked problems.

### Storage

There are as yet no mechanical means of extracting a book from its store and placing it on a mechanized delivery system. The design of the store has therefore to follow simple anthropometric rules – books must be within reach, aisles must be wide enough for people.
The critical vertical dimension is that the topmost shelf must not be higher than 6′4″ from the floor if it is to be reached by a relatively short person. This makes it possible to place six shelves evenly spaced below this height and to allow for a kicking plinth, fig. 4. Such an arrangement giving book shelves at 12″ centres will take 90% of all books as can be seen from Table 2.
The number of books that can be stored on these seven shelves per foot run of shelving will depend on the thickness of the books which in turn is related as a rule to the classification of the book. Fiction averages 8 volumes, history, literature and art 7 volumes, science and technology 6 volumes, medicine, public documents and most bound periodicals 5 volumes and law 4 volumes per lineal foot.
Shelving is normally manufactured in 3′0″ long sections. The capacity of such a section seven shelves high using an average value from the figures in the preceding paragraph is conventionally taken as 125 volumes. This in other words is an assumed average capacity of a single sided standard section when full and is the figure used for the calculations which accompany the diagrams of stack layout (figs. 7–12). Shelving is also made to a standard one metre length for which the average capacity per section can be assumed as 140 volumes.
The critical horizontal dimension is that of the space between two sets of shelves facing each other across an aisle. This passage way has to allow at least for a person to walk down it and for a book trolley to clear the shelving on either side. As the number of people using any one aisle at the same time increases, so the width of that space has to increase so that people can pass each other. The clear space between two sets of parallel shelving is therefore dependent on use.
The width of the shelving itself is related to average book depth. If the same criteria are to be accepted as for book

Diese beiden Vorgänge stehen in direkter Verbindung miteinander. Die Information kann sich nicht mitteilen, solange sie im Magazin zurückgehalten wird: Wir können kein Buch lesen, das im Regal steht, und kein Band abhören, das in seinem Behälter untergebracht ist. Andererseits aber können wir die ungeheuren Quantitäten des verfügbaren Materials nicht so speichern, daß die indirekte Funktion der Beschaffung entfällt und die Kommunikation unmittelbar stattfindet. Selbst wenn die Information nicht in ein Mikroformat gebracht wird, ist sie – der Konzeption des Buches wie auch der Bibliothek entsprechend – so verpackt und gelagert, daß eine direkte Kommunikation nicht möglich ist.
Der Zusammenhang zwischen Magazinierung und Beschaffung zeigt sich auch darin, daß die Methode der Beschaffung sich nach der Größe des Magazins richtet. Eine kleine Volksbücherei kann ihr Magazin dem Benutzer öffnen, der dann die Beschaffung selbst übernimmt; eine große Nationalbibliothek, die den Bestand nach dem Zugang und der Größe geordnet hat, muß beim Beschaffungsvorgang Personal und technische Hilfsmittel heranziehen. Das Problem der Beschaffung steht also in direkter Proportion zur Größe und Komplexität des Magazins.
Außerdem richten sich Organisation und Ausstattung des Magazins danach, ob der Leser oder das Personal die Beschaffung übernimmt. Es ergeben sich also drei voneinander abhängige Probleme.

### Magazinierung

Bis heute gibt es noch keine technischen Hilfsmittel, mit denen sich ein Buch dem Regal entnehmen und auf ein mechanisches Fördersystem plazieren ließe. Deshalb muß die Planung des Magazins einfachen anthropometrischen Regeln folgen – die Bücher müssen sich in Griffhöhe befinden, und die Gänge müssen breit genug für Menschen sein.
Bei den vertikalen Abmessungen ist zu beachten, daß das oberste Fach nicht weiter als ca. 1,90 m vom Fußboden entfernt sein darf, wenn eine relativ kleine Person es erreichen soll. Darunter ist dann Platz für sechs in regelmäßigen Abständen angeordnete Fachböden und für eine Sockelleiste (Abb. 4). Bei einer solchen Anordnung und bei Abständen von 30,5 cm lassen sich, wie Tabelle 2 zeigt, 90% aller Bücher unterbringen.
Wie viele Bücher sich auf diesen sieben Fachböden pro laufendem Meter unterbringen lassen, hängt von der Stärke des Bandes ab, die wiederum meist von der Kategorie des Buches bestimmt wird. Bei Romanen gehen 26 Bände, bei Geschichte, Literatur und Kunst 23 Bände, bei Wissenschaft und Technik 20 Bände, bei Medizin, Publikationen der Öffentlichen Hand und den meisten gebundenen Zeitschriften 16 Bände und bei juristischen Werken 13 Bände auf den laufenden Meter.
Regale werden im allgemeinen in Einheiten von 90 cm Länge hergestellt. Die Kapazität einer solchen sieben Fächer hohen Einheit wird nach einem Durchschnittswert der im vorhergehenden Absatz angegebenen Zahlen gewöhnlich mit 125 Bänden angenommen. Diese durchschnittliche Kapazität einer einzelnen, mit Seitenwangen versehenen Standardeinheit dient als Grundlage für die Berechnungen, die den Diagrammen der Regalgrundrisse (Abb. 7–12) beigegeben sind. Es gibt auch Regale mit einer Standardlänge von 1 m, bei denen die durchschnittliche Kapazität pro Einheit mit 140 Bänden angenommen werden kann.
Das ausschlaggebende horizontale Maß ist das des Raumes zwischen zwei Regalreihen, die durch einen Gang

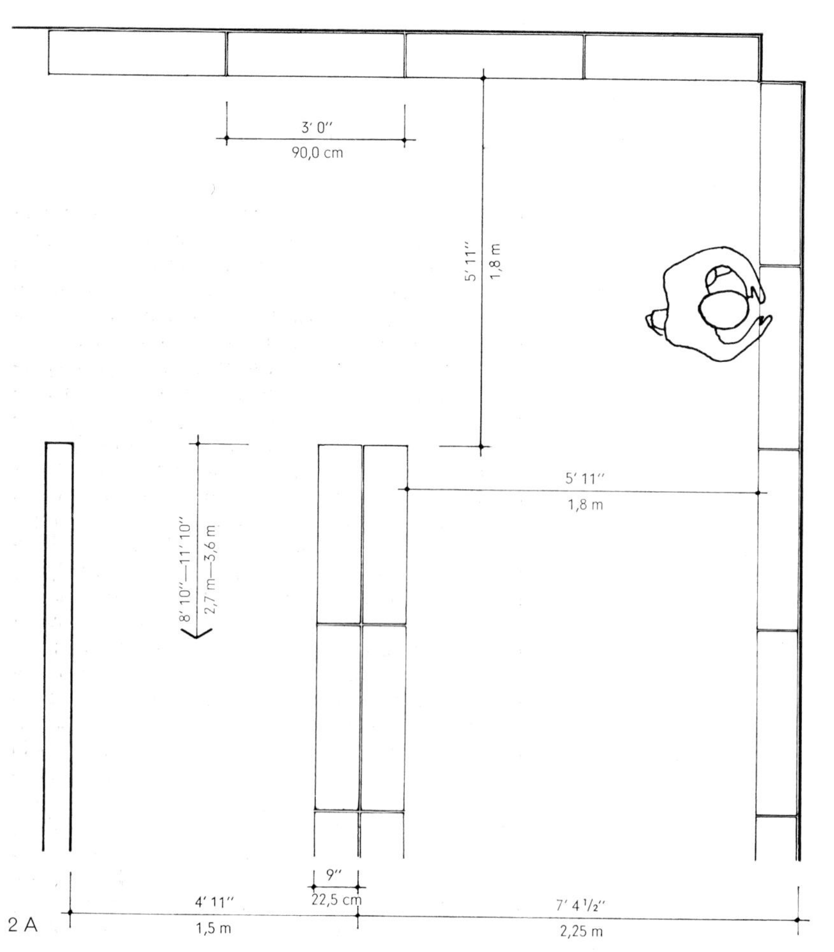


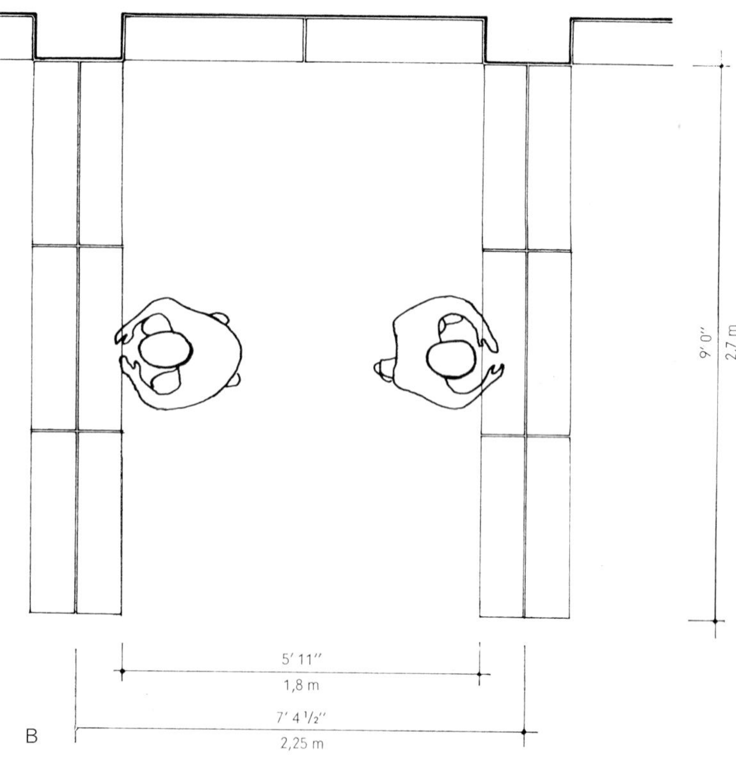


2. Plans of shelving layouts in open access areas.
A. Shelves around walls and free standing.
B. Shelves forming alcoves.

2. Regalgrundrisse in frei zugänglichen Bereichen.
A. An den Wänden angeordnete, frei stehende Regale.
B. Regale, die Lesenischen bilden.

3. Plywood shelves with plywood ends held by aluminium brackets adjustable on vertical aluminium supports which are screwed to blockwork walls; a combination of simple elements which can be put up by any contractor. Theological College, Chichester. Architects: Ahrends, Burton & Koralek.

3. Sperrholzregale mit Wangen aus Sperrholz. Die Fachböden werden von Aluminiumkonsolen getragen, die sich auf vertikalen Aluminiumschienen verstellen lassen. Die Schienen sind an Hohlblocksteine geschraubt. Eine Kombination einfacher Elemente, die leicht zu montieren ist. Theological College, Chichester. Architekten: Ahrends, Burton & Koralek.

4. Recommended shelf heights for different uses (A) bookstacks, (B) public lending libraries and (C) children's libraries.
(Diagrams 2 and 4 based on *The Architects' Journal*, Vol. 147, number 12, March 1968.)

4. Empfohlene Regalhöhen bei Verwendung (A) im Magazin, (B) in öffentlichen Leihbüchereien und (C) in Kinderbüchereien.
(Diagramme 2 und 4 nach *The Architects' Journal*, Band 147, Nr. 12, März 1968.)

3

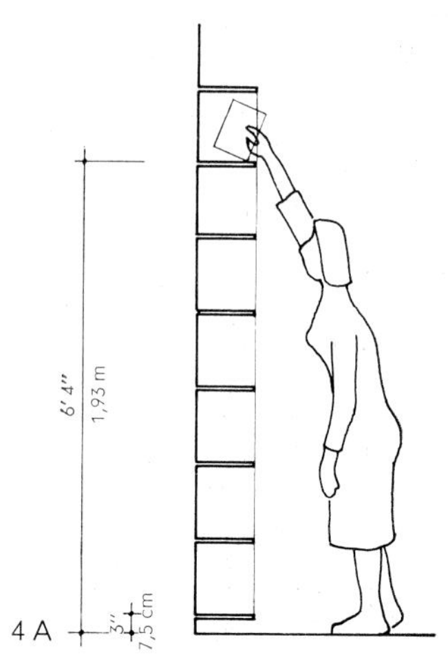


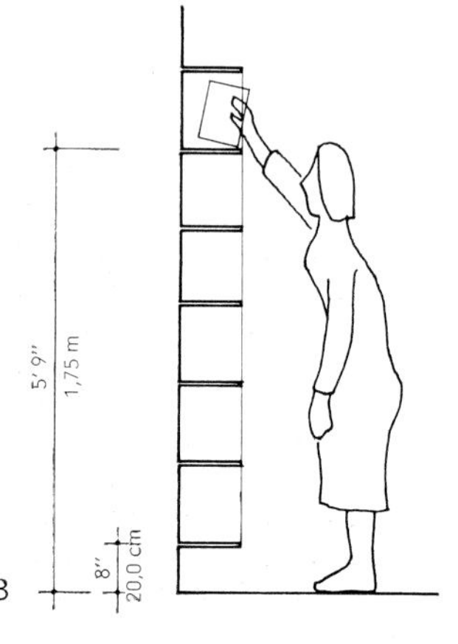


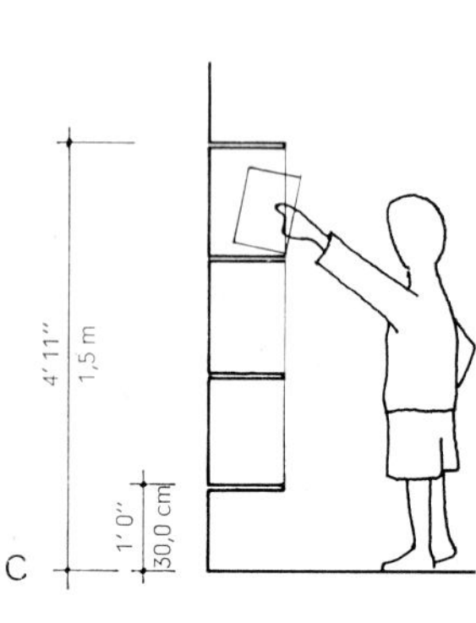

height, shelves should be 8" (or 20 cm) deep to cope with 90% of all books. Shelves for newspapers, the face display of books or magazines and so forth will of course have different depths. Because of the standard dimension of shelf depth for the vast majority of books however, the critical horizontal dimension can be expressed as that between the centre line of adjacent stacks and this is the figure used when relating the spacing of stacks to that of structural columns, for instance.

If there is to be effective use of the floor space, it is important that this relationship is established in such a way that the columns fall within the band width of a stack, in other words that the distance between the centre lines of columns measured at right angles to the direction of the stacks is a multiple of the distance between the centres of the stacks. A number of possible grids is shown in Table 3.

In terms of future changes there is a good deal to be said for a structural grid which allows a number of different stack spacings to occur. There are also some advantages in a square structural grid so that the direction of the stacks can be turned through 90°. There is a further advantage if the structural grid parallel to the direction of the stacks is such that the clear space between columns is a multiple of a standard section length, i. e. 3'0" (900 mm) or 3'4" (1 m) if the wider section is used.

getrennt sind. Dieser Gang muß so breit sein, daß Platz für mindestens eine Person und einen Transportwagen bleibt. Benutzen mehrere Bibliotheksangestellte den Gang zur gleichen Zeit, muß der Raum so verbreitert werden, daß zwei Personen aneinander vorbeikommen. Deshalb hängt der Freiraum zwischen zwei parallel angeordneten Regalreihen von der Benutzungsfrequenz ab.

Die Tiefe der Fachböden richtet sich nach der durchschnittlichen Tiefe der Bücher. Werden die gleichen Kriterien angewandt wie für die Höhe der Bücher, so sollten die Regale 20 cm tief sein, um 90% aller Bücher aufnehmen zu können. Fächer für Zeitungen und für frontal ausgelegte Bücher oder Zeitschriften haben natürlich andere Tiefen. Da jedoch für die meisten Bücher die normale Fachtiefe in Frage kommt, läßt sich als ausschlaggebende horizontale Abmessung diejenige zwischen den Mittellinien gegenüberstehender Regale bezeichnen. Diese Ziffer wird zum Beispiel verwandt, wenn die Anordnung der Regale mit der Anordnung der tragenden Stützen in Verbindung gebracht wird.

Soll die Bodenfläche zweckmäßig ausgenutzt werden, so ist es wichtig, daß die Stützen in eine Regalachse fallen, das heißt, daß die Achsabstände der Stützen, im rechten Winkel zur Richtung der Regale gemessen, ein Vielfaches der Achsabstände der Regale darstellen. Tabelle 3 zeigt eine Reihe möglicher Raster.

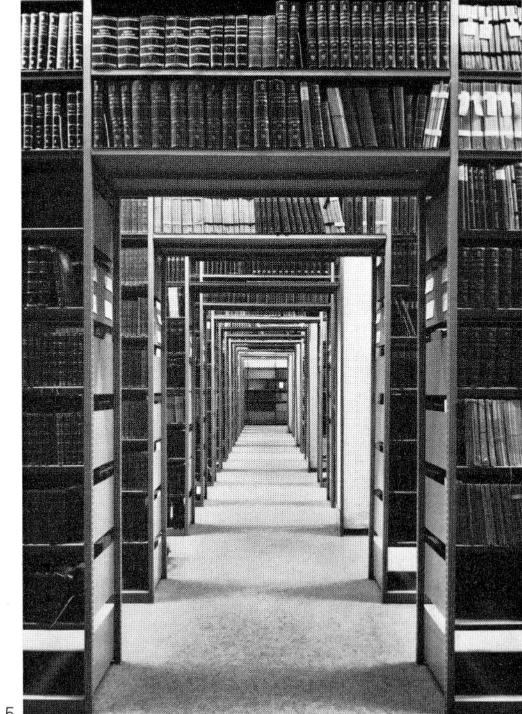

5

5. A system of square slotted uprights and steel shelves with a special infill section over the corridor has been used in the stacks of the State Library in Aarhus, Denmark. Reska Equipment, Birkerød, Denmark.

5. In der Staatsbibliothek von Aarhus, Dänemark, wurde ein System mit Schlitzpfosten und Stahlböden sowie speziellen Einheiten über dem Korridor verwandt. Reska, Birkerød, Dänemark.

Table 3

*Dimensional relationships between stack centres and structural grids of various spans*

| Span of structural grid | Stack centres Closed access | Open access | Periodicals display |
|---|---|---|---|
| 18' | 3'7" | 4'6" | 6'0" |
| 20' | 4'0" | 5'0" | 6'8" |
| 22'6" | 3'5" | 4'6" 5'7" | 5'7" |
| 24' | 4'0" | 4'9 1/2" | 6'0" |
| 25' | 3'7" 4'2" | 5'0" | 6'3" |
| 25'6" | 3'7" | 4'3" 5'1" | 6'4 1/2" |
| 27' | 3'10" | 4'6" 5'7" | 5'7" 6'7 1/2" |

(From Information Sheet 1593, prepared by Sally Odd in *The Architects' Journal*, 28 February 1968.)

Tabelle 3

*Maßbeziehungen zwischen Regalachsen und Konstruktionsraster*

| Konstruktions-raster | Regalachsen Geschlossener / Offener Magazinbereich | | Zeitschriften-auslage |
|---|---|---|---|
| 5,40 m | 1,12 m | 1,35 m | 1,82 m |
| 6,00 m | 1,21 m | 1,52 m | 2,02 m |
| 6,85 m | 1,04 m | 1,35/1,69 m | 1,69 m |
| 7,31 m | 1,21 m | 1,43 m | 1,82 m |
| 7,62 m | 1,12/1,26 m | 1,52 m | 1,89 m |
| 7,75 m | 1,12 m | 1,28/1,37 m | 1,92 m |
| 8,35 m | 1,17 m | 1,35/1,69 m | 1,69/1,99 m |

(Aus dem Informationsblatt 1593, zusammengestellt von Sally Odd in *The Architects' Journal*, 28. Februar 1968.)

6

6. Double-sided free standing steel stacks; the solid ends provide lateral stability. Beatley Library, Simmons College, Boston, Massachusetts. Architects: Campbell, Aldrich & Nulty.

6. Doppelseitige frei stehende Stahlregale. Die festen Seitenwandungen sorgen für Stabilität. Beatley Library, Simmons College, Boston, Massachusetts. Architekten: Campbell, Aldrich & Nulty.

7–11. Plans of some possible stack layouts within a given column spacing; the area considered in the five diagrams is identical.
The calculations assume that this stack area is part of a closed access library, i. e. only minimal circulation space is needed for attendants and that the stacks are made up of standard sections 3′0″ wide, 7 shelves at 12″ centres high. Each section has therefore 21 lineal feet of shelving and an approximate capacity of 125 books.
The column spacing in figs. 7, 9 and 11 assumes a square grid of 25′6″ (7.772 m) with each column 14″ (35.8 cm) square allowing some dimensional tolerance between columns and standard stack sections.

7–11. Verschiedene Regalgrundrisse innerhalb eines gegebenen Stützenabstandes. Die Fläche ist in allen fünf Diagrammen die gleiche.
Die Berechnungen gehen davon aus, daß das Magazin dem Publikum nicht zugänglich ist, so daß die Verkehrswege für die Angestellten nur einen relativ geringen Raum einnehmen. Außerdem bestehen die Regale aus 91,4 cm breiten Einheiten und sind bei Abständen von 33 cm sieben Fächer hoch. Jede Einheit bietet also 6,40 laufende Meter und hat eine Kapazität von ungefähr 125 Büchern.
Der Stützenabstand in Abb. 7, 9 und 11 basiert auf einem quadratischen Raster von 7,772 m. Die quadratischen Stützen haben eine Abmessung von 35,8 cm Seitenlänge, so daß Maßtoleranzen zwischen Stützen und Standardeinheiten ermöglicht werden.

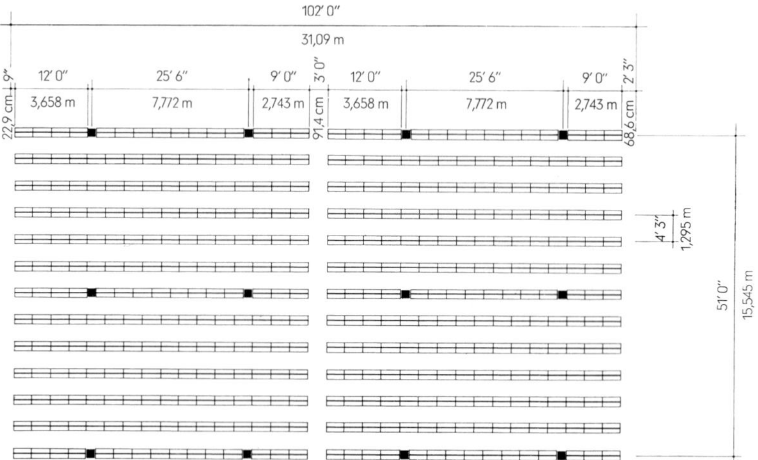


7. Stacks are 4′3″ (1.295 m) on centre line and gangways between groups of stacks are 3′0″ (91.4 cm) wide.
Number of sections: 808.
Number of books: 808 × 125 = 101,000.

7. Die Regale haben Achsabstände von 1,295 m, die Gänge zwischen den Regalgruppen sind 91,4 cm breit.
Zahl der Einheiten: 808.
Zahl der Bücher: 808 × 125 = 101 000.

8. Layout as in fig. 7 but there are no columns, i. e. shelf supports are structural.
Number of sections: 832.
Number of books: 832 × 125 = 104,000.

8. Die Anordnung entspricht der in Abb. 7, es sind jedoch keine Stützen vorhanden. Die Regale sind selbsttragende Konstruktionen.
Zahl der Einheiten: 832.
Zahl der Bücher: 832 × 125 = 104 000.

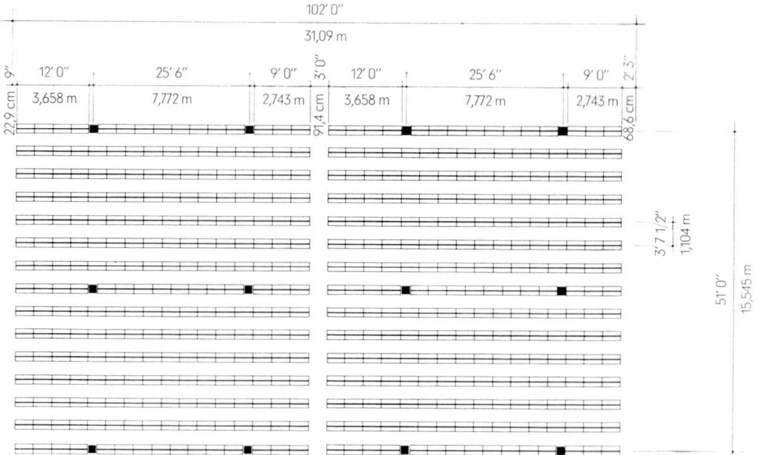


9. Stacks are 3′7½″ (1,104 m) on centre line giving aisles 2′2″ (66.0 cm) wide which is the minimum recommended width if trolleys are to be used.
Number of sections: 936.
Number of books: 936 × 125 = 117,000.

9. Die Regale haben Achsabstände von 1,104 m. Die Gänge haben die Mindestbreite von 66 cm, die bei der Benutzung von Bücherwagen erforderlich ist.
Zahl der Einheiten: 936.
Zahl der Bücher: 936 × 125 = 117 000.

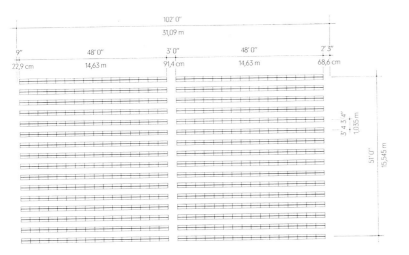

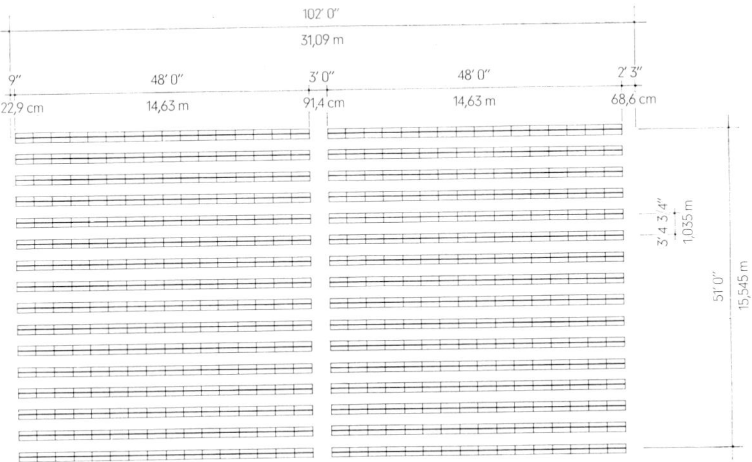


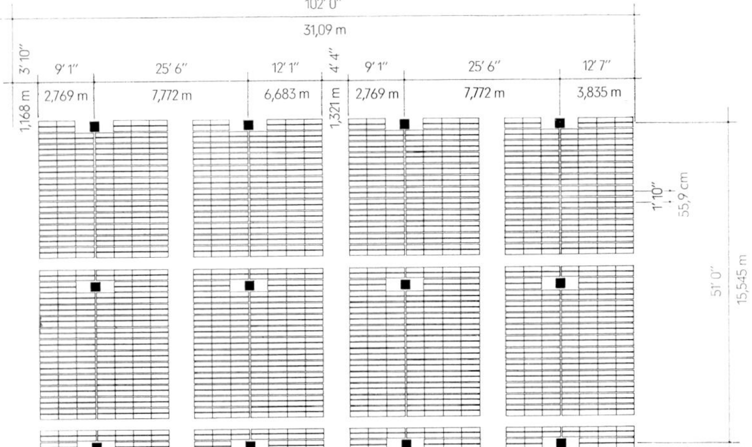


10. Stacks are at 3'4¾" (1.035 m) on centre line. This gives aisles 1'10¾" (57.78 cm) wide which is below the recommended minimum but often found in old libraries. It is also doubtful if a stack length of 48'0" (14.63 m) without cross gangways is tolerable. Shelf supports are structural.
Number of sections: 1024.
Number of books: 1024 × 125 = 128,000.

10. Die Regale haben Achsabstände von 1,035 m. Die Breite der Gänge liegt mit 57,78 cm unter dem empfohlenen Mindestmaß, findet sich jedoch häufig in älteren Bibliotheken. Im übrigen ist es zweifelhaft, ob sich eine Regallänge von 14,63 m ohne quer verlaufende Gänge empfiehlt. Die Regale sind selbsttragende Konstruktionen.
Zahl der Einheiten: 1024.
Zahl der Bücher: 1024 × 125 = 128000.

11. Compact shelving assuming that the portion of stack rolling at any one time is no longer than four sections.
A gap occurs alternatively after every 12 or 13 rows; cross gangways are 4'4" (1.321 m) wide to allow for handles.
Number of sections: 1464.
Number of books: 1464 × 125 = 183,000.
This represents a gain of more than 80% over the layout in fig. 7.

11. Raumsparendes Regalsystem. Vorausgesetzt wird, daß nicht mehr als vier Einheiten zur gleichen Zeit in Bewegung gesetzt werden.
Nach 12 bzw. 13 Reihen ist jeweils freier Raum vorgesehen. Die quer verlaufenden Gänge sind 1,321 m breit, damit das System bedient werden kann.
Zahl der Einheiten: 1464.
Zahl der Bücher: 1464 × 125 = 183000.
Damit ist gegenüber der Anordnung in Abb. 7 ein Raumgewinn von mehr als 80% erzielt.

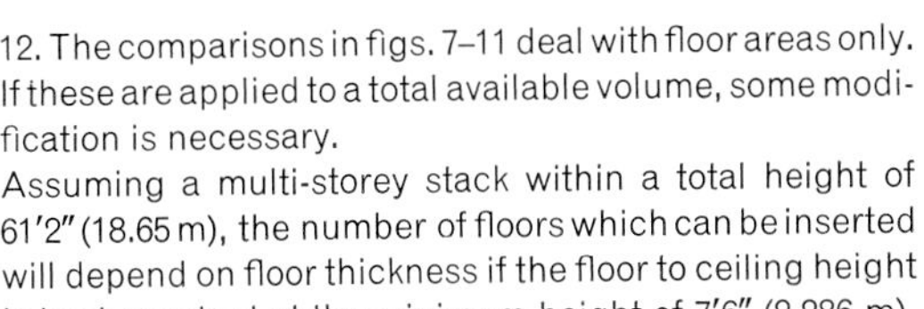

12. The comparisons in figs. 7–11 deal with floor areas only. If these are applied to a total available volume, some modification is necessary.
Assuming a multi-storey stack within a total height of 61'2" (18.65 m), the number of floors which can be inserted will depend on floor thickness if the floor to ceiling height is kept constant at the minimum height of 7'6" (2.286 m).
A. Stacks are on structural shelf supports with metal flooring 2" (5.1 cm) thick.
The number of floors which can be inserted is 8, if stacks are laid out at the maximum possible density as in fig. 10, within the floor area shown on eight floors.
Number of books: 128,000 × 8 = 1,024,000.
B. Compact shelving rolling on structural floors which are 1'1" (33.0 cm) thick to carry this load over 25'6" (7.772 m) spans.
The number of floors which can be inserted is 7, if stacks are laid out as in fig. 11, within the floor area shown on seven floors.
Number of books: 183,000 × 7 = 1,281,000.
This represents a gain of about 25% over the layout shown in fig. 12 A.

12. Die Vergleiche in Abb. 7–11 beziehen sich lediglich auf die Geschoßfläche. Wenn das gesamte Raumvolumen in Betracht gezogen wird, ergeben sich einige Modifikationen.
Bei einem mehrgeschossigen Magazin mit einer Gesamthöhe von 18,65 m hängt die Zahl der Geschosse, die eingefügt werden können, von der Stärke der Decken ab, wenn die lichte Höhe der Geschosse durchgehend die Mindesthöhe von ca. 2,30 m betragen soll.
A. Die Regale sind selbsttragende Konstruktionen, die Metallböden sind 5,1 cm stark.
Es können acht Geschosse eingefügt werden. Wenn die Regale wie in Abb. 10 in größtmöglicher Dichte gestellt werden, ergibt sich bei der gegebenen Geschoßfläche von acht Geschossen als
Zahl der Bücher: 128000 × 8 = 1024000.
B. Das raumsparende Regalsystem wird auf tragenden, 33 cm starken Decken bewegt, die ihre Lasten auf Stützen in Achsabständen von 7,772 m abtragen.
Es können sieben Geschosse eingefügt werden.
Wenn die Regale wie in Abb. 11 angeordnet werden, ergibt sich bei der gegebenen Geschoßfläche von sieben Geschossen als
Zahl der Bücher: 183000 × 7 = 1281000.
Damit ist gegenüber der Anordnung in Abb. 12A ein Raumgewinn von 25% erzielt.

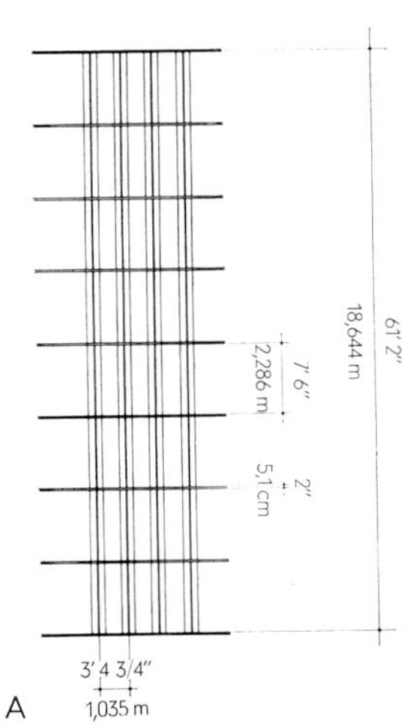


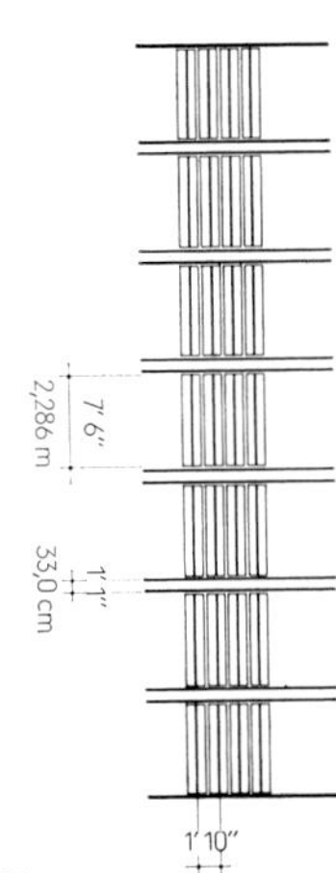

13

14

These conditions are satisfied for example, in a structural grid 25′6″ × 25′6″ (7.75 m × 7.75 m) having columns no greater than 1′6″ × 1′6″ (450 mm × 450 mm) and preferably less to allow for tolerances as shown in figs. 7–11.
The capacity of a book stack within a given floor area will naturally depend on the spacing adopted for the stacks. If it is a multi-storey stack space, the total given volume will have to be considered since the floor thickness needed may also affect the storage capacity. This is particularly the case with compact storage systems where the floor loading is considerably increased. An analysis of a typical volume is given in fig. 12 showing the marked difference in capacity between various designs.
Provided ordinary shelving is being considered, the storage capacity will not be affected by the choice of book shelving. The decision can be made on grounds of adaptability, cost and appearance. It will normally be between timber and steel with various systems available in both materials; some of these are illustrated in figs. 3, 5, 6, 13, 14. On the whole, steel shows at the moment some advantages on adaptability, and, in most countries, also on cost.
Compact shelving is an attempt to use the floor area more efficiently by altering the ratio of circulation to storage which exists in a normal layout. With the centres of stacks 4′6″ apart and shelves 8″ deep, 30% of any aisle is given over to storage, 70% to circulation. Compact shelving alters this relation in favour of storage.
Various designs have in the past been suggested and produced such as having hinged sections fastened to existing stacks and opening into the aisle space like large

Im Hinblick auf spätere Erweiterungen spricht manches für einen Konstruktionsraster, der die Wahl verschiedener Regalabstände zuläßt. Ein quadratischer Raster hat den Vorteil, daß die Richtung der Regale um 90° gedreht werden kann. Von Vorteil ist es auch, wenn der Konstruktionsraster parallel zur Richtung der Regale so verläuft, daß die lichte Weite zwischen den Stützen ein Vielfaches der normalen Regaleinheit (90 cm) beträgt.
Solche Voraussetzungen sind zum Beispiel bei einem Raster von 7,75 × 7,75 m gegeben, wobei die Stützenquerschnitte nicht größer als 45 × 45 cm und möglicherweise sogar kleiner sein sollten, damit Maßtoleranzen gewährleistet sind (vgl. Abb. 7–11).
Die Kapazität eines Regalsystems auf einer gegebenen Grundfläche richtet sich natürlich nach der Spationierung der Regale. Wenn es sich um ein mehrgeschossiges Magazin handelt, muß das Gesamtvolumen berücksichtigt werden, da die erforderliche Deckenstärke ebenfalls die Kapazität beeinflussen kann. Das trifft besonders auf raumsparende Regalsysteme zu, die eine erheblich stärkere Belastung der Decken darstellen. Die Analyse eines typischen Volumens zeigt Abb. 12, die zugleich den Unterschied in der Kapazität der verschiedenen Systeme deutlich macht.
Bei einer normalen Anordnung der Regale wird die Kapazität nicht durch die Wahl des Regalsystems beeinflußt. In einem solchen Fall kann sich die Entscheidung nach Zweckmäßigkeit, Kosten und Aussehen richten. Normalerweise stellt sich vor allem die Frage, ob Holz oder Stahl gewählt werden sollen, wobei in beiden Mate-

13. Steel uprights with wooden shelves which go right through a double-sided section; the absence of a division may make book arrangement awkward. Technische Hochschule, Stuttgart, Germany. Architect: Hans Volkart.
14. Shelving specially made to be part of the general design of the building and its furniture; wooden sides and wooden shelves held by a metal strip with clips let into the uprights. Library, New Zealand House, London. Architect: Robert Matthew, Johnson-Marshall & Partners.

13. Stahlpfosten mit tiefen Fachböden aus Holz, die doppelseitig benutzbar sind. Da eine Unterteilung fehlt, wird möglicherweise die Aufstellung der Bücher erschwert. Technische Hochschule, Stuttgart. Architekt: Hans Volkart.
14. In dieser Bibliothek wurden die Regale entsprechend der Gestaltung des Gebäudes und des Mobiliars entworfen. Holzwangen, Holzbretter und Metalleisten, die in die Vertikalen eingelassen sind. Bibliothek des New Zealand House, London. Architekten: Robert Matthew, Johnson-Marshall & Partners.

15. Steel frames with wooden shelves used as low division between reading spaces and also fixed to a wall. Library, Skedsmo, Norway. Architects: Paul Cappelen and Torbjørn Rodahl.
16. Current magazines displayed on sloping shelves which can be pivotted to reveal back numbers stored on a flat shelf behind. Reska Equipment, Birkerød, Denmark.
17. Sloping wooden shelves for the free display of periodicals set into the same system of uprights as is used for book storage. Technische Hochschule, Stuttgart, Germany. Architect: Hans Volkart.

15. Stahlrahmen mit Holzfächern, zum Teil an der Wand befestigt, zum Teil als frei stehende niedrige Unterteilungen zwischen den Lesebereichen. Bücherei, Skedsmo, Norwegen. Architekten: Paul Cappelen und Torbjørn Rodahl.
16. Die laufenden Zeitschriftennummern sind hier auf abgeschrägten Fächern ausgelegt, die hochgehoben werden können, so daß die dahinter aufbewahrten Nummern zugänglich werden. Reska, Birkerød, Dänemark.
17. Auslegeregal für Zeitschriften mit schräggestellten Fachbrettern. Das Stahlrohrgestell entspricht dem im Magazin verwandten System. Technische Hochschule, Stuttgart. Architekt: Hans Volkart.

doors or rows of fixed stacks with a row of stacks immediately in front which can be slid aside in sections to allow access to the rear part. The most common and probably the most efficient method now in use is made up of closely packed stacks where a complete range of several sections can be slid aside to open up an access aisle. Such stacks are supported on rails in the floor or occasionally hung from overhead rails, and can be moved aside either manually or mechanically. In a well supported system comparatively little effort is needed to slide a range laterally.
Despite the very great increase in storage capacity of such a compact system, it is clearly only suitable when the chance of a demand at the same time for books in nearby stacks is small. The system is therefore at its most useful in large closed access libraries, for little used research material, for reserve collections and similar situations where the material is being retrieved by the library staff.
Compact methods of storage increase storage efficiency without altering the original record. Microcopy alters the record itself by reducing its size. As a result the amount of space used is considerably diminished. To take microfiche as an example, there will be a 97% saving of shelf space compared to books. Microfiche is probably the most easily stored and the simplest to use microcopy so far available and one, for instance, used by NASA (National Aeronautics and Space Agency) in its report distribution programme. It is a transparent film card 105 × 148 mm on which something like 60 pages can be photographed. The top of this card contains the title of the volume which has been copied on the microfiches and it can therefore be located without needing an enlarging device. Assuming that 10,000,000 pages need storing, these can be copied on to about 180,000 microfiches at 60 pages per card. The space needed to file 100 cards is one inch, so that 1,800 inches or 150 feet of linear filing will be needed. If put into filing cabinets, 180,000 microfiches would use up about 55 cu. ft. or with aisles about 100 cu. ft. taking the calculations quoted in *Library Planning for Automation*. If the microfiches are put into boxes each holding 100 cards, the linear space needed is $1^1/_4$" per 100 cards including the box thickness or 190 linear feet for 180,000 cards. If these boxes are placed on six shelves a foot apart with two rows of boxes per foot height, just a little over 15 ft. run of stack will be needed or just over five standard sections. This represents 3% of the storage space required by the original 10,000,000 pages.

rialien verschiedene Systeme zur Verfügung stehen; einige sind in Abb. 3, 5, 6, 13, 14 gezeigt. Im allgemeinen scheinen Stahlsysteme heute vielseitiger verwendbar und in den meisten Ländern auch billiger zu sein.
Raumsparende Regalsysteme nutzen die Bodenfläche besser aus, da bei ihnen im Vergleich zu einem normalen Grundriß ein günstigeres Verhältnis zwischen Zirkulationswegen und eigentlicher Magazinfläche gegeben ist. Wenn die Achsabstände der Regale 1,35 m betragen und die Fachböden 20 cm tief sind, werden 30% des Ganges der Magazinfläche und 70% der Zirkulation zugerechnet. Bei raumsparenden Systemen dagegen fällt dem Magazinbereich ein höherer Prozentsatz zu.
Zu den verschiedenen Systemen, die in der Vergangenheit entwickelt worden sind, zählen beispielsweise die mit Scharnieren an vorhandenen Regalen befestigten Einheiten, die sich wie große Türen auf den Gang öffnen, oder die beweglichen Regalreihen, die sich seitlich verschieben lassen, so daß die dahinterliegenden Reihen erreichbar werden. Die üblichste und wahrscheinlich auch praktikabelste Methode besteht zur Zeit darin, enggestellte Regale mit beweglichen Einheiten zu verwenden, die sich reihenweise seitlich verschieben lassen und dadurch einen Zugang freimachen. Diese Systeme sind entweder auf Gleitschienen im Boden montiert oder gelegentlich an Deckenschienen aufgehängt und können manuell oder mechanisch bewegt werden. Bei einem kontinuierlichen System ist verhältnismäßig wenig Körperkraft erforderlich, um eine Einheit seitlich zu verschieben.
Obwohl raumsparende Systeme die Kapazität des Magazins erheblich vergrößern, lassen sie sich lediglich dort verwenden, wo nur selten Bücher aus nahe beieinander liegenden Regalen zur gleichen Zeit verlangt werden. Sie sind also am nützlichsten in großen, nicht allgemein zugänglichen Bibliotheken, bei wenig benutztem Forschungsmaterial, bei Reservemagazinen und in ähnlichen Fällen, in denen die Bücher vom Bibliothekspersonal herbeigeschafft werden.
Raumsparende Systeme steigern die Kapazität des Magazins, ohne das Originaldokument zu verändern. Mikrokopien dagegen verändern das Dokument, indem sie es verkleinern. Bei Microfiche zum Beispiel ist eine Einsparung von 97% an Regalfläche zu erzielen. Microfiche ist zur Zeit wahrscheinlich die Mikrokopie, die sich am leichtesten lagern und am einfachsten anwenden läßt; sie wird zum Beispiel auch von der NASA (National Aeronautics and Space Agency) benutzt. Microfiche ist eine transparente Filmkarte von 10,5 × 14,8 cm Größe, auf die etwa 60 Buchseiten fotografiert werden können.

15

16

17

18

19

18. An atlas stand with trays on nylon rollers and sloping reading shelf. Brunswick Corporation, Kalamazoo, Michigan.
19. Map chest in timber; it is important to recognize that a variety of material may need storage, each with its own needs. Library. New Zealand House London. Architects: Robert Matthew, Johnson-Marshall & Partners.

18. Atlasschrank mit Fächern auf Nylonrollen und schräger Lesefläche. Brunswick Corporation, Kalamazoo, Michigan.
19. Landkartenschrank aus Holz. In Bibliotheken werden die verschiedensten Materialien aufbewahrt, die jeweils individuelle Lösungen für die Unterbringung erforderlich machen. Bibliothek des New Zealand House, London. Architekten: Robert Matthew, Johnson-Marshall & Partners.

Am Kopf der Karte ist der Titel des kopierten Buches vermerkt, der ohne Vergrößerungsapparat zu entziffern ist. Sollen zum Beispiel 10000000 Seiten gespeichert werden, so lassen sie sich auf etwa 180000 Microfiches mit 60 Seiten pro Karte kopieren. Für 100 Karten werden zur Aufbewahrung 2,5 cm benötigt, so daß insgesamt 45 m erforderlich sind. Nach den Berechnungen in *Library Planning for Automation* würden 180000 Microfiches in Karteischränken etwa 1,5 cbm oder, mit Gängen, etwa 2,8 cbm einnehmen. Wenn die Microfiches in Kästen zu je 100 Karten untergebracht werden, sind pro 100 Karten einschließlich Kasten 3,2 cm erforderlich, was für 180000 Karten 57 m ergibt. Werden diese Kästen zu je zwei Reihen übereinander auf sechs Fachböden mit 30 cm Abstand untergebracht, so sind ca. 4,50 m Regalfläche oder etwas mehr als fünf Standardeinheiten nötig. Das entspricht 3% des Raumes, den die ursprünglichen 10000000 Seiten eingenommen hätten.

20, 21. The steel uprights of a stack system can also be made the structure supporting a number of floors; the book stack becomes a building within a building. The supports can carry floors made of metal decking or a thin concrete slab incorporating electrical services. Pohlschröder & Co., Dortmund, Germany.

20, 21. Die Stahlpfosten eines Regalsystems können auch die Lasten mehrerer Geschoßflächen aufnehmen; das Bücherregal wird dann zu einem Gebäude innerhalb des Gebäudes. Die Stützen tragen Metallböden oder dünne Betonplatten, die elektrische Leitungen enthalten. Pohlschröder & Co., Dortmund.

20

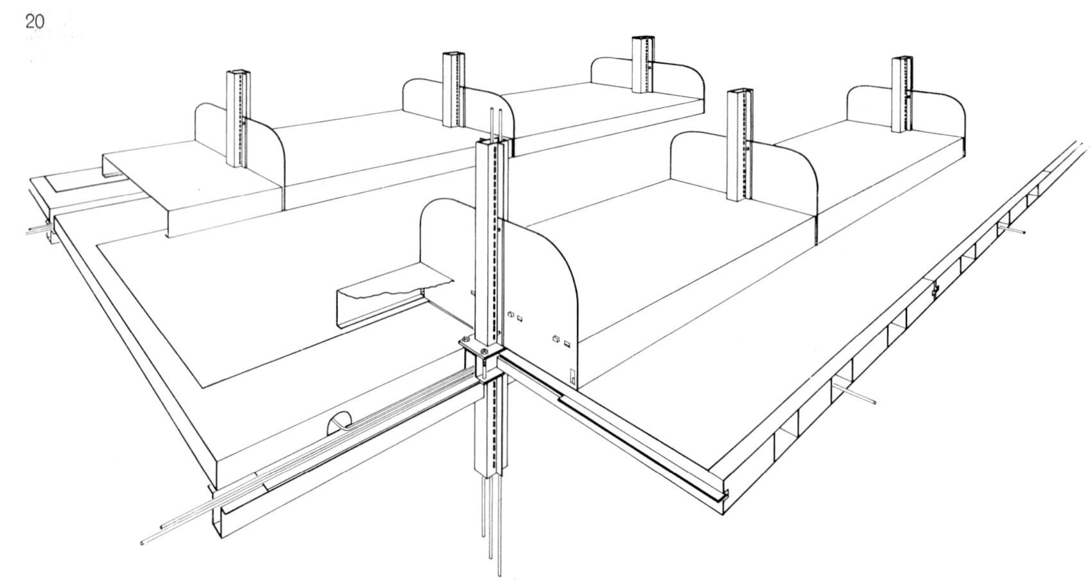

21

22. Book storage used as a defining element in the system of external wall enclosure. Putterham Branch Library, Brookline, Massachusetts. Architects: The Architects Collaborative.
23. Open bins for book storage in children's libraries linked by wooden shelves which can become seats. EKZ Equipment (Central Purchasing Organization for Public Libraries), Reutlingen, Germany.

22. Die Bücherregale sind hier als Gestaltungselement im System der Raumabschlüsse verwandt. Putterham Branch Library, Brookline, Massachusetts. Architekten: The Architects Collaborative.
23. Offene Kästen für die Buchaufbewahrung in Kinderbüchereien. Die Kästen sind mit Holzbrettern verbunden, die als Sitze dienen können. Einkaufszentrale für Öffentliche Büchereien, Reutlingen.

22

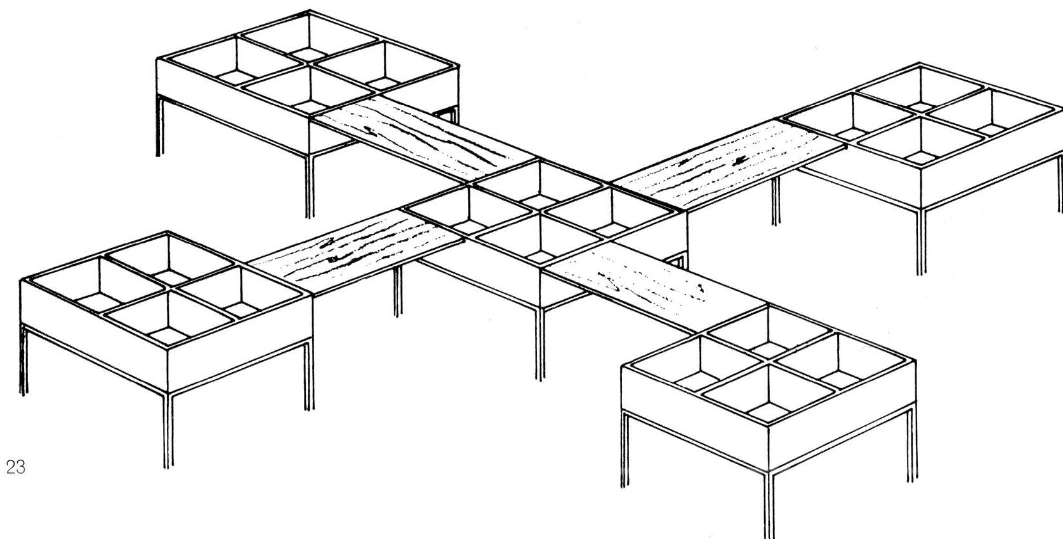

23

24. Bookshelves on metal uprights fixed to partitions making small alcoves. Library for the Danish minority of South Schleswig, Flensburg, Germany. Architects: Tyge Holm and Flemming Grut.
25. Manually operated steel compact shelving; each section can be slid along on a floor-mounted track to allow access. Urajärvi Depot, Helsinki University Library. Architect: O. Hansson.

24. Bücherregale auf Metallstützen, die an Trennwänden befestigt sind. Die Wände bilden kleine Lesenischen. Bibliothek für die dänische Minderheit Südschleswigs, Flensburg. Architekten: Tyge Holm und Flemming Grut.
25. Von Hand bedientes raumsparendes Regalsystem aus Metall. Jede Einheit kann auf einer Gleitschiene am Boden verschoben werden, um den Zugang zu ermöglichen. Urajärvi Depot, Universitätsbibliothek Helsinki. Architekt: O. Hansson.

24

25

### Retrieval

A decision on the way this operation is to be performed will very largely determine a considerable part of the architectural organization of the building. If the book or other information source is to be found and removed from storage by the user, the whole of the stack area must be part of the space accessible from the main lines of movement and must make contact with the reading areas, where these exist. The bulk of the building is, in a sense, a public place. If retrieval is to be done by the library staff, probably helped by mechanical means, storage and reading areas can be dissociated and two clear categories of space – one private, the other public – will exist within the same building organization.

The built forms which result from these two methods are likely to differ a good deal. There are clearly certain kinds of libraries – most small and medium sized public and university libraries – in which closed access has little application just as there are other libraries – the great national collections, research libraries sending off books by post – in which open access is unlikely to play a useful role. There is however a certain no-man's land in which decisions on retrieval and therefore on access are open to debate, not least because these are to some extent dependent on the technology of book handling. It is obvious however that in a building in which these functions have been radically separated it may be extremely difficult to combine them at a later stage; it would seem wise therefore to develop designs which even though assuming closed access at first, do not produce an unalterable separation between stack and reading rooms. Skidmore, Owings & Merrill suggest such a possibility in a design for the University of Chicago Library of Humanities and Social Sciences, in which storage and reading spaces although separated by screens and a possible control position exist on each floor and in which each part can be added to separately. The decision on access will therefore be an administrative one and not dictated by the built form.

### Beschaffung

Die Organisation dieses Vorgangs übt einen starken Einfluß auf die architektonische Disposition des Gebäudes aus. Soll sich der Benutzer das Buch oder eine andere Informationsquelle selbst aus den Regalen beschaffen, so muß das gesamte Magazin in den Bereich einbezogen werden, der von den Hauptverkehrswegen aus zugänglich ist. Außerdem muß das Magazin mit den Lesebereichen in Verbindung gebracht werden, sofern solche vorgesehen sind. Das Gebäude steht also weitgehend dem Publikum offen. Wird die Beschaffung dagegen vom Bibliothekspersonal vorgenommen, das eventuell technische Hilfsmittel zur Verfügung hat, so können Magazin und Lesebereiche voneinander getrennt werden. In diesem Fall entstehen innerhalb eines Gebäudes zwei klar unterschiedene Kategorien von Räumen – die einen der Öffentlichkeit zugänglich, die anderen nicht.

Die gebauten Formen, die sich aus diesen beiden Konzeptionen ergeben, unterscheiden sich im allgemeinen deutlich voneinander. Es gibt zwar Bibliothekstypen – die meisten kleinen und mittleren öffentlichen Büchereien und Universitätsbibliotheken –, in denen das Magazin fast immer zugänglich ist, während etwa in den großen Nationalbibliotheken oder in Forschungsbibliotheken, die Bücher per Post verschicken, Freihandbereiche nicht von Nutzen sind. In anderen Fällen jedoch lassen sich die Beschaffung und damit die Zugänglichkeit des Magazins sowohl in der einen wie in der anderen Weise organisieren. In einem Gebäude, in dem die Funktionen streng getrennt sind, ist es freilich schwierig, sie zu einem späteren Zeitpunkt miteinander zu verbinden; es wäre deshalb angebracht, Grundrisse zu entwickeln, die zunächst einen geschlossenen Magazinbereich vorsehen, zugleich aber eine spätere Verbindung zwischen Magazin und Leseräumen ermöglichen. Skidmore, Owings & Merrill schlagen eine solche Lösung in einem Entwurf für die Library of Humanities and Social Sciences an der University of Chicago vor. Hier sind in jedem Geschoß Magazin-

1. Retrieval at its simplest – the reader looks for the book being guided by labels on the shelves. Hampstead Central Library, London. Architects: Sir Basil Spence, Bonnington & Collins.
2. Personal retrieval is often accompanied by a certain amount of sampling in order to make a choice. Seats near the shelves are a great help. Public Library, Hälsingborg, Sweden. Architects: Arton.

1. Die einfachste Form der Beschaffung: Der Leser wird durch Aufschriften an den Regalen geleitet und sucht sich selbst das Buch heraus. Zentralbücherei Hampstead, London. Architekten: Sir Basil Spence, Bonnington & Collins.
2. Bei der persönlichen Auswahl blättert der Leser häufig mehrere Bücher durch, ehe er sich für einen Titel entscheidet. Sitzplätze in der Nähe der Regale erweisen sich deshalb als sehr nützlich. Öffentliche Bücherei, Hälsingborg, Schweden. Beratende Architekten: Arton.

1

2

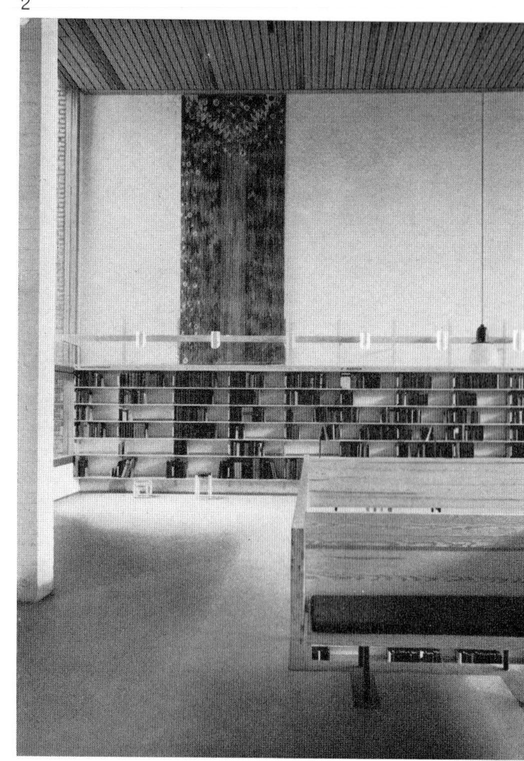

3

3, 4. Closed access libraries require a message from the reader to go to the stacks before retrieval can take place. This message is most commonly sent to positions in the stacks by pneumatic tube. Municipal and University Library, Frankfurt-on-Main. Architect: Ferdinand Kramer.

3, 4. Sind die Magazine nicht für das Publikum zugänglich, so muß der Bestellzettel des Lesers an das Magazin geschickt werden, damit das Buch beschafft werden kann. In den meisten Bibliotheken werden die Buchbestellungen mit Rohrpostanlagen ins Magazin befördert. Universitäts- und Stadtbibliothek, Frankfurt am Main. Architekt: Ferdinand Kramer.

4

Given that retrieval is to be by the reader, the architectural problem is relatively simple. It consists of providing an environment within the storage areas which makes those spaces appear part of the whole building, gives adequate space for movement and arranges the stack in such a manner that the linear consecutive nature of the sequence of books in the catalogue can be understood as a similar consecutive arrangement of the stacks. A progression which has the appearance of continuity and allows of only one interpretation at the corners is obviously the simplest to understand.
Where this space also forms the predominant part of the building, as in a public lending library, the whole feeling of the place will depend on its design. It may be advisable not to treat the shelving as if it were in a tightly laid out storage area, but deliberately to reduce both its height and the distance of the bottom shelf from the floor so as to make retrieval easier and to introduce small seating areas among the shelving in which casual reading is possible. The function of retrieval and an immediate check on whether or not the book is likely to be of interest should be possible within the same space and this double operation is in fact one of the characteristics of the public library.
Given that retrieval is to be performed by the library staff, three distinct components of this operation should be distinguished:
1. Sending a message to the stack area giving the title of the book or its code equivalent including a code for its position.
2. Finding the book within the stack area on the basis of this message and removing it from the shelf.
3. Despatching the book from the stack to the reading room. Mechanical means of assisting the first and third operation are in existence, the middle operation has still however to be done manually though it may be assisted by mechanically operated devices which guide the attendant to the correct shelf.
The most common method of sending the message is to put a demand slip into a metal container which will be put into a pneumatic tube and routed by an operator to the appropriate part of the stack. This routing can be done either by having separate tubes to each station in the stack or having a dialling device on the metal container which automatically directs it by tripping mechanisms to the correct stack section. The first method is rather more foolproof and actually not more space consuming because of the different radii of curvature at the bends needed by the two systems.
The demand slip can also be a thin piece of card which can have its two ends folded down at right angles and then be placed direct into a pneumatic tube with a corresponding thin rectangular cross-section. This method is rather quieter than the one using metal containers and is successfully in use at the Bibliothèque du Musée d'Histoire Naturelle in Paris for example.
The most interesting and potentially the most efficient method of transmitting the message is one which uses an adaptation of a telephone system and which was developed for the Technical University at Delft.
The principle of the system is shown in diagrammatic form on p. 142, fig. 6. It is "an electrical switching system which directly connects the request with the proper stack location. Since the system has been in operation, the waiting time of the library user has been cut down to an average somewhere between one and four minutes." The previous average was between 15 and 20 minutes.
J. Verhoeff, formerly the head of the Research Department of the library, describes the working of the system (fig. 6) as follows: "At convenient points within the catalogue area

und Leseräume vorgesehen, die nur durch provisorische Zwischenwände und eine eventuelle spätere Kontrollposition voneinander getrennt sind und sich gesondert miteinander verbinden lassen. Die Entscheidung über die Zugänglichkeit des Magazins hängt daher von der Bibliotheksverwaltung und nicht von der Architektur ab.
Wird die Beschaffung vom Leser selbst vorgenommen, so ist das architektonische Problem relativ einfach. Das Magazin muß mit den übrigen Bereichen des Gebäudes in visueller Verbindung stehen und genügend Raum für die Zirkulation bieten; außerdem muß die Anordnung der Regale der Aufeinanderfolge der Bücher im Katalog entsprechen. Am übersichtlichsten ist zweifellos eine kontinuierlich wirkende Aufstellung, die auch an den Ecken eindeutig zu interpretieren ist.
Wo dieser Bereich zugleich den beherrschenden Teil des Gebäudes bildet, wie zum Beispiel in einer öffentlichen Leihbücherei, hängt die räumliche Wirkung von der Gestaltung dieser Zone ab. So ist es zum Beispiel ratsam, die Regale nicht wie in einer kompakten Magazinanlage zu behandeln, sondern ihre Höhe wie auch den Abstand des untersten Faches vom Boden zu reduzieren, so daß die Bücher bequem zu erreichen sind. Außerdem sollten kleine Sitzgruppen innerhalb des Regalbereiches eingerichtet werden, damit der Benutzer das Buch, das er sich herausgenommen hat, durchblättern kann. Es sollte möglich sein, innerhalb des gleichen Bereiches die Auswahl zu treffen und sofort zu prüfen, ob das Buch in Frage kommt oder nicht. Die Kombination dieser beiden Vorgänge bildet eines der Charakteristika der öffentlichen Bücherei.
Wird die Beschaffung vom Bibliothekspersonal durchgeführt, so lassen sich drei Phasen unterscheiden:
1. Es wird eine Anweisung ins Magazin geschickt, die den Titel des Buches oder seine Signatur, aus der die Angabe des Standortes hervorgeht, enthält.
2. Das Buch wird auf Grund der Anweisung im Magazin ausfindig gemacht und aus dem Regal genommen.
3. Das Buch wird vom Magazin in den Lesesaal gesandt. Den ersten und dritten Vorgang können technische Hilfsmittel erleichtern, der zweite muß jedoch noch immer manuell ausgeführt werden, obwohl es immerhin technische Vorrichtungen gibt, die das Personal an das richtige Fach führen.
Im allgemeinen wird die Anweisung so erteilt, daß der Bestellzettel in eine Metallkapsel gelegt wird, die über eine Rohrpostanlage in den entsprechenden Bereich des Magazins gelangt. Entweder führen verschiedene Rohrpostanlagen zu den einzelnen Abteilungen des Magazins, oder die Metallkapsel hat eine Wählvorrichtung mit Auslösemechanismen, die sie automatisch zur richtigen Abteilung leiten. Das erste Verfahren funktioniert um einiges zuverlässiger und nimmt im Grunde nicht mehr Raum ein, da die beiden Systeme in den Kurven verschiedenartige Krümmungsradien benötigen.
Bei dem Bestellzettel kann es sich auch um ein dünnes Stück Karton handeln, das an beiden Enden rechtwinklig gefaltet und direkt in eine Rohrpostanlage mit entsprechend schmalem rechteckigem Querschnitt gesteckt wird. Diese Methode verursacht – im Gegensatz zu den Anlagen mit Metallkapseln – wenig Lärm und wird zum Beispiel in der Pariser Bibliothèque du Musée d'Histoire Naturelle mit Erfolg angewandt.
Die interessanteste und vielleicht auch wirksamste Methode, die Bestellung zu übermitteln, wurde für die Technische Hochschule in Delft, Niederlande, entwikkelt und bedient sich eines telefonähnlichen Systems.
Das Prinzip des Systems ist in schematischer Form auf S. 142, Abb. 6, dargestellt. Es handelt sich um »ein elektrisches Schaltsystem, das die Anforderung sofort an den

5. The Catalogue Hall / Blick in den Katalogsaal.

are five Ericsson telephones (1) connected with a switching centre (2). The call number of a desired book is dialled on one of these telephones and switched by the centre to the floor on which the requested book is housed (3). The dialled information causes certain direction lights to be turned on in the stacks. The attendant is guided by these lights towards the stack in which the book is shelved. The correct stack and shelf are identified by the lights, and the book location on the shelf is displayed near the stack on digit indicator tubes. The attendant takes the book from the shelf and lays it in the spiral chute (5) and presses the upper button (4). If the book is not on the shelf, the attendant presses the lower button (4) in which case the book number is automatically typed on the typewriter (10) next to the loan desk. In the first case the book, by its own weight, descends gracefully down the spiral chute (5) and is picked up by a conveyor belt (6). This conveyor brings it to the main building and drops it into another spiral chute (7) which ends on a second conveyor belt (8). This belt deposits the book on the loan desk (9). In both cases the paper tape punch (11) records the call number of the requested book followed by a + if the book was in and by a − if the book was out. Hence, the assistant at the loan desk receives either the requested book or the not-on-shelf message. The switching process and the overall system status can be followed on an automatic display (12). It shows engaged if someone is dialling or if all memories are filled. Otherwise it shows free and library users may dial requests."

The great merits of the system are, apart from its speed and simplicity, that the system contains within it as a subsystem a foolproof guiding mechanism for the attendants in the stacks, and that there is a permanent record of the books which have been in demand which can be translated into data capable of being analyzed by computer.

A considerable improvement of the system would be if the request were dialled to a computer rather than a telephone exchange. Such a computer could store a large number of incoming demands, check these and immediately report back whether or not the book was available. There would then be no abortive search in the stacks. This is technically a perfectly feasible refinement and is being studied at Delft.

The despatch of books from the stack to the reading area can of course be done by attendants on foot, but is more usually done mechanically by some adaptation of light industrial handling devices such as moving belts and paternosters. Books can also be sent in padded containers in large pneumatic tubes such as those below the road

genauen Standort vermittelt. Seit das System verwendet wird, ist die Wartezeit des Bibliotheksbenutzers auf durchschnittlich eine bis vier Minuten verkürzt worden.« Vorher hatte die durchschnittliche Wartezeit 15 bis 20 Minuten betragen.

J. Verhoeff, früher Leiter der Forschungsabteilung an der Bibliothek, beschreibt das System (Abb. 6) wie folgt: »An günstigen Punkten des Katalogbereiches stehen fünf Ericsson-Telefone (1), die mit einer Schaltzentrale (2) verbunden sind. Auf den Telefonen wird die Rufnummer des gewünschten Buches gewählt und von der Zentrale an das Geschoß übermittelt, in dem das Buch aufbewahrt wird (3). Die gewählte Information läßt im Regalbereich richtungweisende Lampen aufleuchten. Diese Signale führen den Bibliotheksangestellten zu dem Regal, in dem das Buch steht. Sie identifizieren Regal und Fach, und der Standort des Buches im Fach wird auf Anzeigern in Regalnähe signalisiert. Der Angestellte nimmt das Buch aus dem Fach, legt es in die spiralförmige Rutsche (5) und drückt auf die obere Taste. Ist das Buch nicht am Fach, drückt der Angestellte auf die untere Taste (4), woraufhin die Schreibmaschine (10) direkt neben dem Tisch der Ausleihe automatisch die Nummer des Buches schreibt. Im ersten Fall gleitet das Buch durch sein eigenes Gewicht sanft die Wendelrutsche (5) hinunter und wird von einem Förderband (6) aufgenommen. Das Förderband transportiert das Buch zum Hauptgebäude und läßt es in eine weitere Wendelrutsche (7) fallen, die auf einem zweiten Förderband (8) endet. Dieses Förderband deponiert das Buch auf dem Tisch der Ausleihe (9). In beiden Fällen registriert der Lochstreifen (11) die Rufnummer des angeforderten Buches, gefolgt von einem +, wenn das Buch am Fach, und einem −, wenn es nicht am Standort war. Der Angestellte an der Ausleihe erhält also entweder das gewünschte Buch oder die Mitteilung, daß das Buch nicht am Standort war. Der Schaltprozeß läßt sich auf einer Kontrolltafel (12) verfolgen. Sie zeigt ›besetzt‹ an, wenn jemand wählt oder wenn alle Speicher belegt sind; anderenfalls gibt sie ein Freizeichen, und die Bibliotheksbenutzer können die Nummern der gewünschten Bücher wählen.«

Abgesehen von der Schnelligkeit und Einfachheit liegt ein großer Vorzug des Verfahrens darin, daß es als untergeordnetes System einen narrensicheren Führungsmechanismus für die Angestellten im Magazin enthält. Außerdem lassen sich die Anforderungen der Benutzer laufend registrieren und in Daten übersetzen, die von einem Computer analysiert werden können.

Das System würde erheblich verbessert, wenn die gewählte Zahl einem Computer und nicht einer Telefonzentrale übermittelt würde. Ein Computer könnte eine große Zahl von Anforderungen speichern und prüfen und sofort bekanntgeben, ob das Buch verfügbar ist oder nicht. Es gäbe dann kein vergebliches Suchen im Magazin mehr. Die Möglichkeit einer solchen Verbesserung, die technisch ohne weiteres durchzuführen ist, wird zur Zeit in Delft geprüft.

Die Beförderung der Bücher vom Magazin zum Lesebereich kann natürlich von Bibliotheksangestellten besorgt werden; häufiger werden jedoch leichte Transportanlagen der Industrie wie Fließbänder und Paternoster eingesetzt, die den Zwecken der Bibliothek angepaßt sind. Die Bücher können auch in gepolsterten Behältern über riesige Rohrpostanlagen befördert werden; eine solche Anlage verbindet zum Beispiel unterirdisch das Hauptgebäude der Library of Congress in Washington, D.C., mit dem Nebengebäude.

Die üblichste Installation ist ein Lift, der die Bücherwagen transportiert, oder ein kleiner Aufzug, der allein die Bücher aufnimmt. Wenn der Weg horizontal oder nur leicht

5–17. The circulation system at the Technical University at Delft, Netherlands. This contains a mechanized and partly automated book retrieval system in which the "Bibliofoon" – a dialling system relaying requests by means of illuminated lights directly to the stacks and keeping a record of requests on punched tape – plays a dominant role. (See J. Verhoeff, *The Delft Circulation System*, in *Libri*, 1966, vol. 16, no. 1, pp. 1–9.)

5–17. Das Zirkulationssystem der Technischen Hochschule in Delft, Niederlande. Bei diesem mechanisierten und teilweise automatisierten System der Buchbeschaffung spielt das »Bibliofoon« – eine Wähleinrichtung, die jede Anforderung durch Lichtsignale an das Magazin übermittelt und die Bestellungen auf Lochstreifen registriert – eine wichtige Rolle. (Vgl. J. Verhoeff, *The Delft Circulation System*, in *Libri*, Band 16, Nr. 1, 1966, S. 1–9.)

6

6. Diagram of the circulation system / Diagramm des Zirkulationssystems.

1 Catalogue with dials / Katalog mit Wählscheiben
2 Bibliofoon switching centre / Schaltzentrale des Bibliofoon
3 Stacks (3 floors) / Magazin (dreigeschossig)
4 Pushbuttons / Drucktasten
5 Spiral chute / Wendelrutsche
6 Conveyor belt 98′ long / Förderband (30 m lang)
7 Spiral chute / Wendelrutsche
8 Conveyor belt 16′ long / Förderband (5 m lang)
9 Loan desk / Ausleihe
10 Automatic typewriter/Automatische Schreibmaschine
11 Paper tape punch / Lochstreifenmaschine
12 Display / Kontrolltafel
13 Public hall / Öffentliche Halle
14 Beacon / Lichtsignal

7

8

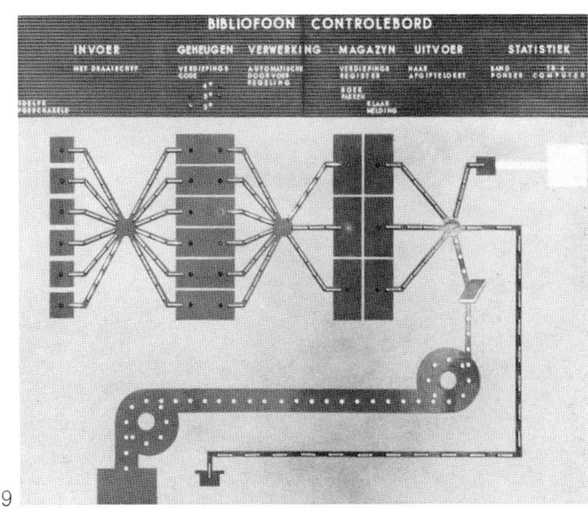

9

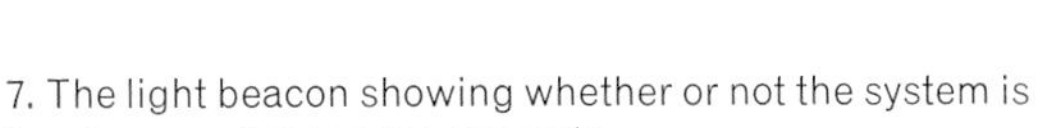

7. The light beacon showing whether or not the system is free to accept incoming requests.
8. The Ericsson telephone on which the request consisting of the books call number is dialled.
9. The automatic display board showing the stages in the circulation system.
10. The switching centre.
11. A section of the stacks showing the digit indicator tube giving the book location on the shelf. The attendant has been alerted by a bell and is guided to the shelf by lights showing the corridor, the row and finally the stack.
12. The push-buttons which are pressed by the attendant to signal whether the book is in or out. If the book is not on the shelf its number is automatically typed on the type-writer next to the loan desk.

7. Das Lichtsignal zeigt an, ob die Anlage eingehende Bestellungen bearbeiten kann.
8. Das Ericsson-Telefon, auf dem der Benutzer die Bestellnummer des gewünschten Buches wählt.
9. Die automatische Kontrolltafel, auf der die verschiedenen Phasen des Beschaffungsprozesses abzulesen sind.
10. Blick in die Schaltzentrale.
11. Blick in das Magazin mit einem Lichtsignal, das den Standort des Buches im Regal anzeigt. Der Angestellte wird durch eine Klingel benachrichtigt und folgt dann den Lichtsignalen, die ihn zu dem Gang, der Reihe und schließlich zu dem Fach leiten.
12. Die Drucktasten, auf die der Angestellte drückt, um mitzuteilen, ob das Buch im Magazin ist oder nicht. Befindet sich das Buch nicht im Regal, so wird seine Nummer von der Schreibmaschine neben der Ausleihe automatisch niedergeschrieben.

10

11

12

13

14

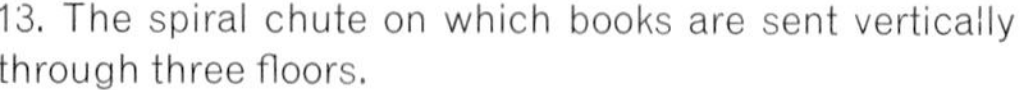

13. The spiral chute on which books are sent vertically through three floors.
14. The spiral chute deposits books on a conveyor belt for lateral movement to a further chute and finally a short second conveyor belt.
15. The second belt deposits the book next to the loan desk.
16. The paper tape punch machine which records all requested call numbers followed by a + if the book was available and by – if it was out.
17. The loan desk and the typewriter next to it which records the call numbers of the books not on the shelf.

13. Die Wendelrutsche, auf der die Bücher vertikal über drei Geschosse transportiert werden.
14. Von der Wendelrutsche gleiten die Bücher auf ein Förderband, das sie zu einer weiteren Wendelrutsche und einem zweiten Förderband transportiert.
15. Das zweite Förderband transportiert die Bücher zur Ausleihe im Katalogsaal.
16. Die Lochstreifenmaschine registriert die Nummern aller bestellten Bücher. Ein + bedeutet, daß das Buch im Magazin, ein –, daß es nicht verfügbar war.
17. Ausleihe mit Schreibmaschine, die die Nummer aller nicht vorhandenen Bücher automatisch niederschreibt.

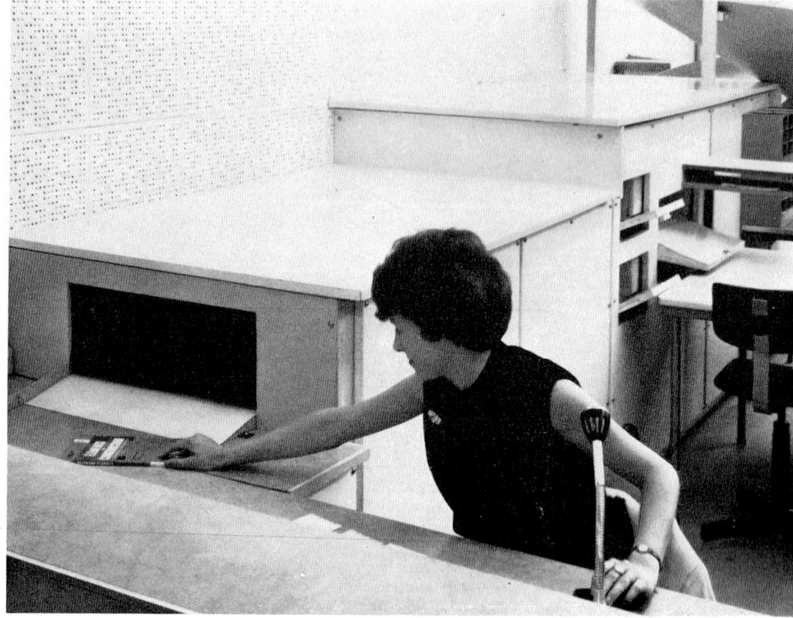
15

16

17

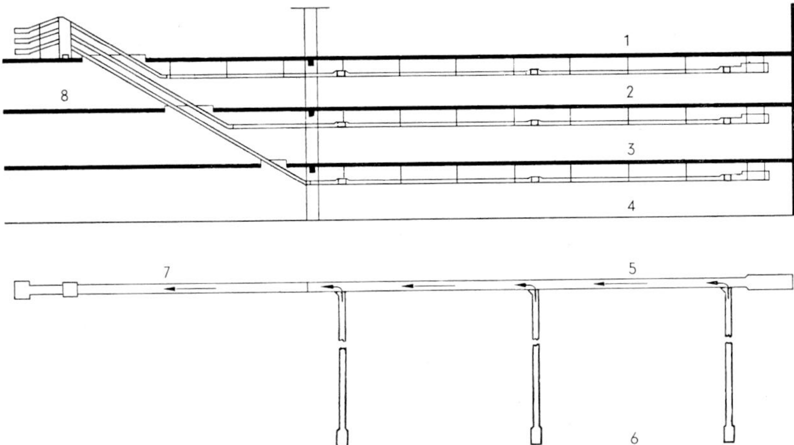


18. A book conveyor belt system / Förderbandsystem.

1 Ground floor / Erdgeschoß
2 Basement 1 / 1. Untergeschoß
3 Basement 2 / 2. Untergeschoß
4 Basement 3 / 3. Untergeschoß
5 Collecting belt / Sammelbänder
6 Delivery belt from stacks / Zubringerbänder
7 Rising belt / Steigebänder
8 Receiving station / Empfangsstelle

19

19. Mechanical systems in the stacks; on the right a pneumatic tube station, on the left at high level a horizontal conveyor belt. Library of the Technische Hochschule, Stuttgart, Germany. Architect: Hans Volkart.
20. Vertical mechanical handling system discharging onto roller tables from which books can be picked up. Library of the Technische Hochschule, Stuttgart.
21. Conveyor belts can move laterally as well as up inclined planes so that a single means of mechanized handling can often be used even in a multi-storey building. Helsinki University Library Extension. Architect: Aarne Ervi.

19. Ein mechanisches System im Magazin; rechts eine Rohrpoststation, links oben ein horizontales Förderband. Bibliothek der Technischen Hochschule, Stuttgart. Architekt: Hans Volkart.
20. Die Förderbänder laufen in Rollenablagen aus, von denen die Bücher heruntergenommen werden können. Bibliothek der Technischen Hochschule, Stuttgart.
21. Förderbänder bewegen sich nicht nur horizontal, sondern können auch Steigungen überwinden, so daß selbst in einem mehrgeschossigen Gebäude ein einziges mechanisches System benutzt werden kann. Erweiterung der Universitätsbibliothek Helsinki. Architekt: Aarne Ervi.

between the main building of the Library of Congress in Washington, D. C. and its annexe.
The commonest device is a book lift either with an attendant and a trolley or a small lift reserved solely for books. For more continuous delivery, books can be placed directly onto a moving belt if the entire journey is to be horizontal or only at a slight incline. If the movement is to be vertical or both horizontal and vertical, books are as a rule carried in buckets. These then travel on horizontal conveyors and can be automatically transferred to paternosters for vertical travel. The speed of such a system can be about 1 ft/sec. for the vertical conveyors and 1.5 ft/sec. for horizontal conveyors and its capacity more than 500 containers per hour, each bucket capable of taking up to 22 lbs. (10 kg) of books. Nor is the system limited to short runs; an installation by Siemens and Halske in Munich runs 400 ft. horizontally and ten floors vertically. It also allows for the buckets to be directed to any one of 936 different addresses by setting a small strip on the side of the bucket. Mechanical handling can at times be avoided if the stack is above the reading area and the books are allowed to slide down a straight or spiral chute. Such a helical chute of bent plastic sheet is in use at the Technical University in Delft, fig. 24, and works well through a height of about 33 ft. (10m).

geneigt ist, können die Bücher direkt auf ein Fließband gelegt werden, das eine kontinuierliche Beförderung ermöglicht; ist der Weg vertikal oder sowohl horizontal als auch vertikal, werden die Bücher gewöhnlich in Behältern untergebracht. Diese Behälter laufen auf horizontalen Fließbändern und können dann für den vertikalen Weitertransport automatisch auf Paternoster überführt werden. Die Schnelligkeit dieses Systems beträgt etwa 30 cm/sec bei vertikalen Paternostern und 45 cm/sec bei horizontalen Fließbändern, die Kapazität liegt bei mehr als 500 Behältern pro Stunde, wobei jeder Behälter bis zu 10 kg Bücher aufnimmt. Zudem ist das System nicht auf kurze Strecken beschränkt; eine Anlage von Siemens & Halske in München läuft horizontal über 120 m und vertikal über zehn Geschosse. Überdies können die Behälter dieser Anlage durch schmale, seitlich befestigte Streifen zu 936 verschiedenen Stationen geleitet werden. Technische Einrichtungen sind nicht erforderlich, wenn das Magazin über dem Lesebereich liegt und die Bücher über eine gerade oder spiralförmige Rutsche nach unten gleiten können. Eine solche Wendelrutsche aus einer gebogenen Kunststoffbahn ist in der Technischen Hochschule in Delft in Gebrauch (Abb. 24); sie reicht über eine Höhe von 10 m und arbeitet ausgezeichnet.

20

21

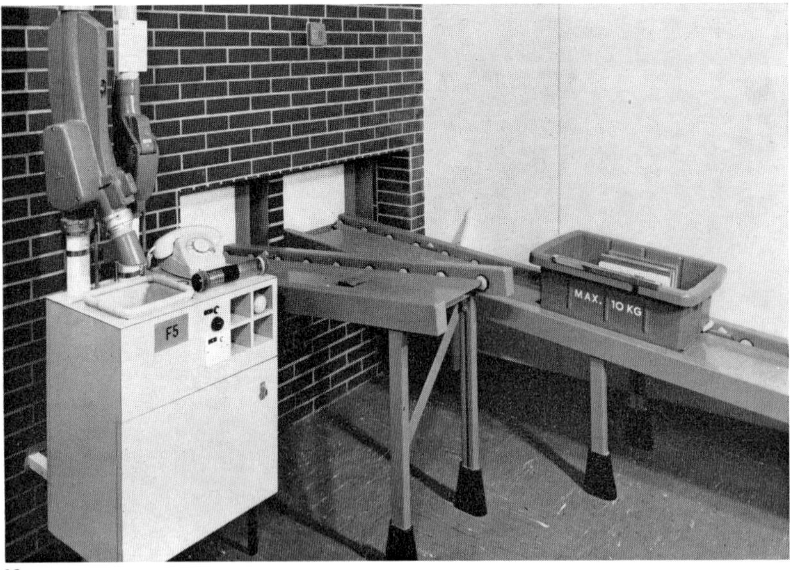


22

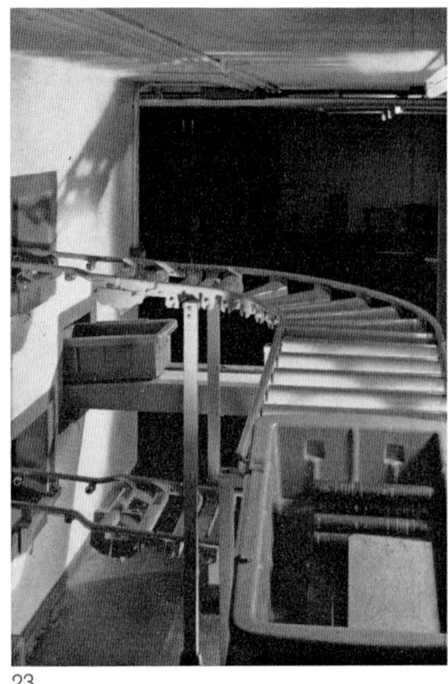

23

24

22. Vertical book handling devices such as paternosters usually employ baskets or boxes to carry books. These are put on and discharged at each floor level. Such an interchange point is here combined with a pneumatic tube station. Municipal and University Library, Frankfurt-on-Main. Architect: Ferdinand Kramer.
23. Book containers after being discharged from a vertical movement device can travel laterally under gravity along roller track or be mechanically taken along a conveyor belt; both are being used in this complex interchange station in the basement of the German Patent Office in Munich. System: Siemens & Halske, Munich.
24. One of the simplest of all book transporting devices, a helical chute which here discharges onto a horizontal conveyor. The chute is made of bent plastic and there are no guiding ridges to damage books. Library of the Technical University, Delft.
25. Retrieval by a member of staff often also implies the delivery of the book to the reader's table. These have in such cases to be clearly labelled and their number entered on the call slip. Each position in this reading area carries a letter and number. Library, Trinity College, Dublin. Architects: Ahrends, Burton & Koralek.

22. Bei vertikalen Förderanlagen wie Paternostern werden die Bücher gewöhnlich in Körben oder anderen Behältern transportiert, die in jedem Geschoß ein- und ausgeladen werden können. Die Förderanlage ist hier mit einer Rohrpoststation kombiniert. Universitäts- und Stadtbibliothek, Frankfurt am Main. Architekt: Ferdinand Kramer.
23. Von einer vertikalen Förderanlage können die Bücherbehälter auf ein horizontales Rollenlager oder auf ein Förderband überführt werden. Bei diesem komplexen Fördersystem im Untergeschoß des Deutschen Patentamtes in München sind beide Einrichtungen vorhanden. System: Siemens & Halske, München.
24. Eine der einfachsten Fördervorrichtungen, eine Wendelrutsche, die hier die Bücher auf ein horizontales Förderband transportiert. Die Rutsche besteht aus gebogenem Kunststoff und hat keine Führungsrillen, die die Bücher beschädigen könnten. Bibliothek der Technischen Hochschule, Delft.
25. Sorgt ein Bibliotheksangestellter für die Beschaffung des Buches, so muß er es häufig auch zum Tisch des Lesers bringen. Jeder Platz muß deshalb deutlich gekennzeichnet und die Platznummer auf dem Leihschein eingetragen werden. In diesem Lesebereich sind die Plätze mit einem Buchstaben und einer Zahl markiert. Bibliothek des Trinity College, Dublin. Architekten: Ahrends, Burton & Koralek.

What is important about all these means of mechanical or gravity conveyance is that they must be able to deal with a flow of material arriving at random intervals without queues being formed. This is quite different from the return of books which can occur in batches.
What is also critical is that a relationship exists between the three components of retrieval in a closed stack – sending the message, finding the book and despatching it – and that this relationship has a bearing on the method of storage which is used and thus on the book capacity of any given area. The efficiency of the retrieval service is measured by the reader as the time which elapses between the moment he orders a volume and the moment it reaches him. Each of the three components of retrieval can have a time ascribed to it. Evidently therefore if a given amount of time is thought to be an acceptable waiting period, then this period could be made up, for example, out of two relatively short components and one slightly longer one. This is a possibility using the Delft system or its computer adaptation together with a rapid mechanical handling system for the first and last stage in retrieval. The intermediate stage, removing the book from the shelf, could then take longer and might therefore make compact storage possible. This would obviously dramatically increase the stack capacity.

Alle diese mechanischen oder auf Grund der Schwerkraft funktionierenden Beförderungsmittel müssen ohne Zeitverlust große Materialmengen bewältigen können, die zu den verschiedensten Zeiten anfallen.
Wichtig ist außerdem, daß die drei Phasen der Beschaffung in einem geschlossenen Magazin – das Einsenden der Anweisung, die Identifizierung des Buches und die Beförderung – in Zusammenhang miteinander stehen und die Methode der Magazinierung, das heißt also auch die Kapazität des Magazinbereichs, beeinflussen. Ob die Beschaffung gut funktioniert, beurteilt der Leser nach der Zeitspanne, die zwischen Bestellung und Erhalt des Buches liegt. Jede der drei Beschaffungsphasen kann eine bestimmte Zeit in Anspruch nehmen. Wird also ein bestimmter Zeitraum als akzeptable Wartezeit angenommen, dann kann sich diese beispielsweise aus zwei relativ kurzen und einer längeren Zeitspanne zusammensetzen. Diese Möglichkeit besteht bei dem Delfter System oder dem entsprechenden Computer-System in Verbindung mit einer schnell arbeitenden mechanischen Hilfsvorrichtung für die erste und letzte Phase der Beschaffung. Die zweite Phase, die Entnahme des Buches aus dem Regal, kann dann mehr Zeit in Anspruch nehmen, so daß eine raumsparende Magazinanlage möglich ist. Dadurch läßt sich die Kapazität des Magazins erheblich steigern.

25

1, 2. Communication in a library is primarily between a reader and a set of information sources; seclusion giving lack of interference aids this process and has traditionally been provided by some sort of cubicle or niche; this can vary in size from a separate room to some enclosure by means of furniture. Max Planck Institute, Munich. Architect: Uwe Breukel.
3. The carrel as a niche within the outer wall was a common medieval form and is now being revived. Nils Yngve Wessell Library, Tufts University, Medford, Massachusetts. Architects: Campbell, Aldrich & Nulty.

1, 2. Die Kommunikation findet in einer Bibliothek in erster Linie zwischen dem Leser und den Kommunikationsquellen statt. Für die Abschirmung gegen Störungen von außen sorgen Kabinette oder *carrels,* die durch entsprechende Möblierung geschaffen werden können oder auch aus einem abgetrennten Raum bestehen. Max-Planck-Institut, München. Architekt: Uwe Breukel.
3. *Carrels* als Nischen in der Außenwand waren im Mittelalter weit verbreitet und werden auch heute wieder entworfen. Nils Yngve Wessell Library, Tufts University, Medford, Massachusetts. Architekten: Campbell, Aldrich & Nulty.

Communication is the key function of the library and the one towards which its other activities are geared. This is true even when the bulk of the communication takes place ouside the building as is likely to be the case in a branch public library without a reading room.
Because communication between source and user is the primary function and since it largely happens in the reading areas, an architectural tradition arose which gave the reading room a hierarchically dominant position. This was normally expressed through a sense of monumentality achieved by height and spatial continuity. Yet it is doubtful whether this accorded with the needs of communication as such.
What appears to be critical to such communication is that it occurs between a single reader on the one hand and the book or other source on the other. All events external to this are in a sense an interference. What would seem to be demanded therefore is seclusion, even a sense of isolation. Many traditional library forms provided this: the medieval carrel or the high-backed benches between the presses of many college libraries. This feeling was also created in some measure in the very large reading rooms where the great volume made each individual seem like a separate, rather isolated, person. This is probably true of the British Museum, for instance, where the individual light and the high back to each desk all helped in making a personal world within a vast space that somehow did not include other readers. It is in no sense true of the large double height reading rooms with ordered rows of tables and chairs under uniform lighting which became a commonplace during this century and which still continue to be built. Spatial arrangement, light and furniture would seem to be the primary elements which need manipulation if an environment suitable for communication is to be devised. The simplest of all methods uses bookshelves to provide separation. Seating is arranged among the books and there is no clear spatial distinction between stack space and reading areas. Quite apart from flexibility in use, this also places the reader near to a good proportion of his likely sources. Because this is obviously such a simple and efficient method of providing a suitable reading environment, it also further reinforces the argument in favour of open access which is of course essential if this arrangement is to be possible.
The most defined situation is that of the carrel, a small enclosure with a table, chair and some shelves, which

Die Kommunikation ist die Hauptfunktion der Bibliothek, auf die alle anderen Tätigkeiten bezogen sind. Das trifft selbst dann zu, wenn die Kommunikation größtenteils außerhalb des Gebäudes stattfindet, wie zum Beispiel bei der Zweigstelle einer öffentlichen Bücherei ohne Lesesaal.
Da nun die Kommunikation zwischen der Informationsquelle und dem Leser die wichtigste Rolle spielt und da sie hauptsächlich in den Lesebereichen stattfindet, entwickelte sich eine architektonische Tradition, die dem Lesesaal einen beherrschenden Platz in der Hierarchie der Bibliotheksräume zuwies. Sie äußerte sich oft in einer gewissen Monumentalität, die durch Höhe und räumliche Kontinuität erzielt wurde, aber wohl kaum günstige Voraussetzungen für eine Kommunikation schuf.
Das wichtigste Kennzeichen der Kommunikation in der Bibliothek ist die Tatsache, daß sie zwischen einem einzigen Leser einerseits und dem Buch oder einer anderen Informationsquelle andererseits stattfindet. Alles, was ringsumher geschieht, bedeutet in gewisser Weise eine Störung. Was also erforderlich scheint, ist Abgeschlossenheit, ja sogar ein Gefühl der Isolation, wie es viele traditionelle Bibliotheksformen – die mittelalterlichen *carrels* oder die Bänke mit den hohen Rückwänden zwischen den Schränken der College-Bibliotheken – vermittelten. Ein Gefühl der Abgeschlossenheit gaben bis zu einem gewissen Grade auch die sehr großen Lesesäle, deren Volumen das Individuum abzusondern und zu isolieren schien. Das trifft beispielsweise auf das British Museum zu, wo zudem die individuelle Tischbeleuchtung und die hohen Rückwände der Tische innerhalb des großen Raumes einen privaten Bereich schaffen, der die anderen Benutzer ausschließt. Anders dagegen die zwei Geschosse hohen Lesesäle mit wohlgeordneten Tisch- und Stuhlreihen und einheitlicher Raumbeleuchtung, die in diesem Jahrhundert allgemein üblich wurden und immer noch gebaut werden. Räumliche Gliederung, Licht und Möblierung sind offensichtlich die wichtigsten Voraussetzungen, wenn eine Umgebung geschaffen werden soll, die eine Kommunikation fördert. Das einfachste Verfahren benutzt Bücherregale als trennende Elemente. Die Arbeitsplätze befinden sich inmitten der Bücher, Magazin- und Lesebereich gehen ineinander über. Diese Anordnung ist nicht nur äußerst flexibel, sondern bringt den Leser auch in die Nähe zahlreicher möglicher Quellen. Da das Verfahren mit einfachsten Mitteln eine für die

1

2

3

4

5

becomes each reader's study cubicle. Where such spaces have been provided, as in many of the recent libraries in America and in the new British Universities, they have been extremely popular and are used in preference to the open reading rooms. For intensive undisturbed study they probably provide the most suitable environment and this is recognized in a sense by the fact that where carrels are scarce they get preferentially allocated to research students and staff.

Carrels do of course take up more space than tables, perhaps 40 sq. ft. as against 15 sq. ft. per person excluding circulation space, see fig. 6, and it may not be possible to use them everywhere. The aedicular feeling of the carrel can to some extent however be provided by enclosure which is part of the furniture. Medieval manuscripts show a whole range of extremely ingenious constructions which supported the heavy manuscripts, gave some adjacent shelf space and provided a measure of screening. When books became lighter and rooms were heated, these designs were abandoned though the problem of enclosure still needed solving. Only very recently has there been a return to a proper consideration of the immediate environment appropriate to a reader.

Some of this may have been prompted by the fact that the equipment needed to read micro-reproductions demands an individual study position and is best placed in a slightly enclosed situation shielding the projected image from excessive light. This also suggests that the more a library is planned around the notion of an individual study place, the more flexible is it likely to be in the future; it will be more capable of absorbing the technological changes which must inevitably relate to its prime function, the communication of an individual with the information source.

Part of the design of the immediate environment will also have to deal with light and sound. Both will affect the feeling of seclusion.

The light intensity recommended for reading is 30 lumens/sq. ft. with glare index 19 (32 lux). It is furthermore suggested that the balance between the brightness of the areas in the field of vision should be in the following ratios:

| | |
|---|---|
| The visual task (the book) | 10 |
| Immediate surround (table top) | 3 |
| Background (walls, bookcases) | 1 |

(Information sheet 1322 *Environmental Standards for Libraries* (from *Architects' Journal,* 17 March 1965.)

Lektüre günstige Umgebung schafft, liefert es zudem Argumente für die Zugänglichkeit des Magazins, die in diesem Fall natürlich Bedingung ist.

Die am klarsten definierte räumliche Situation ist die des *carrel,* eines kleinen, abgeschlossen wirkenden Bereichs mit Tisch, Stuhl und einigen Regalfächern, der zum Studiengehäuse des Lesers wird. Wo solche separaten Zonen geschaffen wurden – zum Beispiel in vielen neueren Bibliotheksbauten der englischen Universitäten und in Amerika –, erfreuen sie sich großer Beliebtheit und werden sehr viel häufiger benutzt als die offenen Lesesäle. Sie bieten die wohl günstigste Umgebung für intensives, ungestörtes Studium, eine Tatsache, die sich auch daran ablesen läßt, daß sie vorzugsweise den Studenten und Universitätsangehörigen mit Forschungsaufgaben zugeteilt werden, wenn nur wenige *carrels* vorhanden sind.

*Carrels* beanspruchen natürlich mehr Raum als Tische, nämlich ungefähr 3,6 qm im Vergleich zu 1,35 qm pro Person einschließlich der Zirkulationswege (vgl. Abb. 6). Es ist deshalb nicht überall möglich, sie einzuplanen. Bis zu einem gewissen Grade läßt sich aber die Abgeschlossenheit solcher Gehäuse auch durch Abgrenzungen erzielen, die einen Teil der Möblierung bilden. Mittelalterliche Manuskripte zeigen zahlreiche höchst kunstfertige Konstruktionen, die die schweren Manuskripte trugen, für Regalraum sorgten und gegen die Umwelt abschirmten. Als die Bücher leichter wurden und die Räume geheizt waren, schienen solche Konstruktionen überflüssig, obwohl das Problem der Isolierung sich damit von neuem stellte. Erst in neuester Zeit sind wieder Bestrebungen im Gange, dem einzelnen Leser einen abgeschlossenen Bereich zu bieten.

Das mag zum Teil darauf zurückzuführen sein, daß die Ausstattung, die zum Entziffern von Mikrokopien nötig ist, einen gesonderten Arbeitsplatz und außerdem eine gewisse Abschirmung erfordert, da das projizierte Bild gegen starken Lichteinfall geschützt werden muß. Auch dieser Aspekt spricht dafür, daß eine Bibliothek um so flexibler künftigen Aufgaben gerecht werden kann, je konsequenter sie auf individuelle Arbeitsplätze hin geplant ist; technische Veränderungen, wie sie sich aus der Hauptfunktion der Bibliothek, der Kommunikation zwischen Individuum und Informationsquelle, stets von neuem ergeben, sind bei einer solchen Planung sehr viel leichter zu berücksichtigen.

4. An element of individual enclosure created as part of the original built form rather than as inserted furniture; this ensures its existence but reduces the possibility for change. Library, Trinity College, Dublin. Architects: Ahrends, Burton & Koralek.

5. A partially delineated and individually lit space created through the design of the furniture. Library, Åbo Academy, Turku, Finland. Architect: Woldemar Baeckmann.

4. Individuelle Abschirmung wird hier nicht durch nachträglich aufgestelltes Mobiliar erreicht, sondern durch Elemente der gebauten Form. Dadurch wird freilich die Flexibilität eingeschränkt. Bibliothek des Trinity College, Dublin. Architekten: Ahrends, Burton & Koralek.

5. Hier schaffen die individuell beleuchteten Tische mit ihren Abgrenzungen einen zumindest teilweise abgeschlossenen Bereich. Bibliothek der Åbo-Akademie, Turku, Finnland. Architekt: Woldemar Baeckmann.

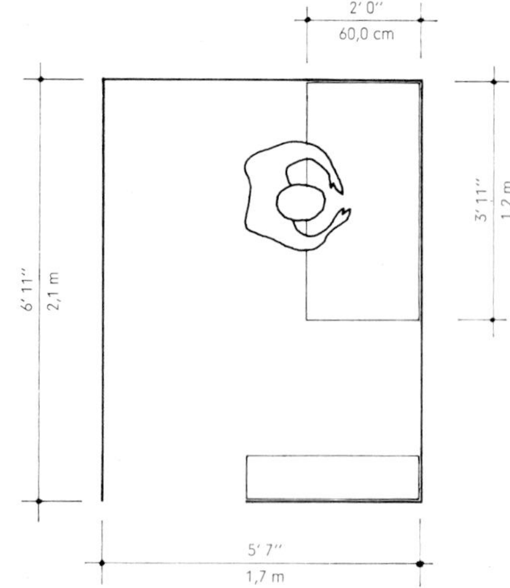


6. Recommended dimensions for a one person enclosed carrel.

6. Empfohlene Abmessungen eines umschlossenen *carrel* für eine Person.

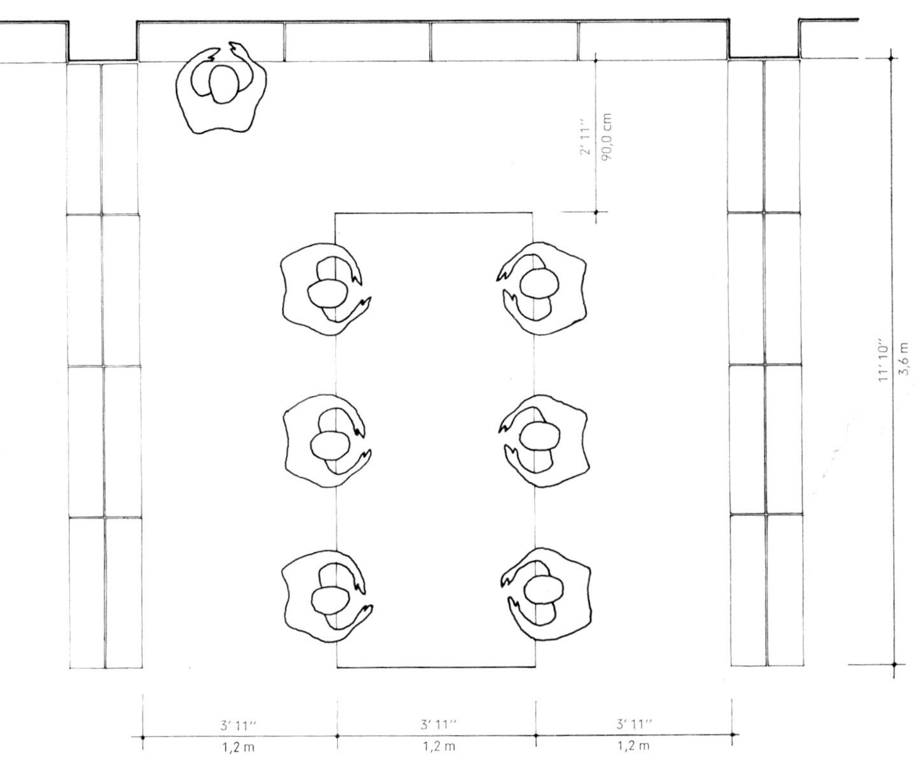


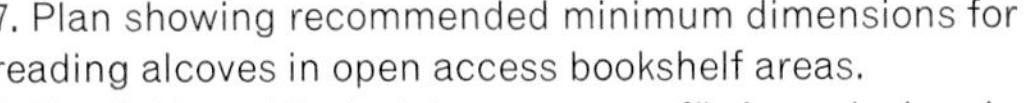


7. Plan showing recommended minimum dimensions for reading alcoves in open access bookshelf areas.
7. Empfohlene Mindestabmessungen für Lesenischen in frei zugänglichen Regalbereichen.

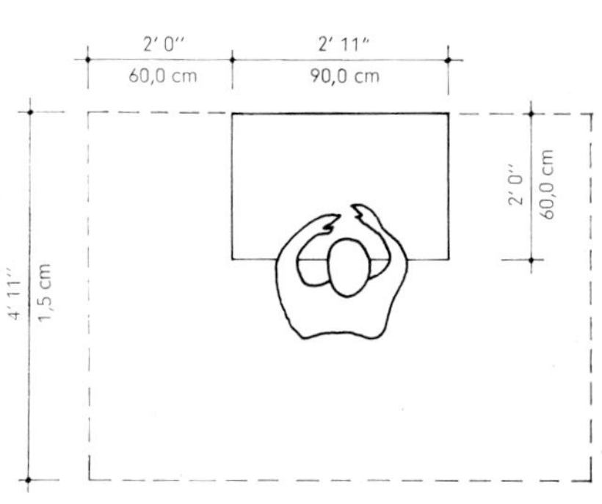


8. Plan of one person reading table giving minimum dimensions for furniture and surrounding space.
8. Lesetisch für eine Person mit den Mindestabmessungen für Möblierung und umgebenden Raum.

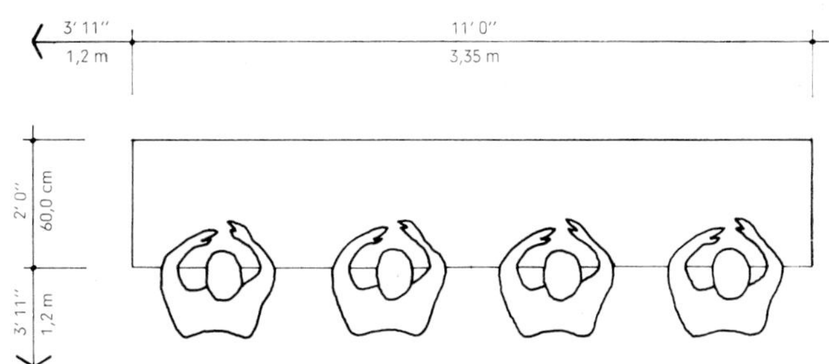


9. Minimum dimensions for single-sided table for four readers.
9. Mindestabmessungen eines einseitig benutzbaren Lesetisches für vier Leser.

(Diagrams 6–13 based on *The Architects' Journal*, Vol. 147, No. 12, 20 March 1968.)
(Diagramme 6–13 nach *The Architects' Journal*, Band 147, Nr. 12, 20. März 1968.)

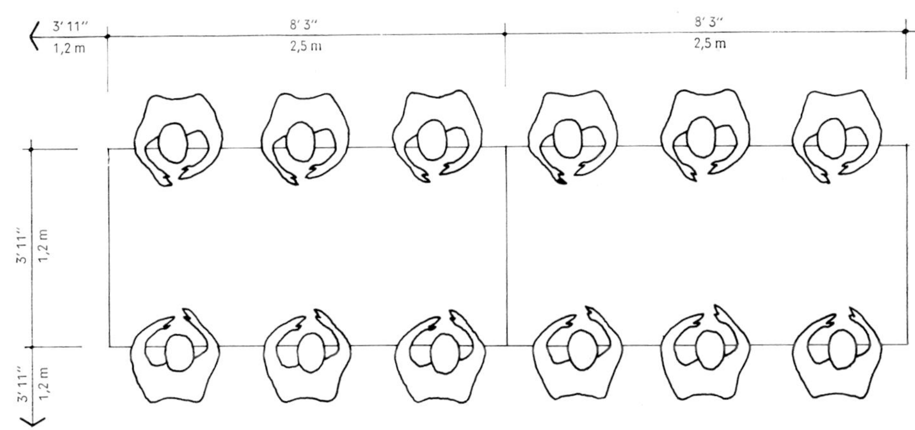


10. Minimum dimensions for six person reading tables.
10. Mindestabmessungen von Lesetischen für sechs Personen.

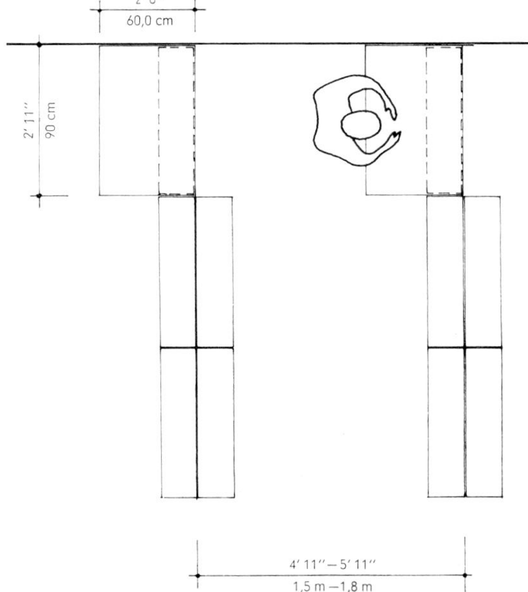


11. Plan of open carrels at ends of stacks.
11. Offene *carrels* als Abschluß der Regaleinheiten.

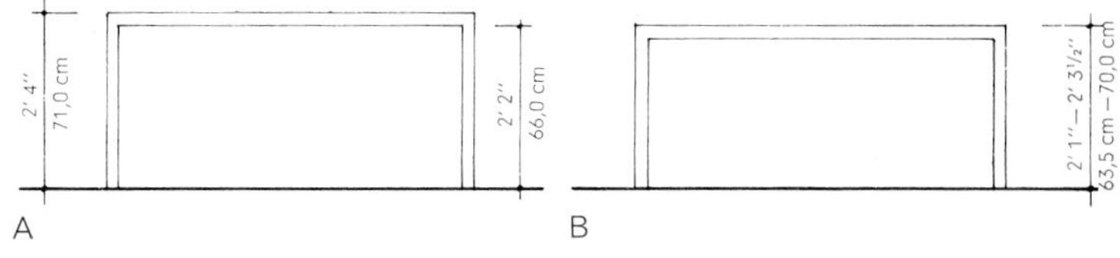


12. Recommended vertical dimensions for tables in (A) adult libraries (B) school libraries.
12. Empfohlene Höhen für Tische in (A) Büchereien für Erwachsene, (B) Schulbüchereien.

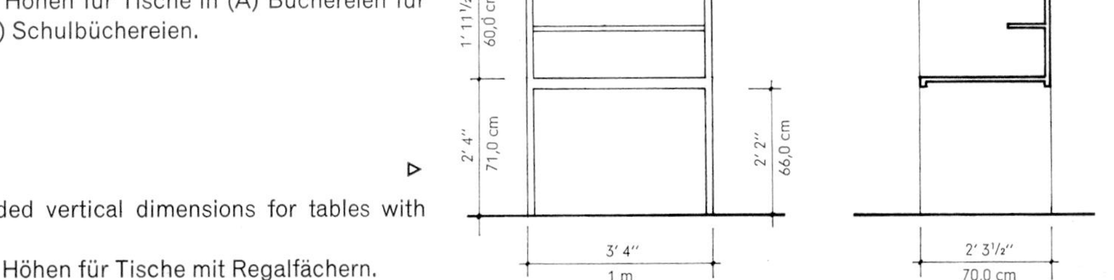


13. Recommended vertical dimensions for tables with shelving.
13. Empfohlene Höhen für Tische mit Regalfächern.

14

15

16

17

18

14, 15. Low partitions sub-dividing groups of tables within a large space; the sense of an individual place is greatly increased by using a light which the reader can control and adjust. Library, Örsted Institute, University of Copenhagen. Architects: Eva and Nils Koppel.
16. A long table facing windows (and sky glare) sub-divided by vertical fins giving a shared reading space. Library, St. Catherine's College, Oxford. Architect: Arne Jacobsen.
17, 18. Readers on opposite sides of a table partly separated by the continuous fluorescent light and its support. Library, Theological College, Chichester. Architects: Ahrends, Burton & Koralek.

14, 15. Niedrige Trennwände unterteilen den großen Raum in einzelne Tischgruppen. Das Gefühl der Abgeschlossenheit wird durch Lichtquellen gefördert, die der Benutzer selbst regulieren kann. Bibliothek des Örsted-Instituts, Universität Kopenhagen. Architekten: Eva und Nils Koppel.
16. Der lange Tisch gegenüber den Fenstern (und mit starkem Blendlicht) ist durch vertikale Bretter unterteilt, die den Arbeitstisch abgrenzen. Bibliothek des St. Catherine's College, Oxford. Architekt: Arne Jacobsen.
17, 18. Die Arbeitsflächen zu beiden Seiten des Tisches werden durch die Halterung der Leuchtstoffröhren teilweise abgegrenzt. Bibliothek des Theological College, Chichester. Architekten: Ahrends, Burton & Koralek.

19. An individual reading space inserted in a run of shelving and supported from the same uprights; reading desks distributed in the stacks can achieve separation through distance and the screening given by bookshelves. Reska Equipment, Birkerød, Denmark. ▷
20. Shelving backed by reading desks; the staggered arrangement increases privacy as well as the structural stability of the unit. Brunswick Corporation, Kalamazoo, Michigan.
21. Readers at individual tables placed near their information sources. Charles Leaming Tutt Library, Colorado College, Colorado Springs, Colorado. Architects: Skidmore, Owings & Merrill.
22. Communication may not always be with a book but may take place with some other source such as a microfilm reader which is best viewed in subdued light. Municipal and University Library, Frankfurt-on-Main. Architect: Ferdinand Kramer.

19. Ein individueller Lesebereich, der in das Regal eingefügt ist und von den gleichen Pfosten gestützt wird. Die räumliche Entfernung und der Sichtschutz der Regale gibt solchen im Magazin verteilten Lesepulten Abgeschlossenheit. Reska, Birkerød, Dänemark. ▷
20. An der Rückwand der Regale sind Schreibtische angebracht. Die gestaffelte Anordnung sorgt für Isolierung und größere Stabilität der Elemente. Brunswick Corporation, Kalamazoo, Michigan.
21. Den Lesern stehen Einzeltische in der Nähe der Informationsquellen zur Verfügung. Charles Leaming Tutt Library, Colorado College, Colorado Springs, Colorado. Architekten: Skidmore, Owings & Merrill.
22. An die Stelle des Buches kann auch eine andere Informationsquelle treten, zum Beispiel ein Ablesegerät für Mikrofilme, das gedämpftes Licht erfordert. Universitäts- und Stadtbibliothek, Frankfurt am Main. Architekt: Ferdinand Kramer.

19

20

22

21

The luminance of a surface – its apparent brightness – is measured as the product of the illumination (lumens/sq. ft. or lux) and the reflectance of that surface. If book and table are lit by the same source and the white book page has a reflectance of .7 to .8 and the table top of .2 to .3, the desirable balance is in fact likely to be achieved.
If the kind of seclusion which is thought to be appropriate is to be provided for a large number of readers, it seems unlikely that all of these can be placed around the perimeter of the building or sufficiently near it to be able to read by daylight. Nor in a multi-storey building is it likely that all of them could be placed under skylights. There is thus a strong likelihood that there will be library spaces which may have a sense of daylight but which will actually rely on artificial light for sufficient illumination. In such areas it will be extremely important to reduce the impact of daylight around the perimeter so as to avoid glare and minimize the contrast between the levels of illumination provided by natural and artificial sources.
The need for such control of daylight is in no way an argument for its total exclusion. In any library and especially a small one, daylight will help to give it that measure of ordinariness which we now believe appropriate to the idea of a library; ordinariness that is in the sense of part of our everyday existence but not in any way suggesting a commonplace architecture. In a large library where there may be a high proportion of artificially lit spaces and where stacks up to 7′6″ (2.3 m) frequently block the view, daylit spaces can provide for a sense of direction and orientate a user in a possibly repetitive and confusing situation.
The need for sound control has long preoccupied library planners. It is where communication occurs that noise will be most disturbing. Yet it is exactly in these reading areas where the spatial arrangements – prompted by a desire for a particular kind of spatial expression – have been such as to allow sound to travel freely from floor to floor or within some other continuous volume. The problem is therefore one of both providing sound barriers and of absorbing sound at its source.
If the acceptable maximum level of background noise in reading rooms is between 30–35 db, then such noise sources as entrances, book issue desks or consultation areas will have to be separated from the quiet zones by dividing walls and doors since it is unlikely that enough of the sound will be absorbed at source or that it will be sufficiently attenuated by distance. The only situation in which such barriers may not be necessary is where there is some continuous acceptable masking noise so that the intermittent interfering noise is barely audible.
In addition to these precautions and the adoption of sensible zoning on plan and section separating noisy areas from quiet ones, it will be most important to absorb sound immediately it is generated so as to reduce interference within any one space. A good deal of this noise is produced by people walking. Soft surfaces underfoot – cork, rubber, carpet – will therefore do more than anything else to reduce the noise level. Of these carpet is unquestionably the most efficient, quite apart from the effect it has on the character of the room. Carpet can be laid direct on concrete floors and though not as long lasting as many other floor finishes, is very economic to maintain and may therefore over a period of time prove no more expensive than other possibly less useful surfaces. Libraries with carpeted reading rooms have been built in Great Britain under the quite stringent financial allocations set by the University Grants Committee, the body responsible for issuing grants for university buildings.
Ceilings with absorbent material, soft furniture, curtains and books on their shelves will also be effective as sound

Bei der Schaffung eines abgeschlossenen Bereichs für den Leser spielen sowohl Licht wie Geräusche eine Rolle.
Die für die Lektüre empfohlene Beleuchtungsstärke beträgt ca. 320 lx bei Blendungsziffer 19 (32 lx). Außerdem sollten die Helligkeitswerte der Bereiche, die innerhalb des Blickfeldes liegen, in folgendem Verhältnis zueinander stehen:

| | |
|---|---|
| Visuelle Aufgabe (Buch) | 10 |
| Unmittelbare Umgebung (Tischfläche) | 3 |
| Hintergrund (Wände, Bücherregale) | 1 |

(Informationsblatt 1322, *Environmental Standards for Libraries*, aus *Architects' Journal*, 17. März 1965.)

Die Helligkeit einer Fläche ist das Produkt aus Beleuchtungsstärke (lumen/qm oder Lux) und der Reflexion dieser Fläche. Wenn Buch und Tisch von der gleichen Quelle beleuchtet werden und wenn die weiße Buchseite eine Reflexion von 0,7 bis 0,8 und die Tischfläche eine Reflexion von 0,2 bis 0,3 hat, läßt sich wahrscheinlich das wünschenswerte Verhältnis erzielen.
Sollen individuelle Bereiche für eine große Zahl von Lesern geschaffen werden, ist es kaum möglich, alle Arbeitsplätze so nahe an die Außenwände des Gebäudes zu plazieren, daß die Benutzer bei Tageslicht lesen können. Ebenso ist es in einem mehrgeschossigen Gebäude kaum möglich, alle Plätze unter Oberlichtern anzuordnen. Infolgedessen werden Bibliotheksräume, die über Tageslicht verfügen, sehr oft für eine ausreichende Belichtung künstliches Licht hinzuziehen müssen. In solchen Räumen ist es außerordentlich wichtig, das einfallende Licht an den Fensterwänden zu dämpfen, damit keine Blendung entsteht und der Kontrast zwischen künstlichem und natürlichem Licht so weit wie möglich reduziert wird.
Das Tageslicht sollte also kontrolliert, aber keineswegs ganz ausgeschlossen werden. In jeder Bibliothek, vor allem in kleineren Gebäuden, verhilft Tageslicht zu jenem Eindruck der Selbstverständlichkeit, der heute der Bestimmung der Bibliothek angemessen erscheint; Selbstverständlichkeit freilich nicht im Sinne einer durchschnittlichen Architektur, sondern vielmehr einer alltäglichen Erfahrung, die der Bibliotheksbesuch darstellen soll. In einer großen Bibliothek mit vielen künstlich beleuchteten Räumen, wo häufig bis zu 2,30 m hohe Regale die Sicht versperren, können Bereiche mit Tageslicht dem Benutzer in einer möglicherweise verwirrenden und unübersichtlichen Situation die Orientierung erleichtern.
Mit dem Problem des Schallschutzes befaßt sich die Bibliotheksplanung schon seit langem. Am störendsten wirkt Lärm dort, wo Kommunikation stattfindet. Doch gerade in diesen Lesebereichen, deren räumliche Verhältnisse häufig von dem Wunsch nach architektonisch bedeutsamem Ausdruck bestimmt sind, können Geräusche sich von Geschoß zu Geschoß oder innerhalb eines kontinuierlichen Volumens verbreiten. Es geht also darum, Barrieren gegen den Lärm zu errichten und zugleich die Geräusche an ihrer Quelle zu absorbieren.
Wenn als zulässige Höchstwerte für Hintergrundgeräusche in Lesesälen 30–35 db angenommen werden, so müssen Lärmquellen wie Eingänge, Ausgabe- und Beratungsstellen durch Trennwände und Türen von den ruhigen Zonen abgetrennt werden, denn es ist unwahrscheinlich, daß die Geräusche an der Quelle absorbiert werden können oder daß sie durch die Entfernung genügend gedämpft werden. Solche Maßnahmen sind nur dort nicht erforderlich, wo ständig ein akzeptabler höherer Geräuschpegel herrscht, der Störgeräusche zum großen Teil überdeckt.

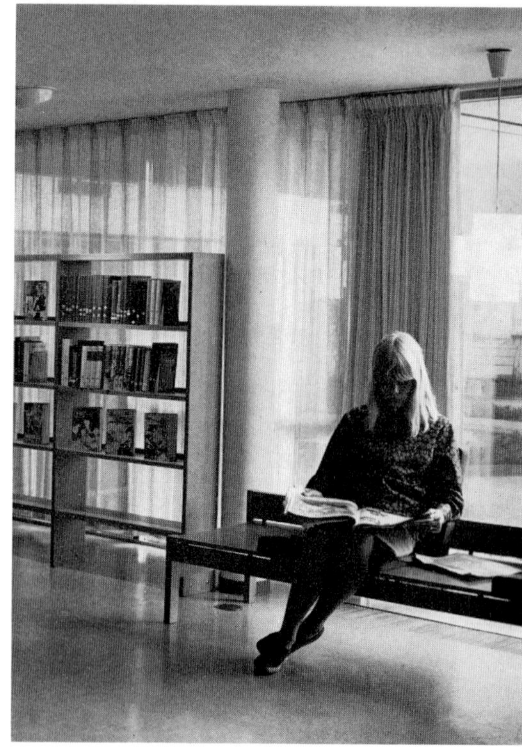
23

23. Readers do not always need the accepted arrangement of a table and chair, particularly if only reading one book at a time. Teenage section, Public Library, Eskilstuna Sweden. Architect: Gustaf Lettström.
24. Carpets absorb airborne sound and prevent the noise of footsteps and thus greatly reduce the noise irritant. Library, New Zealand House, London. Architects: Robert Matthew, Johnson-Marshall & Partners.

23. Die übliche Anordnung von Tischen und Stühlen ist nicht immer unbedingt erforderlich, vor allem dann nicht, wenn der Besucher jeweils nur ein Buch benutzt. Jugendabteilung der Öffentlichen Bücherei, Eskilstuna, Schweden. Architekt: Gustaf Lettström.
24. Teppiche dämpfen die Geräusche und verhindern Trittschall, so daß wenig störender Lärm entsteht. Bibliothek des New Zealand House, London. Architekten: Robert Matthew, Johnson-Marshall & Partners.

24

25

25. Most people reading a book at home will do so in an armchair and there is no reason why they should not frequently do the same in a library. Library, Skedsmo, Norway. Architects: Paul Cappelen and Torbjørn Rodahl.
26, 27. Even within quite a small library it is possible to create a number of different reading conditions. Library, Schlumberger Administration Building, Ridgefield, Connecticut. Architect: Philip Johnson.
28. Armchairs and low upholstered benches are particularly appropriate to magazine and newspaper reading areas. Walnut Hill Branch Library, Dallas, Texas. Architects: J. Herschel Fisher & Donald E. Jarvis.

25. Zu Hause setzen sich die meisten Leute beim Lesen in einen Sessel, und es gibt keinen Grund, warum ihnen nicht auch die Bibliothek diese Bequemlichkeit erlauben sollte. Bücherei, Skedsmo, Norwegen. Architekten: Paul Cappelen und Torbjørn Rodahl.
26, 27. Selbst in einer sehr kleinen Bibliothek lassen sich unterschiedliche Lesebedingungen schaffen. Bibliothek des Schlumberger Administration Building, Ridgefield, Connecticut. Architekt: Philip Johnson.
28. Sessel und niedrige Polsterbänke eignen sich besonders gut für Zeitschriftenleseräume. Walnut Hill Branch Library, Dallas, Texas. Architekten: J. Herschel Fisher & Donald E. Jarvis.

absorbents. Book stacks thus play a crucial role in creating both visual and acoustic isolation and an intermingling of reading spaces and book storage is, it seems, therefore likely to produce the most congenial arrangement for the largest number of users.
Though this juxtaposition has all the appearance of apparent simplicity there are in fact very few examples of its successful application. What matters is the ratio between book and reader areas and the degree to which a special place can be carved out of a general space. It is a problem not confined to libraries; it is one of manipulating the organization of a small zone embedded within a very much larger and relatively undefined space so that the small individual places acquire their own appropriate characteristics. The more the initial design concept tends towards an equality between all areas for reasons of variability, the more difficult such differentiation may become and the more it will have to rely on furniture and local lighting adaptations. It is important therefore that this need for an intermingling of at least two characteristic spaces is recognized as part of the architectural problem and provision made for the total range of requirements. To take a quite simple example, that there are not only overhead tracks for the placement of ceiling lighting in a number of positions related to a changing stack arrangement but that there are also floor outlets for a similarly changing distribution of table lamps.
The problem is further accentuated in those libraries

Auch wenn durch vernünftige Planung in der Horizontalen und in der Vertikalen lärmerzeugende von ruhigen Zonen getrennt werden, ist es außerordentlich wichtig, die Geräusche bei ihrer Entstehung zu absorbieren, damit die Störungen in allen anderen Bereichen so gering wie möglich bleiben. Einen beträchtlichen Lärm verursacht zum Beispiel der Trittschall. Hier tragen weiche Bodenbeläge – Kork, Gummi, Teppich – viel dazu bei, den Geräuschpegel zu senken. Mit Teppichböden – die zudem eine angenehme räumliche Atmosphäre schaffen – ist zweifellos die beste Wirkung zu erzielen. Teppich kann direkt auf Betonböden verlegt werden. Er ist nicht so haltbar wie manche anderen Bodenbeläge, ist aber trotzdem sehr ökonomisch in der Unterhaltung und kostet deshalb über einen längeren Zeitraum gesehen nicht mehr als andere, möglicherweise weniger geeignete Beläge. In Großbritannien sind Bibliotheken mit Teppichbelägen in den Lesesälen sogar unter den strengen finanziellen Bedingungen des University Grants Committee gebaut worden, jener Institution, die Zuschüsse zu Universitätsbauten bewilligt.
Decken aus schalldämmendem Material, gepolsterte Möbel, Vorhänge und Bücherregale helfen ebenfalls, Geräusche zu dämpfen. Bücherregale spielen also nicht nur bei der optischen, sondern auch bei der akustischen Isolation eine wichtige Rolle. Eine Verbindung von Lesebereichen und Büchermagazin schafft deshalb die angemessensten Bedingungen für eine größtmögliche Zahl von Benutzern.
Obwohl eine solche räumliche Organisation nicht schwer zu verwirklichen sein dürfte, existieren nur wenige Beispiele für wirklich gelungene Lösungen. Als ausschlaggebend erweisen sich dabei das Größenverhältnis zwischen Magazin- und Lesebereich und die Aussonderung einer individuellen Zone aus einem großen allgemeinen Raum. Dieses Problem ist nicht auf Bibliotheken beschränkt; bei vielen Bauaufgaben ergibt sich die Notwendigkeit, eine kleinere Zone so in einen sehr viel größeren und relativ undefinierten Raum einzubetten, daß dieser individuelle Bereich seinen eigenen Charakter erhält. Je mehr die Planung um der Flexibilität willen zu einer einheitlichen Gestaltung aller Bereiche hin tendiert, um so schwieriger wird eine solche Differenzierung und um so stärker ist sie von Möblierung und Anordnung der Lichtquellen abhängig. Deshalb sollte die Verbindung mindestens zweier charakteristischer Bereiche von Anfang an in die Entwurfskonzeption einbezogen werden, damit sämtliche möglichen Forderungen Berücksichtigung finden können. Um ein einfaches Beispiel zu nennen: Es sollten nicht nur Deckenschienen für Lichtquellen in verschiedenen Positionen vorgesehen werden, die sich einer variablen Anordnung der Regale anpassen, sondern

26

27

28

which cater for a wide age group. Most public libraries will have users between the ages of 3 and 90. For many at the lower end, communication will not be through reading but through story telling; new spaces may therefore be required. Children's libraries will also need quite different furniture and those for adolescents may equally need a character which marks off a section of the library and where rules of silence are perhaps not too rigidly enforced. For a good many users at the upper end of the age group, the library is a club and a meeting point. They will need comfortable chairs, a chance to look at newspapers, perhaps to talk and smoke. This should be done in spaces which though clearly part of the library are sufficiently detached to make such a social function possible without disrupting the individual communication going on elsewhere.
Some such detachment may also be advisable for specialist sections of the library like those in which rare books can be read, those housing maps or other documents needing special places for viewing, and particularly those dealing with music and gramophone records and tapes which need their own listening booths or equipment for playing music through earphones. A number of these special situations are shown in the accompanying illustrations.
Because clearly so much depends in a library and particularly in the reading rooms on decisions about quite small scale elements, it is most important that library design is not seen as solely the provision of external enclosure. The design of the desk or chair matters as much as that of the wall. Yet it is precisely in the making of this small scale environment that most libraries are so deficient. There is either a feeling of an aggressive anonymity, of a kind of artificial orderliness produced purely by the need to marshal large numbers, or of a pompousness which is both outmoded and needless. The idea that libraries might be places associated with pleasure, that there is in fact joy in communication, is alien to most designs.

auch Bodenauslässe für eine ähnlich variable Verteilung von Tischlampen.
Das Problem der räumlichen Organisation stellt sich besonders in den Bibliotheken, die für Benutzer aller Altersgruppen bestimmt sind. Die meisten öffentlichen Büchereien betreuen Leser zwischen sechs und neunzig Jahren. An der untersten Grenze findet Kommunikation weniger durch Lesen statt als durch Geschichtenerzählen; deshalb sind neuartige Raumformen notwendig. In Kinderbüchereien werden außerdem völlig andere Möbel verwendet, und auch für die Jugendlichen sollte ein gesonderter Bereich eingerichtet werden, in dem möglicherweise das Redeverbot nicht allzu streng eingehalten wird. Für viele Benutzer am oberen Ende der Altersskala ist die Bibliothek ein Club, ein Treffpunkt. Sie brauchen bequeme Stühle und müssen die Möglichkeit haben, Zeitung zu lesen und vielleicht auch zu reden und zu rauchen. Das sollte in Bereichen geschehen, die zwar einen Teil der Bibliothek bilden, aber genügend abgesondert sind, so daß die soziale Funktion nicht die individuelle Kommunikation beeinträchtigt, die an anderen Stellen vor sich geht.
Eine solche Absonderung ist häufig auch für spezielle Abteilungen der Bibliothek zu empfehlen, zum Beispiel bei den Abteilungen für seltene Bücher oder für Landkarten und andere Dokumente, die besondere Arbeitsplätze verlangen, sowie vor allem bei den Musikabteilungen mit Schallplatten und Tonbändern, die mit Kopfhörern oder in Kabinen abgehört werden müssen. Eine Reihe solcher Situationen ist hier in Abbildungen verdeutlicht.
Da in der Bibliothek und vor allem in den Lesesälen so viel von kleinmaßstäblichen Elementen abhängt, ist es außerordentlich wichtig, daß die Bibliotheksplanung sich nicht nur mit der Hülle des Gebäudes befaßt. Die Form eines Pultes oder eines Stuhls spielt keine geringere Rolle als die der Außenwand. Und doch werden gerade solche Umwelt-Elemente in den meisten Bibliotheken sehr vernachlässigt. Die Räume sind entweder von einer aggressiven Anonymität, von einer künstlichen Ordnung, die lediglich die Disziplin einer größeren Menge von Lesern garantieren soll, oder von einem ebenso altmodischen, sinnlosen Pathos. Der Gedanke, daß Bibliotheken Orte sein können, die man mit Vergnügen besucht, daß Kommunikation tatsächlich beglückend zu wirken vermag, hat bei den meisten Bauten offenbar keine Rolle gespielt.

30. Communication need not be confined indoors. Public Library, Eskilstuna, Sweden. Architect: Gustaf Lettström. ▷
31. Libraries are increasingly making it possible to listen to music and speech on gramophone records or tape. Beatley Library, Simmons College, Boston, Massachusetts. Architects: Campbell, Aldrich & Nulty.
32. Earphones allow people to listen in ordinary rooms making it unnecessary to provide special soundproofed booths; plug-in points can then be installed in various places. Public Library, Eskilstuna, Sweden. Architect: Gustaf Lettström.
33. Electric points and preferably also connections for co-axial cables should exist in the floor to make it possible to plug-in individual lights, to connect positions for listening to music or speech or to connect microcopy readers and electronic equipment. Public Library, Växjö, Sweden. Architect: Erik Uluots.
34. Communication between reader and book needs in some instances to be complemented or reinforced by seminars or tutorial meetings and spaces for these should be provided. Francis A. Countway Library of Medicine, Harvard University, Boston, Massachusetts. Architect: Hugh Stubbins & Associates.

30. Kommunikation braucht nicht auf die Innenräume beschränkt zu bleiben. Öffentliche Bücherei, Eskilstuna, Schweden. Architekt: Gustaf Lettström. ▷
31. Immer häufiger kann man in Bibliotheken Musik- und Sprechplatten oder Bandaufnahmen anhören. Beatley Library, Simmons College, Boston, Massachusetts. Architekten: Campbell, Aldrich & Nulty.
32. Kopfhörer mit verschiedenen Anschlußmöglichkeiten machen schalldichte Kabinen auch in normalen Räumen überflüssig. Öffentliche Bücherei, Eskilstuna, Schweden. Architekt: Gustaf Lettström.
33. Im Fußboden sollten elektrische Auslässe und möglichst auch Sammelkabel vorgesehen werden, damit Tischlampen und Grammophone sowie Ablesegeräte für Mikrofilme und elektronische Geräte angeschlossen werden können. Öffentliche Bücherei, Växjö, Schweden. Architekt: Erik Uluots.
34. Die Kommunikation zwischen Leser und Buch muß in manchen Fällen durch Seminare und einführende Vorträge unterstützt werden. Für solche Zwecke sollten geeignete Räume zur Verfügung stehen. Francis A. Countway Library of Medicine, Harvard University, Boston, Massachusetts. Architekt: Hugh Stubbins & Associates.

29

29. Newspaper reading rooms frequently become a kind of social centre within a library and their casual and possibly even noisy character should be recognized. It is probably possible to associate them with a disturbing activity like that in the television room behind the curtains. Public Library, Eskilstuna, Sweden. Architect: Gustaf Lettström.

29. Zeitschriftenlesesäle bilden häufig eine Art informelles – und bisweilen auch lautes – gesellschaftliches Zentrum innerhalb der Bibliothek. Wenn möglich sollten sie mit anderen geräuscherzeugenden Bereichen – wie zum Beispiel dem Fernsehraum hinter dem Vorhang – verbunden werden. Öffentliche Bücherei, Eskilstuna, Schweden. Architekt: Gustaf Lettström.

30

31

32

33

34

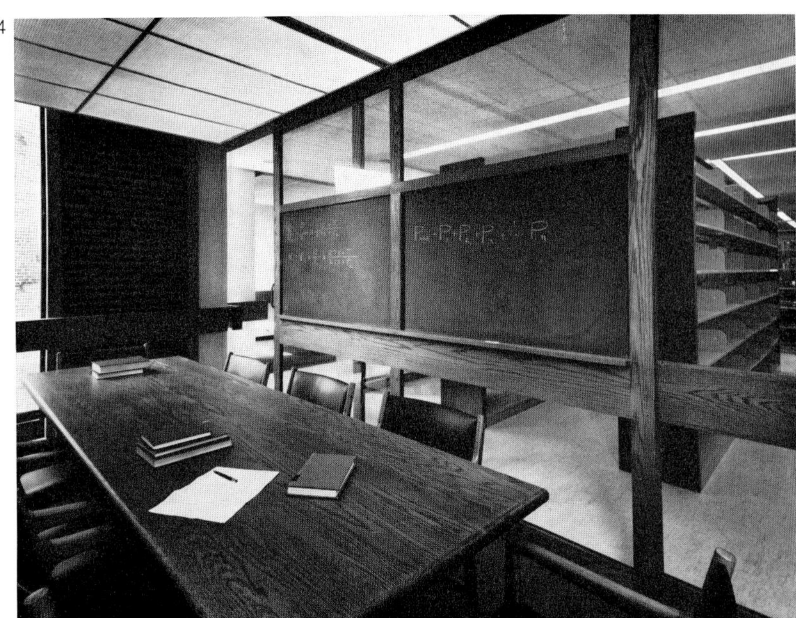

The return of books to storage is not, as far as the main characteristics of the problem are concerned, a simple reversal of the procedure for retrieval. What matters most in the case of book retrieval is that there should be the quickest possible flow of books from shelf to reader either through self-service arrangements or through the use of staff and mechanical handling devices. The speed of the first method depends largely on the reader himself and a sensible stack layout; the speed of the second method is very much affected by whether or not queue formation takes place.
In the case of return, speed is not likely to be critical. Books can therefore be returned in batches. What this implies is that a mechanical conveyor should only be used for book return if this in no way affects the flow from the stack to the reading areas. Any interference with the flow of retrieval is almost certainly going to negate the marginal gain which may have been achieved by using the mechanical system in both directions.
The return of books in batches can take place in trolleys which can be transported vertically in lifts or by mechanized carts which are in fact able to negotiate ramps as at the University of Helsinki Library. It is also of course possible to allow the returning books to accumulate in a sub-store and to use the mechanical system for return at the end of the day or some other period when book retrieval is not taking place.
Whether book retrieval is done by the reader or by a member of the staff and irrespective of the means used to handle flow and return, books are most often returned to their shelf position by the library staff. This in itself is a strong argument for return in batches. What is most important, however, is that the book should reappear in storage in its correct position, related to its catalogued place, so that the next sequence of library operations starting with location and retrieval can take place once more. A library can only function successfully if the linear sequence of its information store is correctly maintained.

Die Rückgabe von Büchern in das Magazin ist nicht als eine Umkehrung des Beschaffungsvorgangs zu interpretieren. Bei der Beschaffung kommt es vor allem darauf an, daß die Bücher so schnell wie möglich vom Fach zum Leser gelangen, entweder durch »Selbstbedienung« des Benutzers oder durch den Einsatz von Personal und technischen Hilfsmitteln. Im ersten Falle hängt die Schnelligkeit weitgehend vom Leser selbst und von einer übersichtlichen Anordnung des Magazins ab; im zweiten Fall richtet sich die Geschwindigkeit der Abwicklung danach, ob starker Andrang herrscht oder nicht.
Bei der Rückgabe spielt die Schnelligkeit dagegen zumeist keine Rolle, so daß die Bücher auch schubweise an das Magazin zurückgehen können. Ein Fließbandsystem sollte also nur dann für die Rückgabe benutzt werden, wenn es die Beförderung vom Magazin in die Lesebereiche nicht behindert. Jede Störung des Beschaffungsvorganges macht den Zeitgewinn zunichte, der durch die Verwendung des Fördersystems in beiden Richtungen erzielt wird.
Die Rückgabe größerer Büchermengen kann entweder in Bücherwagen erfolgen, die vertikal in Aufzügen befördert werden, oder in Förderkarren, die sogar – wie in der Bibliothek der Universität Helsinki – Rampen zu bewältigen vermögen. Es ist natürlich auch möglich, die zurückgehenden Bücher sich ansammeln zu lassen und sie am Ende des Tages oder zu einer anderen Zeit, in der keine Beschaffung stattfindet, über das Fließbandsystem ins Magazin zu befördern.
Ob es sich um eine Freihandbücherei oder eine Bibliothek mit geschlossenem Magazin handelt – die Bücher werden gewöhnlich vom Bibliothekspersonal in die Fächer zurückgestellt, was allein schon für die Rückgabe in Schüben spricht. Wichtig ist aber vor allem, daß das Buch im Magazin wieder den richtigen Platz einnimmt, der dem im Katalog angegebenen Standort entspricht, damit die mit Lokalisierung und Beschaffung beginnende Phase des Benutzungszyklus von neuem einsetzen kann. Eine Bibliothek funktioniert nur dann, wenn die lineare Anordnung der gespeicherten Information korrekt eingehalten wird.

1

1. Bulk return usually takes place in some kind of a trolley which is wheeled to the stacks or taken in a lift. Brunswick Corporation, Kalamazoo, Michigan.
2. Books are normally issued at random intervals; they can, however, be returned to storage at times most convenient to the library staff and can thus go there in bulk. Reska Equipment, Birkerød, Denmark.
3. The moving belt on the left delivers books on demand throughout the day from the stacks to the reading area; the mechanized trolley returns books in bulk perhaps once a day. Helsinki University Library. Addition and renovation: Aarne Ervi.

1. Bei Rückgabe in größeren Mengen werden die Bücher auf einem Wagen gesammelt, der zum Magazin gerollt oder in einem Lift transportiert wird. Brunswick Corporation, Kalamazoo, Michigan.
2. Bücher werden im allgemeinen zu unterschiedlichen Zeitpunkten ausgegeben. Bei der Rückgabe können sie jedoch, der Arbeitseinteilung des Bibliothekspersonals entsprechend, zu größeren Schüben zusammengefaßt und zu bestimmten Zeiten an das Magazin zurückgegeben werden. Reska, Birkerød, Dänemark.
3. Das Förderband links transportiert angeforderte Bücher laufend vom Magazin zum Lesebereich. Der motorisierte Bücherwagen dagegen bringt einmal täglich die Bücher zum Magazin zurück. Universitätsbibliothek, Helsinki. Erweiterung und Renovierung: Aarne Ervi.

2

3

## Service Functions

Two kinds of service functions should be distinguished, those which deal with the reader and books, and those which alter the environment of the building. On the whole the first group is still largely, though not exclusively, performed by people, the second, by mechanical and electrical services.

### Reader Services

1. Control

The most frequent service function which the library staff performs in relation to readers is the control of incoming and outgoing books necessary in a lending library. This is a repetitive checking task which can be simplified and speeded-up through the use of mechanical devices such as microfilming machines, which photograph the borrower's card and a card belonging to the book or some distinguishing mark on the book itself. This task is done at a control desk. Depending on the number of readers likely at peak periods, this control position can be a single desk with separate positions for incoming and outgoing traffic, a U-shaped desk with separate sides for issue and return or two completely detached desks each dealing with only one function.
The process of controlling books in and out of the library can also be done by a computer and this has already been put into action in at least one library area (West Sussex) in England. The great advantage of such a system would be that it would both speed up flow and also provide an automatic print-out service of reminder cards for overdue books as well as being able to produce on demand an analyzed record of the books which have been borrowed over a given period.
The staff on duty at the control desk are usually also available for advice and are as a rule trained librarians. If the library has however a sufficient number of users there is a good deal to be said for separating control from helping readers. It is then possible to remove a potentially noisy control area from the stack and reading zones, and also to employ less skilled staff on control while trained librarians can operate in those parts of the building where readers are in fact likely to need guidance.

## Bibliothekstechnische Einrichtungen

Es gibt zwei Arten bibliothekstechnischer Einrichtungen, diejenigen, die für Leser und Bücher bestimmt sind, und diejenigen, die mit Konstruktion und Organisation des Gebäudes zusammenhängen. Im allgemeinen werden die der ersten Gruppe noch immer weitgehend vom Bibliothekspersonal bedient, während in der zweiten technische Hilfsmittel herangezogen werden.

### Einrichtungen für Benutzer

1. Kontrolle

Die Funktion, die das Bibliothekspersonal in Bezug auf den Benutzer am häufigsten ausübt, ist die Kontrolle der eingehenden und herausgehenden Bücher, die in einer Bibliothek mit Ausleihe erforderlich ist. Diese sich ständig wiederholende Kontrollfunktion kann durch technische Vorrichtungen vereinfacht und beschleunigt werden, zum Beispiel durch Mikrofilmapparate, die den Leserausweis des Benutzers sowie eine zum Buch gehörende Karte oder ein Kennzeichen auf dem Buch selbst fotografieren. Je nach der Benutzungsfrequenz zu Stoßzeiten kann die Kontrollstelle aus einem einfachen Tisch für Ausleihe und Rückgabe, aus einer U-förmigen Theke mit je einer Seite für eingehende und herausgehende Bücher oder aus zwei völlig getrennten Schaltern bestehen, die jeweils nur für eine Funktion zuständig sind.
Die Kontrolle der Bücher kann auch von einem Computer übernommen werden, wie es in England zumindest in einer Bibliothek in West Sussex schon geschieht. Der Computer sorgt für eine Beschleunigung des Verfahrens, liefert automatisch gedruckte Mahnkarten für überfällige Bücher und gibt eine Analyse der Bücher, die innerhalb einer bestimmten Zeit ausgeliehen worden sind.
Die Bibliotheksangestellten an der Kontrollstelle sind gewöhnlich auch für Auskünfte zuständig und sind deshalb in der Regel ausgebildete Bibliothekare. Wenn die Bibliothek jedoch eine große Zahl von Benutzern hat, spricht viel für die Trennung der Kontrolle von der Auskunft. Es ist dann möglich, die geräuscherzeugende Kontrollzone von Magazin und Lesebereichen abzusondern und außerdem weniger spezialisierte Arbeitskräfte an der Kontrolle einzusetzen, während die ausgebildeten Bibliothekare in den Teilen des Gebäudes arbeiten, wo die

1

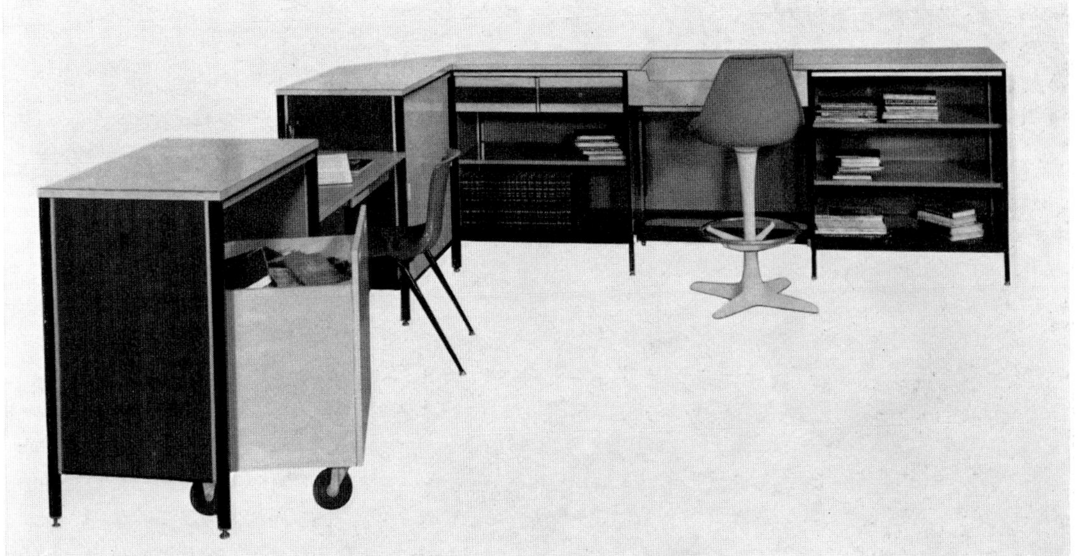

1. A control desk is a work station which needs storage for reserved books, for returned books, for bibliographical reference, for readers' tickets, cash collected from fines, for photographic equipment recording loans, etc. depending on the size of the library and the intensity of use. Brunswick Corporation, Kalamazoo, Michigan.

1. In einem Kontrolltisch müssen je nach der Größe der Bibliothek und der Benutzungsfrequenz reservierte Bücher, zurückgegebene Bücher und Tonbänder, bibliographische Nachschlagewerke, Lesekarten, Bargeld, fotografisches Zubehör und anderes aufbewahrt werden. Brunswick Corporation, Kalamazoo, Michigan.

2

3

2. Library control of books and readers can be exercized from a very small and simple counter in a small library (it would always seem helpful, however, to make it possible for a librarian to sit down on a chair and for children not to have to reach up). Library, Skedsmo, Norway. Architects: Paul Cappelen and Torbjørn Rodahl.
3, 4. A long counter sub-divided for issue, return and enquiries. It overlooks the library for supervision but is also seen by readers needing help. Public Library, Chalfont St. Peter, Buckinghamshire. Architect: Frederick Pooley.
5. Large and medium-sized libraries may have to separate issue, book return and such functions as registering new readers. Public Library, Eskilstuna, Sweden. Architect: Gustaf Lettström.

2. In einer kleinen Bibliothek genügt für die Kontrolle der Bücher und Leser eine einfache Theke. Allerdings wäre es wünschenswert, daß der Bibliothekar einen Stuhl zur Verfügung hat und daß Kinder nicht zu hoch reichen müssen. Bücherei, Skedsmo, Norwegen. Architekten: Paul Cappelen und Torbjørn Rodahl.
3, 4. Eine lange Theke, die in Ausgabe, Rückgabe und Information unterteilt ist. Von hier aus läßt sich die Bibliothek überblicken, aber zugleich liegt die Theke auch im Blickfeld von Lesern, die Hilfe benötigen. Öffentliche Bücherei, Chalfont St. Peter, Buckinghamshire. Architekt: Frederick Pooley.
5. Große und mittlere Bibliotheken müssen Ausgabe, Rückgabe und weitere Funktionen wie die Einschreibung neuer Leser häufig voneinander trennen. Öffentliche Bücherei, Eskilstuna, Schweden. Architekt: Gustaf Lettström.

4

5

6

6. Security may make it necessary to sift readers through a control point where they may have to leave shopping baskets and briefcases, or at least have them inspected. University Library, Edinburgh. Architects: Sir Basil Spence, Glover & Ferguson.

6. Aus Sicherheitsgründen ist es häufig notwendig, daß die Benutzer eine Kontrollstelle passieren, wo sie Einkaufs- und Aktentaschen zurücklassen oder zumindest vorzeigen müssen. Universitätsbibliothek, Edinburgh. Architekten: Sir Basil Spence, Glover & Ferguson.

Such a separation of these functions would in turn considerably affect the library plan – communication and control would not be confused.

2. Consultation

The kind of service which readers need in the reading and reference areas is mainly a matter of consultation – users have to discuss some bibliographical problem, be directed to a particular source, need explanation of a reference. This involves discussion yet there should at the same time be a high degree of accessibility to the advisers. It seems appropriate therefore to provide the greatest possible local sound absorption and perhaps even some screening as a sound barrier, but nevertheless to place the library staff in such a way that they are on the natural routes of movement and near those areas where difficulty is likely to occur: the catalogue, the reference sections, the children's library. The fact that staff positioned in such a way may also exercise some control is an additional benefit but not the critical determinant. Users intent on defacing a book or stealing it will always devise some way of doing so.

3. Information Copying

In many instances users will want to have a personal facsimile of some information source which they have found in the library. To cope with this libraries have installed copying machines which are either operated by putting a coin in a slot or, where the demand is considerable, by members of the staff. In the latter case these are then placed in a small separated space where a copying service can be organized. As users may have to wait for their copy it is helpful if a seating area and perhaps even a coffee machine are nearby.
A quite different form of copying is done by readers who want to use a typewriter either to take down parts of books or to make notes. Because there is as yet no silent typewriter, such users have to work in totally enclosed typing carrels or typing rooms.

Benutzer am meisten auf Beratung angewiesen sind. Eine solche Trennung der Funktionen wirkt sich auch auf die Organisation der Bibliothek aus – Kommunikation und Kontrolle sind in separaten Bereichen untergebracht.

2. Auskunft

In den Lese- und Katalogräumen ist die Leserbetreuung in erster Linie eine Sache der Beratung: Der Benutzer braucht Auskunft über ein bibliographisches Problem, sucht eine bestimmte Quelle, läßt sich einen Hinweis erklären. Damit sind Gespräche verbunden, doch sollte die Auskunft trotzdem zentral gelegen und leicht zugänglich sein. Es ist deshalb ratsam, Maßnahmen zur örtlichen Schalldämmung zu treffen und vielleicht sogar eine Abschirmung vorzusehen, zugleich aber die Bibliotheksangestellten an den Zirkulationswegen und nahe den Bereichen zu plazieren, wo am häufigsten Schwierigkeiten auftreten: Katalog, bibliographischer Apparat, Kinderbücherei. Die Tatsache, daß der Bibliothekar dann zugleich eine gewisse Kontrolle ausüben kann, ist ein zusätzlicher Vorteil, sollte aber nicht ausschlaggebend für die Plazierung der Auskunftsstelle sein. Leser, die es darauf abgesehen haben, ein Buch zu beschädigen oder zu stehlen, finden immer Mittel und Wege.

3. Kopierdienst

Häufig wünschen die Benutzer Kopien einer Informationsquelle, die sie in der Bibliothek gefunden haben. Deshalb sind in den meisten Bibliotheken Kopierapparate installiert, die entweder als Münzautomaten arbeiten oder – wenn die Nachfrage sehr groß ist – vom Personal bedient werden. Im letzteren Falle sind die Apparate in einem abgesonderten Bereich aufgestellt, wo ein Kopierdienst organisiert werden kann. Da die Leser meist auf ihre Kopie warten müssen, sollten sich eine Sitzgruppe und vielleicht auch eine Kaffeemaschine in der Nähe befinden. Eine ganz andere Art des Kopierens wird von Lesern ausgeführt, die eine Schreibmaschine benutzen, um Teile des Buches zu exzerpieren oder Notizen zu machen. Da es bisher noch keine geräuschlosen Schreibmaschinen gibt, müssen die Benutzer in abgeschlossenen Schreibabteilen oder Schreibzimmern arbeiten.

7

8

7, 8. If cases cannot be taken into the library, storage for these must be provided outside the control barrier. Lockers which users can rent or which they are allocated are useful in academic libraries for readers who may want to keep material in a library without having to remove it each day. EKZ Equipment (Central Purchasing Organisation for Public Libraries), Reutlingen, Germany.

7, 8. Wenn Taschen nicht mit in die Bibliothek genommen werden dürfen, müssen außerhalb der Kontrollbarriere Aufbewahrungsmöglichkeiten zur Verfügung stehen. Schließfächer, die den Benutzern zugeteilt oder von ihnen gemietet werden, sind besonders nützlich in wissenschaftlichen Bibliotheken, wo der Leser möglicherweise sein Material hinterlegen will, statt es jeden Tag mit nach Hause zu nehmen. Einkaufszentrale für Öffentliche Büchereien, Reutlingen.

9

4. External Information Sources

No library however vast can ever hope to contain all possible information sources. The problem has normally been dealt with by a system of inter-library loans in which a book would be requested from another library, sent off by it and then issued in the same way as any other book. This is naturally a slow process.
In many instances the user may in any case not want the whole book but merely a single item of information. Libraries are finding an increasing demand for such a service from a wide range of their users: school children checking up on some facts needed for their homework, students doing research, businessmen in need of commercial information. What is required in such instances are links to other information sources which can either relay it by telephone or telex, or display it by close-circuit television or, better still, can produce a facsimile at a distance. Such an information centre within a library will make its own demand on space and will require the service arrangements needed for its telecommunication links.

5. Bookshop

The lending and selling of books should not be seen as competitive but as complementary activities.
Studies have in fact shown that bookshops do not in any way suffer in areas with public libraries. It is useful therefore in some instances to have bookshops attached to libraries which are able to sell material which, for example, is not available on loan. Such a shop exists in the entrance area of the Library and Museum of the Performing Arts at the Lincoln Center, New York. Within a university a bookshop will perform a similar function and need not of course always be part of the library building. The bookstore at the California State College at Long Beach occupies for instance an important position adjacent to the main walk-way connecting the academic buildings and library with the cafeteria and dormitories.

4. Informationsquellen außerhalb der Bibliothek

Keine noch so große Bibliothek kann alle verfügbaren Informationsquellen enthalten. Deshalb gibt es einen Leihverkehr der Bibliotheken untereinander: ein Buch wird bei einer anderen Bibliothek angefordert und, sobald es eingegangen ist, wie jedes andere Buch ausgeliehen. Dieses Verfahren nimmt natürlich Zeit in Anspruch.
In vielen Fällen ist der Benutzer gar nicht an dem ganzen Buch interessiert, sondern nur an einer bestimmten Einzelinformation. Die Bibliotheken verzeichnen eine immer stärkere Nachfrage nach solchen Informationen, wobei die Skala der Leser weitgespannt ist: Schulkinder, die für ihre Hausaufgaben Fakten nachprüfen, Studenten, die ihren Studien nachgehen, Geschäftsleute, die sich über wirtschaftliche Fragen unterrichten wollen. Hier sind Verbindungen zu anderen Informationsquellen erforderlich, die die gewünschte Einzelinformation über Telefon, Fernschreiber oder – bei einem eigenen TV-Netz – über einen Fernsehschirm übertragen oder sogar über die Entfernung hinweg Kopien herstellen. Ein solches Informationszentrum innerhalb einer Bibliothek erfordert entsprechende Flächen und muß die nötigen fernmeldetechnischen Einrichtungen aufnehmen können.

5. Buchläden

Ausleihe und Verkauf von Büchern sollten nicht als konkurrierende Tätigkeiten, sondern als sich gegenseitig ergänzende Vorgänge betrachtet werden.
Tatsächlich haben Untersuchungen erwiesen, daß Buchhandlungen keineswegs unter der Nachbarschaft öffentlicher Büchereien leiden. Es kann also in manchen Fällen ratsam sein, den Bibliotheken Buchläden anzugliedern, die beispielsweise Material verkaufen, das nicht ausgeliehen wird. Eine solche Buchhandlung existiert im Eingangsbereich der Bibliothek und des Museums im Lincoln Center, New York. Auch in einer Universität kann ein Buchladen ähnliche Aufgaben erfüllen, ohne daß er deshalb notwendigerweise zum Bibliotheksgebäude gehören müßte. Die Buchhandlung des California State College in Long Beach nimmt beispielsweise eine wichtige Position an dem Hauptverbindungsweg ein, der von den akademischen Gebäuden und der Bibliothek zur Cafeteria und den Wohnheimen führt.

9. Bookshops and libraries are not in competition with each other, they are complementary in a system of communication. University bookshops selling text books and paperbacks can greatly reduce the load on a library and make it possible for students to read in the privacy of their rooms. Bookstore, California State College, Long Beach, California. Architects: Killingsworth, Brady, Smith & Associates.

9. Buchhandlungen und Bibliotheken stehen keineswegs in Konkurrenz zueinander, sondern ergänzen sich innerhalb des Kommunikationssystems. Universitätsbuchhandlungen, die Textbücher und broschierte Ausgaben verkaufen, können die Belastung einer Bibliothek sehr vermindern und ermöglichen es den Studenten, in der Abgeschlossenheit ihrer Räume zu lesen. Buchhandlung des California State College, Long Beach, Kalifornien. Architekten: Killingsworth, Brady, Smith & Associates.

## Administration and Book Services

### 1. Administration

Every library, however small, will have to cope with a certain amount of administration which in turn will make some demands on space. In a large library this area will assume considerable importance since there will be offices not only for those dealing with the administration of the library as a whole, but also for heads of individual departments and members of their staff. In terms of space allocation it ought to be remembered that librarians frequently perform a double function. They not only carry out the routine administrative duties of control of their departments or of the library as a whole but they are usually also responsible for book selection. This means that a good deal of bibliographical information has to be to hand in their rooms.
In addition to this librarians, including heads of departments and chief librarians, may be asked to advise readers. This suggests that in terms of the organization of the library, administrative areas should be secluded but still

## Verwaltung und Buchbearbeitung

### 1. Verwaltung

Jede Bibliothek, und sei sie noch so klein, verursacht ein gewisses Maß an Verwaltungsarbeit, die ihrerseits einigen Raum beansprucht. In einer großen Bibliothek spielt dieser Bereich eine wichtige Rolle, da er nicht nur die Büros der allgemeinen Bibliotheksverwaltung aufnimmt, sondern auch die Räume der Leiter der einzelnen Abteilungen und ihrer Mitarbeiter. Bei der Bemessung der Räume sollte berücksichtigt werden, daß Bibliothekare häufig eine doppelte Funktion erfüllen. Sie üben nicht nur Verwaltungs- und Kontrollfunktionen aus, die mit ihrer Abteilung oder der Bibliothek im ganzen zusammenhängen, sondern sind gewöhnlich auch für die Buchauswahl verantwortlich. Das bedeutet, daß in ihren Büros ein umfangreicher bibliographischer Apparat zur Verfügung stehen muß. Außerdem können Bibliothekare einschließlich der Abteilungsleiter und Hauptbibliothekare auch zur Leserberatung herangezogen werden. Die Verwaltungszonen sollten also abgeschlossen, zugleich aber für die

10

10. Librarians spend a great deal of time in their offices which they may also use for consultations with readers. Beinecke Rare Book and Manuscript Library, Yale University, New Haven, Connecticut. Architects: Skidmore, Owings & Merrill.

10. Die Bibliothekare verbringen einen großen Teil ihrer Zeit in ihren Büros, die sie unter Umständen auch zur Leserberatung benutzen. Beinecke Rare Book and Manuscript Library, Yale University, New Haven, Connecticut. Architekten: Skidmore, Owings & Merrill.

accessible to readers in a simple and direct manner. The complexity of library administration is very much dependent on its size. The space allocated to it will therefore change considerably as the library increases in size and will do so not only in area but also in character. It may be wise as a rule to consider the administrative zone as part of the adaptable book and reader area and allow a free interchange between these.

2. Book Services

Most libraries will need a working zone which has to do with book delivery and despatch and with the processing of accessions and their care in binderies. In its layout this area should allow for the flow of books in the same sort of way as in an industrial plant. The sequence of spaces should have the same linear progression as the sequence of operations to be performed on the book and should involve the minimum change of levels.
Material normally arrives in batches, is unloaded and unpacked in a shipping room or bay and then goes to an accessions room where it is checked against an order, is recorded and may be sorted in terms of books, newspapers and periodicals. It then goes to a catalogue department where books are classified according to subject headings and given a catalogue entry together with the necessary cross-reference entries. A duplicate library catalogue together with standard bibliographical reference material has to be within this area. Books are then marked, may have book cards and card pockets attached to them and then finally put in the stack or first displayed on shelves reserved for new accessions. Books and periodicals may at some stage during the process also be sent off to a bindery either within the building or elsewhere. All these operations occupy a good deal of space individually though their total is still likely to be only a small proportion of the whole library area. At least 100 sq. ft. (9 sq. m.) per person should be allowed for this processing work apart from any space needed for storage or catalogues.
This sequence of spaces designed for the handling of printed material will usually also be able to cope with the very much less bulky microreproductions which may be arriving. In many libraries there should however be a further service space which deals with the transfer of printed material into microcopy. Cameras and processing equipment specially designed for this purpose will be required and these will need connections to electrical supply, and to cold water and waste. Most equipment is designed to process the material in daylight.

Benutzer ohne große Schwierigkeiten zugänglich sein. Der Umfang der Verwaltungsaufgaben hängt weitgehend von der Größe der Bibliothek ab. Wenn also die Bibliothek erweitert wird, nimmt auch die Verwaltungszone mehr Raum in Anspruch und erhält überdies einen anderen Charakter. Es ist deshalb in den meisten Fällen ratsam, die Verwaltungszone als einen Teil der flexiblen Magazin- und Leseflächen zu betrachten und diese Bereiche gegeneinander offenzuhalten.

2. Buchbearbeitung

Die meisten Bibliotheken benötigen eine Arbeitszone, die für Bucheingang und -versand sowie für die Bearbeitung und das Binden von Neuerwerbungen bestimmt ist. Die Planung dieses Bereichs sollte darauf hinzielen, daß die Bearbeitung der Bücher ebenso flüssig abgewickelt werden kann wie in einer Fabrik. Die Abfolge der Räume sollte der Abfolge der Bearbeitungsvorgänge entsprechen und möglichst wenig Niveauunterschiede aufweisen. Normalerweise trifft das Material in Schüben ein, wird in einem Versandraum entladen und ausgepackt und geht dann in einen Akzessionsraum, wo es mit der Bestellung verglichen, registriert und häufig nach Büchern, Zeitungen und Zeitschriften sortiert wird. Danach kommt es in die Katalogabteilung, wo die Bücher nach Kategorien geordnet werden und einen Katalogeintrag mit den notwendigen Querverweisen erhalten. In dieser Abteilung müssen deshalb ein Duplikat des Kataloges und die wichtigen bibliographischen Nachschlagewerke zur Verfügung stehen. Die Bücher werden dann mit der Signatur versehen, eventuell mit Karten und Kartentaschen ausgestattet und schließlich in die Regale geräumt, falls sie nicht zuvor in gesonderten Fächern für Neuerscheinungen ausgestellt werden. Bücher und Zeitschriften können im Laufe des Verfahrens auch an eine Buchbinderei innerhalb oder außerhalb des Gebäudes geschickt werden. Alle diese Arbeitsvorgänge erfordern nicht wenig Raum, nehmen aber nur einen kleinen Teil der gesamten Bibliotheksfläche ein. Abgesehen von dem Platz, der für Lagerung oder Kataloge benötigt wird, sollten bei der Buchbearbeitung mindestens 9–10 qm pro Person zur Verfügung stehen.
Diese Raumfolge, die für die Bearbeitung gedruckten Materials bestimmt ist, wird in der Regel auch für die eingehenden Mikrofilm-Sendungen ausreichen, die sehr viel weniger umfangreich sind. Für die Übertragung von gedrucktem Material auf Mikrofilme sollte jedoch in den meisten Bibliotheken ein weiterer Raum vorgesehen werden, da das Verfahren Kameras und besondere technische Einrichtungen erfordert, die wiederum auf Strom- und Wasseranschlüsse sowie auf Abfallanlagen angewiesen sind. Die technische Ausrüstung ist zumeist auf eine Bearbeitung bei Tageslicht eingerichtet.

11. Books must undergo a process of unpacking, checking and cataloguing between arrival and being placed on a shelf; this process requires a good deal of space if it is to be done methodically and efficiently and should, if at all possible, be organized as a simple flow process. Charles Patterson Van Pelt Library, University of Pennsylvania, Philadelphia. Architects: Harbeson, Hough, Livingston & Larson.

11. Wenn neue Bücher eintreffen, müssen sie zunächst ausgepackt, kontrolliert und katalogisiert werden, bevor sie in die Regale eingeordnet werden können. Für diesen Prozeß, der möglichst in einer Richtung verlaufen sollte, müssen genügend große Räume zur Verfügung stehen. Charles Patterson Van Pelt Library, University of Pennsylvania, Philadelphia. Architekten: Harbeson, Hough, Livingston & Larson.

11

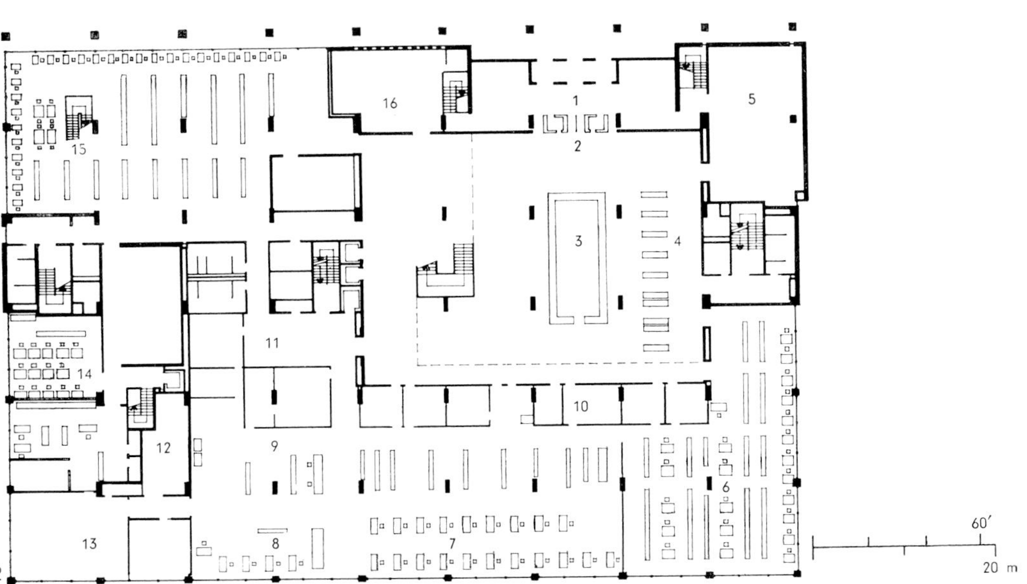


12

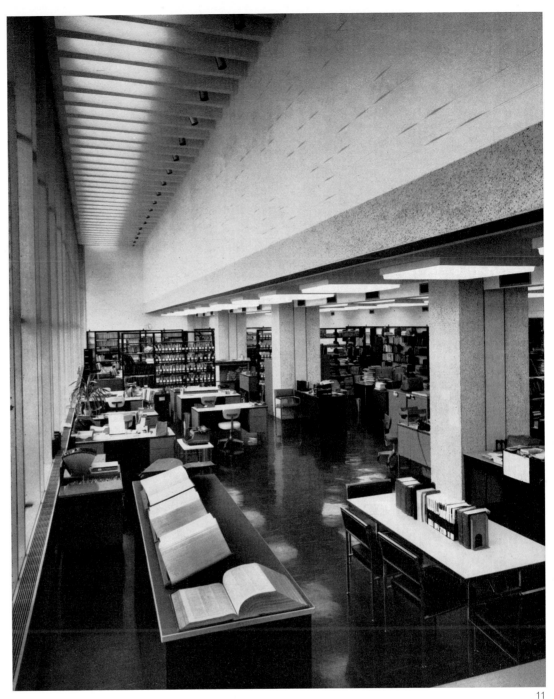

12. University Library, Edinburgh. Architects: Sir Basil Spence, Glover & Ferguson. Plan showing circulation desk, catalogue and administrative areas.

12. Universitätsbibliothek, Edinburgh. Architekten: Sir Basil Spence, Glover & Ferguson. Grundriß Publikumsbereich, Katalog und Verwaltungsbereich.

1 Foyer
2 Control / Kontrolle
3 Circulation desk / Publikumsverkehr
4 Catalogues / Kataloge
5 Exhibition hall / Ausstellungshalle
6 Reference and bibliography / Nachschlagewerke und Bibliographie
7 Cataloguing / Katalogisierung
8 Ordering / Buchbestellung
9 Accessioning / Akzession
10 Heads of department / Abteilungsleiter
11 Trolley park / Bücherwagen
12 Machine room / Maschinenraum
13 Typing / Schreibraum
14 Rare books / Seltene Bücher
15 Periodicals reading / Zeitschriftenlesesaal
16 Browsing / Leseraum

## Building Services and Structure

### 1. Mechanical

The demands of readers and books as regards temperature, relative humidity and air movement are not far apart. The most important control as far as books are concerned is that of relative humidity; excessive moisture will cause mould growth, excessive dryness will make the paper and some bindings brittle. This is particularly true of leather bindings and wood pulp paper with a large residue of acid. It has been suggested that the life span of a very considerable proportion of present day books could be doubled if kept at around 50% relative humidity. Comfort and conservation will therefore be achieved with room temperatures of about 69° F allowing ± 3° F fluctuations (20.6° C ± 1.7° C) and a relative humidity of between 45% and 55%. The number of air changes per hour should be between three and five in winter with mechanical ventilation or throughout the year with air conditioning and higher than this in the summer, if there is only mechanical ventilation.

Natural ventilation is difficult to achieve successfully in most libraries since readers sitting near the perimeter for light and thus near open windows will probably have too much air movement, while those within the building and possibly shielded by stacks will at the same time have inadequate ventilation. Efficient library plans also tend to be deep, often in fact square so as to minimize circulation, and such spaces are difficult to ventilate by opening windows. Excessive air movement is moreover a considerable nuisance not only because it may be unpleasantly cold but because it makes papers move about. Mechanical ventilation also makes it possible to clean the incoming air by filtration. The filters should be capable of screening particles in excess of 1 micron (one millionth of a metre). This will greatly help book maintenance.

All mechanical forms of ventilation will produce some noise. The amount considered permissible should be specified as one of the design criteria. The upper limit thought appropriate in reading areas is 30 NC to 35 NC (noise criteria = the common levels for equal sound pressure over the eight octave bands) unless there is a deliberate decision to introduce grey noise i.e. to use the steady noise of the equipment as a masking noise to the fluctuating sounds in the library.

## Technische Einrichtungen und Konstruktion

### 1. Klimaanlagen

Leser wie Bücher stellen ungefähr die gleichen Anforderungen an Temperatur, relative Luftfeuchtigkeit und Luftbewegung. Für die Bücher ist freilich die Regulierung der Luftfeuchtigkeit am wichtigsten; ein zu hoher Feuchtigkeitsgrad verursacht Schimmel, zu große Trockenheit macht das Papier und manche Einbände brüchig, besonders Ledereinbände und holzhaltiges Papier mit hohen Säurerückständen. Man nimmt an, daß bei einem erheblichen Teil des heutigen Bibliotheksbestandes die Lebensdauer verdoppelt werden könnte, wenn die relative Luftfeuchtigkeit stets etwa 50% betrüge. Physisches Wohlbehagen und günstige Konservierungsbedingungen werden bei Temperaturen von 20,6° C mit einer Toleranz von ± 1,7° C und einer relativen Luftfeuchtigkeit von 45 bis 55% erzielt. Die Luft sollte bei Ventilatoren im Winter und bei Klimaanlagen das ganze Jahr hindurch drei- bis fünfmal pro Stunde ausgetauscht werden; wenn nur Ventilatoren vorhanden sind, muß der Luftaustausch im Sommer noch öfter stattfinden.

Natürliche Lüftung ist in den meisten Bibliotheken schwer durchzuführen, da die Leser, die wegen des Tageslichtes in der Nähe der Fenster sitzen, in einem solchen Fall dem Luftzug ausgesetzt sind, während Leser, die sich im Gebäudeinneren aufhalten und möglicherweise durch Regale abgeschirmt sind, unter unzureichender Lüftung leiden. Gut durchdachte Bibliotheksgrundrisse weisen zudem häufig eine beträchtliche Tiefe auf oder sind sogar quadratisch, damit die Zirkulationswege abgekürzt werden, so daß eine Lüftung durch Fenster schwierig ist. Luftzug ist im übrigen nicht nur unangenehm, weil er Kälte mit sich bringt, sondern auch, weil er Papiere aufwirbelt.

Mechanisch erzeugte Ventilation ermöglicht es, die hereinströmende Luft durch Filter zu reinigen. Die Filter sollten Schmutzpartikel über 1 Mikron (1/1000 mm) abhalten. Luftsauberkeit trägt entscheidend dazu bei, den Bestand zu schützen.

Alle mechanischen Formen der Ventilation verursachen Lärm. Die zulässige Höchstgrenze sollte schon bei der Planung berücksichtigt werden. In Lesebereichen liegt die oberste Grenze bei 30–35 db, wenn nicht das gleichmäßige Geräusch der Anlage bewußt als ein Mittel be-

13

13. External movable blinds help to control both the heat gain within the building and the amount of light falling on books and readers. Excessive light and particularly glare or direct sunlight make reading very difficult. Public Library, Hansaviertel, Berlin. Architect: Werner Düttmann.
14. All books benefit from being kept at a constant relative humidity of about 50%. This becomes crucial in the case of rare books especially if these have leather bindings. Air-conditioning will produce such a constant environment and the load on the equipment will be reduced if varying outside conditions are excluded as much as possible. In this instance the material is within an inner shrine-like case placed within a concrete and translucent marble enclosure. Beinecke Rare Book and Manuscript Library, Yale University, New Haven, Connecticut. Architects: Skidmore, Owings & Merrill.
15. The tall spaces frequently found in the reading areas of libraries may have large high windows exposing a good deal of sky; external louvres greatly help to grade the light. Library, Technische Hochschule, Stuttgart, Germany. Architect: Hans Volkart.

13. Außenjalousien kontrollieren sowohl Hitzeeinstrahlung als auch Lichteinfall. Zu starker Lichteinfall oder direktes Sonnenlicht erschweren das Lesen. Hansabücherei, Berlin. Architekt: Werner Düttmann.
14. Bücher werden am besten bei einer ständigen relativen Luftfeuchtigkeit von etwa 50% aufbewahrt. Das ist besonders wichtig für seltene Bücher mit Ledereinbänden. Für gleichbleibende Luftfeuchtigkeit sorgen Klimaanlagen, die weniger belastet werden, wenn äußere Einflüsse soweit wie möglich ausgeschaltet sind. In diesem Fall wird das Material in einem schreinähnlichen Gehäuse gelagert, das von einer durch Beton und durchscheinende Onyxplatten begrenzten Raumhülle umgeben ist. Beinecke Rare Book and Manuscript Library, Yale University, New Haven, Connecticut. Architekten: Skidmore, Owings & Merrill.
15. Große Räume, wie sie sich häufig in den Lesebereichen der Bibliotheken finden, haben meist hohe Fenster. Außen angebrachte Sonnenschutzblenden mildern das einfallende Licht. Bibliothek der Technischen Hochschule, Stuttgart. Architekt: Hans Volkart.

The arguments for using air conditioning in a library are extremely strong. It is difficult to achieve 45%–55% relative humidity in most places throughout the year, and the cooling may also be needed because of the heat output of the electronic equipment which is likely to become an increasingly important part of a library. Air conditioning also implies clean, washed air which, particularly in industrial and dense urban areas, is a great improvement on simple filtration.

There is no doubt that complete air conditioning is needed for rare books but the dividing line between what to put into the rare bookroom with its special environment and what to leave out, is often an extremely difficult one.

The installation of air conditioning will also create situations for the reader where all parts of the building will be equally comfortable. This seems particularly important if notions of flexibility are to have any meaning.

nutzt wird, die wechselnden Geräusche in der Bibliothek zu überdecken.

Viele Argumente sprechen dafür, Bibliotheken mit Klimaanlagen auszustatten. An den meisten Orten ist es schwierig, während des ganzen Jahres eine relative Luftfeuchtigkeit von 45 bis 55% zu erhalten; außerdem kann Kühlung wegen der Wärmeausstrahlung der elektronischen Installationen erforderlich sein, die eine immer größere Rolle in der Bibliothek spielen werden. Im übrigen bedeutet Klimatisierung zugleich gründliche Reinigung der Luft, was besonders in Industriegebieten und dichtbebauten Stadtteilen einen großen Vorteil gegenüber der einfachen Filterung darstellt.

Es steht außer Frage, daß für die Aufbewahrung seltener Bücher Klimaanlagen benötigt werden, doch ist es häufig schwierig zu entscheiden, welches Material in den besonders ausgestatteten Raum für seltene Bücher aufgenommen werden soll und welches nicht.

Für den Leser schafft die Installierung einer Klimaanlage gleichmäßig angenehme Arbeitsbedingungen in allen Teilen des Gebäudes, was besonders dort wichtig ist, wo Flexibilität angestrebt wird.

14

15

2. Electrical

Loadings for the electrical services should be worked out on the basis of lighting levels between 30–40 lumens/sq.ft. (320–430 lux) on the working plane in reading areas and between 5–10 lumens/sq.ft. (53–107 lux) on the vertical plane in the stack areas. Since however these two spaces should be interchangeable, all areas should be capable of providing at least 30 lumens/sq.ft. (320 lux). In addition to this there may be a need for electrical equipment in the form of micro-reproduction readers or consoles linked to a computer. The network of electrical services must therefore be capable of dealing with such loads and must be arranged in such a way as to provide both floor and ceiling outlets. This is critical in terms of future re-arrangements.

2. Elektrische Anlagen

Die Belastungsfähigkeit der elektrischen Leitungen sollte auf Beleuchtungsstärken zwischen 320 und 430 lx (auf der Arbeitsfläche in Lesebereichen) und zwischen 53 und 107 lx (auf der vertikalen Ebene der Regalbereiche) beruhen. Da diese beiden Bereiche jedoch auswechselbar sein sollten, müssen überall zumindest 320 lx zu erzielen sein. Darüber hinaus sind häufig elektrische Apparate wie Lesegeräte für Mikrofilme oder mit einem Computer verbundene Pulte erforderlich. Das Stromnetz muß also auch solchen zusätzlichen Belastungen gewachsen sein und muß Boden- wie Deckenauslässe ermöglichen. Das ist besonders für künftige Umbauten wichtig.

18. A projecting tungsten light fitting is attached to each ▷ section of book shelving and different sources are used for general room lighting and for reading. Reska Equipment, Birkerød, Denmark.
19. Continuous linear sources of illumination running at right angles to the direction of the stacks make it possible to place stacks at any distance apart unrelated to a ceiling module. Public Library, Heidelberg, Germany. Architects: Johannes Grobe & Karl-Heinz Simm.

18. Über jeder Regaleinheit sind auskragende Leucht- ▷ körper angebracht. Für die Allgemeinbeleuchtung und für die Tische sind jeweils verschiedene Lichtquellen vorgesehen. Reska, Birkerød, Dänemark.
19. Durchlaufende Lichtbänder im rechten Winkel zu den Regalen ermöglichen es, die Regale ohne Rücksicht auf einen Deckenraster in beliebiger Entfernung voneinander aufzustellen. Stadtbücherei, Heidelberg. Architekten: Johannes Grobe und Karl-Heinz Simm.

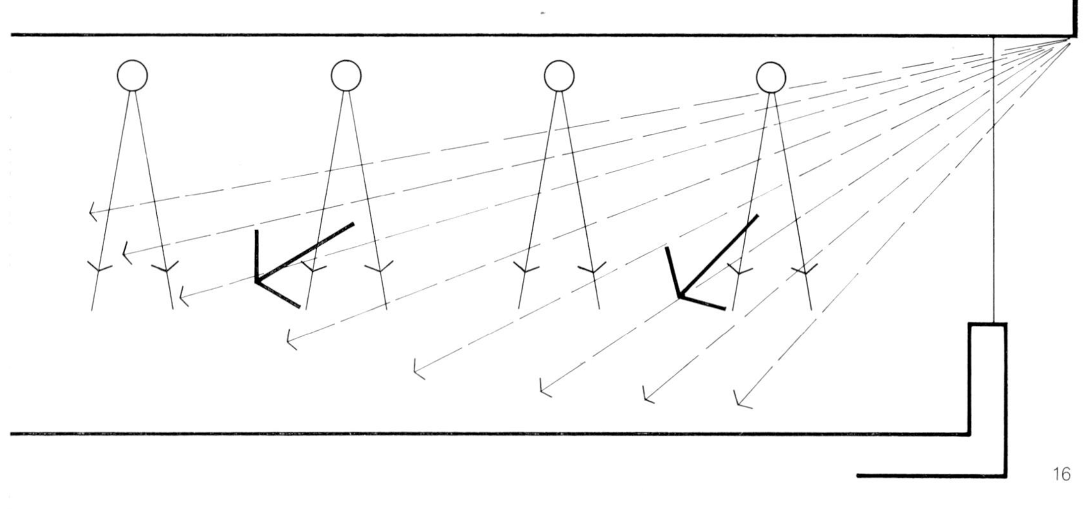

16

◁ 16. Artificial light may often be necessary in reading areas throughout the day especially where glass surfaces have been reduced to cut down glare or to reduce the load on an air-conditioning system. This artificial light should reinforce daylight so that the resultant illumination is such as still to provide some modelling. This gives a greater sense of reality than completely diffused lighting.
17. Lights may be a very considerable heat source in a library which may cause serious difficulty in the summer. Where mechanical ventilation or air conditioning is provided it may be an advantage to extract air through the fittings so that the minimum amount of heat is allowed to reach readers.

◁ 16. In vielen Lesebereichen ist auch tagsüber künstliche Beleuchtung erforderlich, vor allem dort, wo die Fensterflächen klein gehalten wurden, um Sonnenblendung zu vermeiden oder die Klimaanlage zu entlasten. Das künstliche Licht sollte das Tageslicht so ergänzen, daß ein gewisses Maß an modellierender Wirkung erhalten bleibt. Die Beleuchtung ist dann natürlicher als bei völlig diffusem Licht.
17. Beleuchtungskörper in Bibliotheken stellen eine starke Wärmequelle dar, was sich im Sommer sehr unangenehm auswirken kann. Wo mechanische Lüftung oder Klimaanlagen vorhanden sind, kann es sich als vorteilhaft erweisen, Luft durch die Auslässe der Lichtquellen abzusaugen, damit den Leser so wenig Wärme wie möglich erreicht.

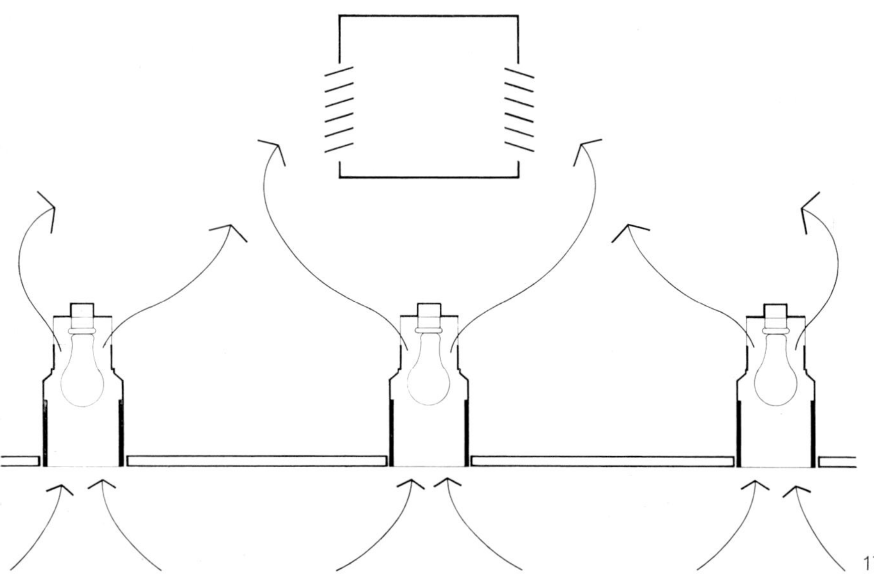

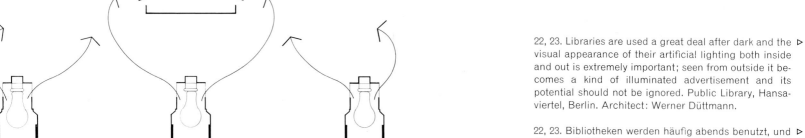

17

22, 23. Libraries are used a great deal after dark and the ▷ visual appearance of their artificial lighting both inside and out is extremely important; seen from outside it becomes a kind of illuminated advertisement and its potential should not be ignored. Public Library, Hansaviertel, Berlin. Architect: Werner Düttmann.

22, 23. Bibliotheken werden häufig abends benutzt, und ▷ die visuelle Wirkung der künstlichen Beleuchtung innen und außen ist deshalb besonders wichtig. Von außen her gesehen, kann die Bibliothek wie eine Leuchtreklame wirken, ein Effekt, der nicht außer acht gelassen werden sollte. Hansabücherei, Berlin. Architekt: Werner Düttmann.

18

19

20. Lights cantilevered from bookcases and directed at the shelves. Library, National Pensions Institute, Helsinki. Architect: Alvar Aalto.
21. Fixed continuous lighting of books is attached to the top of the supports holding the shelves; adjustable point sources of light for readers are at the tables. Library, Örsted Institute, University of Copenhagen. Architects: Eva and Nils Koppel.

20. Die Lampen sind an den Regalen angebracht und auf die Fächer gerichtet. Bibliothek der Staatlichen Volkspensionsanstalt, Helsinki. Architekt: Alvar Aalto.
21. An den oberen Regalträgern sind durchgehende Leuchtkörper für die Fächer befestigt; für die Lesetische stehen verstellbare Punktleuchten zur Verfügung. Bibliothek des Örsted-Instituts, Universität Kopenhagen. Architekten: Eva und Nils Koppel.

20

21

22

23

3. Structure

In any library which has mechanical ventilation or air conditioning there is liable to be a conflict between the continuity of hollow spaces needed to carry the air supply and the continuity of solid members needed for the supporting structure. Because this conflict has to be resolved through proper design, it is important that this problem is considered from the start even if such mechanical services cannot be installed at first. It seems very likely that the air distribution system will require some overhead space and that it will therefore not be possible to have the minimum floor to floor heights which have been traditional in the stack area. There is some advantage to this additional height which is useful in reading areas and which allows fluorescent light fittings to be placed at right angles to the bookstacks. These have to be at least 18″ (45 cm) above the top of the stack if the light is to be evenly distributed. Fittings at right angles allow the centres of bookstacks to be determined independently of the lighting layout.
The horizontal spacing of columns has already been discussed on page 131.
The structural floors of a library have to carry considerable superimposed loads. With bookstacks 7′6″ (2,28 m) high spaced about as close as possible, 3′4″ (1 m), this load will be 150 lbs/sq.ft. (680 kg/qm).
In a vast number of libraries the possibility of using compact shelving should not be excluded. This is true of every large public library, all university and research libraries and all sections of a national library. Although compact shelving may not be used throughout every floor of such institutions it seems extremely wise to take the precaution at the time of design to allow for this. The superimposed loading of compact systems will be about 225 lbs/sq.ft. (1 000 kg/m). The increased cost of the structure due to this additional loading is, in relation to the total cost of the building, not very great. It is an important investment in future flexibility.

4. Fire

Paper really only burns easily if it is in a loose form surrounded by oxygen. In the tight form of a book it is not a great fire hazard. Large parts of a stack may however remain unvisited for a long time and there is therefore the chance of a fire starting due to an electrical fault or some other cause, without being noticed. Where this is at all probable and also where valuable material is being stored it is advisable to install fire detection equipment. The most suitable, because likely to give the earliest warning, works by detecting any smoke content in the air. The use of sprinklers does not seem appropriate since books are likely to be damaged more severely by water than fire.

3. Konstruktion

In jeder Bibliothek mit Ventilatoren oder Klimaanlage ergibt sich ein Konflikt zwischen der Kontinuität der Hohlräume, die für die Luftzufuhr bestimmt sind, und der Kontinuität der massiven Bauteile, die zur tragenden Konstruktion gehören. Da dieser Konflikt nur durch entsprechende Planung zu lösen ist, muß er von vornherein berücksichtigt werden, selbst wenn solche technischen Einrichtungen zu Beginn noch nicht installiert werden können. Im allgemeinen erfordert ein Belüftungssystem zusätzliche Raumhöhe, so daß sich die übliche geringe Geschoßhöhe im Magazinbereich nicht beibehalten läßt. Vor allem in Lesebereichen erweist sich diese zusätzliche Raumhöhe als nützlich; sie ermöglicht es zum Beispiel, Leuchtstoffröhren im rechten Winkel zu den Regalen anzubringen. Die Leuchtkörper müssen mindestens 45 cm über dem obersten Fachboden montiert sein, wenn das Licht gleichmäßig gestreut werden soll. Bei rechtwinkliger Anbringung können die Achsabstände der Regale unabhängig von der Verteilung der Lichtquellen festgelegt werden.
Von der Stützenstellung in der Horizontalen war bereits auf Seite 131/133 die Rede.
Die tragenden Decken einer Bibliothek müssen beträchtliche Lasten aufnehmen. Bei 2,28 m hohen Regalen, die so eng wie möglich gestellt sind (Achsabstand 1 m), beträgt die Nutzlast beispielsweise 680 kg/qm.
In vielen Bibliotheken, vor allem in großen öffentlichen Bibliotheken, Universitäts- und Forschungsbibliotheken und in allen Abteilungen einer Nationalbibliothek sollte die Verwendung raumsparender Regale nicht ausgeschlossen werden. Auch wenn nicht in jedem Geschoß Kompaktsysteme benutzt werden, ist es ratsam, diese Möglichkeit bei der Planung zu berücksichtigen. Die Nutzlast beträgt bei platzsparenden Systemen etwa 1 000 kg/m². Die höheren Kosten für die Konstruktion, die sich aus dieser zusätzlichen Belastung ergeben, fallen im Vergleich zu den Gesamtkosten des Gebäudes kaum ins Gewicht. Sie bedeuten eine Investition, die sich in der flexiblen Nutzung des Gebäudes auszahlt.

4. Brandschutz

Papier entzündet sich nur dann leicht, wenn es sich um lose Blätter handelt, die von viel Sauerstoff umgeben sind. In der festen Form eines gebundenen Buches ist es nicht sonderlich feuergefährdet. Wenn jedoch große Teile eines Magazins lange Zeit nicht benutzt werden, kann beispielsweise auf Grund eines Kurzschlusses unbemerkt ein Feuer entstehen. Wo diese Möglichkeit gegeben ist und wo wertvolles Material aufbewahrt wird, ist es ratsam, Feuermeldeanlagen zu installieren. Die wirksamste Anlage, die am schnellsten Alarm geben dürfte, basiert auf der Prüfung des Rauchgehaltes der Luft. Die Verwendung von Sprinkleranlagen ist nicht unbedingt zu empfehlen, da Wasserschäden größer sein können als Brandschäden.

24

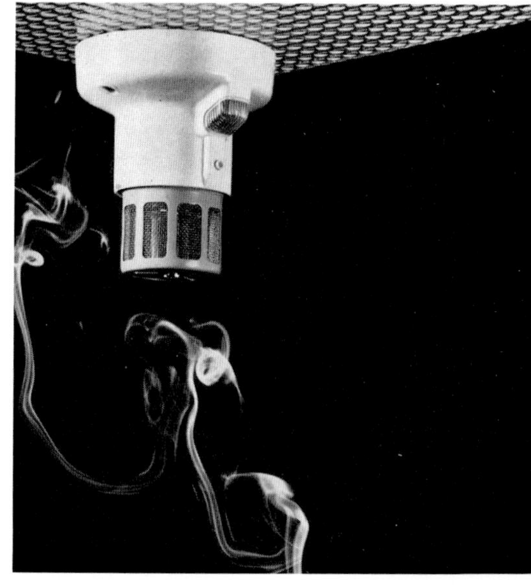

24. Smoke detection probably gives the earliest possible warning among commercially available systems and makes it likely that a fire is located and extinguished before much damage is done. Ceiling mounted detecting device: Siemens & Halske Co., Munich.

24. Unter den im Handel verbreiteten Systemen ist das der Rauchwarnung wahrscheinlich das wirksamste, da es am frühesten Alarm gibt. An der Decke befestigte Kontrollvorrichtung von Siemens & Halske, München.

## THE SETTING

Decisions on library siting are frequently made by committees long before the appointment of an architect. As a result it may happen that either extremely difficult sites are selected or potentially exploitable sites are overlooked. It is precisely at the time of deciding on a location that advice on possible built forms is needed. Such advice should therefore be one of the many factors influencing the discussions of the committee considering the placing of a new building. The nature of the site may moreover have a very direct bearing on the cost of the building.
What is of primary importance, however, is that the chosen site should be appropriate to the function of the library. Though one understands, for example, the sentiment that led to the building of what is the National Library of Germany in Berlin, it is by no means, at the moment, as accessible to the population as a whole as one might wish. Conversely arguments about siting the Library of the British Museum, the effective National Library of Great Britain, outside London seem to disregard all principles of accessibility and of the actual centre of gravity of the country. The principles which apply at the national scale are relevant downwards through the range of scales to the placing of a library within a school building. All the more recent secondary school plans, for instance, in which the library is thought of as a vital information centre essential to the process of learning, put the library space in a critical central position. If a social benefit is to be derived from the functioning of a library such considerations would appear essential.

## DIE LAGE DES BIBLIOTHEKSGEBÄUDES

Lange, bevor ein Architekt den Bauauftrag erhält, wird meist von Ausschüssen die Entscheidung über die Lage des Gebäudes gefällt. Bisweilen werden deshalb außerordentlich schwierige Grundstücke ausgewählt oder günstige Grundstücke übersehen. Gutachten über mögliche Gebäudeformen sind also bereits dann notwendig, wenn die Auswahl des Grundstücks zur Debatte steht, damit der Ausschuß diesen Faktor berücksichtigen kann. Die Art des Grundstücks wirkt sich übrigens häufig auch direkt auf die Baukosten aus.
Von besonderer Bedeutung ist freilich, daß das ausgewählte Grundstück der Funktion der Bibliothek entspricht. Obwohl zum Beispiel die Motive für die Placierung der neuen deutschen Staatsbibliothek in Berlin durchaus verständlich sind, wird das Gebäude für die Bevölkerung zunächst keineswegs so leicht zugänglich sein, wie es wünschenswert wäre. Und wenn die Forderung erhoben wird, die Bibliothek des British Museum, die eigentliche Nationalbibliothek Großbritanniens, außerhalb Londons und damit außerhalb des Aktivitätszentrums des Landes unterzubringen, so wird damit das Prinzip der Zugänglichkeit völlig außer acht gelassen. Dieses Prinzip gilt nicht nur auf nationaler Ebene, sondern bezieht sich auf alle Bibliothekstypen bis hinab zur Bücherei in einem Schulgebäude. So nimmt zum Beispiel in allen neueren Projekten für Höhere Schulen, bei denen die Bücherei als wichtiges und für den Lernprozeß unerläßliches Informationszentrum betrachtet wird, der Bibliotheksbereich eine zentrale Position ein. Wenn eine Bibliothek also von gesellschaftlichem Nutzen sein soll, so ist der Faktor der leichten Erreichbarkeit entscheidend.

2. The library of Säynätsalo, a community living on an island in a lake in Central Finland, forms part of the town hall and some shops which have been built at a central location. The library, on the right of the plan, is at first floor level. This grouping of facilities at a highly accessible point prevents the isolation of what would otherwise be a very small building. Community Library, Säynätsalo, Finland. Architect: Alvar Aalto. ▷

2. Die Bücherei von Säynätsalo, einer Inselgemeinde in einem See Mittelfinnlands, bildet einen Teil des Rathaus- und Ladenkomplexes, der in zentraler Lage errichtet wurde. Die Bibliothek (auf dem Plan rechts) nimmt das erste Obergeschoß ein. Durch eine Zusammenfassung verschiedener Einrichtungen an einem leicht zugänglichen Ort läßt sich die Isolierung eines Gebäudes vermeiden, das im Falle dieser Bibliothek sehr klein ausgefallen wäre. Gemeindebücherei, Säynätsalo, Finnland. Architekt: Alvar Aalto.

3. The clustering of activities may have equal validity at the urban scale especially if certain facilities can be shared. The library at the Cultural Centre in Wolfsburg is in the same building as a group of auditoria and clubrooms and there is obvious interaction between the various uses. Accessibility is ensured not only by central location but by providing car parking on a scale appropriate to the town manufacturing Volkswagens. Cultural Centre, Wolfsburg. Architect: Alvar Aalto. ▷

3. Die Verbindung verschiedener Funktionen ist auch in einer größeren Stadt durchaus sinnvoll, vor allem, wenn bestimmte Einrichtungen gemeinsam genutzt werden können. Die Bibliothek des Kulturzentrums in Wolfsburg ist mit mehreren Vortragssälen und Klubräumen zusammen in einem Gebäude untergebracht, und die unterschiedlichen Funktionen sind miteinander verzahnt. Leichte Zugänglichkeit ist nicht nur durch die zentrale Lage gewährleistet, sondern auch durch Parkplätze, deren Größe der Volkswagenstadt Wolfsburg angemessen ist. Kulturzentrum, Wolfsburg. Architekt: Alvar Aalto.

1. Accessibility is of prime importance to any library which has users coming to it; this is as true of a small suburban library as a large university one. A great many of the new universities have made the library one of the nodal buildings of the development. The plan of the University of Warwick, for example, shows in black the first stage of the library lying at the centre of the entire university site. Further expansion space is shown hatched. University of Warwick, Coventry. Architects: Yorke, Rosenberg, Mardall.

1. Bei jeder Bibliothek, die von den Benutzern aufgesucht wird, ist leichte Zugänglichkeit von größter Bedeutung. Das trifft auf kleine Vorortbüchereien ebenso zu wie auf große Universitätsbibliotheken. Bei vielen der neuen englischen Universitäten bildet die Bibliothek das Zentrum der gesamten Anlage. Der Lageplan der Universität Warwick zeigt zum Beispiel in Schwarz die erste Bauphase der Bibliothek, die den Mittelpunkt des Universitätsgeländes einnimmt. Der Bereich für spätere Erweiterungen ist schraffiert. Universität Warwick, Coventry. Architekten: Yorke, Rosenberg, Mardall.

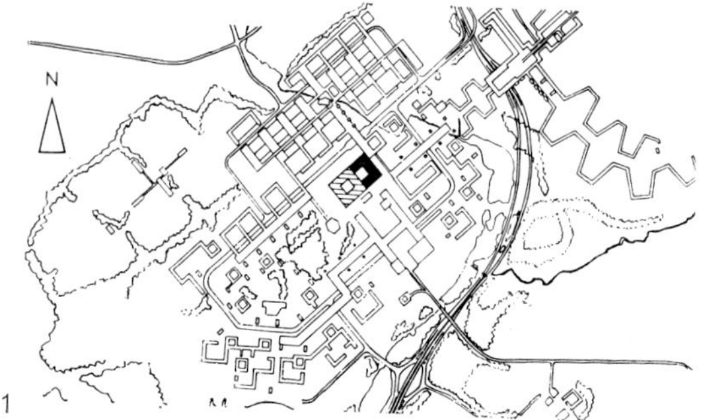


1

4. In low density areas accessibility will depend not so much on being at the centre of the area the library serves, as at some point that is linked to the main lines of movement, since in most cases readers will go there by car or, possibly, public transport. This also implies adequate car parking and a bus or train stop adjacent to the library. Putterham Branch Library, Brookline, Massachusetts. Architects: The Architects Collaborative. ▷

4. In Gebieten geringer Wohndichte bedingt leichte Zugänglichkeit nicht so sehr eine zentrale Lage der Bibliothek als ihre günstige Anbindung an die wichtigsten Verkehrswege, denn in den meisten Fällen werden die Leser ein Auto oder öffentliche Verkehrsmittel benutzen. Deshalb müssen genügend große Parkplätze und eine Bus- oder Bahnhaltestelle in der Nähe der Bibliothek vorgesehen werden. Putterham Branch Library, Brookline, Massachusetts. Architekten: The Architects Collaborative.

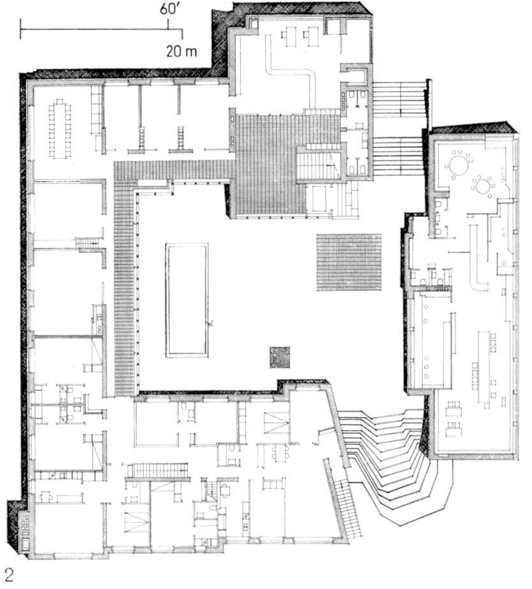


2

5. The branch library is often a very small building and apt to look insignificant. A link to some other building may therefore help. This branch library in a new housing area forms an outlying pavilion to a block of maisonnettes. It is at the entrance to a very large housing group and on the other side of the road is a shopping area. Just round the corner are the local bus stops. Public Library, Alton Estate, Roehampton, London. Architect: Hubert Bennett, Architect to the Greater London Council.

5. Eine Zweigbücherei ist oft ein sehr kleines Gebäude und sieht leicht unbedeutend aus. Eine Verbindung mit anderen Bauten kann deshalb von Nutzen sein. Diese Zweigbücherei einer neuen Siedlung bildet einen Pavillon, der einem Wohnblock mit Maisonnettewohnungen vorgelagert ist und am Zugang zu einem großen Häuserkomplex liegt. Auf der anderen Straßenseite befindet sich ein Einkaufszentrum, um die Ecke eine Bushaltestelle. Public Library, Alton Estate, Roehampton, London. Architekt: Hubert Bennett, Greater London Council.

5

3

6. Libraries ought not to be shy about advertising their wares, either during the day or at night. The library at Växjö not only lights up its large sign but reveals the whole of its ground floor. Although the building is set within a small municipal park, its brightly lit areas are visible over a considerable distance. Public Library, Växjö. Architect: Erik Uluots.

6. Bibliotheken sollten sich nicht davor scheuen, ihre Waren anzupreisen, tagsüber ebenso wie abends. Bei dieser Bücherei in Växjö wird nicht nur ein großes Schriftband beleuchtet, sondern auch das ganze Erdgeschoß gezeigt. Obwohl das Gebäude in einem kleinen städtischen Park liegt, sind die hell erleuchteten Fenster auf eine beträchtliche Entfernung sichtbar. Öffentliche Bücherei, Växjö. Architekt: Erik Uluots.

6

4

7. Readers ought to be encouraged to return books promptly so that others may use them. Usually, of course, they will want to do this when borrowing the next book. It ought, however, to be possible to return books even when the library is closed and a deposit box on the outside acting like a rather large letter box is undoubtedly helpful. Public Library, Orlando, Florida. Architect: John M. Johansen.

7. Leser sollten dazu ermutigt werden, die Bücher schnell zurückzugeben, damit auch andere sie benutzen können. Gewöhnlich warten sie damit natürlich, bis sie das nächste Buch leihen. Es sollte aber möglich sein, auch dann Bücher zurückzugeben, wenn die Bibliothek geschlossen ist. Ein Kasten an der Außenseite, der wie ein großer Briefkasten funktioniert, ist zweifellos eine nützliche Einrichtung. Public Library, Orlando, Florida. Architekt: John M. Johansen.

7

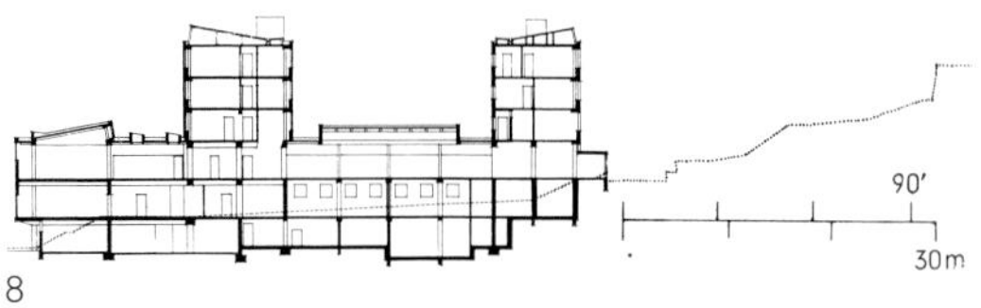

8

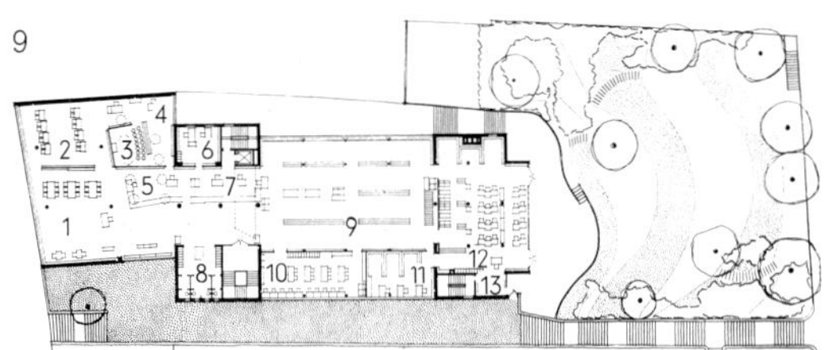
9

8–10. A central urban location may pose a conflict between accessibility and the kind of environment suitable for a library. The library for the Danish minority of South Schleswig resolves this by being a narrow building on plan, making contact at one end with the busy shopping street and then climbing up the hill to a sloping garden at the rear. The library is entered from the street like a shop; the reading room opens onto a terrace at the back. Library for the Danish minority of South Schleswig, Flensburg. Architects: Tyge Holm and Flemming Grut.

8–10. Eine zentrale Lage in der Stadt kann zu einem Konflikt zwischen dem Faktor der leichten Zugänglichkeit und der für eine Bibliothek angemessenen Umgebung führen. Die Bibliothek für die dänische Minderheit Südschleswigs ist ein im Grundriß schmales Gebäude, das auf der Vorderseite in eine belebte Einkaufsstraße einbezogen ist und sich auf der Rückseite an einen ansteigenden Hügel lehnt. Die Leser betreten die Bücherei wie einen Laden von der Straße her. Der Lesesaal öffnet sich auf eine Terrasse auf der Rückseite. Bibliothek für die dänische Minderheit Südschleswigs, Flensburg. Architekten: Tyge Holm und Flemming Grut.

Section and ground floor plan / Schnitt und Grundriß Erdgeschoß.

1 Children's library / Kinderbücherei
2 Children's reading room / Lesesaal für Kinder
3 Story-telling room and TV / Vorleseraum und Fernsehen
4 Book set collection / Sammlung von Buchserien
5 Children's lending counter / Ausleihe für Kinder
6 Office / Büro
7 Adults' lending counter / Ausleihe für Erwachsene
8 Cloakroom / Garderobe
9 Lending library / Leihbücherei
10 Newspaper reading room / Zeitschriftenlesesaal
11 South Schleswig collection / Sammlung Südschleswig
12 Reading room / Lesesaal
13 Office / Büro

10

13. Out-door reading is an enjoyment which ought not to be denied. If it takes place in an enclosed courtyard or on a balcony or roof top the security arrangements of the library need not be infringed. Such out-door reading spaces should give some shelter from wind and sun and also create some sense of seclusion. Library, Gakushuin University, Tokyo. Architect: Kunio Mayekawa. ▷

13. Lesen im Freien bietet Annehmlichkeiten, auf die man nicht verzichten sollte. Wenn dafür ein umschlossener Hof, ein Balkon oder eine Dachterrasse vorgesehen ist, können auch die Sicherheitsmaßnahmen einer Bibliothek eingehalten werden. Lesebereiche im Freien sollten Schutz gegen Wind und Sonne gewähren und zudem ein Gefühl der Abgeschlossenheit vermitteln. Bibliothek der Gakushuin-Universität, Tokio. Architekt: Kunio Mayekawa.

14. Withdrawal to a quiet outdoor zone can also take place upwards. The roof level can in fact easily become a slightly different area with a coffee bar or club rooms exploiting the particularity of that situation. Public Library, Orlando, Florida. Architect: John M. Johansen. ▷

14. Wer sich hier in einen ruhigen Bereich im Freien zurückziehen möchte, kann auf das Dach steigen. Das Dachniveau läßt sich häufig für eine Cafeteria oder Clubräume nutzen, die von der Besonderheit der Situation profitieren. Public Library, Orlando, Florida. Architekt: John M. Johansen.

11, 12. The Children's Library at Pimlico follows the same principle as the library at Flensburg. It takes up two bays of a line of shops under a new block of housing. It is entered through one bay, like any of the other shops, immediately off the pavement; the front part of the other bay is taken up by service rooms. At the rear the library is open to a courtyard which occupies the area given over to service yards in the standard shopping unit. Children's Library, Churchill Gardens, Pimlico, London. Architects: Powell & Moya.

11, 12. Die Kinderbücherei in Pimlico folgt dem gleichen Prinzip wie die Flensburger Bücherei. Sie nimmt zwei Fensterachsen innerhalb einer Reihe von Läden ein, die im Erdgeschoß eines neuen Wohnblocks untergebracht sind. Der Leser betritt in einer der beiden Achsen die Bibliothek wie jeden Laden direkt vom Bürgersteig aus. In der anderen Achse liegen Nebenräume an der Vorderfront. An der Rückseite öffnet sich die Bücherei auf einen Hof, der den Lieferhöfen der Ladeneinheiten auf beiden Seiten entspricht. Children's Library, Churchill Gardens, Pimlico, London. Architekten: Powell & Moya.

11

12

15. Although actual seclusion may be very difficult to achieve, particularly when an outdoor area is next to the pavement, some sense of separation may still be helpful. This partial enclosure may, in addition, help to shield the indoor library spaces on the other side of the glass wall. There is also something about these outdoor carrels which may make them act like a sign for the library. Prefectural Library, Oita. Architects: Arata Isozaki & Associates. ▷

15. Völlige Isolation ist zwar meist sehr schwierig zu erreichen, vor allem, wenn die Lesezone unmittelbar an der Straße liegt. Trotzdem läßt sich wenigstens eine gewisse Abgeschlossenheit erzielen. Darüber hinaus schirmt ein solcher Bereich die inneren Bibliotheksräume auf der anderen Seite der Glaswand ab. Solche *carrels* im Freien können wie eine Werbung für die Bibliothek wirken. Präfektur-Bibliothek, Oita. Architekten: Arata Isozaki & Associates.

13

14

15

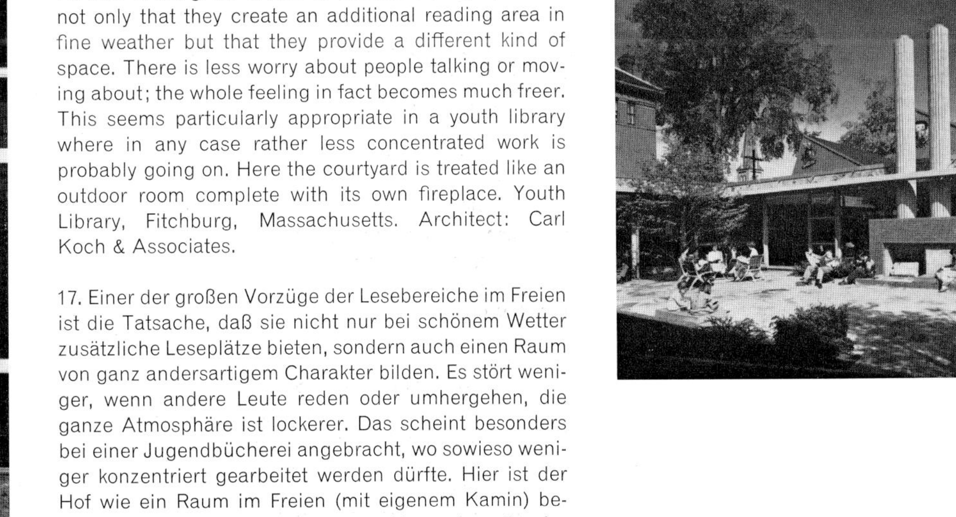

16. Expansion is one of the crucial problems in deciding on a library site. Very frequently the decision will have been made a long time ago and an extension will have to be fitted into an existing situation which only allows for a limited number of possibilities. The new library for Trinity College, Dublin had to make an attachment to the existing library and then go off at right-angles to continue the sequence of grass courts which make up the university. The connection between the two buildings is made below ground level, the roof of this space making an entrance terrace to the new building. Library, Trinity College, Dublin. Architects: Ahrends, Burton & Koralek.

16. Bei der Auswahl des Grundstücks ist die Möglichkeit der Erweiterung ein wichtiges Kriterium. Häufig ist die Entscheidung bereits vor langer Zeit gefallen, und der Erweiterungsbau muß der bestehenden Situation angepaßt werden, die nur bestimmte Lösungen erlaubt. Das neue Bibliotheksgebäude des Trinity College in Dublin mußte an die bestehende Bibliothek angeschlossen und dann im rechten Winkel weitergeführt werden, da die Folge der grasbewachsenen Höfe auf dem Universitätsgelände fortgesetzt werden sollte. Die beiden Gebäude sind unterirdisch miteinander verbunden. Die Decke dieses Verbindungsbereichs bildet die Eingangsterrasse der neuen Bibliothek. Bibliothek des Trinity College, Dublin. Architekten: Ahrends, Burton & Koralek.

16

17. One of the great virtues of outdoor library spaces is not only that they create an additional reading area in fine weather but that they provide a different kind of space. There is less worry about people talking or moving about; the whole feeling in fact becomes much freer. This seems particularly appropriate in a youth library where in any case rather less concentrated work is probably going on. Here the courtyard is treated like an outdoor room complete with its own fireplace. Youth Library, Fitchburg, Massachusetts. Architect: Carl Koch & Associates.

17. Einer der großen Vorzüge der Lesebereiche im Freien ist die Tatsache, daß sie nicht nur bei schönem Wetter zusätzliche Leseplätze bieten, sondern auch einen Raum von ganz andersartigem Charakter bilden. Es stört weniger, wenn andere Leute reden oder umhergehen, die ganze Atmosphäre ist lockerer. Das scheint besonders bei einer Jugendbücherei angebracht, wo sowieso weniger konzentriert gearbeitet werden dürfte. Hier ist der Hof wie ein Raum im Freien (mit eigenem Kamin) behandelt. Youth Library, Fitchburg, Massachusetts. Architekten: Carl Koch & Associates.

17

## CHANGE AND INCREASE

Very few buildings remain in the state in which they were first designed, or are used in quite the same way as when first occupied. This is after all not unexpected, for the life span of most buildings is greater than the length of time a particular function remains static either as regards size or character. This is particularly true in the case of libraries and has now been emphazised by librarians for a considerable number of years. Whether all library design has acted on the basis of such a viewpoint is, however, another matter. Even when it has, this need has often been treated in too simple a fashion.

A number of quite clear and separate aspects ought to be distinguished. A building will become in some measure obsolete for the function it houses if the building itself deteriorates, if the function changes, or, perhaps most commonly, if our expectation of what constitutes a proper functional relation between a building and its usage alters through time. To take a particular component of a library which is not peculiar to it, the heating system, as an example, one can see that this will need maintenance from time to time and at some point the maintenance costs will become greater than the amortization cost of a new heating system or there will be a complete breakdown, and as a result a replacement system will be installed. As the library increases in size its heating plant may be working perfectly efficiently but will be unable to deal with the increased load and may therefore need alteration or additional equipment. Similarly if even within the existing envelope of the building a rare book collection, for instance, is placed in an area previously used as ordinary stack space, the heating equipment in that section may be obsolete and need replacement. Equally, however, our expectation of what represents acceptable comfort levels – how warm, cool, humid and clean the air is – and what is thought to be an appropriate environment for the safe keeping of books, is liable to alter quite as rapidly as the rate at which the heating equipment itself is deteriorating. The same will be true of an element particular to a library such as the conveyor system handling books. This will for example, similarly become obsolete through mechanical failure, through lack of capacity or through an inability to meet the criteria of efficiency demanded in a changed situation. Such alternative possibilities of obsolescence will in some way or other be true of most building elements. What is important to discover, therefore, is how many of these possibilities are likely to affect each element and what the probable rate of obsolescence is for each.

Such an analysis will yield a hierarchy of permanence which will permit an ordering of the elements making up the library building. It is as a result of such an ordering that the need for variability and increase can be foreseen, and that decisions about the likely nature of these changes can be made.

Even a very simple examination will show that structure is likely to be the most permanent element and the idea of flexibility is therefore most often seen as needing those kinds of structure which will interfere least with the probable variations. In practice this suggests a grid of columns with supports spaced so as to relate to the dimensions most likely to be critical, the spacing of stacks or office partitions for example. The structure should however not only be seen as something that may get in the way but also as an element which makes certain uses possible. This is particularly true of floor loading and obviously the greater the permissible loading the greater is the range of uses which becomes feasible. Floors designed to take only readers will not take stacks and those designed to carry ordinary stacks will not support compact shelving. Design criteria imposed at the building stage can therefore set limits on future flexibility.

The capacity to change a space is moreover not solely dependent on the freedom given by the structural system. This would after all pre-suppose that the use demands nothing more than columns, floor and roof. Not even in the simplest bookstorage space is this true. A whole set of other building elements is involved but, more important still, there is a relationship of different kinds of spaces linked to a movement system within any building which exercises an organizational control and which therefore places limits on variability.

Among non-structural building elements the most important as regards flexibility are those dealing with mechanical and electrical services. These also show the highest rate of obsolescence and, perversely, are also amongst the most expensive. In an air-conditioned building, mechanical and electrical services may together with the space needed by them (plant rooms, ducts, etc.) account for as much as half the total cost of the building. This is obviously critical since any ability to change in the future may demand a provision of facilities at the time of construction which will not be used immediately or which are an alternative facility, and which thus increase still further the building cost. To have electrical floor outlets, for instance, in the stack area to allow table lamps or electronic equipment to plug in at some future date when the space becomes used for communication rather than storage, will inevitably raise the cost of the library. The decision on whether such expenditure is worthwhile could be guided by the hierarchy of permanence established for the elements within the project. If, on the assumption that it is safe to forecast that communication spaces will need electrical outlets distributed on a grid at floor level, it can be seen that the area being used for book storage temporarily, will be used as a reading room immediately the second phase of the library is built, such expenditure may well be worthwhile. If the likelihood on the other hand is remote, it may be more sensible to lay conduits in the floor screed but not to provide any electrical connections. If the probability is more remote still, it may only be necessary to make sure that the screed is sufficiently thick to permit the insertion of an electrical distribution system when it is needed.

Such changes apply to ideas about possible functional variations within a space. That space, however, does not exist in isolation; it is part of an organization of spaces which forms the library building. The limit on variability may depend not only on the actual and potential characteristics of each area but on the relationships which may have to exist between them. A good many of these relationships are given by the internal movement system – entrances, routes, lifts, conveyor belts – which has been established. Given, to take an obvious example, that there are to be closed access stacks, a certain sequence of spaces has to exist from the entrance inwards which precludes the possibility of the space immediately beyond the front door being used as stack; the established movement system has in fact set limits on the degree of variability. Radical conversions of buildings as a result frequently demand a change in the existing layout of entrances and routes.

This is very much the case in libraries. Attempts have been made, as in the studies by Sir Leslie Martin and Colin St. John Wilson for the Oxford group of libraries (page 104) to suggest forms which would in fact allow an increase in size but demand very little, if any, restructuring of the spatial relationships of the library.

There are, however, limits even within the most favourable organization of extendible spaces to the amount by which a library can increase before it needs not only just more floor area but requires to function within a changed

Nur wenige Gebäude bleiben in dem Zustand, in dem sie geplant wurden, oder werden stets in der gleichen Weise genutzt. Das ist nicht anders zu erwarten, denn bei den meisten Gebäuden ist die Lebensdauer länger als die Periode, in der eine bestimmte Funktion dem Charakter oder dem Umfang nach unverändert bleibt. Bibliotheksexperten haben schon seit einer Reihe von Jahren darauf hingewiesen, daß dies besonders auf Bibliotheken zutrifft. Ob die Bibliotheksplanung sich immer danach gerichtet hat, ist freilich eine andere Frage. Selbst wenn dieser Aspekt berücksichtigt wurde, sind die Lösungen häufig nicht gründlich genug durchdacht.

Ein Gebäude vermag die Funktion, der es dient, nicht mehr in vollem Maße zu erfüllen, wenn es veraltet ist, wenn die Funktion sich wandelt oder wenn – was am häufigsten vorkommt – die Auffassung von der angemessenen funktionalen Beziehung zwischen Gebäude und Verwendungszweck sich im Laufe der Zeit ändert. Das Heizungssystem zum Beispiel, ein Bestandteil der Bibliothek, der jedoch nicht für Bibliotheksbauten charakteristisch ist, muß von Zeit zu Zeit repariert werden. An einem bestimmten Punkt werden die Reparaturkosten höher als die Amortisierungskosten eines neuen Heizsystems, oder aber die ganze Anlage fällt aus und muß durch eine neue ersetzt werden. Wenn die Bibliothek sich vergrößert, muß möglicherweise ein durchaus noch leistungsfähiges Heizsystem verändert oder erweitert werden, da es sonst der höheren Belastung nicht gewachsen ist. Auch wenn beispielsweise innerhalb eines Gebäudes eine Sammlung seltener Bücher in einem Bereich untergebracht wird, der zuvor als einfaches Magazin gedient hat, kann die Heizanlage in dieser Zone sich als unzureichend erweisen. Ebenso schnell wie das Heizsystem selbst veraltet, wandeln sich freilich auch unsere Vorstellungen von physischem Wohlbehagen – Wärme, Kühle, Feuchtigkeit und Sauberkeit der Luft – und von den angemessenen Bedingungen für eine sichere Aufbewahrung der Bücher. Ähnliches gilt für die Förderanlagen, die ein charakteristischer Bestandteil der Bibliothek sind. Sie veralten beispielsweise durch technische Defekte oder durch mangelnde Kapazität oder infolge neuer Ansprüche, die sich aus einer veränderten Situation ergeben. Solche verschiedenen Möglichkeiten des Verschleißes finden sich bei den meisten Bauelementen. Deshalb muß bei jedem einzelnen Element untersucht werden, wie viele dieser Möglichkeiten in Betracht kommen und wie schnell der Prozeß des Verschleißes vor sich geht.

Aus einer solchen Analyse ergibt sich eine Hierarchie der Dauerhaftigkeit, die allen Elementen des Bibliotheksgebäudes ihre Rangordnung zuweist. Ist diese Rangordnung festgestellt, so lassen sich auch Reorganisation und Erweiterung vorausplanen.

Schon eine oberflächliche Untersuchung zeigt, daß die Konstruktion im allgemeinen das dauerhafteste Element ist. Flexibilität bedeutet daher zumeist, daß die Konstruktion eventuelle Veränderungen so wenig wie möglich behindert. In der Praxis ist ein Raster zu empfehlen, in dem die Stützenabstände auf Abmessungen bezogen sind, wie sie sich beispielsweise aus der Anordnung von Regalen oder den Achsmaßen von Büros ergeben. Freilich sollte die Konstruktion nicht nur als etwas betrachtet werden, das hinderlich werden kann, sondern auch als ein Element, das bestimmte Funktionen überhaupt erst ermöglicht. Das gilt vor allem für die Tragfähigkeit der Decken, denn je stärker die Decken sind, desto vielfältigeren Zwecken können die Räume dienen. Zwischendecken, die für Lesesäle geplant sind, können keine Magazine tragen, und wo normale Regale vorgesehen waren, können keine kompakten Regalsysteme untergebracht werden. Deshalb setzen bestimmte Entwurfskriterien im Planungsstadium möglicherweise einer späteren Flexibilität Grenzen.

Ob sich ein Gebäude variabel nutzen läßt, hängt im übrigen nicht allein davon ab, wieviel Freiheit das Konstruktionssystem gewährt. Das würde nämlich letzten Endes bedeuten, daß das Bauwerk nur durch Stützen, Decken und Dach bestimmt würde, was nicht einmal auf den simpelsten Magazinbereich zutrifft. Zahlreiche andere Bauelemente spielen eine Rolle, vor allem aber die Kombinationen unterschiedlicher, durch ein Zirkulationssystem verbundener Raumbereiche, die jedes Gebäude organisieren und deshalb in seiner Variabilität eingrenzen. Von der Konstruktion abgesehen, sind die technischen Einrichtungen und die elektrischen Anlagen am wichtigsten für die Flexibilität des Gebäudes. Sie sind zugleich am meisten dem Verschleiß ausgesetzt, gehören aber paradoxerweise zu den kostspieligsten Bauelementen. In einem Gebäude mit Klimaanlage können beispielsweise die technischen und elektrischen Installationen mit dem Raum, den sie beanspruchen (Leitungen, Maschinenräume usw.) die Hälfte der gesamten Baukosten ausmachen. Diese Tatsache ist deshalb wichtig, weil Flexibilität unter Umständen zusätzliche Installationen, die eine Alternativlösung bieten oder nicht sogleich in Anspruch genommen werden, schon während der Errichtung des Baus verlangt und weil damit die Baukosten noch mehr in die Höhe getrieben werden. Eine Bibliothek wird beispielsweise zwangsläufig teurer, sobald im Magazinbereich elektrische Auslässe für Tischlampen oder elektronische Apparate installiert werden, die sich vielleicht zu einem späteren Zeitpunkt als notwendig erweisen, wenn der Bereich nicht mehr für das Magazin, sondern für die Kommunikation benutzt wird. Ob eine solche Ausgabe sich lohnt, sollte entsprechend der unterschiedlichen Lebensdauer der einzelnen Projektelemente entschieden werden. Geht man davon aus, daß Kommunikationsbereiche Auslässe mit einem elektrischen Netz auf Fußbodenniveau benötigen, so ist die zusätzliche Ausgabe durchaus gerechtfertigt, wenn etwa der Bereich vorübergehend als Magazin und nach Vollendung des zweiten Bauabschnitts als Lesesaal genutzt wird. Liegt die Möglichkeit einer andersartigen Nutzung fern, so ist es empfehlenswerter, Leitungen im Unterboden zu verlegen, aber keine elektrischen Anschlüsse vorzusehen. Scheint eine solche Möglichkeit ausgeschlossen, so genügt es, dafür Sorge zu tragen, daß der Unterboden stark genug ist, um zu einem späteren Zeitpunkt ein elektrisches Leitungssystem aufzunehmen.

Solche Veränderungen ergeben sich aus dem Wandel der Funktionen innerhalb eines bestimmten Bereichs. Dieser Bereich ist jedoch nicht isoliert, sondern bildet einen Teil der gesamten Raumfolge, aus der das Bibliotheksgebäude besteht. Flexibilität hängt daher nicht nur von den gegenwärtigen oder künftigen Charakteristika der einzelnen Bereiche ab, sondern auch von ihren räumlichen Beziehungen zueinander, die wiederum weitgehend durch das interne Zirkulationssystem – Eingänge, Verkehrswege, Aufzüge, Förderbänder – bestimmt sind. Wenn zum Beispiel das Magazin dem Leser nicht zugänglich ist, kann der Bereich unmittelbar hinter der Eingangstür nicht als Magazin genutzt werden, da eine Folge von Räumen vom Eingang ins Innere des Gebäudes führen muß; das vorhandene Zirkulationssystem setzt also der Variabilität Grenzen. Wird die Organisation eines Gebäudes grundlegend geändert, so müssen häufig auch die Eingänge und Verkehrswege verlegt werden. Das trifft vor allem auf Bibliotheken zu. Es wurden jedoch Versuche unternommen – wie zum Beispiel die Studien Sir Leslie Martins und Colin St. John Wilsons für den Bibliothekskomplex in Oxford (Seite 104) –, Gebäudeformen zu

organizational framework. Libraries exhibit a problem of magnitude; there is, that is to say, a preferred system related to particular ranges of size. This relationship has sometimes been masked by the fact that for probably historical reasons libraries differing in size tend to belong to different administrations; small branch libraries to local government, regional libraries to counties or metropolitan government, national libraries to national government. But as earlier sections have tried to make clear, the essential differences are not those dependent on the source of financial support but on the particularity of the principal library function. Within each of these again, size will exercise a controlling influence. To take a very obvious example, it is perfectly feasible to suggest an institution dealing primarily with very similar kinds of users reading books outside the library which could have a stock of 10,000 volumes or 10,000,000. The first could be a very small departmental library of a research group, the second a national lending library of scientific literature. To be efficient they would have very different library organizations as a result of this difference in size: one would be an open access room, the other a closed access and mechanized storage space.

The magnitude of the problem is very evident in the growth of university libraries. It is part of the debate between those advocating central library facilities because of the impossibility of parcelling up knowledge, and those suggesting the need for libraries within each of which a reader can find his way and have free access to all parts. Not enough work has been done on libraries in use to know at which points along the magnitude scale new ways of dealing with the problem have to be introduced. There is only a hunch that the graph is not a straight line progression. This difficulty of sub-division within the university library system may be solved, at least partially, if some of the new techniques of reproduction which are becoming increasingly inexpensive are used to copy books and create duplicates. It should then be possible for large unified libraries to create subsidiary libraries almost on demand to cater for specific interest groups; what Frederick Goodman of the University of Michigan has called a mother library producing specialized offsprings.

The facts regarding increase itself are well documented and often considered alarming. As a first consideration it is important to realize that no library can function effectively if 100% of its shelf space is occupied. A library should be considered as having reached its maximum capacity when it is about 85% full. This leaves roughly 5 inches (12.5 cm) free on each shelf. If less than this amount of space is left free it will not only mean that a considerable number of books has to be moved at a large labour cost each time there is a new accession but also that binding will be damaged when books are pulled out of a too tightly packed shelf. The combined cost of these effects is sizeable and cumulative and suggests that new space should be available immediately this stage is reached. The number of years it will take for a library to reach 85% capacity assuming it is half full is given in table 4.

Many libraries are designed so that at the time the building is occupied they are about half full. It takes, however, a considerable number of years to plan, finance and build a library building and the alarm should, therefore, be sounded when the stack space is about two-thirds full depending, of course, on the rate of growth and the complexity of the decision-making process needed to acquire new space. The number of years left are shown in table 5, also taken from Keyes D. Metcalf.

The percentage rates of growth selected for these tables are not at all unusual and show very clearly how soon in the total life span of the library building expansion is likely to be needed. Even a rate of growth of 2% exponential implies that the library roughly doubles in size in 35 years. The kind of rates of increase which are frequently experienced are suggested by the following examples:

| | 1947 | 1957 | 1967 |
|---|---|---|---|
| University of London, Senate House Library | 385,000 | 680,000 | 800,000 |
| Public Library, Newcastle | | 365,000 | 610,640 |
| Ministry of Agriculture, Fisheries and Food, London | 30,000 | 70,000 | 140,000 |

(From Library Association, London.)

This continuous numerical increase can be dealt with by providing more floor space, by altering the method of storage and thus utilizing a given floor space more intensively or, clearly, a combination of both of these. Altering the method of warehousing the material may take the form of shelving by size, of reducing the spacing between stacks, of changing to compact shelving or of replacing the material with some micro-reproduction. The implications of these alternatives are elaborated in a hypothetical example of library expansion on page 178. The example is only meant to show the kind of questions which need consideration and naturally the situation would be quite different in most instances. In many cases the possibility of alternatives does not arise; expansion simply has to be more space of the same kind.

Change and increase have so far been discussed as a progression through time measured in years with appropriate action taken at each relevant stage on the initiative of the library staff. There is, however, another kind of change which is measured in hours and which has to do with the needs of users for different kinds of situations during a library visit: for muffled seclusion, for sun and view, for coffee, cigarettes and talk, for sitting out of doors, for the acoustic isolation of a listening booth, for pacing up and down after hours of sitting. The possibility for these different experiences has to co-exist. It is not often that these and many similar needs are considered and provided for. One of the reasons why the possibility of such short-term variability is disregarded is due to the notion that it would limit long term changes, that only total uniformity makes flexibility possible.

This is a sad but frequent misreading of the meaning of flexibility. What the idea should imply is an extended range of possibilities. an enlargement of the potentials of a spatial organization; what it far too frequently turns out to be is an extremely limited opportunity of performing very much the same sort of thing in a number of quantitatively different ways. The ability of an area to take stacks at different spacings is a typical example. This does very little, if anything, however to make possible different qualitative experiences in a library. Yet these are as important to the, proper and full functioning of the building as the simple changes in disposition.

What such a more complex approach may, therefore, suggest is that there is an argument for designing a built form made up of a number of categories of space, each with its own particular characteristic. Within each of these, certain activities will seem more appropriate, will be able to be performed in a manner which enhances rather than just tolerates those activities. A total equality between all spaces may indeed in theory at least make it possible to allocate any area to any use but may in fact be appropriate

Table 4

*Years required for a collection to increase from 50 to 85 per cent of full capacity*

| | Years | | | | | |
|---|---|---|---|---|---|---|
| Rate of Growth | 3 1/3% | 4% | 5% | 6% | 8% | 10% |
| Geometric | 16+ | 13+ | 11+ | 9+ | 7+ | 5− |
| Arithmetic | 27+ | 18− | 14+ | 12− | 9− | 7+ |

Geometric or exponential increase is the increase each year by the stated percentage of the total number in existence at the end of the immediately preceding year. Like compound interest, the effect is, therefore, cumulative.

Arithmetic increase is the increase each year by the stated percentage of the number which was in existence at the beginning of the period of calculation. The same amount is thus added each year.

Table 5

*Years required for a collection to increase from 66 to 85 per cent of full capacity*

| | Years | | | | | |
|---|---|---|---|---|---|---|
| Rate of Growth | 3 1/3% | 4% | 5% | 6% | 8% | 10% |
| Geometric | 7+ | 6+ | 5+ | 4+ | 3+ | 2+ |
| Arithmetic | 8+ | 7+ | 6− | 5− | 4− | 3− |

(Tables from Keyes D. Metcalf, *Planning Academic and Research Library Buildings*.)

finden, die eine Erweiterung ermöglichen, ohne daß zugleich die räumlichen Verhältnisse der Bibliothek von Grund auf geändert werden müßten.
Selbst bei der günstigsten Anordnung der erweiterten Räume sind einer Ausdehnung freilich Grenzen gesetzt, denn von einem gewissen Punkt an braucht die Bibliothek nicht nur zusätzliche Fläche, sondern auch einen anderen organisatorischen Rahmen. Bei Bibliotheken spielt das Problem der Größenordnung eine wichtige Rolle, denn jede Kategorie hat ihr bevorzugtes System. Die Beziehung zwischen Größe und Organisation wird bisweilen dadurch verdeckt, daß verschieden große Bibliotheken aus möglicherweise historischen Gründen in die Kompetenz verschiedener Verwaltungsorgane fallen: Kleine Zweigbüchereien unterstehen der Ortsverwaltung, Landesbibliotheken den Regionalbehörden oder den Großstadtverwaltungen, Nationalbibliotheken dem Staat. Wie jedoch schon früher gesagt wurde, lassen sich die Bibliothekstypen weniger nach ihren Trägern unterscheiden als vielmehr nach ihrer wichtigsten Funktion. Auch innerhalb dieser Funktionen ist dann die Größe ein bestimmender Faktor. Es ist zum Beispiel denkbar, daß zwei Institutionen sehr ähnliche Lesergruppen ansprechen, aber über verschieden große Bestände verfügen; die kleine Fachbibliothek einer Forschungsgruppe besitzt 10000 Bände, die nationale Leihbibliothek für wissenschaftliche Literatur 10000000. Dieser Größenunterschied führt zwangsläufig zu unterschiedlichen Organisationsformen; in dem einen Fall ein Freihandmagazin, in dem anderen Fall ein mechanisierter und für den Benutzer unzugänglicher Magazinbereich.
Das Problem der Größenordnung macht sich vor allem bei den ständig wachsenden Universitätsbibliotheken bemerkbar. Während einerseits zentrale Bibliothekseinrichtungen befürwortet werden, da es unmöglich sei, den Wissensstoff aufzusplittern, werden andererseits Bibliotheken gefordert, in denen sich jeder Leser zurechtfinden kann und in denen alle Bereiche frei zugänglich sind. Bisher ist noch nicht genügend erforscht, bei welchen Schwellenwerten jeweils andere Lösungen gefunden werden müssen. Es läßt sich nur vermuten, daß die Progression nicht regelmäßig verläuft.
Das schwierige Problem der Gliederung innerhalb der Universitätsbibliotheken dürfte sich zumindest teilweise lösen lassen, wenn einige der neuen und in zunehmendem Maße wirtschaftlichen Reproduktionstechniken zur Herstellung von Duplikaten und zum Vervielfältigen von Büchern angewandt werden. Es müßte dann möglich sein, daß große Einheitsbibliotheken nach Bedarf Spezialbibliotheken schaffen, die für bestimmte Interessengruppen bestimmt sind; Frederick Goodman von der University of Michigan spricht von einer »Mutterbibliothek«, die spezialisierte »Sprößlinge« hervorbringt.
Was die Wachstumsraten selbst angeht, so steht ausreichendes Zahlenmaterial zur Verfügung, das häufig als alarmierend betrachtet wird. Zunächst muß festgestellt werden, daß eine Bibliothek nicht funktionsfähig ist, wenn ihre Regalflächen zu 100% besetzt sind. Sie hat ihre höchste Kapazität erreicht, wenn die Regale zu etwa 85% ausgenutzt sind. Das bedeutet, daß in jedem Fach etwa 12,5 cm frei bleiben. Steht weniger freier Raum zur Verfügung, so müssen bei jedem Neuzugang unter beträchtlichem Aufwand an Arbeitslohn Bücher bewegt werden; außerdem werden die Einbände beschädigt, wenn Bücher aus einem zu eng besetzten Regal herausgezogen werden. Diese zusätzlichen Kosten summieren sich, so daß neuer Raum bereitgestellt werden sollte, sobald ein solches Stadium erreicht ist. Wie viele Jahre es dauert, bis eine zur Hälfte ausgenutzte Bibliothek auf 85% ihrer Kapazität kommt, ist in Tabelle 4 angegeben.

Viele Bibliotheken werden so geplant, daß sie bei der Inbetriebnahme etwa zur Hälfte besetzt sind. Da es jedoch viele Jahre dauert, ein Bibliotheksgebäude zu planen, zu finanzieren und zu bauen, sollte bereits Alarm geschlagen werden, wenn das Magazin zu zwei Dritteln ausgenutzt ist. Wie viele Jahre dann noch bleiben, zeigt Tabelle 5.
Die Prozentzahlen dieser Tabellen sind keineswegs ungewöhnlich. Sie illustrieren deutlich, wie schnell im allgemeinen eine Erweiterung des Bibliotheksgebäudes notwendig wird. Selbst eine Wachstumsrate von 2% (exponential) bedeutet, daß die Bibliothek in 35 Jahren ihren Bestand ungefähr verdoppelt.
Als Beispiele für häufig auftretende Wachstumsraten seien die folgenden englischen Bibliotheken genannt:

| | 1947 | 1957 | 1967 |
|---|---|---|---|
| University of London, Senate House Library | 385 000 | 680 000 | 800 000 |
| Public Library, Newcastle | | 365 000 | 610 640 |
| Ministry of Agriculture, Fisheries and Food, London | 30 000 | 70 000 | 140 000 |

(Nach Library Association, London.)

Um diesen ständigen Zuwachs aufzufangen, wird entweder zusätzliche Stellfläche geschaffen, oder die vorhandene Fläche wird durch andere Methoden der Magazinierung besser ausgenutzt, oder beide Verfahren werden miteinander kombiniert. Andere Methoden der Magazinierung können darin bestehen, daß die Bücher nach Formaten geordnet werden, daß der Abstand zwischen den Regalen verringert wird, daß raumsparende Regalsysteme angewendet werden oder daß das Material teilweise durch Mikrofilme ersetzt wird. Was diese Alternativen jeweils bedeuten, ist in dem hypothetischen Beispiel einer Bibliothekserweiterung auf Seite 179 erläutert. Das Beispiel soll lediglich zeigen, welche Probleme in Erwägung gezogen werden müssen; häufig liegt die Situation natürlich ganz anders. In vielen Fällen gibt es gar keine Alternativen, weil die Erweiterung nicht anders als durch Bereitstellung zusätzlicher Flächen durchzuführen ist.

Bisher sind Veränderungen und Erweiterungen als langfristige, in Jahren zu messende Prozesse beschrieben worden, die jeweils auf die Initiative des Bibliothekspersonals hin in Gang kommen. Es gibt jedoch noch eine andere Art der Veränderung oder des Wechsels, die nach Stunden bemessen wird: Der Benutzer hat während des Bibliotheksbesuches das Bedürfnis nach wechselnden Situationen, er sucht Stille und Abgeschiedenheit oder Sonnenlicht und Ausblick, er braucht Kaffee, Zigaretten und Gespräche oder die akustische Isolation einer Abhörkabine. Diese Möglichkeiten sollten nebeneinander gegeben sein. Es kommt jedoch nur selten vor, daß solchen und ähnlichen Bedürfnissen Rechnung getragen wird. Einer der Gründe liegt darin, daß die Möglichkeit kurzfristigen Wechsels als Hindernis für langfristige Veränderungen betrachtet wird und daß nur totale Uniformität als Voraussetzung für Flexibilität gilt.
Hier liegt ein bedauerliches, aber weitverbreitetes Mißverständnis vor. Flexibilität sollte bedeuten, daß eine größere Skala von Möglichkeiten geboten und das Potential einer räumlichen Organisation vergrößert wird. Allzu häufig jedoch wird unter Flexibilität nicht mehr verstanden als die sehr begrenzte Möglichkeit, die gleiche Sache in nur quantitativ verschiedener Weise auszuführen. Ein

Tabelle 4
*Zahl der Jahre, in denen sich der Bestand von 50% auf 85% der Kapazität vermehrt*

| | Jahre | | | | | |
|---|---|---|---|---|---|---|
| Wachstumsrate | 3¹/₃% | 4% | 5% | 6% | 8% | 10% |
| Geometrisch | 16+ | 13+ | 11+ | 9+ | 7+ | 5− |
| Arithmetisch | 27+ | 18− | 14+ | 12− | 9− | 7+ |

Geometrisches Wachstum oder Exponentialwachstum ist das jährliche Wachstum um einen Prozentsatz, der vom Gesamtbestand am Ende des vorhergehenden Jahres gerechnet ist. Wie bei Zinseszinsen handelt es sich also um eine Kumulation.
Arithmetisches Wachstum ist das jährliche Wachstum um einen Prozentsatz, der von dem zu Beginn der Rechnungsperiode vorhandenen Bestand gerechnet ist. Es wird also jedes Jahr der gleiche Betrag hinzugefügt.

Tabelle 5
*Zahl der Jahre, in denen sich der Bestand von 66% auf 85% der Kapazität vermehrt*

| | Jahre | | | | | |
|---|---|---|---|---|---|---|
| Wachstumsrate | 3¹/₃% | 4% | 5% | 6% | 8% | 10% |
| Geometrisch | 7+ | 6+ | 5+ | 4+ | 3+ | 2+ |
| Arithmetisch | 8+ | 7+ | 6− | 5− | 4− | 3− |

(Tabellen nach Keyes D. Metcalf, *Planning Academic and Research Library Buildings.)*

to none. The condition is summarized in Aldo van Eyck's phrase: "The glove that fits every hand, fits no hand". The demands of variability will in general suggest that each of these characteristic spaces should be as large as possible since the number of permutations of usable spaces within a given volume will be proportional to the size of that volume. Clearly, for example, if one is considering naturally side-lit office spaces or seminar rooms or reading areas within 20 ft. (6 metres) of a window, then the greater the length of that characteristic space the larger will be the number of different possible sub-divisions of that zone. One of the important considerations in the design of a library which assumes the need for such a characteristic space would be, for instance, to maintain an appropriate ratio between this kind of a space on the perimeter and a rather different top lit or artificially lit internal space.
Perhaps fortunately for library design many of the differences between one kind of characteristic usage and another can be resolved at the non-structural scale. Frequently the change can be brought about by differences in lighting related to different kinds of personal enclosure and especially through the use of furniture. This stems, of course, from the basic fact that within a library the relation of an individual to the information source is the crucial activity. While this is also likely to be true in the future it may not hold equally for all spaces within the library building.

### A Possible Trend

It is on present evidence most unlikely that the function of the library system will remain in the same state as we know it in the late 1960s. Changes will be due to both technical and social causes. This is to put quite to one side those changes which may happen in building techniques or building expression and which will undoubtedly be reflected in libraries as one of the many current built forms. What is of interest to this discussion are developments in the usage of the library service and the effect of these on design.
Writing the foreword to A. K. Mukherjee's *Librarianship: Its Philosophy and History* (London 1966), S. R. Ranganathan suggested that "a library is now recognized to be a centre for socializing books". This definition is undoubtedly a useful and important concept. It may however, unless analyzed critically, leave out certain aspects even if some other word is substituted for "book". Its importance lies in the fact that it suggests that any library exists to provide a service and that although this service is contributed in effect to individuals, it deals with sections of society. There is, in other words, a difference between having individual information sources in one's possession – having books, tapes, magazines in the house or the laboratory – and having access with numbers of other people to such sources. The difference is both a matter of the number and kind of information sources readily usable. It is clear that libraries are institutions dealing with a certain aspect of communication. Traditionally this has been verbal communication encoded in written form, together with such pictorial information as may have been necessary to amplify or explain the written texts. Traditionally also the library as a collection of such encoded sources has existed to bridge the gap in time between the information being issued by its initiators and it being received on demand by a user. Information transfer is thus possible within a library over an extremely extended period of time. This period is certainly measurable in centuries.
Analysis would, moreover, also demonstrate that this information transfer covers a wide range of demands. Not all are best suited by taking a book from a shelf and reading the whole text or large portions of it. While this is a delightful experience in the case of a novel it is not appropriate where the search is for a specific item of information. To read a book in that case may provide a great deal of redundant information and may in fact have been completely wasteful, since the book did not contain the sought item. In addition to this it must be recognized that information transfer at the more or less instantaneous level now takes many different forms and that there should, therefore, be a way of storing these sources so that subsequent transfers can take place. If the prime function of the library is thus seen as the storage and dissemination of verbal and certain kinds of pictorial communication in order to make possible an information transfer at times chosen by the user, certain extensions to its present function become likely. It is important to emphasize here the notion of dissemination in order to distinguish a library and the social service it provides from a private store of information, and equally the notion of unspecified times of use so as to make quite clear the difference between such a use of communication media and the use by a mass audience receiving the information simultaneously at a moment selected by the initiators of the communication. In both cases the differences are not only technical but also moral.
The changes which we expect will probably have repercussions on the design and siting of the building and are, therefore, relevant to the subject of this book. Given that the assumption just described is correct, libraries will have to deal with material other than books, periodicals, newspapers or miniaturized versions of these. Libraries, of course, already deal with gramophone records and tapes in rather small numbers but this is likely to be only the beginning of a reduction in the dominance of the printed word. A good many of the forms which are likely to be introduced may indeed not need storage of the information within the library building, but may be able to be connected to a central information store. A system such as that known as *Walnut*, developed by IBM for the United States Central Intelligence Agency, stores millions of pages in the form of film. Each item is coded and a computer has been programmed to remember its location and to search through the total store given certain key words about the subject. As a result of its search the computer presents a list of documents. The user then "indicates which he wants. When he does, the computer locates the item and activates a mechanical device that extracts the appropriate film. The images of this film may then be enlarged and read on a viewer, or may be photographically enlarged and converted into so-called hard copy – i. e. a duplicate of the original". (Toffler) The whole process may take no longer than five seconds. Such a system would obviously deal with a certain kind of rather frequent library demand but would be connected to a centralized computer allowing multiple access.
The likelihood of such systems occurring within library buildings designed in the late 1960s is extremely high. Hasan Ozbekhan, Director of Planning at the System Development Corporation in California, suggests the following probable dates for the introduction of certain technological applications based on computers within libraries:

| | |
|---|---|
| Automatic bibliography generation | 1970–1975 |
| Question answering | 1975–1980 |
| Text abstraction and reproduction | 1975–1980 |
| Home access and retrieval (reproducing copy) | 1985 |

(From Hasan Ozbekhan, *Automation,* in *Science Journal,* London, October, 1967.)

### Example of Library Expansion

An existing collection of 200,000 volumes is growing exponentially at the rate of 4%. A new building is to be provided for the collection.

*Year 1.* Architect selected; design and approval of the scheme by its users, relevant committees and local authorities.
*Year 2.* Preparation of constructional drawings, specifications, Bills of Quantities and tendering.
*Years 3 and 4.* Construction of building.
*Year 5.* The Library moves into its new building. It has by now grown to 234,000 volumes. If the building is to be half full on occupation, the library should have a capacity for 468,000 volumes.
*Year 11.* The library has grown to 308,000 volumes, i. e. just over 66% of its total capacity. Action is required to deal with further expansion.
Assuming that it would be possible to shelve 10% of the collection on compact shelving: Approx. 30,000 volumes would then take up an area equivalent to about 17,000 volumes shelved on stacks at 4'3" centres (see comparative layouts on pages 134 and 135); space would thus have been liberated for a further 13,000 volumes shelved normally.
Assuming moreover that a further 10% of the collection could be copied onto microcopy: Approx. 30,000 volumes (or about 6,000,000 pages) would take up the equivalent of 900 volumes shelved normally (see page 137 for comparative calculations); space would thus have been liberated for a further 29,000 volumes. Total gain = space for 42,000 volumes.
*Year 15.* During the year the library will reach 350,000 volumes and have used up the space gained by transfer to compact shelving and microcopy. New action is required.
The past rate of growth ought to be extrapolated, decisions made on what proportion of the new acquisitions have to be shelved on normal shelving, on compact shelving or can be transferred to microcopy immediately. In addition to this some acquisitions may be received as microcopy from their publishers.
These figures should produce a new effective growth rate measured as an annual increase of shelf length.
It can then be seen whether new space is required or whether the usefulness of the existing building can be extended by further use of compact shelving or microcopy.
*Year 16.* A decision has been made to build an extension. The library now has 360,000 volumes. The new effective growth rate is 3%.
*Year 20.* The library can move into its extension. Its collection is now 371,000 volumes. On the principle that the shelf space available at the opening should be 50% of total capacity, the combined space available in the original building and the extension should be for 742,000 volumes.
At the end of 20 years the space demands of the collection given the suggested growth rates are about 3¾ times the number of books existing at the beginning of the period.

These calculations deal with book storage only and take no account of any increase in the number of readers.

## Beispiel einer Bibliothekserweiterung

Eine Bibliothek mit einem Bestand von 200000 Bänden hat eine exponentiale Wachstumsrate von 4%. Es soll ein neues Gebäude für die Bücher geschaffen werden.

*Jahr 1.* Auswahl des Architekten; Entwurf und Billigung des Projekts durch die zuständigen Ausschüsse und örtlichen Behörden.
*Jahr 2.* Vorbereitung der Konstruktions- und Detailzeichnungen, Spezifikationen und Ausschreibung.
*Jahr 3 und 4.* Errichtung des Gebäudes.
*Jahr 5.* Die Bibliothek zieht in das neue Gebäude ein. Der Bestand ist inzwischen auf 234000 Bände angewachsen. Wenn das Gebäude bei Bezug zur Hälfte ausgenutzt sein soll, müßte die Bibliothek über eine Aufnahmekapazität von 468000 Bänden verfügen.
*Jahr 11.* Der Bestand ist auf 308000 Bände, das heißt etwas mehr als 66% der gesamten Kapazität, angewachsen. Es müssen Maßnahmen für eine weitere Steigerung der Aufnahmefähigkeit getroffen werden.
Wenn 10% des Bestandes in raumsparenden Regalsystemen untergebracht werden können, nehmen etwa 30000 Bände so viel Raum ein wie zuvor 17000 Bände auf Regalen mit Achsabständen von 1,30 m (vgl. Grundrisse auf Seite 134 und 135). Es finden also 13000 Bände mehr Platz als bei normaler Aufstellung.
Wenn außerdem weitere 10% des Bestandes auf Mikrofilme übertragen werden können, nehmen etwa 30000 Bände (oder ungefähr 6000000 Seiten) so viel Raum ein wie zuvor 900 Bände (vgl. Seite 137/138). Es finden also 29000 Bände mehr Platz. Insgesamt wäre damit Raum für weitere 42000 Bände geschaffen.
*Jahr 15.* Im Laufe dieses Jahres wächst der Bestand auf 350000 Bände, so daß der durch raumsparende Systeme und Mikrofilme gewonnene Raum ausgenutzt ist. Neue Maßnahmen sind erforderlich.
Die frühere Wachstumsrate sollte überprüft werden. Es muß entschieden werden, welcher Prozentsatz der Neuerwerbungen auf normalen oder raumsparenden Regalsystemen untergebracht oder sofort auf Mikrofilme übertragen wird. Außerdem werden eine Reihe neuer Titel bereits als Mikrofilme von den Verlagen eingesandt.
Aus diesen Zahlen ergibt sich eine neue effektive Wachstumsrate, die als jährliche Zunahme der Regalflächen gemessen wird.
Danach läßt sich feststellen, ob mehr Raum erforderlich ist oder ob das Gebäude durch weitere Verwendung raumsparender Systeme oder Mikrofilme noch besser ausgenutzt werden kann.
*Jahr 16.* Es ist entschieden worden, eine Erweiterung zu bauen. Die Bibliothek umfaßt nun 360000 Bände. Die neue effektive Wachstumsrate beträgt 3%.
*Jahr 20.* Die Bibliothek kann in den Erweiterungsbau einziehen. Sie umfaßt nun 371000 Bände. Nach dem Prinzip, daß die verfügbare Regalfläche bei Bezug 50% der Gesamtkapazität entsprechen sollte, muß der im ursprünglichen Bau und im Anbau gegebene Raum 742000 Bänden Platz bieten.
Nach 20 Jahren sind die Raumanforderungen des Bücherbestandes bei den genannten Wachstumsraten etwa 3³/₄ mal größer als die des Bücherbestandes im Jahre 1.

Diese Berechnungen gehen nur von der Magazinierung aus und berücksichtigen nicht ein eventuelles Anwachsen der Leserzahlen.

typisches Beispiel dafür ist die Wahlmöglichkeit verschiedener Regalabstände innerhalb eines Magazinbereichs. Eine solche Variabilität verhilft dem Leser freilich nur selten zu jenen unterschiedlichen qualitativen Erfahrungen, die für das Funktionieren einer Bibliothek ebenso wichtig sind wie simple Umdispositionen.
Es spricht also vieles dafür, ein Bibliotheksgebäude so zu planen, daß es eine Reihe verschiedener Raumkategorien bietet, die alle ihre eigenen Charakteristika aufweisen. Jede dieser Kategorien sollte bestimmten Tätigkeiten angemessen sein und sie fördern statt sie lediglich zu tolerieren. In der Theorie mag eine völlige Uniformität aller Räume dazu führen, daß jeder Bereich jedem Verwendungszweck zugeordnet werden kann, doch in der Praxis kann sich erweisen, daß keiner der Räume seiner Bestimmung angemessen ist. Um Aldo van Eyck zu zitieren: »Der Handschuh, der jeder Hand paßt, paßt keiner Hand.« Um der Variabilität willen sollte jeder dieser charakteristischen Bereiche so groß wie möglich sein, denn die Wandlungsmöglichkeiten des nutzbaren Raumes innerhalb eines gegebenen Volumens sind der Größe dieses Volumens proportional. Wenn zum Beispiel Büroräume oder Seminarräume oder Lesesäle mit natürlichem Seitenlicht in einer Entfernung bis zu 6 m vom Fenster geplant sind, ist die Zahl der möglichen Unterteilungen um so größer je länger sich der charakteristische Bereich erstreckt. Ist eine solche charakteristische Zone vorgesehen, so muß bei der Planung freilich auch darauf geachtet werden, daß ein angemessenes räumliches Verhältnis zwischen dem Bereich an der Peripherie des Gebäudes und den andersartigen, durch Kunstlicht oder Oberlicht erhellten inneren Räumen besteht.
Unterschiede zwischen verschiedenen charakteristischen Bereichen lassen sich häufig auch mit nicht-konstruktiven Mitteln hervorheben. Individuelle Bereiche entstehen zum Beispiel durch unterschiedliche Beleuchtung sowie vor allem durch verschiedenartige Möblierung. So wird der Tatsache Rechnung getragen, daß die Kommunikation zwischen Individuum und Informationsquelle die wichtigste Aufgabe zumindest der Bibliothek als Ganzes ist und wohl auch in Zukunft bleiben wird.

## Ausblick

Nach dem gegenwärtigen Stand der Dinge ist anzunehmen, daß das Bibliothekssystem in Zukunft anders funktionieren wird als in den späten sechziger Jahren. Es werden sowohl technisch als auch gesellschaftlich bedingte Veränderungen eintreten, ganz abgesehen von bautechnischen oder stilistischen Fortentwicklungen, die zweifellos auch in der Bibliothek, einer der vielen gängigen Bauaufgaben, ihren Niederschlag finden. An dieser Stelle soll jedoch nur von bibliothekstechnischen Neuerungen und ihren Auswirkungen auf die Architektur die Rede sein.
In seinem Vorwort zu A. K. Mukherjees Werk *Librarianship: Its Philosophy and History* (London 1966) schrieb S. R. Ranganathan, daß »die Bibliothek heute als der zentrale Ort gilt, an dem Bücher vergesellschaftet werden«. Diese Definition ist zweifellos treffend. Sie geht davon aus, daß jede Bibliothek eine Dienstleistung zu erbringen hat und daß sie sich, obwohl ihre Dienstleistung Individuen zugute kommt, an Teile der Gesellschaft wendet. Es ist also ein Unterschied, ob man individuelle Informationsquellen besitzt – Bücher, Tonbänder, Zeitschriften, die zu Hause oder an der Arbeitsstätte zur Verfügung stehen – oder ob man zusammen mit vielen anderen Menschen Zugang zu solchen Quellen hat. Der Unterschied liegt sowohl in der Art wie in der Anzahl der Informationsquellen.

Bibliotheken sind Institutionen, die sich mit einem bestimmten Aspekt der Kommunikation befassen. Traditionsgemäß handelt es sich um verbale Kommunikation, die in schriftlicher Form niedergelegt ist, sowie um bildliche Information, soweit sie notwendig ist, um den geschriebenen Text zu erläutern oder zu vervollständigen. Es gehört ebenso zur traditionellen Aufgabe der Bibliothek, als Sammelstelle solcher schriftlicher Quellen den Zeitraum zwischen der Veröffentlichung der Information durch den Verfasser und ihrer Benutzung durch den Leser zu überbrücken. Die Informationsvermittlung durch eine Bibliothek kann sich daher über eine sehr lange Zeitspanne, oft sogar über Jahrhunderte, erstrecken.
Eine genauere Analyse würde darüber hinaus auch ergeben, daß diese Informationsübermittlung vielen Bedürfnissen gerecht werden muß. Nicht allen ist damit gedient, daß sie ein Buch aus dem Regal nehmen und den ganzen Text oder große Teile daraus lesen. Das mag im Fall eines Romanes durchaus angenehm sein, ist aber keineswegs angebracht, wenn eine bestimmte Einzelinformation gesucht wird. In einem solchen Fall liefert die Lektüre eines Buches möglicherweise zahlreiche überflüssige Informationen und bleibt unter Umständen völlig ergebnislos, weil die gesuchte Tatsache nicht in dem Buch enthalten ist. Im übrigen muß angemerkt werden, daß die kurzfristige Übermittlung von Informationen heute viele verschiedene Formen annimmt und die Informationsquellen deshalb so gespeichert werden sollten, daß eine schnelle Übermittlung möglich ist. Sieht man die Funktion der Bibliothek darin, daß sie verbale und in bestimmten Fällen auch bildliche Kommunikation speichert und verbreitet und die Informationsübermittlung zu dem vom Benutzer gewünschten Zeitpunkt ermöglicht, so ist eine Ausweitung ihres bisherigen Aufgabenbereichs wahrscheinlich. Die Funktion der Verbreitung muß hier besonders betont werden, da sie die Bibliothek mit ihren gesellschaftlichen Aufgaben von einem privaten Informationsspeicher unterscheidet. Die Möglichkeit, zu beliebigen Zeiten über die Information zu verfügen, macht dagegen den Unterschied zwischen der Benutzung eines solchen Kommunikationsmittels und der eines Massenmediums deutlich, bei dem die Zuhörer eines Auditoriums die Information zur gleichen Zeit und in einem von den Urhebern der Kommunikation gewählten Augenblick empfangen. In beiden Fällen ist der Unterschied nicht nur technischer, sondern auch moralischer Natur.
Künftige Entwicklungen werden sich wahrscheinlich auch auf die Planung und die Lage des Bibliotheksgebäudes auswirken und stehen deshalb in engem Zusammenhang mit dem Thema dieses Buches. Falls sich der Aufgabenbereich der Bibliothek tatsächlich ausweitet, so bleibt das Informationsmaterial nicht mehr auf Bücher, Zeitschriften, Zeitungen oder Mikrofilme beschränkt. Zwar verfügen die Bibliotheken auch heute schon über eine geringe Anzahl von Schallplatten und Tonbändern, aber das gedruckte Wort wird in Zukunft wahrscheinlich weit mehr in den Hintergrund treten. Ein großer Teil des neuen Informationsmaterials braucht nicht in der Bibliothek selbst aufbewahrt zu werden, sondern kann von einem zentralen Informationsspeicher abgerufen werden. Ein System wie *Walnut,* das von IBM für die United States Central Intelligence Agency entwickelt wurde, speichert Millionen Buchseiten in der Form von Filmen. Jeder Titel ist mit einer Signatur versehen, und ein Computer ist darauf programmiert, den entsprechenden Film zu lokalisieren und auf bestimmte Schlagworte hin den gesamten Speicher nach Informationen zu dem gewünschten Thema zu durchsuchen. Als Ergebnis seiner Suche präsentiert der Computer dann eine Liste von Titeln und der Benutzer »gibt an, welchen er haben möchte. Daraufhin

These dates coincide fairly closely with similar forecasts made by the Rand Corporation.

Some developments in the printing industry may have very considerable influence on this timetable. It is very probable that computer-aided printing will become much more general and will in fact be used because it will lower costs. If information which has been printed is also in existence as magnetic tape it can be used for a great number of other purposes: "actually it introduces a new and important principle which can help to extend bibliographical control over the ever-growing output of recorded literature and information contained in it. It makes possible the integration of two functions: primary publication and secondary retrieval of content – an information system becomes a by-product of the original publication system at hardly any extra cost." (Herbert Coblaus, *Documentation, Print and the Relevance of Hardware,* in *The Penrose Annual,* Vol. 61, London 1968.)

For quite different purposes and in quite a different way we now expect to go to the library and borrow a book, or a score, or a recording of a musical performance but not a recording of a television play. The economics of making and using videotape do not as yet allow of this. This is obviously again a matter of time. The same is probably also true of cinematic film. What may therefore happen is a diversification of the library service and the inclusion within the library of different kinds of media. The important thing would be that each medium of communication would be used for the job best suited to it. The efficiency of the library in meeting the demands put on it is thus likely to increase and this in turn may mean a greater use of libraries. Such a diversification and expansion would probably hold true for public libraries as much as academic and research institutions; national libraries would have an increased responsibility to store at least one copy of the whole extended range of information sources. Given that libraries provide an information transfer service in the widest sense – encompassing both the most esoteric research and the most frivolous pleasure – they may acquire functions which are by-products of their primary use. If, for instance, there is to be a University of the Air, offering courses on a national basis to students through television, and if these viewing sessions are to be complemented by occasional discussion meetings, it would seem extremely appropriate to hold such meetings in a library building and, when necessary, make use of the communication facilities available. There is very likely to be a greatly increased demand for such services. It is a well established case that in most developed countries the provision for education and for leisure pursuits shows a faster rate of growth than for almost any other service. This diversification and very probable expansion makes it all the more important that libraries are located at points of high accessibility. It does not necessarily imply, however that the whole group of facilities should always be put in a single building. The range of facilities provided should be geared to the particular location. Nevertheless it can be seen that when many of these services depend on a central storage system and only need a console consisting of a colour television screen and possibly a teleprinter locally, the quality of service which it will be possible to provide in quite a small branch library will be much higher. We are thus likely to get much closer to the kind of interconnected library service to which librarians have aspired for a considerable time.

High levels of accessibility imply, of course, something quite different in a compact town within a Swiss valley, a growing regional centre in West Africa or a Californian suburb. What these, however, may have in common, is that the ease of getting to a specific point, both in a physical time – distance sense and a psychological sense of feeling nearness, is produced by the routes of movement leading to a place with a high level of activity. This is likely to be the case because either the activity was in the first place generated by easy access or alternatively access has been planned to cope with an established and important activity. This suggests that libraries should be placed at points which exert a strong gravitational pull on the population – shopping centres, schools, recreational areas. This would seem especially important in view of the fact that libraries are much used by two age groups – the very young and the old – who may have to rely on public transport which would normally only be provided to such important localities.

It could be said that this argument takes an unduly pessimistic point of view of the role of the library and ascribes to it too low an attractive force. While this is undoubtedly partly true and may, of course, change for many kinds of libraries as our ideas about education as a leisure pursuit alter, it could nevertheless be maintained that for many libraries the service they provide is part of its users' general day to day activity and is most useful if it can be combined with it. It is obviously rather easy if one can borrow a novel from the branch library at the same time as one goes shopping, or take out a book on the reading list as one goes from study-bedroom to seminar.

Such locations frequently imply high land costs and possibly constricted sites. In any social accounting system they can be justified without difficulty and in fact become economic propositions since they increase the use of the facility and thus increase its social benefit. The possible planning difficulties of such sites in terms of noise exclusion have already been discussed, page 152, and are by no means insuperable. The problem of expansion may be far more serious and is again largely an economic one in terms of the amount of land allocated initially. In many instances, however, and particularly in the case of libraries most likely to be in urban centres with high land values, there may well be a diversification and increase of functions without a correspondingly large increase in floor area.

The possible trend which has just been outlined was partly influenced by the introduction of a computer-based technology into the library and partly by social changes in education and leisure. Both are in some measure also connected with the changes which are already under way in libraries due to the very great numerical increase in the collections and the demands this puts on the library service. The problem of maintaining up-to-date catalogues of the national collections in some form which could be distributed, for example, became just about impossible. The British Museum Catalogue of Printed Books was until recently a conventionally printed series of volumes. A revised version was started in the early 1930s but by 1954 the project had only reached the letter D; "a rate of progress which would have seen the edition completed some time in the middle of the twenty-first century – by which time the earlier alphabetic segments would have been some 100 years out of date". (John Commander, *The Abstracting Process and the British Museum Catalogue of Printed Books* in *The Penrose Annual,* Vol. 61, London 1968.) A photographic process using specifically designed equipment was developed which transformed the pasted entries in the working catalogues which existed in book form into printed pages and which were then published at the rate of a 500 page volume a week. The experience which has been gained is now being used to design cameras which will be highly automatic and which will be capable of dealing

lokalisiert der Computer den Titel und setzt eine technische Vorrichtung in Gang, die den entsprechenden Film herausgibt. Der Film kann mit Hilfe eines Lesegerätes abgelesen werden, oder er wird fotografisch vergrößert und in eine sogenannte harte ›Kopie‹ verwandelt – das heißt, in das Duplikat eines Originals« (Toffler). Das ganze Verfahren benötigt meist nicht mehr als fünf Sekunden. Ein solches System würde bestimmte, relativ häufig auftretende Arbeitsvorgänge innerhalb der Bibliothek übernehmen, müßte aber mit einem zentralen Computer in Verbindung stehen, der von vielen Seiten in Anspruch genommen werden könnte.

Daß solche Systeme künftig in Bibliotheksgebäuden eingesetzt werden, die in den späten sechziger Jahren entstanden, ist sehr wahrscheinlich. Hasan Ozbekhan, Planungsdirektor der System Development Corporation in Kalifornien, gibt für die Einführung technischer Einrichtungen, die auf Computer basieren, die folgenden ungefähren Daten an:

| | |
|---|---|
| Automatische Bibliographie | 1970–75 |
| Beantwortung von Fragen | 1975–80 |
| Exzerpte und Reproduktion von Texten | 1975–80 |
| Übermittlung ins Haus des Benutzers mit Herstellung von Kopien | 1985 |

(Aus Hasan Ozbekhan, *Automation,* in *Science Journal,* London, Oktober 1967.)

Diese Daten entsprechen weitgehend ähnlichen Voraussagen der Rand Corporation.

Neue Entwicklungen in der Drucktechnik können diesen Zeitplan freilich entscheidend beeinflussen. Es ist anzunehmen, daß Druckverfahren mit Hilfe von Computern immer mehr Verbreitung finden, da sie geringere Kosten verursachen. Wenn gedruckte Information zugleich als Tonband existiert, kann das Band zahlreiche zusätzliche Aufgaben erfüllen: »Auf diese Weise wird ein neues und wichtiges Prinzip eingeführt, das dazu verhelfen kann, die bibliographische Kontrolle über die ständig wachsende Zahl erfaßter Literatur und die darin enthaltene Information auszuweiten. Es ermöglicht die Verbindung zweier Funktionen: erstens die Publikation, zweitens die Magazinierung des Inhalts – das ursprüngliche Publikationssystem wirft als Nebenprodukt ohne nennenswerte zusätzliche Kosten ein Informationssystem ab.« (H. Coblaus, *Documentation, Print and the Relevance of Hardware,* in: *The Penrose Annual,* Band 61, London 1968.)

Der Benutzer einer Bibliothek kann heute zwar ein Buch, eine Partitur oder die Schallplattenaufnahme eines Konzerts ausleihen, nicht jedoch die Aufzeichnung eines Fernsehstücks. Die Herstellung und Verwendung von Kopien ist vorläufig noch zu kostspielig, was freilich ebenso wie beim Spielfilm lediglich eine Frage der Zeit sein dürfte. Die Bibliothek wird also auf die Dauer wahrscheinlich ihr Programm erweitern und die verschiedensten Medien umfassen. Wichtig ist dabei, daß jedes Kommunikationsmedium dort eingesetzt wird, wo es seinen Zweck am besten erfüllt. Dadurch steigt auch die Leistungsfähigkeit der Bibliotheken, was wiederum dazu führen könnte, daß sich die Benutzungsfrequenz erhöht. Eine solche Ausweitung der Funktionen wird sich wahrscheinlich bei öffentlichen Bibliotheken ebenso vollziehen wie bei akademischen Institutionen und Forschungsbibliotheken; Nationalbibliotheken werden die Aufgabe übernehmen müssen, mindestens je ein Exemplar sämtlicher neuer Informationsquellen aufzubewahren.

Da die Bibliotheken Informationen im weiteren Sinne übermitteln – von der esoterischen wissenschaftlichen Arbeit bis zur oberflächlichen Unterhaltungslektüre –, können sie auch Funktionen ausüben, die nicht direkt mit ihrer primären Nutzung zusammenhängen. Wenn zum Beispiel eine Fernsehuniversität ihren Studenten Vorlesungen auf nationaler Basis bietet und das Programm durch gelegentliche Zusammenkünfte mit Diskussionen ergänzen will, so erscheint es durchaus angebracht, diese Zusammenkünfte in einem Bibliotheksgebäude abzuhalten und eventuell die erforderlichen Kommunikationsmittel zur Verfügung zu stellen. Solche Aufgaben werden in Zukunft sicherlich immer häufiger an die Bibliothek herangetragen werden. Es ist erwiesen, daß Einrichtungen für Fortbildung und Freizeitbetätigung in den meisten hochentwickelten Ländern eine steilere Wachstumsrate aufweisen als fast alle anderen Institutionen.

Diese Ausweitung des Programms läßt es um so wichtiger erscheinen, daß Bibliotheken verkehrsgünstig gelegen sind. Die verschiedenen Einrichtungen müssen freilich nicht unbedingt in einem einzigen Gebäude untergebracht werden, sondern lassen sich auch an den jeweils günstigsten Standort verlegen. Wenn die meisten dieser Einrichtungen mit einem zentralen Speichersystem in Verbindung stehen, so daß an Ort und Stelle nur ein Pult mit einem Farbfernsehschirm und eventuell ein Fernschreiber erforderlich sind, wird die Leistungsfähigkeit auch der kleinsten Zweigbücherei gesteigert. Eine solche Lösung bedeutet einen weiteren Schritt auf dem Wege zu einem engmaschig verknüpften Bibliothekssystem, wie es die Bibliothekare schon seit langem erstreben.

Ein hoher Grad an Zugänglichkeit stellt natürlich in einer dichtbesiedelten Stadt eines Schweizer Gebirgstales andere Bedingungen als in einem wachsenden regionalen Zentrum Westafrikas oder einem kalifornischen Vorort. In allen Fällen hängt jedoch die Leichtigkeit, mit der ein Ort zu erreichen ist – physikalisch gesehen im Sinne der Relation von Zeit und Entfernung, psychologisch gesehen im Sinne eines Gefühls der Nähe –, von den Verkehrswegen ab, die zu Bereichen mit großer Aktivität führen. Entweder wurden diese Verkehrswege geschaffen, um ein vorhandenes aktives Zentrum leichter zugänglich zu machen, oder aber die Aktivität entstand gerade durch die leichte Zugänglichkeit. Bibliotheken sollten daher an Punkten liegen, die eine starke Anziehungskraft auf die Bevölkerung ausüben – Einkaufszentren, Schulen, Erholungsgebiete. Das ist vor allem deshalb wichtig, weil Bibliotheken viel von zwei Altersgruppen – den sehr Jungen und den Alten – benutzt werden, die häufig auf öffentliche Verkehrsmittel angewiesen sind und nur viel frequentierte Gegenden leicht erreichen können.

Man könnte hier einwenden, daß die Rolle der Bibliothek zu pessimistisch beurteilt und ihre Attraktivität zu gering eingeschätzt wird. Das mag zum Teil zutreffen, und die Situation vieler Bibliotheken wird sich zweifellos wandeln, wenn sich neue Auffassungen von der Fortbildung als einer Freizeitbeschäftigung durchsetzen. Dennoch ist es für einen großen Teil der Benutzer ein Vorzug, wenn sie den Bibliotheksbereich in ihren normalen Tagesablauf einbeziehen können, indem sie nach dem Einkauf einen Roman aus der Zweigbücherei holen oder auf dem Wege vom Studentenheim zum Seminar ein Buch entleihen.

Eine günstige Lage wird häufig durch hohe Kosten und geringere Größe des Grundstücks erkauft. In jeder sozial orientierten Gesellschaftsordnung sind solche Kosten jedoch durchaus zu rechtfertigen und erweisen sich auf die Dauer als rentable Investition, denn bei einer zentral gelegenen Bibliothek erhöht sich die Benutzungsfrequenz und damit auch der soziale Nutzwert. Welche Lärmschutzmaßnahmen in solchen Fällen getroffen werden müssen, wurde bereits auf Seite 152 erwähnt. Schwieriger ist die Frage der Erweiterung, die wiederum wirtschaftliche Probleme bietet, wenn das ursprüngliche Grundstück zu klein bemessen war. In vielen Fällen und vor

with the National Union Catalogue of pre–1956 imprints containing something like twelve and three-quarter million entries recording books in the major libraries of North America.
The kind of automated processes which are increasingly being used in business also have an application to libraries, particularly as regards inventory keeping from the moment the book is ordered to its arrival on the shelf. If this procedure is dealt with by some punched card or punched tape process it then becomes a relatively simple operation to transfer this information into the computer memory bank which forms the continuously up-to-date library catalogue. In other words the mechanization of the clerical process of a library may have very beneficial effects on its total efficiency and in particular as regards to its ability to keep information about its current stock up-to-date.
These procedures assume for the moment that the kind of information which is dealt with by a library is in some printed form or originated in such a form because it is the simplest method of dissemination. The suggestion has been made by J. C. R. Licklider in *Libraries of the Future* that information could both as regards input and output be handled entirely by a computer system without taking an intermediate printed form for purposes of distribution. A research worker wanting to "publish" his findings would type these direct into the computer (which would immediately check the findings against the existing state of knowledge and report back discrepancies) and someone needing that information would ask for a print-out from the computer. Licklider has outlined the hierarchical structure of what he has called a procognitive system and described its possible operation in some detail. Since the publication of his work in 1965, some of the technical and intellectual problems have been reduced if not necessarily overcome. The likelihood of some such system being operational within the next quarter century is therefore extremely high.
The important question as regards library design is whether this high probability means the extinction or at any rate considerable reduction in importance of the printed book. While it is extremely dangerous to make forecasts at a time when information technology is in a state of rapid advance, there is little at present to suggest a fast obsolescence of the book. The increase in the total number of communications is so rapid that even a very considerable growth in a new sector does not produce a reduction in the existing forms measured as absolute numbers. The percentage each has of the total will naturally vary. The situation is perhaps analogous to that of personal mobility; although the number of passenger miles flown shows a sharp rate of increase this does not in any way produce a reduction in the number of miles travelled by car. The general rate of increase is so great that only a variety of modes can cope with such a growth. The important thing is that each must be efficient within the sector most appropriate to it.
This criterion of efficiency is also likely to be applicable in the field of communication and in particular to that part affecting libraries. If the present rate of information increase were to continue and be encoded solely in the form of books and periodicals it is very probable that libraries would become unworkable or at least grossly inefficient and uneconomic. Collections of 100,000,000 volumes would not at all be out of the question. The Lenin Library in Moscow already houses 23,000,000 volumes and is acquiring about 1,100,000 each year. Diversification of communication storage and transmission becomes therefore simply a matter of survival. Only in this way will the library be able to fulfil its role.
The effect of such diversification on library design may be complex but will most of all require a shift in the way the problem is tackled. Traditionally libraries have been rather simple buildings consisting of a warehouse, a large reading area and a service zone or, alternatively, of undefined floor space capable of holding books, readers and staff. This allocation of space was true throughout the entire hierarchy of library buildings. As a result of this simplicity library buildings were also, unless covered in marble or bronze, relatively inexpensive. The square foot cost of floor space with few partitions and not many services was low. Not until air-conditioning was introduced did this change. To continue to think of libraries in such a way may however be to ignore their probable development. Their function is likely to become much more diversified both in terms of the techniques used to transfer information and in the social role the library will perform within its particular community, irrespective of whether that community is a suburban area, a university or a nation state. It may well be that this widening in the range of functions will also need a corresponding increase in the numbers of characteristic spaces within the building. What is likely to hold, however, is that within these characteristic spaces the communication transfer will always take place between an individual and a source. This is the hall-mark of the library. The more present arrangements, therefore, make possible and enhance such a situation, the more likely is the library building to remain a functioning organization in the years to come.

allem bei Bibliotheken in Stadtgebieten mit hohen Grundstückspreisen läßt sich freilich eine Ausweitung der Funktionen durchführen, ohne daß die Gesamtfläche entsprechend vergrößert werden müßte.

Die künftige Entwicklung, wie sie hier skizziert wurde, hängt einerseits von der Einführung neuer technischer Hilfsmittel wie Computer ab, andererseits aber auch von gesellschaftlichen Veränderungen in Erziehung und Freizeitgestaltung. Beide Faktoren stehen in einem gewissen Zusammenhang mit den Veränderungen, die sich auf Grund der beträchtlichen Zunahme des Bestandes und der entsprechend höheren Anforderungen an die bibliothekstechnischen Einrichtungen schon jetzt in den Bibliotheken vollziehen. Es wurde zum Beispiel nahezu unmöglich, Kataloge der Nationalbibliotheken auf den jeweils letzten Stand zu bringen und in einer übersichtlichen Form zu publizieren. Der Catalogue of Printed Books des British Museum bestand bis vor kurzem aus einer Reihe normal gedruckter Bände. Zu Beginn der dreißiger Jahre wurde eine verbesserte Version in Angriff genommen, doch im Jahre 1954 war erst der Buchstabe D erreicht, so daß »die vollständige Ausgabe irgendwann in der Mitte des 21. Jahrhunderts vorgelegen hätte – zu einem Zeitpunkt, an dem die früheren Teile des Alphabets um etwa hundert Jahre veraltet gewesen wären«. (John Commander, *The Abstracting Process and the British Museum Catalogue of Printed Books,* in: *The Penrose Annual,* Band 61, London 1968.) Dann wurde jedoch ein fotografisches Spezialverfahren entwickelt, mit dessen Hilfe sich die eingeklebten Eintragungen in den Arbeitskatalogen, die in Buchform existieren, in gedruckte Seiten verwandeln ließen. Nun konnte jede Woche ein Band von 500 Seiten publiziert werden. Die dabei gewonnenen Erfahrungen werden heute bei der Entwicklung weitgehend automatischer Kameras verwendet, mit deren Hilfe der National Union Catalog (Bestand aus der Zeit vor 1956) ausgearbeitet werden soll. Dieser Katalog enthält ungefähr 12750000 Titel aus den wichtigsten Bibliotheken Nordamerikas.
Automatisierte Verfahren können auch in Bibliotheken von Nutzen sein, vor allem für die Bestandskontrolle von der Bestellung des Buches bis zu seiner Rückkehr ins Fach. Wenn ein Lochkarten- oder Lochstreifensystem benutzt wird, ist es verhältnismäßig einfach, eine solche Information an den Speicher des Computers weiterzugeben, der den ständig auf den neuesten Stand gebrachten Katalog der Bibliothek enthält. Die Mechanisierung bürotechnischer Vorgänge vermag also die Leistungsfähigkeit einer Bibliothek zu steigern und ermöglicht vor allem den Überblick über den jeweiligen Bestand des Magazins. Diese Verfahren setzen freilich zur Zeit noch voraus, daß die Information, wie eine Bibliothek sie vermittelt, in gedruckter Form vorliegt, weil sie sich auf diese Weise am leichtesten verbreiten läßt. J. C. R. Licklider ging dagegen in seiner Untersuchung *Libraries of the Future* davon aus, daß die eingehende wie die ausgehende Information einem Computer übertragen werden kann, ohne daß eine gedruckte Zwischenform für Zwecke der Verbreitung erforderlich wäre. Ein Wissenschaftler, der seine Forschungsresultate »publizieren« möchte, würde den Computer direkt mit seinen Ergebnissen füttern (der sie sofort mit dem Stand des Wissens vergleichen und Unstimmigkeiten melden würde). Wer diese Information benötigt, beschafft sich über den Computer eine ausgedruckte Fassung. Licklider hat in seinem Buch die hierarchische Struktur des *procognitive system,* wie er es nannte, skizziert und das mögliche Verfahren detailliert beschrieben. Seit dem Erscheinen seines Werkes im Jahre 1965 haben sich einige der technischen und intellektuellen Probleme reduziert, wenn sie nicht sogar schon gelöst worden sind. Es ist also wahrscheinlich, daß ein solches System innerhalb der nächsten fünfundzwanzig Jahre realisiert wird. Für die Bibliotheksplanung ergibt sich die entscheidende Frage, ob die Einführung dieser Systeme dazu führt, daß das gedruckte Buch völlig an Bedeutung verliert oder zumindest in den Hintergrund tritt. Zwar ist es höchst gefährlich, Voraussagen zu wagen, während die Informationstechnik sich rapide entwickelt, doch spricht zur Zeit nicht viel dafür, daß das Buch seine Rolle bald ausgespielt haben wird. Die Zuwachsrate auf allen Gebieten der Kommunikation ist so groß, daß sogar eine beträchtliche Zunahme auf einem neuen Sektor in absoluten Zahlen gemessen nicht zu einer Verminderung der bestehenden Formen führt. Der prozentuale Anteil der einzelnen Kommunikationsformen kann natürlich variieren, ähnlich wie etwa im Verkehrswesen: Zwar nimmt die Zahl der Flugkilometer ständig zu, doch die Zahl der im Auto zurückgelegten Kilometer wird dadurch keineswegs vermindert. Die allgemeine Zuwachsrate ist so groß, daß sie nur durch eine Vielfalt der Verfahrensweisen bewältigt werden kann. Wichtig ist freilich, daß jede Methode dort eingesetzt wird, wo sie am meisten zu leisten vermag. Dieses Kriterium der Leistungsfähigkeit läßt sich auch auf das Gebiet der Kommunikation und insbesondere auf Bibliotheken anwenden. Wenn die Information in gleichem Maße weiter zunimmt und nur in Form von Büchern und Zeitschriften gespeichert wird, ist es sehr wahrscheinlich, daß die Bibliotheken auf die Dauer funktionsunfähig werden oder zumindest höchst unökonomisch arbeiten. Bestände von 100000000 Bänden wären dann keineswegs ungewöhnlich. Die Lenin-Bibliothek in Moskau verfügt zum Beispiel bereits über 23000000 Bände und erwirbt jedes Jahr ungefähr 1100000 dazu. Es ist also unerläßlich, daß verschiedene und neuartige Wege für die Speicherung und Übermittlung der Information gefunden werden, wenn die Bibliothek ihre Aufgabe erfüllen soll.
Werden solche neuen Möglichkeiten entwickelt, so muß auch die Bibliotheksplanung andere Lösungen suchen. Bisher waren Bibliotheken jeder Größenordnung relativ einfache Gebäude mit einem Magazin, einem großen Lesebereich und technischen Nebenräumen, oder sie bestanden aus undefinierten Geschoßflächen, auf denen Bücher, Leser und Personal untergebracht werden konnten. Wegen dieses unkomplizierten Raumprogramms waren Bibliotheksgebäude verhältnismäßig billig, sofern sie nicht mit Marmor oder Bronze verblendet wurden. Die Quadratmeterkosten der großräumigen Flächen mit wenig Unterteilungen und wenig Installationen waren niedrig. Erst mit der Einführung der Klimaanlagen begannen die Kosten zu steigen. Die Frage der Baukosten sollte freilich nicht im Vordergrund stehen, wenn es um die künftige Entwicklung der Bibliothek geht. Die Funktionen der Bibliothek werden immer vielfältiger werden, einmal im Hinblick auf die Techniken der Informationsübermittlung, zum anderen im Hinblick auf die soziale Rolle, die die Bibliotheken innerhalb ihres Einzugsbereiches – sei es ein Vorortgebiet, eine Universität oder ein Land – zu spielen vermag. Diese Ausweitung der Aufgaben wird wahrscheinlich dazu führen, daß die Zahl der charakteristischen Zonen innerhalb des Gebäudes entsprechend erhöht werden muß. Allerdings wird auch in den charakteristischen Bereichen die Kommunikation aller Voraussicht nach stets zwischen einem Individuum und einer Informationsquelle stattfinden. Je mehr deshalb die heutige Planung eine solche Kommunikation – das wichtigste Merkmal der Bibliothek – ermöglicht und fördert, desto wahrscheinlicher ist es, daß ein Bibliotheksgebäude auch in den kommenden Jahren seine Aufgaben erfüllen kann.

## Some References

The number of books about libraries and librarianship is very large. Although many of these deal with problems which may only be peripheral to the design of the building, some general knowledge of library science is essential before an attitude to the design of the building can be established. Most libraries contain recent bibliographies which should be consulted for available references. The following list is a short selection of some titles which are immediately relevant to the architecture of libraries or which contain descriptions of important new developments.


Ralph E. Ellsworth. *Planning the College and University Library Building.* Pruett Press, Boulder, Colorado, 1960.

Ralph E. Ellsworth and Hobart D. Wagener. *The School Library.* Educational Facilities Laboratories, New York, 1963.

Barbara Evans Markuson (editor). *Libraries and Automation.* Library of Congress, Washington, D.C., 1964.

Hoyt R. Galvin & Martin Van Buren. *The Small Public Library.* UNESCO, Paris, 1959.

John Harrison and Peter Laslett (editors). *The Brasenose Conference on the Automation of Libraries.* Mansell, London, 1967.

K. C. Harrison. *Libraries in Scandinavia.* André Deutsch, London, 1961.

J. C. R. Licklider. *Libraries of the Future.* MIT Press, Cambridge, Mass., 1965.

Keyes D. Metcalf. *Planning Academic & Research Library Buildings.* McGraw-Hill, New York, 1965.

Werner Mevissen. *The Public Library Building/Büchereibau.* Ernst Heyer, Essen, 1958.

Carl F. Overhage and R. Joyce Harman (editors). *Intrex: Report of a Planning Conference on Information Transfer Experiments.* MIT Press, Cambridge, Mass., 1965.

Nikolaus Pevsner. "Libraries: Nutrimentum Spiritus," article in *Architectural Review,* October 1961, London.

Gunther Pflug and Bernhard Adams. *Elektronische Datenverarbeitung in der Universitätsbibliothek Bochum.* Schürmann & Klagges, Bochum, 1968.

Rainald Stromeyer. *Europäische Bibliotheksbauten seit* 1930. Otto Harrassowitz, Wiesbaden, 1962.

A. Thompson. *Library Buildings of Britain & Europe: An International Study.* Butterworth, London, 1963.

Alvin Toffler. "Libraries," article in *Bricks and Mortarboards: a Report on College Planning and Building.* Educational Facilities Laboratories, New York, 1964.


Library buildings are frequently illustrated in architectural magazines as well as the journals of most national library associations. Reference should also be made to developments in information and communications theory.

## Kurzbibliographie

Die Zahl der Bücher über Bibliotheken und das Bibliothekswesen ist sehr groß. Zwar befassen sich viele von ihnen mit Problemen, die mit der Planung von Bibliotheksgebäuden nur am Rande zu tun haben, doch sind einige grundlegende Kenntnisse in der Bibliothekswissenschaft unerläßliche Voraussetzung für den Entwurf. Die meisten Bibliotheken verfügen über neuere Bibliographien zu diesem Thema.
Die folgende Liste ist eine kurze Auswahl von Titeln, die sich unmittelbar auf den Bibliotheksbau beziehen oder wichtige neue Entwicklungen beschreiben.


Ralph E. Ellsworth. *Planning College and University Library Building.* Pruett Press, Boulder, Colorado, 1960.

Ralph E. Ellsworth und Hobart D. Wagener. *The School Library.* Educational Facilities Laboratories, New York, 1963.

Barbara Evans Markuson (Herausgeber). *Libraries and Automation.* Library of Congress, Washington, D.C., 1964.

Hoyt R. Galvin und Martin Van Buren. *The Small Public Library.* UNESCO, Paris, 1959.

John Harrison und Peter Laslett (Herausgeber). *The Brasenose Conference on the Automation of Libraries.* Mansell, London, 1967.

K. C. Harrison. *Libraries in Scandinavia.* André Deutsch, London, 1961.

J. C. R. Licklider. *Libraries of the Future.* MIT Press, Cambridge, Mass., 1965.

Keyes D. Metcalf. *Planning Academic and Research Library Buildings.* McGraw-Hill, New York, 1965.

Werner Mevissen. *Büchereibau/The Public Library Building.* Ernst Heyer, Essen, 1958.

Carl F. Overhage und R. Joyce Harman (Herausgeber). *Intrex: Report of a Planning Conference on Information Transfer Experiments.* MIT Press, Cambridge, Mass., 1965.

Nikolaus Pevsner. »Libraries: Nutrimentum Spiritus«, in *Architectural Review,* Oktober 1961, London.

Gunther Pflug und Bernhard Adams. *Elektronische Datenverarbeitung in der Universitätsbibliothek Bochum.* Schürmann & Klagges, Bochum, 1968.

Rainald Stromeyer. *Europäische Bibliotheksbauten seit* 1930. Otto Harrassowitz, Wiesbaden, 1962.

A. Thompson. *Library Buildings of Britain and Europe: An International Study.* Butterworth, London, 1963.

Alvin Toffler. »Libraries«, in *Bricks and Mortarboards: a Report on College Planning and Building.* Educational Facilities Laboratories, New York, 1964.


Bibliotheksbauten werden außerdem häufig in Architekturzeitschriften und in den Publikationen der meisten nationalen Bibliotheksgesellschaften veröffentlicht. Auch die Entwicklungen der Informations- und Kommunikationstheorie sollten berücksichtigt werden.

Library planning must take into account current developments in information and communication technology as these may seriously affect the use, and thus the organization, of the building. Reference should therefore be made to the literature on these topics as well as to the information put out by manufacturers. Olivetti TCV 250 alphanumerical real-time terminal; an autonomous video unit with its own screen, able to operate at a considerable distance from a central computer and using normal telephone or telegraph lines. Olivetti, Milan.

Die Bibliotheksplanung muß die jeweils neuesten Entwicklungen auf dem Gebiet der Informations- und Kommunikationstechnik in Betracht ziehen, die großen Einfluß auf Funktion und Organisation des Gebäudes ausüben können. Deshalb sollte die entsprechende Literatur ebenso zu Rate gezogen werden wie das Informationsmaterial der Herstellerfirmen. Alphanumerisches Real-Time-Gerät Olivetti TCV 250; autonome Fernseheinheit mit eigenem Bildschirm, die in beträchtlicher Entfernung von einem zentralen Computer arbeiten kann und an das normale Telefon- oder Telegraphennetz angeschlossen ist. Olivetti, Mailand.

# Index of Names · Namensverzeichnis

Numbers in *italics* denote illustrations.

Die *kursiv* gedruckten Seitenzahlen verweisen auf Erwähnungen mit Abbildungen.

## Photo Credits · Fotonachweis

Alinari, Firenze 11, 13 (7, 8)
Ingrid Amslinger, München 87–89
Lala Aufsberg, Sonthofen 15 (12, 13)

Bibliothèque Nationale, Paris 16 (15–17)
British Museum, London 19
de Burgh Galwey 172 (11, 12)

André Chatelin, Paris 20 (22, 23)

John Donat, London 106–108, 111 (6–8, 10), 132 (3), 146 (25), 150 (17, 18)

Richard Einzig, Brecht-Einzig Ltd., London 100, 102, 103

Walter Faigle, Stuttgart 136 (13), 137 (17), 145 (19, 20), 165 (15)
Finsk Kommunaltidskrift, Helsinki 29 (48)
Fitzwilliam Museum, Cambridge 13 (9)
Reinhard Friedrich, Berlin 114–116

Gerald Gard, Grand Rapids 3, Michigan 45
García Garrabella y Cia. 14 (10)
Keith Gibson, Malton, Yorks. 99
Greater London Council, Photographic Unit Dept. of Architecture and Civic Design, London 171 (5)
Cecil H. Greville Ltd., Slough, Bucks. 158 (3, 4)

Robert Häusser, Mannheim-Käfertal 167 (19)
Heikki Havas, Helsinki 148 (5), 167 (20)
H. Heidersberger, Wolfsburg 24, 171 (3)
Keld Helmer-Pedersen, København 37 (1, 2, 4)
Cortlandt V. D. Hubbard, Philadelphia, Pennsylvania 163

Ihle-Werbung, Foto-Atelier, Frankfurt am Main 146 (22), 151 (22)

Phokion Karas, Melrose, Massachusetts 128 (3), 147 (3), 155 (31)
Foto-Kessler, Berlin-Wilmersdorf 46, 47, 48 (7), 49 (9–11), 130 (8)

Edward Leigh, Cambridge 121–123

Mann Brothers, London 124
Foto Marburg, Marburg 14 (11)
Eric de Maré 15 (14), 150 (16)
Milmoe 151 (21)
Moncalvo, Torino 41–43
Osamu Mural, Tokyo 173 (15)

National Gallery, London 8
National Monuments Record, London 12
Sigrid Neubert, München 65–68

Thomas Pedersen og Poul Pedersen, Århus 37 (3), 39, 133 (5), 137 (16), 139 (24), 150 (15), 151 (19), 156 (2), 167 (21), 172 (10)

Louis Reens, New York 85, 139 (22), 155 (34), 171 (4)
K. E. Roos, Helsinki 139 (25)

Matti Saanio, Rovaniemi 26–28, 29 (48)
Ben Schnall, Hewlett Harbor, L. I., N. Y. 153 (26, 27)
Rolf Schroeter, Zürich 136 (13), 137 (17), 145 (20), 165 (15)
Karro Schumacher, Stuttgart 159 (7, 8)
Herbert Schwöbel, Tübingen 76 (9)
Julius Shulman, Los Angeles, California 160
Siemens-Pressebild, München 141, 168
Henk Snoek, London 95–97, 129 (5), 136 (14), 138 (19), 140 (1), 152 (24)
Sonnenburg Fotografi, København 130 (7), 150 (14), 159 (6)
R. Stahman 90, 91, 93
Stearn & Sons, Cambridge 13 (9)
Ezra Stoller, Mamaroneck, N. Y. 81–83, 161, 165 (14), 173 (17)
Ateljé Sundahl, Stockholm 57–59, 61–63, 69–71, 140 (2)
Suomen Rakennustaiteen Museo, Helsinki 22 (25–27), 23 (28–31) (Photo Welin); 25 (Photo Ingervo)

Teigens Fotoatelier, Oslo 137 (15), 153 (25), 158 (2)

Erik Uluots, Stockholm 51–55, 128 (2), 155 (33), 171 (6)

Verlag für Radio-Foto-Kinotechnik GmbH, Helios-Verlag GmbH, Berlin-Borsigwalde 48 (6), 49 (8), 167 (22, 23)
Roger Viollet, Paris 18

G. Wade Swicord, Micanopy, Florida 171 (7), 173 (14)
Makoto Watanabe, Tokyo 173 (13)
Erik Wilk, Helsinki 17, 145 (21), 156 (3)

W. M. Zeijlemaker, Zutphen 13 (6)